Let's Eat in Green Pastures

A Practical Guide to Healthy Living

Valerie J. Whatley, Ph.D.

(A Servant of Jesus Christ)

Mill City Press, Inc.

212 3rd Avenue North, Suite 290

Minneapolis, MN 55401

612.455.2294

www.millcitypublishing.com

Editor: Marna Poole

Photographer: Sandra L. Jackson-Brugger

ISBN - 978-1-936107-49-0

ISBN - 1-936107-49-x

LCCN - 2010935698

Cover Design by Wes Moore

Printed in the United States of America

Contents

Part III: Designing a Healthy Diet That Fits You

Part IV: Medicine, Common Health Issues, and Diet

Part V: My Favorite Recipes Created by My Family

I dedicate this book to my dear and loving mother, Jennie James Whatley, and to my beloved and compassionate son, Jonathon Luther Sweeney.

Prologue

And the LORD *answered me, and said, Write the vision, and make it plain upon tables, that he may run that readeth it. For the vision is yet for an appointed time, but at the end it shall speak, and not lie: though it tarry, wait for it; because it will surely come, it will not tarry.*
(Habakkuk 2:2–3)[1]

Vision Statement: I envision a nation in which everyone everywhere bows before God as they accept their God-given gift of good health and begin living the healthy lifestyle that is required to maintain it.

My Abba Father spoke to me and said, "I want you to be my servant and help people."

I humbly replied, "Yes, Lord."

Then my Abba Father said, "I will give your mother the idea of how I want you to help others. As you listen to what she says, I will reveal the vision to you."

I humbly replied, "Yes, Lord."

This book is the product of my obedience. God was the writer; I was the pen. As this book begins to help others and the vision begins to manifest itself, I will humbly fall on my knees and say (just as I have done so many times before), "Thank you, my Abba Father, for your faithfulness. In Jesus name I pray. Amen."

Acknowledgments

In writing this book, I first give honor and thanks to God, my Father, who inspired my writing, blessed me with every good thing, and is my everything.

I give thanks to all who are ready to begin their journey to better health. I salute you!

To my mom, Jennie Whatley, a pillar who keeps fueling my writing efforts and all of my dreams, is my faith counselor, speaks constant jewels of wisdom, creates healthy meals with much love, and bakes the best sweet potato pies on both sides of the Mississippi River.

To my dad, Pastor Luther Whatley, who keeps the faith, constantly gives me words of encouragement to continue in my writing and future endeavors, provides excellent enduring advice, and teaches me how to persevere through example.

To my son, Jonathon Sweeney, who supports all of my decisions and dreams and always gives me a therapeutic dose of his wonderful sense of humor. I thank God that you have matured into a fine young man!

To my sister, Veronica Ware, who is a motivator and initiator of wonderful and insightful ideas, a most appreciated consultant in my writing efforts, a good friend, and a creator of delicious healthy recipes.

To my brother-in-law, Jerry Ware, who gave helpful suggestions and provides a good income so his family can afford to eat healthy meals.

To my little nephew, Jerry Ware, Jr., and niece, Victoria Ware, who knew absolutely nothing about my writing project and allowed me to take breaks and laugh.

To my brother and sister-in-law, Pastor Theodore and Ella Thompson, my nephew, Tony, and niece, Ashton, who provided prayers at crucial junctures.

To my uncle, Pastor Cordell Phillips, who gave insightful ideas and encouraging words of endurance.

To my editor, Marna Poole, who used her wonderful talents and offered much of her time. Your efforts will always be sincerely appreciated.

To my dear friends, Pamela-Joyce Jones, Atty. Eleanor Towns, Sandy Hansen, Marilee Wick, Ph.D., and Pastor Robert Johnson who took the time and effort to read my manuscript and give constructive criticism.

To my uncles, aunts (especially Aunt Angie Hull and Aunt Mae Jones), cousins, and friends who supported me. I love you all.

To all my brothers and sisters at Our Faith Baptist Church for all the lessons I continue to learn as we grow together in faith, improve our health, and complete our God-given purpose.

Introduction (The Change)

We are a nation of unhealthy people. We have a problem. Let us solve it together. Let us accept responsibility for our health by eating right and exercising. Let's commit to changing this nation to a smorgasbord of healthy foods as we protect our food from becoming products of toxic waste and guarantee its growth in fertile soils. Let's seek and gain the knowledge we need to engage in healthy living as we motivate others to do the same.

Let's Eat in Green Pastures is a practical guide that will lead us to the path of healthy living. The journey to healthy living begins once we choose to listen, as dear children, to God's voice and words about health. When we reject God's voice, doubt His healing power, or neglect to take care of ourselves, we then choose to be unhealthy. On the other hand, when we choose to listen to and obey His words, God our Father will speak to us and tell us that good health is a God-given gift offered to all. If we want to live our life in wellness, we must choose to accept our gift and then maintain it. Obtaining good health is to accept our gift; maintaining our gift requires a lifestyle change. Together, let us take hold of this message and complete the journey from an unhealthy existence to a healthy one. To help guide you on this journey, I have divided this message into five parts.

- **Part I**: *"Sheep, Who Is Your Shepherd?"* illustrates how human beings are like sheep in need of direction. Unlike sheep, however, we are free to choose our shepherd, and this choice determines our state of health and purpose in life.
- **Part II**: *"Health = You + Your Village"* describes mechanisms and gives personal illustrations on how you can choose good health, live a healthier lifestyle, and spread good health to family members and others within your circle of influence.
- **Part III**: *"Designing a Healthy Diet Fit for You"* characterizes the different types of foods and helps you tailor a healthy diet that suits your personal needs.

- **Part IV**: *"Common Health Problems and Food"* defines the role of medicine and faith in the healing process and gives suggestions that will help eliminate the symptoms of various health problems generally triggered or controlled by diet.
- **Part V**: *"My Favorite Family Recipes"* lists yummy, healthy recipes my family and I use to curb our appetites from the unhealthy foods we used to love.

Completing the path that leads to healthy living involves a two-step process. The *first step* will equip you with basic tools and practical skills required to build a solid relationship with Jesus Christ so you can acquire the faith needed to accept your God-given gift of good health. This book is filled with information and personal stories to help you:

- **Evaluate** yourself and your belief system.
- **Understand** your choices in life.
- **Form** an intimate relationship with God.
- **Accept** responsibility for your health.
- **Break** old habits.
- **Choose** a healthy lifestyle.
- **Inspire** others to do the same.

The *second step* will empower you to maintain your God-given gift of good health as you use your newly acquired tools and skills to successfully live a healthy lifestyle. In this book, you will learn how to:

- **Make** new life decisions.
- **Intensify** your commitment to healthy living.
- **Take** steps to help you and others become healthier.
- **Organize** methods to build healthier communities.
- **Increase** your awareness of health foods and physical fitness.
- **Design** your own personal healthy diet and exercise regimen.
- **Use** medicine not as the solution but as a tool to help sustain life.

The message—that good health is a God-given gift that requires a lifestyle change to maintain—is presented throughout this book to help you gain faith in the message and then live it. The Bible says faith cometh by hearing and hearing by the Word of God (Romans 10:17). Generally, information, read only once, is soon forgotten, or it forms a fragmented memory buried deep within the brain. Yet repetitively reading, hearing, studying, and meditating on positive information establishes permanent memories, creates new visions, transforms minds, and improves lives. I hope the information shared in this book will help you understand and take responsibility for your own health struggles as you help your family and others within your circle of influence to do the same.

At the end of each chapter there is a work-study section to help you apply what you have read—you'll find questions on various issues and situations that relate to beginning and maintaining a healthy lifestyle. You may choose to simply think about the answers to each question, or you may prefer to write out your responses in a journal so that you can keep track of your personal growth. The questions also lend themselves to group discussions, particularly if you, your family, and your friends are on the path to healthy living together. However you choose to use the work-study sections, enjoy the journey as you change your life to a healthy one.

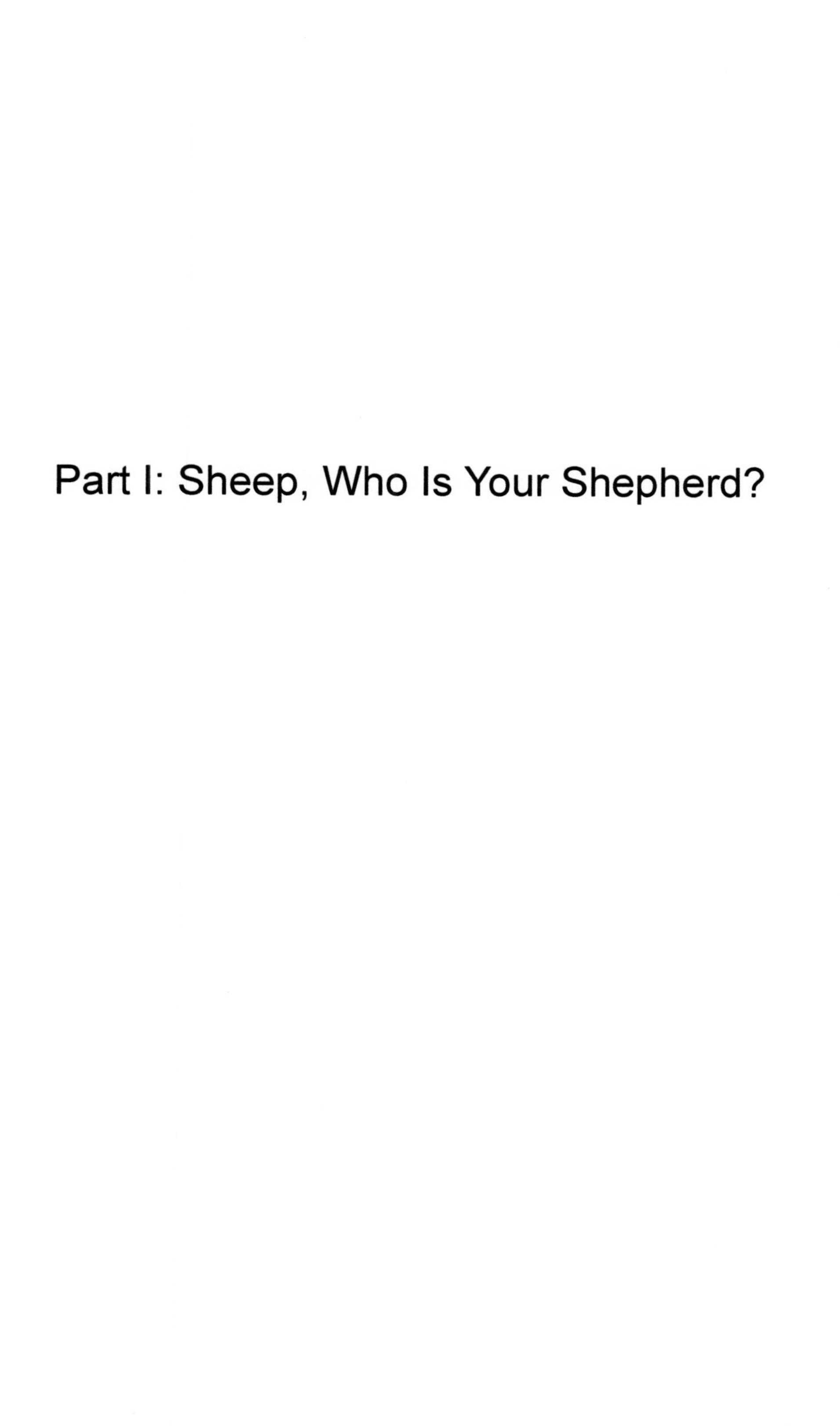

Part I: Sheep, Who Is Your Shepherd?

Chapter 1

In All Your Getting, Get Understanding

Happy is the man that findeth wisdom, and the man that getteth understanding, for the merchandise of it is better than ... silver and ... fine gold. (Proverbs 3:13-14)

This first chapter focuses on the health problems we as a nation obtained from living unhealthy lifestyles, and also on our sense of responsibility to seek answers to these problems as we take action to solve them.

Healthy—what does it mean? Do you know of anyone who is actually healthy? I am not sure if anyone experiences optimal health anymore. I know of people whose health is satisfactory; thus, they are relatively healthy compared to a large portion of the population. Yet the reality is that these people still have health issues—their issues may be few and minor, but they still have issues. Unfortunately, a large percentage of the population suffers from a long list of health complaints. Some of these health complaints are due to unfortunate circumstances, such as genetic abnormalities, pathogenic (e.g., bacterial, viral, and fungal) infections, exposure to toxic chemicals, and bodily injuries. The majority of these health complaints, however, are consequences of the choice to live an unhealthy lifestyle. Many of us seem to blame our unhealthy lifestyles on our economic status, society, government, family, and environment, instead of blaming ourselves. Only our defenseless infants and small children own the right to blame others for their unhealthy lifestyles, as they have no means to independently provide for themselves. Yet as adults, teenagers, and children (all of whom are old enough to read and comprehend), we need to understand that no excuse—no matter how valid the excuse may seem—should stop us from gaining better health. We all must take the initiative towards making good health a priority.

All people are created equal. It is important to understand and agree on this fact. No one is more or less important than you. It is important for you to value yourself by taking the time to know who you are, and to define your strengths and weaknesses. You should take the time to seek out your beliefs, discover your purpose in life, and listen and grow from the knowledge, wisdom, and thoughts of others. Yet do not allow the lies and half-truths of others to influence your moral standards and beliefs. Before you accept the words of others, study their words and develop a method for screening out untruths. Be selective and make the right choices. Ask yourself, *Does what they say make sense? Does it agree with the truth?* If it is an untruth, then delete it. Say "next," and move on. If it is the truth, then use the information to benefit your life and the lives of others.

You also should not speak lies and half-truths to yourself and others. Do not think that just because a thought or idea pops into your mind that it must be the truth. Just because you consider yourself to be intelligent or to have high moral standards does not automatically mean that all the thoughts and ideas in your mind are good and beneficial to you and others. Study the thought or idea. Find out the origin of it. Be selective and make the right choices. Remember to ask yourself, *Does it make sense? Is it the truth?* If it is an untruth, then delete it, get over yourself, and move on. If it is the truth, then keep it; let it absorb deep within your mind, and use it to induce change in yourself and others.

The information I have collected in this book has been very beneficial to me and my loved ones as we began to transform our lives from unhealthy habits and health issues to a healthier lifestyle. Although we have not yet arrived to the place of complete health, we are definitely headed in the right direction. We are now striving to be healthier than ever before, and we are not about to turn back. I believe and pray that the information in this book will do the same for you. Being both a Christian and a scientist, I am a seeker of the absolute truth. Tired of suffering from certain health issues, I studied, searched, and researched for years and have become one with what I present to you in this book, and that is: *God desires that we all choose good health.* No matter which health problems we inherited or developed over the years, each of us can choose to be healthy. Good health is a God-given gift offered to all. The Bible says, "By Jesus' stripes (i.e., the thirty-nine lashes through which Jesus suffered on the day of His crucifixion) we were healed" (I Peter 2:24), which means He had healed all parts of our existence—our hearts, souls, minds, and bodies. Yet it is up to us to believe this by faith, accept our God-given gift of good health, and then live a healthy lifestyle to maintain it.

As you develop a method for discovering the truth, I advise that you carefully examine the information in this book. Be selective, and make the right choices. Ask yourself, *Does it make sense? Is it the truth?* If the answer is no, then delete it, and move on. But if the answer is yes, I challenge you to use it to change your life by grasping it, planting it, nurturing it, and letting it take root in your heart, and then, grow throughout your mind, soul, and body. Begin to take responsibility for your life and enjoy the fruit of your choices. Make the right choices to accept your God-given gift of good health, eat healthy, move your body, live a healthier lifestyle, and encourage others to do the same as you reach your God-given purpose in wellness.

* * *

Work-Study: Points to Ponder

We have a problem. It is well understood that we are nation of unhealthy people. The solution to this problem, however, depends on how committed we are, both individually and as a united voice, to change. Yet it is important for us all to understand that before we can commit to change, we must first learn how to accept change. We all must be willing to take responsibility for our own health as we help others do the same. Please read the following statement and—*if you are ready to help solve this problem and commit to change*—sign your name. If you are not quite ready, don't be discouraged, but continue to search for and hear the truth until you find the willpower to change.

My Promise

I, ______________________________, promise that I will

- Take the time to read this book,
- Commit to making the right choices,
- Gain the knowledge required to maintain good health, and
- Complete the path to a healthy lifestyle.

I will encourage others (e.g., spouse, children, relatives, friends, neighbors, coworkers, acquaintances, and strangers) to do the same.

I will devote myself to changing my village and the villages of others to places of healthy living.

Signature _________________________ Date______________________

Congratulations! You are now well on your way to living a healthy life. Remember the above commitments and meditate on them as you enjoy walking the path to living a healthy lifestyle!

Chapter 2

Healing the Heart and Soul Before the Mind and Body

But now being made free from sin, and become servants to God, ye have your fruit unto holiness, and the end everlasting life. (Romans 6:22)

At times, it has been difficult to deal with the internal problems that are embedded in my heart and soul as I mature into the person of my desire, which is to be a servant of Jesus Christ. I didn't realize, at first, that my transformation from the person I used to call me would require such a major undertaking. Through the years, my transformation process has been healing not only my heart and soul but also my mind and body. I am glad and long for my continuous transformation as I reach wellness and accomplish my God-given purpose.

I was brought up in a Christian family. As children, my sister and I were privileged to be nurtured by loving parents who worked hard to provide for their family and to help those in need. Before I was born, Dad accepted his calling to the ordained ministry, and when I was eight, he began pastoring the church that he and Mom established. Throughout my childhood, he never received a dime from the ministry but financially supported his family by being a school teacher, buying real estate, and at times, working a second (nighttime) job. Mom, being full of great wisdom and much faith, has been a continuous blessing to my family and many other people. When I was growing up, she valued being a stay-at-home mom, fulfilled many ministries in the church, became a certified watch- and clock-repair person, supported Dad's career and pastoral duties, and was an equal partner in the real estate investments. My parents were far from rich, but my sister and I grew up with our needs met and with many of the things we wanted. Throughout my childhood, God has truly blessed my family. Yet like all of us, I was born with issues of the heart and soul. When I was a child, I didn't know these issues existed; ignorance was bliss. But God, showering me with His love, brought me to a point where I gained the desire and strength to search and deal with my imperfections.

I accepted Jesus Christ as my personal Savior at a very young age, and throughout my life, I have engaged in intimate yet straightforward conversations with my Heavenly Father. Years ago, I remember I had asked God out of a sense of fear, dissatisfaction, and emptiness to make me complete as His servant. I was hoping that He would respond by revealing a couple of my character flaws, readily removing them from me, and then starting me on my way. However, this was not the case at all. Instead, He replied that He had much work for me to do, but first I had some major changes to make. He then proceeded to let me know that I was in constant fear of failure and needed to embrace His love. Starting with my childhood, God began to reveal how my character flaws had brought me to this point. Unfortunately, I had been in fear of failure as far back as I can remember. Although I don't remember exactly when this character flaw first revealed itself, I do know it was fueled by my constantly hearing compliments from many of the important people in my life about my being smart. My parents would tell people how smart I was. My teachers would tell me, the other students, and my parents how smart I was. My relatives and friends would tell me I was smart. Members of my church would tell me I was smart. My I.Q. score indicated I was smart. My medical physicians would tell me I was smart. Strangers in grocery and department stores would walk up to my parents and tell them how smart I was. Everyone—except for my sister, who, out of love, typically called me a "dingbat"—told me that I was smart, and I needed to hear it, longed to hear it, and worse yet, lived to hear it. Hearing these compliments should have given me a healthy self-image, but because of my fear of failure, these words fueled my obsession to be smart. I always read books, rarely played, studied all the time, and earned excellent grades.

Without knowing it, I lived to be the "smart one." To make matters worse, people would add to the "smart one" compliments by saying I was also a "good girl." Throughout my years in school, my principals and teachers always considered me to be a model student. In the second grade, my teacher invented, especially for me, a new award category titled the "Trustworthy Award." When I was a little girl, people at church would repeatedly tell my parents, "Teachers' kids are always dumb, and preachers' kids are known to be rebellious, but not your girls; they are both smart and well-behaved." Growing up, I never rebelled, smoked a cigarette, drank alcohol, used drugs, or partied. I constantly lived up to a high standard so that God, my parents, other people, and I would think of me as the smart/good girl and love me for my accomplishments.

Being a college graduate, married, and then divorced, I soon realized that I wasn't as smart or good as I had hoped. But I fearfully attempted to solve this dilemma by comparing myself to others who I thought made more mistakes than I did, so that I could regain my position as the smart/good one. This, however, didn't last long. Out of a sense of emptiness, I realized that the standards I used to identify myself as a smart and good person were judgmental and illusional, for in my imagination, it was always possible to create or define someone who had more faults and troubles than I had. It was at this point that I sought God for help by asking Him to make me complete as His servant. Not only did I want to become closer to God, but I, being a mother of a wonderful son, needed to be whole for him. When God revealed the character flaws of my smart/good girl syndrome, it was bittersweet, for I was relieved to finally have these flaws identified and to begin my transformation towards wholeness; yet at the same time, it hurt to know that I wasn't smart or good enough to keep myself from having these flaws. Fortunately, over the years God has continued to heal my heart and soul, remove my fears, and fill the void with His love. By exposing other flaws that link back to my fear of failure such as bad eating and exercise habits, God has also started to heal my mind and body so that I shall soon reach a place of wellness. My transformation is definitely not complete, but it is by the grace of God that I am now His servant.

Knowing that He loves me for who I am (flaws and all), I no longer put myself in bondage by using my own merits and efforts to define my intelligence and goodness. I now choose to surrender myself to the all-knowing and holy God, who, through His grace, gives me the knowledge and goodness to grow and become all that I desire in Him as I complete my God-given purpose.

We must first deal with the issues of the heart and soul before we can complete our God-given purpose in a healthy body. The process of healing the heart and soul is not easy and sometimes can be quite painful; the truth often hurts. Those of us who are wise consistently strive to seek, hear, and understand the truth, even if it causes discomfort, because correction brings growth. Yet those of us who are unstable, prideful, or overly sensitive may often find the truth to be offensive and end up living in constant fear of it. In an attempt to protect our own evolved beliefs or our unwillingness to change, many of us may block our ears from the absolute truth and seek to have our ears tickled by a stretched-out, sugar-coated, and watered-down version of it. But because God is love, He always presents us with the unadulterated, absolute truth. He speaks sharp, distinct, and cleansing words as He strategically reveals the flaws responsible for our pain and sufferings. We then have the choice to either ignore our flaws or surrender ourselves to God and let Him mercifully remove them through our transformation to the new us. Our transformation process can be either quick or slow; the choice is ours. If we completely surrender all to God, our entire transformation process can occur instantaneously. But if we are hesitant to change or slow about surrendering all to Him, our transformation process may be divided into many phases and even take years to complete. Before we enter each phase of our transformation, God gives—to those of us who gradually surrender all to Him—the time to make choices, recuperate, and grow in His grace. As you read and complete Part I, embrace the truth as certain character flaws are revealed, and then allow your transformation process to heal your heart and soul, along with your mind and body, as you progress toward wellness.

***

Work-Study: Points to Ponder

1. Before we can receive our God-given gift of good health and maintain a healthy lifestyle, we must first deal with the issues of the heart and soul. Are you willing to deal with these issues? Do you feel a void that you want to be filled?

2. What character flaws do you currently know about? How have you dealt with them? If you have not yet dealt with them, are you ready to start? Would you be willing to go through a transformation process?

Chapter 3

The Lord Is My Shepherd

The Lord is my shepherd; I shall not want.
He maketh me lie down in green pastures.
He leadeth me by the still waters.
He restoreth my soul: He leadeth me in the path
of righteousness for His name's sake. Yea, though I walk
through the valley of the shadow of death, I will fear no evil:
for Thou art with me: Thy rod and Thy staff they comfort me.
Thou preparest a table before me in the presence of my enemies:
Thou anointest my head with oil; my cup runneth over.
Surely goodness and mercy shall follow me all the days of my life:
and I will dwell in the house of the Lord forever. (Psalm 23, KJV)[1]

You may not believe in God; you may have problems with surrendering yourself to a higher being. Being a scientist, I am familiar with these struggles. Yet if you desire to live a fulfilled life, then it is to your benefit to seek a relationship with God, the One who created you in His own image for a specific purpose and thus knows everything about you. But before you can do this, you must first choose to believe in God and surrender your all to Him. Chapters 3 and 4 are designed to help you work through your struggles as you establish or reevaluate your belief system and faith in a higher being. This is extremely important because the first step in receiving wellness requires that your human spirit becomes one with God (the Good Shepherd) as you surrender all to Him and accept your God-given gift of good health through faith.

The Lord is the one who knows all and takes care of us all. He is the controller of the universe. Why should we look or seek for another when there is no other? He doesn't need anything or anybody else to make Him God. He is God all by Himself.

Because many of you may believe only in yourselves, in your own intelligence, you may not believe that there is a God. Many of you may believe it is your conscience that totally directs your destiny and your intelligence that controls your being. But if your intelligence is not able to create your being, then your intelligence is not in total control of your being. Your intelligence was created by the one who can define its measurements; by the one who can control and usurp its power. The one with ultimate intelligence is the greatest force in existence and has the power to create your intelligence and all other intelligence. The Ultimate Intelligence is the only one that possesses the capacity to create something from absolute nothingness. In the beginning, it was impossible for something to come forth out of nothing until the Ultimate Intelligence who envisioned something in the midst of nothing said, "Let there be light," and there was light (Gen. 1:3b). The Ultimate Intelligence is the Almighty God, the Greatest Someone who created all things from nothing.

As you ponder over the creation of all things, you may ask yourself, "If all things came in existence by the Almighty God creating something from nothing, then who was the 'Someone' greater than God that created God and His Ultimate Intelligence?"

It is at this point where my attempt to complete an argument abruptly ends for there is no human argument, reasoning, logic, concept, deduction, or theory that can define God's existence. There is only faith. The Bible explains that no one created God. He was, is, and always will be. He is Alpha and Omega, the beginning and the end. He and His Son are one, the "I Am" from the beginning to eternity (see Rev. 1:8). Belief in God's existence requires faith in God. Faith in God is not up for debate. It is a choice; either you choose to have faith in Him or you don't.

God desires for you to have faith and surrender your all to Him. The purpose of your surrendering all to God is not to rob you of your intelligence, identity, and choices but to make you whole and complete. Your intelligence standing alone as a mere human is incomplete for God, through His love, purposely designed you to be in a close relationship with Him. Choosing to surrender yourself to the Almighty interconnects you to the divine source of all truth, knowledge, and wisdom. God created you in His own image and made you an intelligent being so that you will desire to seek and understand who He is, discover the mysteries of the universe, and take proper dominion and authority over the earth. God made you intelligent so that He can instruct you on how to glorify Him with your entire existence and complete your God-given purpose in a healthy body. But the choice to have faith in God and surrender all to Him is yours. It is your choice to believe that He loves you and wants to give you peace, prosperity, and good health. The Bible says that God gives every man the measure of faith (see Rom. 12:3), and as man looks at creation he knows deep within his heart that there must be a God somewhere (see Rom. 1:20); I believe this by faith. In the Old Testament, King David, a great patriarch who sought the very heart of God (see I Samuel 13:14), said, "The Lord is my shepherd I shall not want; He maketh me to lie down in green pastures" (Psalm 23:1); I believe this by faith.

The question is, do you?

* * *

Work-Study: Points to Ponder

1. I believe that one cannot convince another to believe in God through arguments or debates, because it doesn't work. The only way one can lead another to God is to speak the Word of God, the words found in the Bible, without arguing and debating. The truth can only be spoken and accepted through faith; nothing more and nothing less. Have you or do you know of anyone who tried to persuade others to believe in God through arguments and debates? Did it work?

2. Being human, it is important that you know who or what controls your being and your destiny. Who or what do you think controls you and your destiny? Is it God, your intelligence, or something else?

3. How do you think the universe and humans were formed? Do you

believe God is the creator of all things? Do you believe in Jesus Christ, in a religion, or in a theory such as evolution?

4. Do you believe that the structure of the universe and life are so complex that it had to be created by design? Or do you have a different belief?

5. The Bible says that we should not have a superior attitude for it is God, the Creator of all things, who gives each of us the measure of faith needed to believe in Him and complete our God-given purpose (see Rom. 12:3-6). I believe this to be true. Do you? Yet it is our choice to decide what we will do with our measure of faith. What have you decided to do with your measure of faith? Are you using it to believe in God or in something else?

6. Many people think that to have faith in God is a sign of weakness. They think that it keeps the weak from facing reality. What do you think?

7. Are you willing to surrender your all to God and use your faith so He can help you discover your God-given purpose and teach you how to live a healthy lifestyle?

Chapter 4

Have Faith

Have Faith in God ... (and) whosoever... shall not doubt in his heart, but shall believe those things which he says shall come to pass; he shall have whatsoever he saith. (Mark 11:22–23)

Having faith in God is something that is difficult for many of us to understand. We may think that it is necessary to see a thing with our eyes or perceive tangible information through our five senses before we can gain enough evidence to prove or believe a thing exists. Yet this is actually false. The truth is that every human being has faith in something. For instance, it is a fact that the brain is a normal part of the human anatomy. But most of us, without ever having seen a brain in our heads, undoubtedly believe we have one. As we think and control the movement of our bodies, each of us has convinced ourselves that a brain rests between our ears. Since childhood, we may have been told by our parents, teachers, and others that we each have a brain. Each of us may have studied diagrams of the human brain in textbooks or watched images of it on television. Others of us may have dissected the human brain in cadavers or seen images of our own brain, acquired from medical technology, such as magnetic resonance imagery (MRI). Some of us may have even gained information about our own brain from the neurosurgeon that operated on it. Yet the reality is that we have not seen, heard, smelled, tasted, or touched our own brain. In short, we continue to have faith that our brain exists without ever experiencing its existence through our five senses.

The manner in which I continue to have faith that a brain exists in my head is not much different from the way in which I continue to have faith in God. God is a Spirit. I cannot touch His spiritual form with my hands. I have not seen Him with my physical eyes or heard His voice audibly. Yet I know He exists. I have faith that He is God because He said so in His Word found in the Bible. I have faith that He exists because I have a relationship with Him. He speaks to me, and I to Him. He is my Abba Father (*Abba* is an endearing term for father, similar to *Daddy*; see Galatians 4:6); He is my shepherd. I know His Spirit dwells in me. My actions and deeds should show evidence to others that He exists. The peace and joy I experience from God's Spirit living in me should attract others to desire the same.

Faith is what it takes for us to believe that the Bible, the Word of God is true, and then act accordingly. As we hear His Word, we must believe in Him, have faith in Him, and obey Him. Because we believe in Him, we have the faith that He loves us and wants the best for us. We obey Him because we have faith that "he who comes to God must believe (that) He is, and that He is a rewarder of them that diligently seek Him" (Hebrews 11:6). Regardless of our present health condition or the hand that has been dealt to us in the past, we must have faith and believe that He wants us all to accept our gifts of salvation and good health.

* * *

Work-Study: Points to Ponder

1. How do you know you have a brain? Do you depend on faith, facts, or both?

2. Do you think believing you have a brain requires faith similar to that needed to believe that God exists?

3. Faith is not mind over matter. Faith is to believe in and then obey the Word of God. Because God said it, we believe it, we speak it, and we act upon it. Many individuals find themselves in trouble because they confuse having faith in God with being presumptuous, which is assuming that a desired thing will be received without first hearing a word from God. You should not assume that your wishes will become reality just because you desire them to be so. Before faith

can operate, it is required that the thing you desire or ask God for is in complete agreement with the Word of God found in the Bible. Then, you must have faith in God and confess with your mouth that you have received the thing you desire, before you see it with your physical eyes.

a. Have you ever believed that something was going to happen before you heard a word from God? If so, what happened?
b. Have you ever heard a word from God that required you to keep the faith? If so, how did you demonstrate your faith? What were the results?
c. Do you believe that having faith in God and in His Word is required before God will answer your prayers and bless you with the things you desire, such as salvation, love, peace, joy, good health, and prosperity, or do you believe being presumptuous is enough to bring forth results?

Chapter 5

We Are Who We Are, and We All Are Like Sheep

All we like sheep have gone astray. (Isaiah 53:6a)

Chapter 5 discusses the biblical metaphor that relates humans to sheep, and chapter 6 explains the choice we have as humans to make either God (the Good Shepherd) or Satan (the Evil One) the shepherd over our lives. God desires that we choose Him as our shepherd so that we can accept our God-given gifts of salvation and good health.

Sheep are not the most intelligent of creatures. They have very poor vision and are very timid. They are easily led and will respond to the voice of their shepherd without hesitation. I once heard a wise elderly man say that if a shepherd leads his sheep to the edge of a cliff without commanding them to stop, his sheep will continue to proceed forward and fall off the cliff. We are all like sheep (see Isaiah 53:6 and I Peter 2:25); every human being has a shepherd. We are led by a spiritual force; and we hear and follow that voice. Yet it is difficult for many of us to admit that we are like sheep. We do not want to identify ourselves with such stupid and timid creatures. We want to think that we are very intelligent beings, originating ideas and formulating decisions all on our own. I am not saying that we are not intelligent beings, but everything is relative. Compared to sheep, we are superior in intelligence; we are the shepherds. Yet compared to Jesus, the Good Shepherd, our intelligence leaves much to be desired. We cannot choose to be like sheep, because we are like sheep. The way we were born into this world was not our choice. Our parents' gene pools came together at our conception, the time at which an egg was fertilized by an energetic sperm. Before I was conceived, I doubt that anyone consulted with me about my preference of which physical features and personality traits should be used to design the wonderful me. No matter if right or wrong, I would have probably chosen some different selections than those with which I was born.

Many years ago, my family adopted an Australian sheepdog as a pet for my son. This was not the dog of my son's choice. He made it very clear that he wanted a poodle mix, a little dog that would follow him around. Being the parent, I thought I knew best. I thought my young son needed a hearty, energetic sheepdog, but I was dead wrong. This female dog was impossible for us to train; instead, she trained us. She never showed or wanted much affection. Her instinctive behavior led her to constantly herd us. She just wanted to eat, sleep, and herd. It did not matter who or how many of us were in the backyard or what we were doing, before long, we found ourselves herded together like sheep in the center of the yard as this hyperactive dog was constantly encircling us. We were supposedly the masters over this dog, but instead, we allowed this dog to control us. Friends and relatives thought that we were exaggerating; they could not comprehend how a dog could herd people. All doubts soon ended when they came over for a visit and before long, found themselves herded together with us like sheep in the center of the yard. This went on for months until we finally gave her away to a family who owned a big animal farm. I learned three great lessons from this dog. One: my son, although young, knows what he wants the majority of time. Two: we as human beings are easily led. And three: some of us will even allow a lesser power to lead us. I am glad I recognized early in life that I am like a sheep; thus, I chose to surrender all to the Good Shepherd, the one who understands everything about me and knows all things. We are who we are, and we all are like sheep.

* * *

Work-Study: Points to Ponder

1. The metaphors about people being like sheep, and God being our Shepherd are used throughout the Bible (see Psalm 23, Isaiah 53:6, Ezekiel 34:11-31, Hebrews 13:20, I Peter 2:25, and John 10:1-11).

Do you agree that people have many characteristics that resemble sheep, or do you think there are no similarities?

2. Do you believe we need Jesus to lead us, or do you think we are intelligent enough beings to control our own lives?

Chapter 6

Choose Your Shepherd

Choose you this day whom you will serve... but as for me and my house, we will serve the Lord. (Joshua 24:15)

We are like sheep; this is the way God created us. Although God created us to be intelligent beings, we are not able to create an idea, thought, or intent all on our own. We are not able to use our own intelligence to independently originate any good or evil thing. God purposely designed our brains in this fashion. Before we can conceive a thought, idea, or intent, a spiritual voice must first speak to our hearts, the site where choices are made. A spiritual voice must first speak to our hearts before we can develop a thought from written information, test a hypothesis through an experimental design, or formulate an opinion from spoken words. Thus, we should not think too highly of ourselves, as it is a spiritual voice and not our own intelligence that initiates the entire thought process.

We are like sheep, but we are not sheep. There are obvious characteristics that separate us from being sheep. One main difference is that we were born to be thinkers and make choices; thus, we were given the capacity to decide who will be our shepherd, God (the Good Shepherd) or Satan (the Evil One). There are only two spiritual voices from which to choose. We can either choose to follow the voice of God or that of Satan but not both simultaneously. Our heart is the central site of our choices. The heart, as mentioned here, does not define the organ that constantly pumps blood throughout our body but refers to the site that begins within the center of our brain. It is at this site where choices that control our thoughts, intents, emotions, willpower, and intelligence are made. It is at this control site where we choose the voice that we will follow—the voice of the Good Shepherd or the Evil One. Without a spiritual voice, there is no choice.

We have a choice; we can either accept the Good Shepherd, or we can reject Him. If we reject God, we are *not* free agents, controlled by our own intelligence. The Evil One sits at the heart of those who reject God. The Evil One speaks; they follow him. If they deny God, it is because their hearts are in bondage by the Evil One. Many who are dissatisfied with the reality of being in bondage by the Evil One may ask the following, "Why was man created if he is not in total control of his own being? Why is man given the choice to choose between only two voices, and why is one of these voices that of the Evil One? If God is love, then why is the Evil One, by default, in control of those who choose to reject God? Furthermore, what about those individuals who want to live an independent life completely free of a shepherd?"

These questions may seem profound but the answers to them are quite simple. Again, the answers are based on faith. *God created man in his own image … male and female he created them* (Genesis 1:27). God made man (as defined in Genesis 1:27, "man" is often used as a non-gender term that is inclusive of both men and women) in His own likeness. God is a Spirit. Man is a spirit within a body. God breathed into man and made man a living soul. Through the spirit, man was created to commune with God and to have a close relationship with Him. God is love, and God loves man. God wants man to reciprocate that love, not out of force, but because man chooses to love Him (God) and desires to have an intimate relationship with Him. God permits evil; He allows Satan to tempt us, because He wants us to choose between good and evil. He gave us a free will so that we can choose for ourselves who and what we will follow. He could have designed us to be nothing more than mere robots, serving Him without any knowledge of a choice. He could have created us so that we would not be exposed to or tempted by anything evil and would always serve Him out of ignorance. Yet He wants us, as intelligent beings, to choose him freely without force. Forcing someone to serve is a form of bondage. Forcing someone to give love is not an expression of love; rather, it is a form of rape, produced out of fear. God is love, and in Him is no fear (see I John 4:8 and 18).

Man was not designed to be a separate entity from God. Man was created to be one with God. Yet after man chose to be deceived by

Satan, his relationship with God was severed, his spirit died, and his heart began to harden. Because of Adam's sin, we are all born as sinners and enslaved by Satan, the tempter. Yet because of Jesus' love, we can choose to be born again and become adopted into the family of our Heavenly Father. Jesus sacrificed His life for us and defeated the Evil One for all eternity. Desiring to be our Good Shepherd, Jesus speaks to our hearts and gives us the opportunity to receive Him as our personal Savior. Waiting patiently and longing for an invitation to commune with us, Jesus stands at the door of our hearts and knocks, but it is our choice to either reject Him or open the door (see Revelation 3:20).

We must choose between the Good Shepherd and the Evil One. If we submit ourselves to Jesus and resist the voice of Satan, Satan will flee from us (see James 4:7). Those of us who receive Jesus Christ as our personal Savior become the children of the Heavenly Father. Our spirits become born again as the Holy Spirit (the Spirit of the Son) begins to live in us, comfort us, and fill our hearts. The Holy Spirit knows the way of the Father, for they are one, and the way of the Father He teaches us (see I Corinthians 2:10–14). He teaches us how to form a close relationship with the Father, obey His voice, and discern between lies and truth. Crying "Abba Father," the Holy Spirit constantly prays for us (see Galatians 4:6 and Romans 8:26) and teaches us how to pray for ourselves. He teaches us how to comprehend the written Word found in the Bible and complete our God-given purpose in wellness. But those of us who reject Jesus remain controlled by Satan, who, as a roaring lion, seeks whom he can devour (see I Peter 5:8). Jesus speaks, and Satan speaks. Whose voice will you choose? Whose words will you follow? Choose this day whom you will serve; choose whose words you will follow.

* * *

Work-Study: Points to Ponder

1. Do you believe man is a spirit in a body, or is he just a body?

2. Do you believe evil and good thoughts are products of your own intelligence? Or do you believe evil thoughts originate from Satan and good thoughts from God?

3. Do you believe man is a separate and complete entity all on his own? Or is man designed to have a close relationship with God?

4. Whose voice do you believe you are following—that of the Good Shepherd, the Evil One, or something else? If you are following the voice of the Good Sheherd, do you believe in the Holy Spirit? If so, are you willing to listen to Him and allow Him to teach you on how to live a fulfilled and healthy life?

CHAPTER 7

Are We Like Aggressive-Passive Sheep?

Why boasteth thou thyself ... O mighty man ... that made not God his strength: But trusted in the abundance of his riches, and strengthened himself in his wickedness. (Psalms 52:1 and 7)

I used to be a confused little lamb who believed that if I worked hard and long enough to be good and smart, God would reward my efforts with His love and blessings. Now, I am a submissive sheep who understands that God loves me unconditionally and without Him, I can do nothing. What kind of sheep do you think you are? Before you can accept your God-given gift of good health and improve your lifestyle, it is important to take the time to define who you are, determine which shepherd is currently controlling your life, and make the decision to form a close relationship with God. At the present time, you may feel that just because you believe there is a God, this automatically qualifies you as an obedient sheep, and there is nothing more you need to do. However, as you read about the different types of sheep described in chapters 7 through 11, you may discover that you're one of God's wayward sheep and that your relationship with Him is not as close as you hope for it to be. If you find this to be the case, then listen as God invites you to submit your all to Him and be one of His dear and obedient children (see chapter 11 for description). Then you will be ready to accept your gift of salvation and good health and become empowered to fulfill your purpose and maintain a healthy lifestyle.

There exists a group of individuals who refuse to believe that they are like sheep. This group is like aggressive-passive (not to be confused with passive-aggressive) sheep, who are individuals that unknowingly display passiveness in an aggressive manner. They are only sheep, blinded-aggressive sheep passively being led by the voice of Satan, the Deceiver. Satan has deceived these aggressive-passive sheep to believe that their intelligence is controlling their inner being, surroundings, and destiny. Because the Deceiver disguises his voice as the voice of their intelligence, the aggressive-passive sheep remain blinded by the Deceiver and have not identified him as the one who speaks ideas into their minds. They continue to believe that the Deceiver's voice is actually the voice of their own intelligence that is speaking, forming, and originating ideas and thoughts. They are the bureaucrats who believe it is the voice of their own intelligence leading them to build, organize, and gain the power to obtain wealth and take control of the masses, those whom the aggressive-passive sheep define as less intelligent because they are followers (see chapter 8 for details). They are the opportunists who believe it is the voice of their own intelligence that led them to leech onto and drain the masses for financial gain. They are the business owners within the food industry who believe it is their own voice telling them to eat healthy foods at every meal, but then to go ahead and market junk food to the masses for profit. Living in a delusional world as the aggressors, they hold fast to the pretense that their intelligence gave them the ability to obtain success and the things of their pleasure. Yet in actuality these thoughts and ideas were not conceived by their own intelligence but by Satan, which is the prince of this world, a system founded on power and wealth.

Unfortunately, as the deception intensifies, the Deceiver convinces many aggressors to gain success by any means necessary. These aggressors are often defined as hard-hearted individuals who continue to exploit the masses with a guiltless conscience until their hearts become hard as stone. There are aggressors, however, who find this type of lifestyle to be extremely stressful. The adverse effects of the intense stress on their health cause them to realize that they need to escape from this lifestyle to one that allows them to become conscience-driven leaders. Although these aggressors are usually known to be avid runners and dedicated dieters, the intense stress from their daily routine often compromises their health and causes health issues such as high blood pressure, heart attacks, and strokes. Other aggressors may become burdened with insurmountable guilt and resort to abusive behaviors and addictive habits, such as child abuse, spousal abuse, drug abuse, alcoholism, sexual immorality and assaults, and eating disorders. Yet it is never too late for aggressors to escape this lifestyle and become the trustworthy, decisive, and caring leaders who will commit to completing their God-given purpose in a healthy body. God will always rescue and provide refuge to all who will come to Him with a repentant heart.

* * *

Work-Study: Points to Ponder

1. Do you or does someone you know have characteristics that resemble the aggressive-passive sheep? If so, what do you believe is the driving force behind the aggressiveness? Is there a willingness to change to a more caring individual without the aggressiveness?

2. Are you in a leadership position? If you are, do you put wealth and success before the welfare and health of others? If so, is there a willingness to change to a leader who has a deep concern for the welfare of others?

3. Do you know of an aggressor with an addictive or bad habit? If so, why do you think he or she developed this habit? If this person is you, do you feel guilty for your aggressive behavior towards others? Does your guilt constantly lead you to continue your addictive or bad habits? Are you willing to break these habits? Are you willing to stop your aggressive behavior towards others?

4. Do you eat a healthy diet and exercise regularly but find that you still have health problems? If so, why? Is it because of excess stress?

Chapter 8

Are We Like Masses of Passive Sheep?

Thus saith the Lord; cursed be the man that trusteth in man, and maketh flesh his arm, and whose heart departeth from the Lord. (Jeremiah 17:5)

The word passive describes the masses of individuals who tend to go with the flow, follow the crowd, believe the majority is always right, and conform to the views of society. These individuals are like the masses of passive sheep. Fearful of change, the masses would rather drown in the familiar than be rescued by the unknown. Afraid of confrontation and controversy, the masses prefer to stay within the gray area and never move out of the box. Satisfied with the status quo, the masses lack the courage to step across boundaries. Great financial success is defined as and limited to those who are employed by the aggressive-passive sheep. Financially, they dare not seek or ask for anything more than a middle-class income, and many readily settle for government assistance or even less. The masses live in the here and now without thinking about tomorrow. Their desire to receive immediate gratification, without changing the familiar, drives their lack of ambition.

The masses prefer to follow the rules and guidance of others rather than support any opinions of their own. They believe that a good citizen is a loyal follower of the aggressive-passive sheep. Attempting to satisfy their urge to comply, the masses passively follow the standards, rules, regulations, and laws set before them by capitalism, religious leaders, employers, and the government. Without asking questions, the masses will allow themselves to be easily persuaded by propaganda and will buy any product marketed by the industry or advertised by the media. They will take medication without asking their physicians the proper questions, accept the junk-food market without demanding the food industry to change, and sit around as couch potatoes without gaining the willpower to exercise. If any of them do question anything out of the ordinary, they will only murmur amongst themselves and refuse to take a stand toward producing a change for the betterment of all.

Unfortunately, members within the masses are often found to be the victims of sexual, mental, or physical abuse. They are usually the chosen prey of their abusers for they tend to cope with pain by repressing their feelings and silencing their voice instead of fighting back. Being victimized and afraid, they fear the process of being transformed to wholeness. They'd rather remain in bondage by the pain buried deep within their hearts and souls than to take the risk of releasing it during the transformation that bears their freedom. This is because they fear that the transformation will force them to relive past violations, forgive their abusers, and discover unknown demons that they dare not encounter or face alone. But God is waiting with open arms to help them through their transformation process. If they will call out to their Heavenly Father for help, God will penetrate their hearts with His love and invite them to rest in His embrace as He casts out their demons into utter darkness, fills their souls with the light of redemption, gives them the desire to forgive, and restores their minds and bodies to wellness.

Over time, as many of the masses continue to find themselves so burdened down from the heaviness of mediocrity or the torrent of abuse, they may fall into a sense of hopelessness and develop mental disorders (e.g., depression, self-mutilation, and preoccupation with food), addictive habits (e.g., drug abuse, alcoholism, sexual immorality, Internet addiction, and junk-food addiction), and abusive behaviors (e.g., child abuse, spousal abuse, victim tendencies, and "couch potato syndrome"). Suffering from low self-esteem, others within the masses may strive for the affection, attention, acceptance, and approval of others by becoming a perfectionist, which often leads to compulsive patterns of behavior, such as excessive cleaning, studying, working, organizing, and exercising, and also eating disorders, such as anorexia, bulimia, compulsive overeating, and binge eating. Yet if the masses will surrender their all to God, God will replace their low self-esteem with confidence of who they are in Him and heal them from the heartaches that are often linked to past depression and abuse. Moreover, God will not only lead them to their purpose but give them the motivation, blessings, and wellness required to complete it.

The masses do not comprehend that in reality, they are following the voice of the Evil One. They do not realize that they are deceived by the Evil One into following the aggressive-passive sheep, who are also deceived and controlled by the Evil One. The Bible explains that in the days of Samuel, the judge, the masses of Israelites were no longer satisfied with the Almighty God being their only leader (see I Samuel 8). As their sins continued to increase, they desired for much less than the sovereign leadership of the Almighty God. They longed for the leadership of a physical king, a mere man. Because of the hardness of their hearts, God permitted them to be ruled by a succession of physical kings for many generations. Unfortunately, the majority of these physical kings, being nothing more than aggressive-passive sheep led by the Evil One, ruled with an iron hand and brought idolatry and much sorrow to the masses. But whenever the masses became tired of the turmoil and hardships and called with a repentant heart upon the name of the Lord, God would always, in spite of all of their unfaithfulness, reach out His merciful hand of deliverance and shower them with blessings and wellness.

* * *

Work-Study: Points to Ponder

1. Are you or do you know of someone who is one of the masses of passive sheep? If so, what is the driving force causing this passive behavior?

2. If you are a follower of the aggressive-passive sheep, are you content with being a follower? Are you more concerned about pleasing others than doing what you believe is right? Are you happy with your life? Do you want a change? If you are dissatisfied with being a follower, then why?

3. Are you content with following the negative ways of others and society? If not, have you developed abusive, addictive, and unhealthy habits because of your dissatisfaction? If so, which habits? Are you willing to stop these habits?

4. If you are a victim of abuse, how are you dealing with it? Did you seek help from reliable sources or professional counselors? Did you ask God to help you through the pain, heal your heart and soul, and bring your mind and body to wellness? If not, are you willing to start? If you are ready, God is waiting to help you through it.

Chapter 9

Are We Like Frustrated Sheep?

For rebellion is as the sin of witchcraft, and stubbornness is as iniquity and idolatry. Because thou hast rejected the word of the Lord, He hath also rejected thee from being king. (I Samuel 15:23)

Committing acts of rebellion is often the choice of individuals who feel trapped in a society that doesn't allow enough room for their existence. Refusing to identify themselves as one of the masses, these individuals rebel against the authority of the aggressive-passive sheep. These individuals are like frustrated sheep. Suppressed by the aggressors and rejected by the masses, these frustrated sheep are soon labeled as the misfits of society. As the frustrated sheep feel they are deprived of opportunities to live up to their potential, the Deceiver feeds them ideas that constantly fuel the flames of frustration. Once the pressure from suppressed frustration begins to intensify, the frustrated sheep often choose to pursue a life of crime. At first, they rebel by committing minor misdemeanors, but as the frustration continues to escalate, their criminal acts rise to more serious and violent offenses. Through efforts to stop imitators, protect citizens from violence, and maintain justice, the frustrated sheep are convicted, punished, and imprisoned by our judicial system. Failing to escape their punishment, these frustrated sheep find themselves caged by the Evil One, as he prepares for the kill. Being imprisoned causes the frustrated sheep to continue to bottle up frustration and release hatred that triggers abusive behaviors and violent acts against themselves and those incarcerated with them.

Those who survive the penitentiary and are introduced back into the mainstream of society often remain imprisoned within their tormented souls. After being released from prison, these individuals generally do not have much interest in taking care of their personal welfare or practicing healthy lifestyle habits; their minds and bodies remain fixed in survival mode. When incarcerated, however, many often develop the habits of pumping iron and bodybuilding. Then, as ex-prisoners, they usually continue with these habits, not because they are so concerned about their health but because they want to maintain the physique that others often find threatening. Unfortunately, many ex-prisoners will either return to a life of vengeful crimes against society or resort to abusive, addictive, and unhealthy habits (e.g., child abuse, spousal abuse, drug abuse, alcoholism, sexual immorality and assaults, victim tendencies, compulsive overeating, junk-food addiction, "couch potato syndrome," and no health insurance) that are detrimental to themselves and those closest to them. Yet thank God for second chances; God gives every frustrated sheep that chooses to stop listening to the wrong voice and start following the voice of the Good Shepherd the opportunity to transform into productive and healthy individuals with the ability and talents needed to complete their God-given purpose.

* * *

Work-Study: Points to Ponder

1. Have you ever been frustrated? If so, what do you think caused it? What mechanism did you use to help end the frustration?

2. Do you have problems with authority? Do you find yourself rebelling against authority because you want to do things your own way?

3. Are you, overall, a calm person? If so, what method do you use to remain calm and at peace? Do you think it is you who is in complete control of your calm attitude, or do you think it is because you listen to the voice of the Good Shepherd?

4. When ideas come into your mind that build up frustration, do you choose to meditate on these ideas, or do you choose to reject them?

5. Do you or does someone you know resemble a frustrated sheep?

6. Have you ever been frustrated to the point that you committed a crime or an abusive act? If so, do you remember what thoughts were going on in your mind at the time? Do you believe the Evil One initiated these thoughts, or do you believe you conceived them all on your own? Do you remember if any good thoughts were also in your mind at the time? If so, why did you choose the evil thoughts over the good ones?

7. If you have committed a crime or an abusive act, are you willing to stop your life of crime and abusiveness and not repeat the offense? If so, what are you willing to do about it? What steps are you willing to take to end your frustration, rebellion, abusiveness, or criminal acts?

8. Have you ever been frustrated but did not commit a crime or display abusive behavior? How did you release your frustrations? What thought process did you go through? Do you believe the Good Shepherd is responsible for the thoughts that stopped you from committing the crime or abusive act, or do you think it was your own conceived thoughts that stopped you?

9. Do you possess years of repressed frustration that is released through abusive behavior or an addictive habit? If so, what is the behavior or habit? What steps are you willing to take to help you release this frustration without resorting to abusive behaviors or addictive habits? Are you ready to surrender your all to God and allow Him to help you remove the frustration?

10. If you are a frustrated sheep, how is your health? Do you have health insurance? How are your eating and exercise habits? If you have poor health, what things are you willing to do to improve it?

Chapter 10

Are We Like Sheep Trying to Serve Two Masters?

No man can serve two masters: for either he will hate the one, and love the other; or else he will hold to the one, and despise the other. (Matthew 6:24)

It is impossible to serve two masters. The two masters in existence are the Almighty God and the Evil One. We can only cling to one and hate the other. We cannot serve both. However, there are several different groups of individuals who are like sheep trying to serve both masters. One group of sheep attempting to serve both consists of aggressive-passive individuals who try to link their wealth gained by power, opportunistic means, and other worldly devices as blessings received from God. These sheep try to convince themselves that they are God's true sheep, but in reality they want God to follow their own agenda. Not being concerned about the purpose that God specifically assigned to them before the world was framed, they greedily give God a long list of their personal desires and then wait anxiously for Him to deliver. Their main goal is to acquire wealth, health, and power in the here and now by trying to manipulate God, as if He is a genie in a bottle waiting to grant their every wish.

Another group of sheep trying to serve two masters is those who want to be members of the masses of passive sheep and still be considered as God's servants. These sheep are those who claim to have submitted their all to God but in actuality they prefer practicing the worldly ways of society. These are the sheep that will go to church every Sunday but do unethical (yet legal) acts on their jobs to keep their positions and satisfy their bosses. These sheep will pray when someone is being mistreated but will not put forth the effort to extend a helping hand. They are the sheep that will pray to God for healing but continue to eat junk food in front of the TV set every night as couch potatoes. They will ask God for a job but expect to remain on government assistance. As God sees all, God knows their hearts are divided and will not answer their requests.

Within the masses, there is another group of sheep that desire to serve two masters; these sheep strive to be the perfectionist through serving God and satisfying others, especially those in authority. These sheep long to maintain their position as upright, law-abiding citizens with high morals standards here on earth, not only so that they will earn God's approval but also that of others. They believe they are justified and made righteous by their own good works and deeds (e.g., helping the poor, visiting the sick, acquiring much success, and living up to high moral standards) and not by their faith in the Redeemer, Jesus Christ. They yearn to be loved and justified by God, but they fail to understand that God loves them unconditionally and that they need to depend on His grace and not on the worth of their own merits to save them and make them righteous (see Ephesians 2: 8-9). As they attempt and fail to reach perfection, they often end up battling compulsive behaviors (e.g., excessive exercising, cleaning, organizing, and working) and eating disorders (e.g., anorexia, bulimia, compulsive overeating, and binge eating). They do not understand that if they will stop trying so hard to be perfect, surrender their all to God, and accept His unconditional love, then God will give them righteousness through His grace and the passion, strength, and health required to complete their God-given purpose without the fear of failure. The Bible says that only God is righteous, and all have come short of the glory of God, but all can receive salvation, righteousness, and wellness through their redemption in the Savior, Jesus Christ (see Romans 3:22-24).

A third group of sheep trying to serve two masters includes those who, through acts of frustration, attempt to be servers of God. These sheep want to justify their rebellious behavior and criminal offenses by either trying to persuade others that they are ordained by God to perform these heartless acts or to convince themselves that God, regardless of their wrong actions, will always bless them as His dear children. Because it is impossible for God to be associated with any hate and sin, the consequences of this type of double-mindedness often result in much mental distress and physical sickness. Truly, God is a God of love and peace and not of hatred and rebellion. Nevertheless, there will be times when God's children are required to speak the truth and stand against opposition, but God will only lead and protect those whose hearts are founded in peace, kindness, and love.

It is impossible to simultaneously follow the voice of the Good Shepherd and that of the Evil One; we must choose. It is best to be cold or hot, but not lukewarm, for God is extremely displeased with those who choose to be lukewarm. In the Bible, Jesus says, "I know thy works that thou are neither cold nor hot; I would that thou were cold or hot. So then because thou are lukewarm, and neither cold nor hot, I will spue [vomit] thee out of my mouth" (Revelations 3:15-16). But if the "lukewarmers" will decide to surrender their all to God, God will then accept them with open arms, heal their entire being, and set their souls on fire for their God-given purpose.

* * *

Work-Study: Points to Ponder

1. Do you confess to be a Christian? If so, have you submitted your all to God, or are you trying to convince Him to follow your own agenda of acquiring wealth and power?

2. Are you following God only, or are you also conforming to the negative ways of society? Do you find it difficult to completely separate yourself from the negative ways of others and society and commit yourself totally to God?

3. Are you a person who believes that God saves and blesses people based on their own goodness and merits?

4. Are you a frustrated person who claims to demonstrate rebellious behavior and commit criminal acts in the name of God?

5. If you are lukewarm, are you ready to submit your all to God and let Him lead you to a place of wellness?

Chapter 11

Are We Like Submissive Sheep of the Good Shepherd?

O come, let us sing unto the Lord: let us make a joyful noise to the rock of our salvation ... for He is our God; and we are the people of His pasture, and the sheep of His hand. (Psalm 95: 1 and 7)

Jesus said that He is the Good Shepherd and His sheep hear and know His voice (see John 10: 4 and 11). Those who follow the voice of Jesus are like submissive sheep of the Good Shepherd. These submissive sheep are nothing more than deceived, lost sheep (e.g., the aggressive-passive sheep, the masses of passive sheep, the frustrated sheep, and the server-of-two-masters sheep) that at one point in time became *sick and tired of being sick and tired*, and came to the realization that they need salvation, deliverance from sin by our Savior, Jesus Christ. Being fed up with all of the lies, sins, and deceptions, they dethroned the Evil One from the seat of their hearts and welcomed the sovereignty of Jesus Christ. They chose to quench the voice of the Evil One, obey the voice of the Good Shepherd, and surrender their lives, hearts, and all to Jesus. Because of God's love for mankind, He gave His only begotten Son so that all who believe in Him can receive salvation and become one of His dear children. He becomes Abba Father to all who accept Jesus Christ as their personal Savior (see Rom. 8:15-17 and Gal 4:6-7). Those of us who are His dear children are Christians, which means Christ-like. We accepted Jesus Christ as our personal Savior and became adopted into the family.

Many deceived sheep believe that Christianity is just another form of religion used by the aggressive-passive sheep to control the masses. Unfortunately, this often seems to be the case, as many leaders of Christian churches prove to be nothing more than corrupt aggressive-passive sheep blinded by the Deceiver. These leaders are false prophets who seek only personal gain and do not represent the true definition of Christianity. Religion does not define Christianity. Different than religion, which is centered on a list of laws and regulations often devoid of love, Christianity is centered on one commandment and that is to love—to love God with all your heart, soul, and mind; to love your neighbor as yourself; and to love your enemies (see Matt. 22:37-39 and Matt. 5:44). Christianity is love because God is love.

Salvation is not received by following a set of laws. We failed the law. Our actions and works cannot save us. Thus, we are saved by grace. Grace is a gift from God, not of works, lest anyone should boast (see Eph. 2:8–9). As our Heavenly Father, God gives us unconditional love that is impossible for us to comprehend with our carnal minds. As the Good Shepherd, Jesus teaches us through His Spirit how to love God, ourselves, and all people. He teaches us how to become leaders as we choose to follow His leadership and learn how to serve Him. As we learn how to serve Him without frustration and a boastful attitude, He gives us minds of perfect peace. He keeps our minds in perfect peace, as we strive to complete our God-given purpose by showing love to others. By accepting God's love and learning how to love as God, God gives us the desires of our hearts. As we grow in love, our desires become founded in love. Showing love to God first and then to others becomes the main desire of our hearts, and against such love there is no law (see Gal. 5:22-23). There are no laws that prohibit us from performing good deeds, giving to those in need, and helping ourselves and others to become better people.

Expressing our love as Christians does not mean we are to be nice all of the time, but it does require that we live and speak the truth. Being nice by avoiding confrontational situations often causes the truth to be hidden. Sometimes, hearing the truth hurts and causes discomfort. Yet hearing the truth, not lies and deceptions, is what sets us free, heals our hearts and souls, and transforms our minds and bodies to wellness. Accepting the truth is what leads us to our purpose and gives us the understanding and strength to complete it in a healthy body as we love God and ourselves enough to eat right and exercise. Practicing the truth by fulfilling our God-given purpose of helping others, as we accept and maintain our gift of wellness, is an unselfish expression of love that compels others to do the same. The Bible says that no one profits when our neighbors come to us in need of help and we do nothing more than say depart in peace and be in good health, without providing them with the desire and means to obtain peace and good health (see James 2:15-16). In order to show love to others and effectively change lives, we must be an example for others to follow, not only by speaking the truth but also by practicing what we speak.

* * *

Work-Study: Points to Ponder

1. Do you believe Jesus Christ is God the Son? If so, do you have a personal relationship with Him? How can you be sure that you do?

2. If you do not have a personal relationship with Jesus, do you desire to have one? If the answer is yes, then follow these steps:

    - Realize that you are a sinner who needs a Savior; in other words, repent.
    - Confess Jesus Christ as your personal Savior who died for your sins.
    - Believe that you are saved by His grace through faith.
    - Be baptized and filled with the Holy Spirit by faith.
    - Become a member of a Bible-teaching church.

    Welcome! If you have completed these steps, you are now a Christian, a follower of Jesus Christ. How do you feel? Do you feel any different? What things are you doing differently?

3. Anyone can read the Bible and formulate personal opinions about its content, but guidance by the Holy Spirit (the third person of the trinity) is required before one can study and comprehend its true meaning.
    a. Do you have the Holy Spirit dwelling in you? If so, have you

experienced any evidence of Him? Are you willing to listen to and obey His voice? If so, what changes are you willing to make in your life?

b. Do you read the Bible and pray? Are you able to comprehend the Bible by listening to the voice of the Holy Spirit? Does the Holy Spirit talk to you directly? If so, what methods of communication are used?
c. Are you willing to listen to the Holy Spirit as He leads you to your purpose? Are you ready to complete your purpose in a healthy body by accepting your God-given gift of good health and living a healthy lifestyle?

4. I used to be a sheep, trying to serve two masters, who believed that God gives salvation and blessings based on my own merits and goodness. If you are a Christian, what type of sheep were you before you submitted your all to Jesus? Since you have been a Christian, how has your life changed?

5. If you are a Christian in a leadership position, such as a pastor, supervisor, manager, or business owner, how have your management or leadership skills grown? How have your attitude and actions toward your followers or employees improved?

6. If you are a Christian follower or employee, do you follow the leadership of others as you first follow God? Do you put God before everything and everybody else?

7. If you are a Christian, do you care about the welfare and health of others? If so, why? Do you help those less fortunate than you? If you do, then describe how. If not, are you willing to start?

8. Do you refer to Christianity as a religion, or is it different than a religion?

9. Do you believe it takes grace or works to save us from our sins? Or do you believe in something totally different?

10. I encourage you to always speak the truth in love, not only because God is with you, but because hearing the truth is what encourages people to change.
    a. What is your definition of love? Do you believe that the truth should always be spoken in love? Or is it okay to hide the truth if it keeps one from experiencing hurt and being offended?
    b. Are you willing to give constructive criticism? Are you receptive to constructive criticism?

11. It is important to practice the truth and not give just lip service so that others can see how to follow your example. Do you live the truth? Are you completing your purpose in a healthy body and living a healthy lifestyle? Does your life serve as an example for others? Or do you only speak the truth without living it?

Chapter 12

The Good Shepherd Provides Prosperity and Good Health

Trust in the Lord with all thine heart; and lean not unto thine own understanding. In all thy ways acknowledge Him and He shall direct thy paths. Be not wise in thine own eyes; fear the Lord, and depart from evil. It shall be health to thy navel, and marrow to thy bones. Honour the Lord with thy substance, and with thy first fruits of all thine increase: so shall thy barns be filled with plenty and thy presses shall burst out with new wine. (Proverbs 3:5–10)

The last three chapters of Part I (chapters 12–14) discuss the benefits of listening to God's voice as we surrender our all to Him, releasing ourselves from our past bad habits and addictive nature, and having the faith that He desires to bless His children with prosperity and good health. Unfortunately, many people who are born in poverty expect to remain so for their entire life. In addition to this, many also think that addictive and bad habits, poor health, and sickness are consequences of life that they must accept and cannot change. In contrast, some people believe they can receive their God-given gift of good health through faith and prayer and then maintain it without ever adopting a healthy lifestyle. Others think that adopting a healthy lifestyle, without first accepting their God-given gift of good health, is all that is required to reach wellness and then maintain it. Adopting a healthy lifestyle, however, only increases the odds of living a long life in good health but does not guarantee it. I am sure we all know of someone who lived a healthy lifestyle but still died early in life as a result of health issues. In short, wellness is guaranteed only to those of us who accept our God-given gift of good health through faith and then take action to maintain this gift by living a healthy lifestyle.

Many Christians fear the thought of being completely led by God. They fear they will end up living a life that is unfulfilled, miserable, and absent of materialistic things. Afraid to submit all to God, many think He will take everything away from them and not give anything back in return. This is because they are allowing the Deceiver to plant ideas of fear in their minds. They fear that if they surrender their all to God, He will transform them and their lives to something with which they do not want to identify. They fear that God will strip them of their happiness and leave them poor and destitute in some foreign land, or coerce them to become missionaries in some Third World country. These possibilities are far from the truth. God is a God of love and does not operate in fear. We must release our fears before we can become free through faith. If we are called to be a missionary, it is because our purpose in life agrees with the desires of our hearts. God does not strip us of our desires; He gives us our desires. As we choose to follow God, our desires become one with our purpose, which is full of every good thing. The words of King David, "The Lord is my shepherd I shall not want" (Psalms 23:1), are so very true. Those of us who are willing to submit all to God and endure life's challenges shall be blessed not only with heavenly treasures in the next life but with peace, joy, health, wealth, family, houses, and land right now in this life (see Mark 10:29–30). If we seek God first, all things shall be added onto us (see Matt. 6:33). All who accept God as their Good Shepherd and freely give to others in need are never found lacking or without but have more than enough of every good thing.

Many Christians think they are following the Good Shepherd by living in lack here on earth as they patiently wait for their blessings in the next life. Working every day, religiously attending church every Sunday, singing, shouting, and waiting for God to take them home to heaven, they try to demonstrate their love and devotion to God by living in poverty and without material things. They also believe that suffering through sickness and disease is the duty of a strong Christian. None of these beliefs, however, is supported by the Word of God found in the Bible. His Word fully explains how He desires that His children not only live with Him throughout eternity but also that they are abundantly blessed here on earth. God created man to be healthy, but sin brought sickness into the world. If we find that we are sick and in sin, then we need to pray the prayer of faith for our healing and become whole (see James 5:14-15). Through Jesus sacrificing His life, we were not only cleansed from our sins by the shedding of His precious blood, but by His stripes we were healed from all sicknesses and diseases (see I Peter 2:24). It doesn't matter who we are or how we were born; we all were healed by Jesus' stripes.

Many believe that before they can depart from this life they must die from physical complications such as sickness, trauma, or organ failure. Yet this is far from the truth. Through being obedient to God's Word, it is possible to live a long, healthy life and not experience death until our God-given purpose has been fulfilled (see Ephesians 6:2–3 and Proverbs 3:5–8). The Bible explains that when Moses died at the old age of 120, he had excellent eyesight and his health was not abated (see Deuteronomy 34:7). Completing his God-given purpose and maintaining God's laws of healthy living (see Leviticus 11 and Deuteronomy 14), Moses had the faith that God would bless him with good health and long life. After living for 120 years, God took Moses to the next life, not because he was physically weak, sick, or injured but because he had completed his purpose. Moses died peaceably with the testimony that he pleased God.

During Jesus' life here on earth, He went about healing people with all kinds of health problems and infirmities (see Matthew 8:16-17). He healed the blind, the lame, the mentally disturbed; whatever the problem, He healed it. After He was crucified, the risen Jesus Christ returned to the right hand of the Father and sent down to us the Holy Spirit (the Comforter), who through our faith empowers us to be obedient and receive the blessings of prosperity and wellness. Jesus came and completed His mission here on earth so that we all can have life—and life more abundantly (see John 10:10). Thus, a life of constant disobedience, lack, and sickness is a consequence of following the voice of the Evil One. It is beyond my understanding why anyone would think that such a loving God would want us to stay depressed, poor, and sick. We need to have enough faith in God to desire and plant obedience, prosperity, and good health in our hearts and then begin speaking them into existence (see III John 1:2). The Bible says that whosoever has faith in God, "doubt not in his heart, but shall believe those things which he saith shall come to pass, he shall have whatsoever he saith" (Mark 11:23). Then, once we are obedient and blessed with prosperity and good health, we must continue to keep the faith so that each one of us shall become channels overflowing with blessings, meeting the needs of others.

* * *

Work-Study: Points to Ponder

1. Many Christians believe that once they have accepted Jesus Christ as their personal Savior and have allowed Jesus Christ to reign in their hearts that Satan will no longer confront them with lies. This is very far from the truth. As long as people have breath in their bodies, the temptations and lies will never cease. After submitting all to God, however, a Christian has the power, through the Holy Spirit, to reject the temptations and lies by speaking truths of victory (the Word of God).
   a. If you are a Christian, do you find that Satan still speaks lies and tempts you? If so, is the intensity of the temptations stronger than before you became a Christian?
   b. If you are a Christian, are you willing to resist Satan's lies and surrender your all to the Good Shepherd? If not, why? Is it because you are afraid? Are you afraid God might ask you to do something that is not listed on your personal agenda, such as become a missionary?

2. Do you believe God uses depression, sickness, and poverty as a means for Christians to express their devotion to Him? Do you believe God uses depression, sickness, and poverty as a method to make Christians stronger?

3. Do you believe you have to be sick or physically injured to die, or do you believe you can die in good health without pain and suffering?

4. God's blessings and prosperity include not only good health and money but also peace, joy, happiness, love, kindness, obedience, patience, friendships, etc. Do you believe God wants people to be depressed, sick, and poor, or do you believe God wants people to be blessed with good health, prosperity, and all good things?

5. As God blesses you with prosperity, good health, and all things, what are you planning to do with your blessings? Will you use your blessings to be an example for others to follow as you complete your God-given purpose and help others in need, or will you only use them to satisfy your personal pleasures?

CHAPTER 13

Breaking Old Habits Requires a New Mind-set

Be not conformed to this world: but be ye transformed by the renewing of your mind, that ye may prove what is that good, and acceptable, and perfect will of God. (Romans 12:2)

What causes an addiction? How is an addiction formed? It starts with the Evil One; he presents an idea into your mind, and you hear it. As this idea is received, it becomes materialized into a thought. You have a choice to either reject or entertain this thought. If you reject the thought, the temptation to act is quenched. But if you choose to continually entertain the thought, before long, you will yield to the temptation to act. Soon, every time opportunity presents itself, you immediately act upon it. The thought is now a constant temptation that begins to invade your heart, as you plant, water, and nurture it until it sprouts and takes root. As you begin to fertilize and till the ground of your heart, soon the temptation becomes rooted deep within it. Then, the temptation starts to branch out into your mind and soul and poison your entire being. Your mind becomes set, and your body is programmed to automatically satisfy the temptation; an addictive habit is born. The addictive habit becomes a stronghold as it saturates every part of your being. A single idea has been transformed into an addiction.

The first step in breaking an addiction requires you to be completely fed up with it. It requires reaching a cathartic moment when you become *sick and tired of being sick and tired*, and realize *enough is enough*. It requires listening to the voice of the Good Shepherd and choosing to obey His words, one day at a time. Each and every time you hear the voice of the Evil One, you must recognize that it is his voice and then reject it. More and more each day, as you begin to follow the voice of the Good Shepherd and reject the voice of the Evil One, a new mind-set starts to form and the old one begins to deteriorate. The old signals and pathways rooted deep within your heart and branching throughout your body are replaced with new ones. You become controlled by a new word. You are reprogrammed to follow a new voice, the voice that speaks encouraging words within your heart, such as *Stop it! Stop the bad habit; stop the destruction!* You choose to follow the voice that teaches you the significance of living your life to the fullest, loving yourself and others, and completing your God-given purpose in a healthy body.

As you break an addiction, flashbacks of the addictive habit may consistently haunt your mind, but don't give up. The Evil One will not stop without a fight; it is war. As you struggle to shake the monkey off your back, Satan is determined to keep your mind in bondage. The Evil One keeps a mean bag of tricks, and he is never afraid to use them. At times, Satan's voice and the tendency to repeat old actions will be extremely strong. Beware—as certain visions trigger flashbacks, old friends stimulate urges, and haunting memories quench your ability to erase past offenses and forgive yourself and others. Also, be careful of the temptation to replace old addictions with brand new ones. For example, many find in their attempt to stop their sexual, drug, alcohol, or cigarette addiction that they are often tempted to replace it with compulsive overeating (a bad habit often chosen as the lesser of two evils). As Satan constantly speaks lies to your mind, you must be prepared to fight temptation with the truth, the Word of the Good Shepherd. If you constantly speak and hear the Word and submit all to the Good Shepherd, you will gain the willpower to say no to Satan, and Satan will flee from you (see James 4:7). It is important to practice meditating on and reciting Bible scriptures, such as, *I can do all things through Christ Jesus which strengthens me* (Phil. 4:13), and *I am more than a conqueror through Him that loves me* (see Rom. 8:37). The more you practice this, the more the truth of the Good Shepherd will fill your heart and give you the strength to form healthy, productive habits.

As time passes, fighting the temptation to relapse into an old addictive habit may seem like a never-ending battle. At first, as your body continues to scream *Satisfy me!*, the temptation to relapse may intensify in magnitude, but as you become stronger in the Word, this temptation will possess less power over your mind and body. However, be careful not to become overly confident, because Satan will always wait for the opportune moment to try to defeat you. This is his job, and he is very good at it. If you do trip and fall, don't be discouraged and stop the fight. Ask God for forgiveness and keep going, keep fighting. Keep fighting the good fight of faith (see I Tim. 6:12). As you continue to seek God, you will gain the strength to starve the lusts of the flesh and the power to resist Satan. Furthermore, if you release it all to God, He will heal you from the addiction and transform your entire being to one of wellness. Satan, the tempter, is as a roaring lion seeking whomever he can devour (see I Peter 5:8). Yet God is a loving Father that will never allow you to be tempted more than you can bear (see I Cor.10: 13). If you choose to listen to God's voice, He will empower you to be victorious over temptation. When God is your Good Shepherd, you will always have the strength to escape the temptation and replace it with the desire to develop healthy habits, but the choice to do so is yours.

* * *

Work-Study: Points to Ponder

1. Addictive and bad habits can be detrimental to the health, safety, and well-being of ourselves and others around us. Some common addictive or bad habits are drug abuse, alcoholism, sexual immorality, gossiping, cigarette smoking, caffeine addiction, sugar addiction, self-mutilation, eating disorders, "couch potato syndrome," being in bad or abusive relationships, and hanging around troublemakers. Do you have an addictive or bad habit? How tired are you of the habit? Are you willing to stop? How detrimental do you believe this habit is to your well-being or that of others around you?

2. Are you willing to listen to the voice of the Good Shepherd that says stop the addictive or bad habit? Are you willing to follow the steps to recovery? Describe how you would be willing to ask and receive help from God and others.

3. Breaking an addictive habit can be quite painful. Are you willing to suffer through cravings or hard withdrawal symptoms? When necessary, are you willing to be rehabilitated or receive medical attention?

4. Living in unforgiveness often hinders us from stopping addictive habits. After Satan has planted ideas in our minds and orchestrated our performances of sins and immoral acts, he then turns around and makes us feel guilty about them. As we experience pain from the hurt and guilt, we often find it hard to forgive others, and especially difficult to forgive ourselves. Before we know it, we have formed an addictive habit (e.g., sexual immorality, drugs, alcoholism, smoking, and eating disorders) in an unsuccessful attempt to bury the hurt, guilt, and shame. Our Heavenly Father is a God of forgiveness (that is why He sent His only Son to save us from our sins and free us from our past). If unforgiveness has you in bondage, give it all to God, and He will give you a new spirit and free your heart, soul, and mind.
   a. Are you haunted by your past and find it difficult to forgive yourself and others? If so, how have you dealt with it? Has this caused you to form an addictive habit?
   b. Do you find it difficult to let go of the past? Do you want to forgive? If you do want to forgive, describe the method you are willing to use to begin the process of forgiveness.

5. People with addictive tendencies often relapse into old addictions or are easily tempted to start new ones. As you attempt to break the old addictions, do you find yourself relapsing or replacing them with new addictions? Or are you recovering and disciplining yourself by replacing these addictions with new good and healthy habits?

6. Do you know of someone with an addictive habit? Does he or she want to break this habit? If so, explain how you would be willing to give that person the needed support to break this habit without causing any damage to your own well-being or to that of your family.

Chapter 14

Good Health Requires Listening to the Right Voice

Labour not to be rich: cease from thine own wisdom. Will thou set thine eyes upon that which is not? For riches certainly make themselves wings; they fly away as an eagle toward heaven. Eat thou not the bread of him that hath an evil eye, neither desire thou his dainty meats: for as he thinketh in his heart, so is he: eat and drink, saith he to thee; but his heart is not with thee. Be not amongst winebibbers; amongst riotous eaters ... for the drunkard and the glutton shall come to poverty: and drowsiness shall clothe a man with rags. (Proverbs 23: 4–7 and 20–21)

Junk food is a major problem in today's society. Obesity is an American epidemic. Our health in America is declining rapidly as we constantly eat unhealthy foods and eliminate exercise from our daily routine. The combined activity of eating junk food and watching television has become the favorite American pastime. Preparing home-cooked meals is rapidly becoming obsolete as fast-food restaurants are found on almost every corner and packaged processed foods are stocked heavily in almost every kitchen cupboard. Although we are responsible for the modern-day troubles, we are not the first to introduce problems into the world. Our forefather Adam is responsible for making that mistake. However, just like Adam, we have control over our choices. We are not mere robots forced to do good or evil. We have the choice of following the voice of the Good Shepherd or that of the Evil One. God does not force us to be healthy. If we want to be healthy, then we must choose to be healthy. We must listen to God's voice guiding us to receive His gift of good health and live a healthier lifestyle now. We need to have faith and believe that God wants us all to aim for the best, which is to be healthy. It is to be hoped that we (the members within the food industry and all of the consumers) will follow the voice of the Good Shepherd, the right voice, and learn how to work together and become a nation of healthy people. However, before this can be done, we need to understand and be accountable for the role we each play in our nation's health epidemic.

Within the food industry, there are certain aggressive-passive sheep that have commercialized the food industry by bombarding the masses (the consumers) with junk food. Junk food is manufactured to be tasty, addictive, unhealthy, sensually and conveniently packaged, affordable, and widely distributed. Without questioning the aggressive-passive sheep's motives, the masses of passive sheep just buy and eat it. The aggressive-passive sheep need to stop exploiting the masses and begin to be more concerned about everyone's welfare and health. They need to listen to the voice that will value the health of others more than their own financial gain.

The food industry is often seen as a flawed entity that has spiraled completely out of control. It is true that the food industry has many problems, but these problems can be corrected. The food industry is nothing more than an "it" that is controlled by a group of members who are the owners, board of directors, chief executive officers, and stockholders of businesses and major corporations, such as farms, food manufacturing plants, restaurants, and grocery stores. These members can choose to take responsibility for their actions and work together to provide this nation with an ample supply of affordable health food. Fortunately, within the food industry, there are responsible members who listen to the right voice by producing, processing, manufacturing, and marketing healthier foods. Yet many more members need to listen to the right voice and follow suit. Furthermore, businesses and major corporations need to provide more funds to educate and encourage the masses to eat healthier. Small-business farmers also need to be provided with more financial assistance so that they can grow healthy produce and raise healthy livestock and still make a reasonable profit. The list of improvements and concerns that needs to be addressed is long, but the greatest contribution that members within the food industry can give to all consumers is to cease the junk-food market.

My message to you, the members within the food industry, is that it will be more profitable in the long run for you, your customers, and your nation's economy to replace the junk-food market with a health-food one. This can be achieved by allowing God to help you reconstruct your strategic decision-making processes. Listen to the right voice, the voice of the Good Shepherd, as He teaches methods and supplies avenues that will allow you to market health food and still earn big profits. It is important to realize that if the majority of your satisfied customers keeps eating your junk food, they will probably become sick, obese, physically unfit, unemployed, and financially dependent, either on the income of their physically fit family members (who don't eat your junk food) or on government assistance. In other words, if the majority of your customers becomes sick, morbidly obese, and physically unfit, then who will be the healthy, fit, employed, satisfied customers that will spend money on your junk food?

The Deceiver has convinced the masses of passive sheep (the majority of the consumers) that the aggressive-passive sheep (a large percentage of the members within the food industry) are the only ones to blame for their unhealthy habits and junk-food addictions. The masses blame the aggressive-passive sheep for not being able to afford the high prices of health food. The masses need to stop listening to the voice of the Deceiver that has them playing the blame game. They need to stop listening to the voice that totally blames the food industry for all of their unhealthy habits and for being physically out of shape. The masses need to stop listening to the voice that says that junk food is great company and eating it is their favorite pastime. The masses need to stop listening to the voice that leads them into a state of depression or denial as they look at their unhealthy bodies in the mirror.

My message to you, the consumers, is that you need to listen to a new voice—the right voice of the Good Shepherd that says your health depends on your choices. You need to listen to the voice that tells you to accept responsibility for your own health, take care of your bodies, and speak good health into existence. You need to listen to the voice that teaches you to love yourselves and others enough so that you will transform your homes and communities into places of healthy living. And above all, you need to love God enough to become physically fit and healthy so that you will have the energy to complete your God-given purpose.

It is essential for you, the consumers, to understand that if you want to be healthy you must learn to not only eat right and exercise but to also depend on God through faith. Sure, living a healthy lifestyle increases your odds of being healthy, but it does not guarantee good health. Believing that Jesus healed you by His stripes (Isaiah 53:5) literally means what it says: Jesus healed you—all of you (i.e., your heart, soul, mind, and body). If your spirit has been renewed and your faith is intact, there are no limitations or restrictions on the problems God will heal. In the four Gospels (Matthew, Mark, Luke, and John) of the Bible, you will find many cases in which Jesus healed people from all manner of sicknesses and diseases. There was never a case where Jesus turned someone away because the sickness, disease, or handicap was too difficult for Him to heal. Many were not healed, however, because they chose not to be; they chose not to have enough faith in God (see Matthew 13:58). Just as it was for people in biblical times, the choice to be healed is yours. You must first accept your gift of healing and good health through faith, and then be obedient to God's voice and do the work that demonstrates your beliefs. If you have the faith to believe you are healthy, then you must do the work to be healthy. The Bible says that works (i.e., actions) without faith are meaningless (see Gal. 2:16) and faith without works is dead (see James 2:17). Faith merged with works is the tool you must use to demonstrate your belief in healing and to progress towards wellness. A person who says he believes that he is healed and healthy but continues to sit on the couch every night while eating a quart of ice cream is living a lie, and the truth is not in him. As you receive your gift of good health, I can guarantee you that God will advise you to eat right and exercise. If you agree to be obedient to this, then God will give you the understanding, strength, provisions, and finances required to live a healthy lifestyle. In addition, your increasingly buying more healthy foods will give the food industry the incentive to manufacture and market them. The formula to good health is simple: have faith that God made you healthy, and then live it.

* * *

Work-Study: Points to Ponder

The below Points to Ponder are divided into two groups. Points 1 through 4 are addressed to individuals within the food industry, and Points 5 through 7 are directed to the consumers.

1. Are you an owner of a business or major corporation within the food industry? Do you own stock in the food industry? Does your business or corporation produce, process, manufacture, or market healthy or unhealthy foods? If only unhealthy foods are supplied, then why?

2. Does your business or corporation manufacture or market junk food? Is your place of business exploiting the junk-food problem? If so, what steps are you willing to take to cease this problem? If stopping the junk-food problem initially results in lost profits or requires donating funds, are you and others at your place of business still willing to address this problem? Are you or others at your place of business willing to educate your customers to eat healthier?

3. As a business owner, do you believe if you have the faith to make the health of your customers a priority and market healthy products that God will reveal and provide mechanisms to increase your profits? Describe your thoughts.

4. For those of you who already own a business or corporation that produces, processes, manufactures, or markets health food, we as a nation thank you. Yet what improvements can still be made? How can you help convince other businesses to do the same?

5. As a consumer, are you a person who eats junk food on a regular basis? Are you overweight or unhealthy? Are you willing to stop eating junk food? Describe the ways in which you would be willing to increase fitness and eat healthy foods.

6. Are you willing to stop being a consumer who buys junk food? Are you willing to take responsibility for your community and help motivate others to eat healthier? How would you be willing to help convince business owners to produce, process, manufacture, and market health food?

7. As a consumer, do you believe that eating right and exercising guarantee good health, or that these things only increase the odds of good health? How do you feel about the statement that good health is a God-given gift that requires faith to receive and a healthy lifestyle to maintain? Do you have faith in God to believe that He will renew your spirit and then heal your heart, soul, mind, and body?

Part II: Health = You + Your Village

Chapter 15

Good Health Requires That We Change Ourselves and Our Villages

Ye are the light of the world. A city that is set on a hill cannot be hid. Neither do men light a candle, and put it under a bushel, but on a candlestick; and it giveth light unto all that are in the house. Let your light so shine before men, that they may see your good works, and glorify your Father which is in heaven. (Matthew 5:14–16)

It is to be hoped that this chapter will encourage you to take responsibility for your health by changing your "village" to a place of healthy living. Here, your "village" is more than just a group of houses surroundings your place of residence; it includes the entire territory within your circle of influence. You define the size of your circle of influence. For example, you may choose to limit it to an area within your neighborhood or to take the challenge of extending it as far as over your entire nation. What's most important, however, is not to focus on the size of your circle of influence, but on your willingness to accept responsibility for improving your "village" to become a healthy place to live.

I have come to the realization that once we—people of all socioeconomic classes—understand that our standard of health is defined by the decisions we make, we can begin to take ownership of our right to be healthy. Our poor health does not have to be a function of our socioeconomic class. We should not allow population demographics to locate large pockets of unhealthy people. Our bodies do not have to be products of junk food, just because we live in a particular area. The choice to be healthy is ours. If we want to be healthy and discard the bad habits we've developed over the past, along with the bad hand that has been dealt to us, we must be ready for change. Once we are motivated to follow the voice of the Good Shepherd and become empowered through His strength, we then must execute change. We must use this power to seek good health, find it, grab it, possess it, and demand it. Then, we must not stop there, but accept responsibility for changing the condition of our villages. As defined here, a "village" includes the entire area (e.g., town, state, county, nation, country, city, metropolitan area, suburbs, rural area, urban area, ghetto, neighborhood, industrial area, residential area, business sites, apartments, houses, schools, and churches) and community (e.g., family members, neighbors, business owners, government officials, consumers, teachers, students, relatives, friends, acquaintances, coworkers, church-goers, and homeless people) in which each of us lives and is willing to help change by our influence. If our villages consist of mostly unhealthy foods and areas that are unsafe for exercising, then it becomes difficult for us and our fellow villagers to be healthy. Thus, it is our responsibility to change our villages to places that support healthy living. This change requires all of us to work together, and in time, no matter our economic statuses or social positions, we all can live in villages that portray a nation of good health. As we evolve to a healthy nation, we can then begin reaching out to villages in other nations and help them to also become places of green pastures.

* * *

Work-Study: Points to Ponder

1. Fill in the blank below.
   My health (good, average, or poor) is dependent on ________.
   a) Me
   b) My village
   c) Me + my village

2. What level of health do you think you have? Rate your health on a scale of 1 to 10 and fill in the blank. ____________
   9–10 (good)
   7–8 (above average)

5–6 (average)
3–4 (below average)
1–2 (poor)

3. There are all types of people (e.g., short, tall, skinny, fat, old, young, red skin, brown skin, yellow skin, white skin, black skin, brunette, redhead, and blonde). Describe yourself.
   Me = ____

4. Everyone lives in a village. There are all types of villages. Describe your village, which includes your entire circle of influence (e.g., family, neighbors, homeless people, houses, apartments, town, city, rural area, schools, churches, businesses, suburbs, inner city, ghetto, and nation).
   My village = ________________________________

5. It is your responsibility to take action by improving your health and changing your village, regardless of its demographic location, to a place that supports good health.
   True or False ________

6. Is the condition of your village influencing your level of health and that of others? If the answer is yes, describe how it does this. If you are unhealthy, what problems in your village are influencing your poor health? Describe your willingness and motivation to get involve and change these problems.

CHAPTER 16

Repent: The 6 R's

As many as I love, I rebuke and chasten: be zealous therefore, and repent. Behold, I stand at the door, and knock: if any man hear my voice, and open the door, I will come in to him, and will sup with him, and he with me. (Revelation 3:19–20)

Before the lifestyle change, I was a Christian who was physically sick. I did not accept my God-given gift of good health. This chapter describes the day of change. By turning from my unhealthy lifestyle, I began to accept my gift of good health and proceed with the work required to maintain a healthier lifestyle. Today, I am still not totally healthy, as my transformation to wellness is still not complete. Yet I am definitely healthier than I was, and I am looking forward to the day when my faith has matured to the level of completely accepting my entire gift of good health.

I was deeply disgusted with myself. Sitting in my office as I completed a technical report, I was tired, sluggish, and miserable. It was St. Patrick's Day 2005, and I had just finished eating my holiday sweets. Out of desperation, I cried out silently to God, *My Abba Father, I am sick and tired of being sick and tired! What is my problem?* He replied in a soft yet firm voice, "Your diet. Your diet of white sugar and white flour is your problem. Stop it! Stop it and accept your gift of good health!"

I sat there, pretending to be mortified beyond disbelief. Yet in reality, I was suffering from nothing more than hurt feelings. The intense sting of hearing the truth had pierced my pride and left me wallowing in self-pity. I already knew that eating "white stuff" (white sugar and white flour) was my problem. I was not a stranger to the health problems involved with eating "white stuff"; I'd known of them since childhood. I was the prototype of a "white-stuff-oholic." But I had tried to bury all the negative repercussions associated with eating white stuff deep within my subconscious. I loved my white stuff and I didn't want to stop it! I always devoured it—two or three times a day at work and then at least two more times at home. Satisfying my addiction for white stuff perpetually fueled a roller-coaster ride that raced throughout this body of mine, and I didn't want the addictive ride to end.

But that day was different; I wanted to change. Thank God for cathartic moments! I came to myself and chose to obey the voice that said *"Stop it!"* Suddenly, I rose from my seat, went to the nearest health-food store, grabbed an organic salad for lunch and a few groceries for dinner, and began my quest of healthy living. That was the day of repentance. For me, "repenting" was more than being sorry; it involved a six-step process: regret, realize, release, replace, repeat, and then remember. On March 17, 2005, I had performed all six steps. I was very excited because I knew my life would never be the same. I had done more than start a new healthy diet, for I had chosen a new healthy lifestyle —I had begun the Repent 6 R's Step Process to wellness.

* * *

Work-Study: Points to Ponder

Below is my description of the Repent 6 R's Step Process. I routinely meditate on it as I progress towards wellness.

R1) **Regret:** I regretted being unhealthy. I was sorry for the role I played in my sickness and wanted to change.

R2) **Realize:** I realized the source of my problem was consuming a diet of white sugar and white flour and not accepting my gift of good health.

R3) **Release:** I released myself from my old diet, bad habits, and many health issues. I eliminated foods with white sugar, white flour, and other simple carbohydrates.

R4) **Replace:** I replaced my old diet, bad habits, and illnesses with healthy foods, good habits, and good health, respectively.

R5) **Repeat:** Since March of 2005, I have consistently repeated my new diet, habits, and lifestyle, and I am committed to do so for the rest of my life.

R6) **Remember:** To keep motivated and moving forward (especially on those days when I make mistakes), I remember and meditate on that great day of repentance.

1. Are you happy with your health? Is your diet healthy? If you need to change your lifestyle to a healthy one, describe how willing you are to start the Repent 6 R's Step Process.

2. If you are ready to change your lifestyle, describe below your own experiences of the Repent 6 R's Step Process as you continue on the path to healthy living!

R1) **Regret:**

R2) **Realize:**

R3) **Release:**

R4) **Replace:**

R5) **Repeat:**

R6) **Remember:**

Chapter 17

My Village Starts at Home

The just man walketh in his integrity: His children are blessed after him. (Proverbs 20:7)

She [a just woman] looketh well to the ways [attends to the needs] of her household, and eateth not the bread of idleness. (Proverbs 31:27)

Chapter 17 demonstrates the importance of introducing your family to a healthy diet and staying on task until your entire family achieves good health.

My family was not sure, at first, if I was serious about my new healthy lifestyle. But I continued to be committed, and soon my family joined me in the effort. I am a divorcée and a mother of one son. My immediate family also includes my parents, who play important roles in our lives. I knew it wouldn't be difficult to convert my parents. My parents had dietary demands associated with related health conditions, and they supported decisions that would improve our health. As a parent, I also knew it was extremely important to teach my child to eat healthy. Fortunately, my son ate practically any healthy thing placed before him. My sister, who lives nearby with her husband and two children, was also a great support at this crucial time of change. She and my mom created delicious home-cooked dishes and desserts baked with healthy ingredients (see Part V for recipes) that kept me from cheating when the temptation for the "white stuff" reared its evil head.

When Mom was growing up, she was all legs and a bushy head of long, jet-black hair. Living on a farm in Goodman, Mississippi, her family grew peanuts, along with many different types of vegetables and fruits, but my mom loved to eat only peanuts—raw, roasted, salted; however they were prepared, she loved them. Being a busy little bee who didn't eat much for pleasure, it was difficult to persuade her to sit down and eat a healthy meal. She would snack on peanuts all day and eat little of anything else. Her parents would always sternly explain to her that she needed to stop eating "those goobers" but never really insisted in the matter.

One day, at the age of seven, with her mouth stuffed full of peanuts, Mom attempted to jump off a chair and onto her oldest sister's back. Instead, she hit the floor face-first, and the peanuts lodged in her throat. The severe choking exacerbated a series of health issues that would be discovered soon after—her parents took her to the nearest hospital as fast as their two mules and wagon could take them. Eating a diet of mostly peanuts, she was not a strong and healthy child; her immune system was weak. Unknowingly contracting at least one case of strep throat that was left untreated in the past, Mom was now found suffering from rheumatic fever, a disease that caused inflammation of her heart and serious heart damage. This disease also unmasked congenital heart complications that were extremely difficult to diagnose. As a result, her doctor gave her no more than two weeks to live. Owning no fear, my mother refused to accept this as the truth. As she watched her family weep in despair, she prayed and asked God to let her live and not die as a little child. Through her faith, much prayer, and eating foods that were healthy (e.g., vegetables, fruit, cocoa, eggs, and cod liver oil), Mom's prayers were answered. Not only did God miraculously heal her from this disease, but to this day, she still is a busy little bee.

* * *

Work-Study: Points to Ponder

1. As you decide to start a new lifestyle of good health, discuss this change with your family and let them know that you really need their support. How did your family respond to your decision to live a healthy lifestyle? Are they willing to support your new healthy lifestyle? If so, how?

2. Are any of your family members willing to change their diet to a healthy one? If so, how? How can you support them? If you have children, will it be an easy or difficult task to encourage them to eat healthy? Are you willing to put forth the effort?

3. Growing up, did you and your family eat healthy? Did your parents provide healthy meals? Did they insist that you and your siblings eat healthy? If you ate unhealthy foods, how did this affect your health? What things would you do differently?

4. Regardless of the food cravings and unhealthy habits that you and your family possess, how do you think you can motivate yourself and your family to start practicing good eating habits? Are you willing to find, create, and introduce your family to new healthy recipes? Will you insist, if necessary, that your children eat healthy foods, even when they do not want them?

5. Do you have any relatives or friends who will support your new healthy lifestyle? If so, list their names here, and explain how they will help you and how you will help them.

Chapter 18

My Village Turned from Perfect to Average

I can do all things through Christ Jesus which strengtheneth me. (Philippians 4:13)

Chapter 18 illustrates how unexpected life changes test commitment and teach flexibility.

I was an overweight person, whom most people would have considered average in size. During my process of obtaining good health, I lost a substantial amount of weight (twenty-six pounds). Good health, not weight loss was my priority, but I was glad I lost the unwanted pounds. I enjoyed my new lifestyle of good health. I ran longer and ate healthy foods until I was full without gaining weight. This lifestyle was not extremely difficult to maintain, because at the time I was employed as a research scientist at a biotechnology company in Boulder, Colorado.

Boulder is a suburban village that markets a healthy lifestyle: a place where employers and government give health incentives, and riding bicycles and running are common modes of exercise and transportation. There are several well-stocked health-food stores and also many restaurants and grocery stores with a large selection of healthy foods. When I worked in Boulder, I never had a problem buying a fast and healthy lunch. For convenience, there was a healthy fast-food joint with a drive-through. Within walking distance from my job site, there was a deli that featured great salads. In general, the food in Boulder is somewhat more expensive than most suburban towns, but the high prices didn't bother me. I wanted to eat healthy and, at the time, I could well afford it.

Then it happened: on March 9, 2007—almost two years after I started my new diet and healthy lifestyle—I was laid off, and I soon found it difficult to maintain my healthy lifestyle. As I no longer worked or commuted to Boulder, my ability to benefit from Boulder's smorgasbord of healthy foods was limited and hard on my budget. I found myself gradually adding simple carbohydrates back into my diet. It wasn't that I craved simple carbohydrates, for my cravings were still gone. The problem was that simple carbohydrates were cheap, and I was hungry. Before I was laid off, I had become accustomed to keeping my stomach full with healthy foods. Also, routine exercise now became more difficult, as I encountered few enthusiasts in my neighborhood.

Six months after my layoff, I had regained ten pounds, and I began to feel disappointed. I felt bloated and fat (although in reality the extra ten pounds did not increase my body size that much), and my digestive system began to deteriorate again. I was disappointed, yet determined not to go back to the old me. I had buried that person more than two years ago, and resurrection was not an option. I had to do something and fast—but what? Out of desperation, I began to flex: I experimented with different foods and evaluated their prices to form a diet that allowed me to reestablish and maintain good health on a budget. Based upon observations, I began to empathize: I realized that my problem was similar to that of many people who live on a fixed, middle, or low income and want to eat healthy but think they cannot afford it. Ready to take action, I began to commit: I became passionate about wanting to help people change their lifestyles to a healthy one.

* * *

Work-Study: Points to Ponder

1. What is the income level of your household (fixed, low, middle, upper, or wealthy)? Do you feel you can afford to eat healthy? If not, then why?

2. In your village, do you have health-food stores?

3. In your village, do the supermarkets and grocery stores sell healthy foods?

4. In your village, at which restaurants do you frequently eat? Do any of these restaurants serve healthy foods? If so, which restaurants?

5. In your village, from which fast-food restaurants do you buy food? Which ones provide healthy foods on the menu?

6. Do you see or know of people in your village who exercise on a regular basis? In what ways do they exercise?

7. Describe the ways in which you feel safe or unsafe about running or walking outside in your village.

8. Describe the ways in which you feel safe or unsafe about allowing your children to play outside in your village.

9. What type, if any, of affordable recreational activities or fitness centers does your village provide?

Chapter 19

Which Came First: The Obesity or the Junk Food?

My people are destroyed for lack of knowledge. (Hosea 4:6a)

Chapters 19 through 21 describe how my ancestral heritage and parental habits influenced both my health and lifestyle. In the work-study sections at the end of each of these chapters, you are given the opportunity to identify your cultural and dietary habits that are affecting your health.

Eating junk food, which contains white sugar, white flour, saturated fats, trans fats, preservatives, and other unhealthy additives, is legal, even though it is slowly yet surely killing many. The more junky the food, the cheaper and more readily available it is to buy. I initially thought this junk-food problem evolved from the revolution of modern-day conveniences and technology, working parents being too busy to cook, continuous population expansion, and healthy foods being high priced. But my mother pointed out that people craved junk food long before I was born. My great-grandmother Angeline (my mother's maternal grandmother) was a perfect example of someone who craved white flour, white sugar, and saturated fats. My great-grandmother was far from rich—her husband, my great-grandfather, made a modest living as a farmer, which was a great accomplishment, especially in those days. Because he was a good provider, my great-grandmother was able to buy the types of food that she wanted. She always made sure that her household was supplied with plenty of white flour, white sugar, and white "light" bread from the town grocery store. My great-grandparents also raised many hogs that were slaughtered for food. My great-grandmother loved pork fatback, chitlins (i.e., chitterlings or pig intestines), and white "light" bread sopped in pork gravy. Being descendants of slavery and poverty, my great-grandmother, like many of my ancestors, equated wealth and good health with acquiring enough money to overeat and gain weight. Young mothers were also praised for giving birth to "fine" (i.e., fat and overweight) babies rather than "poor" (i.e., normal and healthy weight) babies. As a sign of her modest prosperity, my great-grandmother constantly ate the foods of her delight, with limited daily exercise. Loving his wife very much, my great-grandfather worked extremely hard every day so that she could stay at home and not work in the fields. After birthing many "fine" babies and much eating and sitting, this led to an obesity that she defined as a sign of much wealth and good health. Unfortunately, her obesity led to hypertension, which caused her to die of a stroke in her early sixties.

The occurrence of my great-grandmother's death is etched into my mother's memory. Reminiscing, my mother told me the story: She remembers that day started as any other ordinary day. My mother, a little scrawny girl, was combing her grandmother's hair, just as she had done so many times before. Yet this particular day, my mother experienced something unusual, something disturbing, something difficult to explain. Then in a moment of deep clarity, the little girl proclaimed silently, *My grandmother's gray hair looks like it's blooming for her grave!*

Sure enough, within hours after the last stroke of the comb through her hair, my great-grandmother died of a stroke. Today, after acquiring much wisdom, my mother realizes that my great-grandmother's flower of life withered before its time because of a lack of understanding. The foods that my great-grandmother thought proved prosperity were a poison that slowly led to her death. Today, the lack of understanding is still the main reason why many people suffer from poor health.

* * *

Work-Study: Points to Ponder

1. Do you and your family routinely eat junk food? If so, approximately how many times a day? A week?

2. Did any of your ancestors eat an unhealthy diet? If so, describe each one's economic status. How healthy were they? Did they exercise? How long did they live?

Chapter 20

Yesterday's Po' Man's Diet Is Today's Healthy Man's Diet

Ashpenaz, the chief officer, had ordered a guard to watch over Daniel, Shadrach, Meshach, and Abednego [the four Hebrew boys]. Daniel said to the guard, "Please give us the test for ten days: Don't give us anything but vegetables to eat and water to drink. After ten days compare how we look with how the other young men look who ate the king's food. See for yourself and then decide how you want to treat us, your servants."

So the guard agreed to test them for ten days. After ten days they looked healthier and better fed than all the young men who ate the king's food. So the guard took away the king's special food and wine, feeding them vegetables instead. (Daniel 1:11-16; NCV)[1]

The husband of my great-grandmother Ella (my mother's paternal grandmother) died when their eldest son (my grandfather) was very young. As a single parent, my great-grandmother worked hard for her family. She worked long hours in the fields and walked everywhere she went without complaint. On Sunday mornings, she walked to church in her high-top patent leather shoes with the little heels and was always the first to open up the church doors before she started Sunday school class. In the summer months, she and her family worked in the fields and enjoyed eating fresh vegetables, fruits, and nuts as often as possible. During the winter, she worked as a maid for upper-class families for next to nothing. Sometimes her pay would be nothing more than pieces of old scrap lean meat, a small sack of coarse cornmeal, and a pitcher of buttermilk. After working hard all day, she would carry the sack of food on her long journey home while balancing the pitcher of buttermilk on her wrapped head. She was always happy and gladly shared this food with her family. Sometimes, to save the best for her children, she would eat dried-up tainted meat and crunchy buttermilk that was so spoiled it made crackling noises.

I was a little girl when my great-grandmother Ella passed away; I will never forget her. She was an amazing woman who lived life to the fullest. Until she was ninety-nine years old, she lived alone and had excellent eyesight. Then, she moved in with my grandparents (her son and daughter-in-law) and enjoyed life for several more years. Even after she was blessed with enough money to afford groceries, she still continued to eat scrap lean meat, coarse cornmeal, and crunchy buttermilk—old habits were hard to break. My mother defines her grandmother's diet of poverty as a life preserver. The scrap pieces of meat were a great source of protein without much fat. The coarse cornmeal, fruits, and vegetables provided much fiber and nutrition, and the crunchy buttermilk maintained a healthy bacterial flora within her digestive system. Accepting her God-given gift of good health through faith, she was a living witness that a person can live a long healthy life without dying from sickness or disease. She died at a ripe old age of 104 (1875–1979), with no pain and having the testimony that she pleased God.

* * *

Work-Study: Points to Ponder

1. Do you, your family, or relatives eat healthy foods? If so, approximately how many times a day? A week?

2. Do you know if any of your ancestors had healthy diets? If so, describe each one's economic status? How healthy were they? Did they exercise? How long did they live? Did they die from health issues, or did they pass away peacefully?

Chapter 21

Live to Eat, or Eat to Live

Hear counsel, and receive instruction, that thou mayest be wise in thy latter end. (Proverbs 19:20).

"I eat to live; you live to eat. If you do not change the way you eat, food will cause you many health problems when you get old." These are the words of wisdom that my thin paternal grandfather gave his son (my dad) when he was a husky little boy, living in the hot Sonora Desert of Coolidge, Arizona. Grandpa was a small, healthy man. Dad was born big, and he always ate as much food as he wanted without his parents restricting his food intake. At the young age of eight, my dad wore the same size overalls as his middle-aged father. After graduating from high school and being drafted in the army, he accepted a football scholarship to San Diego State College (this was before it expanded into an university) as one of the best and largest linemen on the football team. Throughout the majority of his life, Dad worked and ate long and hard without suffering from any major health issues. My mom says that my dad must've been blessed at birth with an extra-strong body, for she never saw a man who could eat, in one lifetime, as many cows as my dad and still remain relatively healthy. However, as Dad became older, he realized that the words of my grandfather were wise and hauntingly true. Now in his winter years, Dad restricts the variety and quantity of foods that he eats in his effort to maintain a leash on certain health issues (i.e., diabetes and gout). As he realizes that living a quality life is more important than food, he now is eating to live, instead of living to eat.

Many years before she passed away, my paternal grandmother went through a similar experience. My grandmother was overweight the majority of her life. But in her old age, she lost a tremendous amount of weight, as she changed her unhealthy diet to one consisting of mostly pinto beans, "yogie" (this is what she called yogurt), and watermelon. In addition to adopting a healthier diet, she started frequent walks in the Sonora Desert for exercise as she helped clean the environment by picking up cans and other litter along the way. She listened to the right voice and decided that a quality life was more important than food; she began eating to live.

My dad says that my mom reminds him of his father; she also eats to live. Mom wants her food to taste good, but she never wants to eat much of it. She can go the entire day without a bite of food before realizing that she did not eat. Calling Mom a little busy bee, Dad often says that he wonders how my mom can keep generating the energy to work and help those in need all day without taking the time to eat. Throughout her life, Mom, much like her parents, has practiced the unselfish habit of putting the welfare of others before her own. Yet as Mom is now older, she understands that if she wants to be healthy, she has to eat an adequate supply of healthy foods throughout every day, even when she doesn't feel like it or is busy helping others.

I have learned eating habits that fall somewhere in between those of my parents. I do not *live* to eat, but I do *love* to eat. Like many Americans, when I sit down to eat, I want to fill up on food that tastes good. Typically, the foods we Americans rate as tasty seem to be high in calories, saturated fats, white sugar, and white flour; whereas, the healthy foods are usually low on the tasty list. In your lifetime, how many people have you seen in the middle of a workday take a spinach break? Or do you know of anyone in the middle of watching a movie who will say, "Right now I am really craving some florets of broccoli"?

People who crave healthy foods like this, however, really do exist; I actually know of a couple. You may never be like these people who crave healthy foods, like vegetables and fruit, but it is important that you take ownership of your responsibility of being healthy and eat many of them anyway.

* * *

Work-Study: Points to Ponder

1. What types of foods do you crave?

2. Do you always satisfy your cravings, or do you ignore them at times? Did your parents help you control your cravings when growing up? If you always satisfy your cravings, how has this affected your health?

3. Do you ever eat food just because you know it is healthy? If so, describe these foods and how often you eat them.

4. Select the answers below that describe the reasons why you eat.

    ____ Always hungry. Never seem to have enough.
    ____ A voice in your head tells you to eat.
    ____ Eat only to maintain nutrition.
    ____ Eat as a method to relieve stress and tension.
    ____ Eat only when hungry.
    ____ Love to eat. Enjoy eating.
    ____ Addicted to or crave food.
    ____ Food is a friend, good company.
    ____ Eating is a favorite pastime.
    ____ Social eater. Enjoy eating with family and friends.
    ____ Other (describe here) ____________________________

Chapter 22

Obesity Is All Genetic—Not!

For when I shall have brought them into the land which I sware unto their fathers, that floweth with milk and honey; and they shall have eaten and filled themselves, and waxen fat; then will they turn unto other gods, and serve them, and provoke me, and break my covenant. (Deuteronomy 31:20)

Chapters 22 through 23 describe the role that your environment, socioeconomic status, and demographic location, along with the food industry, plays in the lifestyle you choose to live. Chapter 23 also gives examples of how you can change your surroundings so that you will be readily supplied with what you need to maintain a healthy lifestyle.

Is obesity a genetic disorder? This question has been debated among scientists for years. Scientists have performed extensive research to locate the obesity genes. Yes, certain individuals may have a predisposition (propensity) for obesity, because they inherited genetic traits that slow down body metabolism or increase fat deposition. Yet an obese person's genetic makeup is only partially responsible for the obesity; environmental factors also play a major role in it. Over the years, I have witnessed people's hunger, in this country and abroad, and I have never seen an obese person suffer from starvation. Many of us would love to blame all of our weight issues on our genetic makeup, but the truth of the matter is if we intake fewer calories than what we burn off, we will not gain weight but will lose it.

The weight of a person is dependent on the amount and type of calories that are consumed (which is dependent mostly on environmental factors) and the person's metabolism rate (which is dependent on both genetic and environmental factors). It is true an inactive person with a slow metabolism (much like a hibernating bear) cannot eat as much as an active person with a fast metabolism (such as a hummingbird) without gaining weight. But if a person with a slow metabolism adjusts the amount and type of calories consumed, exercises to burn off extra calories, and builds up muscle mass to increase the metabolism rate (muscle mass burns energy; fat tissue stores energy), then overweight fat would not be gained. A person can also be compared to an automobile. A small economic car with no frills gets more gas mileage to the gallon than a sport utility vehicle with all of the frills. This is the same with people—a short-statured person with a slow metabolism rate burns fewer calories each day than a tall person with a fast metabolism rate. Thus, a short, overweight couch potato should not consume as many calories as a tall, professional basketball player that efficiently burns calories (i.e., has a "green body").

In this country, junk food is low in cost, found everywhere, and is appetizing. It is almost impossible to live in a village where junk food is not heavily promoted. Fast-food restaurants are at almost every corner, grocery stores are in every neighborhood, and television commercials entice everyone to buy and eat more and more. Yet you must be willing to meet the challenge head-on and control your eating habits. If you are overweight and want to become healthy, then you must be willing to burn off more calories than you consume. As you continue to read this book, you will gain the information needed to design a healthy diet and an exercise regimen that fits you.

* * *

Work-Study: Points to Ponder

1. Do you consider yourself to be underweight, at a healthy weight, overweight, obese, or morbidly obese? Do you have a fast or slow metabolism? By approximately how many pounds are you underweight or overweight?

2. Describe the health conditions of your family—are your parents

overweight or obese? Are your siblings? Are your children?

3. Do you have the same eating habits as your parents? Do you eat the same foods; eat as much and as often; and eat for the same reasons as they do?

4. Do you and your family exercise? If so, how often and how long?

5. Describe your parents' exercise habits. Are your exercise habits similar to theirs?

Chapter 23

Hello ... Where Is the Healthy Stuff?

When thou sittest to eat with a ruler, consider diligently what is before thee: And put a knife to thy throat, if thou be a man given to appetite. Be not desirous of his dainties: for they are deceitful meat. (Proverbs 23:1–3)

Who's responsible for the junk-food craze in America today? Is it the food industry that is pushing to market it, or is it the consumer that is demanding to buy it? The answer is both—the food industry and the consumer are both responsible for the junk-food craze.

The food industry escalates the junk-food craze in this country for profit by manufacturing junk food so that is cheaper and has a longer shelf life than health food. Junk food also often includes addictive additives, which entice the consumer to keep buying them. Yet I do not believe the food industry is the main culprit in the junk-food craze. The main goal of the food industry, just like all of the other industries, is to gain profit. The food industry is just following the principle of supply and demand (give the consumers what they will buy) as it produces and processes junk food as much and inexpensively as possible to supply the demand of an ever-increasing population that is willing to buy the junk presented to them. As consumers will buy junk food, the food industry will sell junk food. The consumers passively allow the food industry to dictate to them what they will crave, buy, and eat. Thus, it is the consumers, not the food industry, that are mostly responsible for the downfall of the American diet.

We, the consumers, should strategically work with the food industry so that our villages are provided with an ample supply of healthy foods. The food industry should not control which foods we eat; we should convince the food industry, through our actions of living healthy, that we are committed to buying healthy foods. If we demand (request and buy) healthy foods, then the food industry will supply them. It doesn't benefit us for the federal government or nonprofit health organizations to promote and urge the food industry to supply more health food if we do not demand to buy health food. We need to stop, or at least tremendously decrease, the amount of junk food we consume. Therefore, we need to not only demand that the food industry supply more health food in the grocery stores, restaurants, fast-food chains, schools, and at our job sites, but we also need to commit to eating it.

We cannot eat healthy unless there are healthy foods in our villages. If our villages do not supply healthy foods, then it is our responsibility to change this problem. If healthy foods are not in our villages, then we must demand that the food industry supply them. Most important, once healthy foods are supplied, we must be committed to buying and eating them. If we pass by the healthy foods on the grocery shelves to buy the soda and chips, or if we constantly buy hamburgers, fries, and chocolate shakes for lunch instead of salads, then the food industry will ignore our insincere request for healthy foods. We must do more than just request healthy foods in our villages; we must become loyal customers who buy and eat healthy foods, day after day, month after month, and year after year. We must be committed to living a healthy lifestyle.

When I was a little girl, I visited my maternal grandparents' farm in Kosciusko, Mississippi. My grandparents were very old yet still led happy, productive lives. Growing, preparing, and eating organic foods was their normal way of life. There were fruit and nut trees all over their wooded land. For fun, my cousins, my sister, and I would go out into the woods with our grandpa for long walks. Along the way, we would pick berries and nuts and then put them in Grandpa's hat. On their land, my grandparents also grew a big garden and raised many farm animals. We enjoyed eating the fresh vegetables, fruits, and nuts. My grandma cooked all types of fresh organic vegetables and organic beef, pork, and chicken. She usually prepared the meat by boiling it in water, pouring off the fatty broth, seasoning the meat with a few slices of onion and garlic, and then sautéing it in its juices until well done. She also would cook corn bread that consisted of very little flour and sugar. Its consistency was not like cake; it was heavy, unsweetened, and coarse.

In the summer of 2006, my parents, my son, and I went to our family reunion in Kosciusko. I enjoyed the family reunion celebration very much, and I had a wonderful time visiting everyone. My grandparents had long since passed away, and it was great to see my relatives and the land of the old family farm. However, I made a few surprising observations. On the land my grandparents had farmed, there was no garden and no farm animals, and all of the fruit and nut trees had disappeared. This seemed to be a common occurrence across the entire woods. The majority of the people no longer grew gardens or raised farm animals. There were a few fruit and nut trees but very few indeed.

When we went shopping at the nearest town grocery store in Kosciusko, I discovered that the variety of vegetables and fruits was scarce, not fresh, and very expensive. The packaged meat was extremely overpriced. Finding a fast-food chain restaurant was not a problem, and the sit-down restaurants served foods high in fats, white sugar, and white flour. Eating healthy was a challenge. I did not see a health-food store anywhere, and the supply of organic and whole foods in grocery stores was very limited. Fortunately, however, I did find much relief by eating my relatives' home-cooked meals. This is because some of my relatives' past diets resulted in health problems that now led them to eat healthier diets, consisting of baked chicken, vegetables, and fruit.

Many people in Mississippi are unhealthy because of their diets. In a news update in the summer of 2007, CNN announced that Mississippi had the leading adult obesity rate, whereas Colorado had the lowest adult obesity rate. After observing eating habits in both states, this announcement didn't surprise me. I also noticed in Mississippi that obesity seemed to be extremely prevalent among Southern Christians and African Americans (both of these groups commonly eat richly seasoned, highly sweetened, and fattening foods). However, obesity has become a constantly escalating problem, not only in Mississippi, but also in Colorado and all the other states. Obesity has become a national epidemic that is rampantly infecting all races, ages, and economic classes, and thus demands the concern of every citizen.

It is hoped that you—the people of all generations, socioeconomic statuses, and demographic locations—will learn to eat healthy, build villages that supply healthy foods, and eliminate the health problems that stem from unhealthy diets. You must start by bringing good health to yourself and to your family. Learn which foods are healthy; then buy, prepare, and cook them. If your village does not have health-food stores or supply healthy foods in the local markets, then find time to carefully plan a grocery list and take a trip to the health-food store nearest you; make it a family outing. Instead of eating fast food and junk food, dine at restaurants that offer relatively healthy entrees.

Once you have helped yourself and your family, it is important to expand the health horizons of your relatives, neighbors, friends, colleagues, church members, and coworkers by introducing them to healthy foods. Grow an organic garden, and plant fruit trees in your backyard or in designated lots in your village, and share the fresh produce with others. Bake healthy dishes and desserts, and then bring them to family picnics, celebrations, school and church functions, and parties at your place of employment. If many seem hesitant about eating your healthy cooking and do not give you any raving compliments about it, don't be offended. Be patient and persistent. It often takes time for some to acquire a taste for the healthy foods.

If your children need to eat healthier meals and snacks in their neighborhood schools, then write a letter of petition (including the signatures of concerned parents), requesting healthy foods and volunteering the services of committed parents. Start off by discussing your concerns with the school principal and sending this letter to the school district's director of Food and Nutrition Services. If you need more assistance, send the letter to the superintendent, the School Board of Education director, and then, if necessary, to the State Department of Education, the state legislators, and the governor. When starting to volunteer your services to help improve school meals, make sure you are a concerned parent that works together as a team with members of the school district, including that of the Food and Nutrition Services, and not against them. It is important that the Food and Nutrition Services has your support, especially since it is not easy to provide nutritional, cost-effective meals that appeal to the students' taste. You can help the Food and Nutrition Services meet this challenge by assisting in the organization of school wellness teams under the leadership of your school district's wellness coordinator, whose main incentive is to direct the teams in developing wellness plans for their schools. If your school district does not yet have a wellness coordinator, then organize a group that will help gain funding for one. It is important for each school to have a wellness team that will join forces in seeking funds and ideas to help improve nutrition and physical activities, and in increasing the health awareness of parents and students. The members of each wellness team may consist of parents, resourceful volunteers, students, principals, teachers, and other concerned citizens. As a team, be creative and seek funding and services from outside sources such as private organizations, nonprofit organizations, the Department of Public Health and Environment, major corporations, small businesses, healthcare providers, health-food stores, and concerned citizens.

Organize a support group that promotes good health and campaigns for health awareness in your village. If the grocery stores and supermarkets in your village do not provide health-food items, then send to the owners of these businesses a petition letter that includes a list of requested health food items, along with the signatures of customers who are committed to buying them. If your village does not have health-food stores, then petition the owners of well-known health-food stores located in other areas to start building stores in your village. Send them a long list of signatures from potential patrons that would frequent new health-food stores built in your village. If your list of potential customers is short in number, then request that the health-food store owners establish a system for ordering and shipping out supplies to a designated site in your village or to the homes of those who lack transportation. Also look to see if you have a food cooperative grocery store (food co-op) in your village that you can patronize, and then, determine if you want to become a member of it. A food co-op is owned by its members, thus is a village-owned grocery store. The owners are able to determine which products are sold in the store, buy items on discount, and respond to the needs of their customers and village. The main goal of the food co-op is to provide customers with affordable organic and whole foods and increase the health awareness of the villagers. In addition to the grocery stores and markets, write petition letters to the owners of different restaurants, requesting that they add healthy entrees and side dishes to their menus. Where there is a will, there is a way. Let us all—merchants and consumers alike—listen collectively to the right voice and build together villages of green pastures.

* * *

Work-Study: Points to Ponder

1. How committed are you to changing your village? Are you willing to bring healthy foods to different functions? Are you willing to grow a garden in your backyard? Are you willing to find an empty lot and do the work required to have it designated as land for a community garden?

2. Do the schools that your children attend serve healthy meals and provide healthy snacks? If not, how will you help solve this problem?

3. Do the grocery stores in your village have an adequate supply of health food? If not, what are you willing to do about it?

4. Does your village have health-food stores or a food co-op? If not, what are you willing to do about it?

5. In your village, do you have restaurants that serve healthy foods? If not, how could you help change this problem?

6. In your village, is there someone whom you can help to understand the importance of good health? Is there someone whom you can encourage to change his or her lifestyle to a healthy one? If so, how will you go about doing this?

7. Do you bake healthy dishes or desserts and bring them to functions? If not, are you willing to start? Describe how you would feel about doing this.

Chapter 24

Water Is to Dry as Healthy Is to Fat

For I [God] will pour water upon him that is thirsty, and floods upon the dry ground: I will pour my spirit upon thy seed, and my blessing upon thine offspring: and they shall spring up as among the grass, as willows by the water courses. (Isaiah 44:3–4)

Chapters 24 through 26 describe what it means to have good health, maintain a healthy weight, and eat right. Many underweight, overweight, obese, and even normal-weight people think they can be unhealthy eaters and still remain healthy. However, once you have accepted your God-given gift of good health, the only way you can remain in good health is to maintain a healthy lifestyle.

Unfortunately, the majority of the population has devalued the importance of being at a healthy weight. Most overweight people are focused on satisfying either their uncontrollable urge to eat or their desire to lose weight just to be skinny more than their need to be healthy. A skinny individual may be healthy, an overweight person is not necessarily healthy, but an obese person is definitely unhealthy. It is impossible to remain healthy and be obese. You may love yourself and all of your overweight fat. You and everyone else should love you, all of you, no matter your physical features, skin color, shape, and size. The problem is, though, that overweight fat doesn't love you. Overweight fat is unhealthy, and you should not love being unhealthy. Your inner self may be comfortable with your overweight fat, but your body isn't. If you want to be healthy, then you must be at a healthy weight for someone of your gender and with your height and bone structure. The more overweight you are, the unhealthier you are. It is impossible to be simultaneously obese and healthy. Even if the results of your most recent physical exam showed that you are an obese person with relatively good health, eventually, your obesity will catch up with you.

When something that is totally dry absorbs water, it becomes wet; dryness disappears. The more water it is exposed to, the wetter it becomes. This is the same with health. If a healthy person gains fat and becomes obese, he becomes unhealthy; good health disappears. Yet before this person can regain good health, the overweight fat must disappear. The more fat that is lost the greater the potential one has of becoming healthy. Although being thin doesn't guarantee good health, being obese does guarantee bad health. The key to good health is to focus not on the weight loss but on your health. If your main goal is to be skinny, then eating an unhealthy, low-calorie diet as you lose the extra pounds will still keep you unhealthy. Yet if you strive to be healthy, you will eat right, exercise, and still lose the extra pounds.

* * *

Work-Study: Points to Ponder

1. Are you thin or overweight? Is your main concern your size, weight, or your overall health?

2. If you are overweight, do you want to lose the extra pounds? If yes, what are your reasons for wanting to lose them? If no, then why do you *not* want to lose them?

Chapter 25

Eat as Much as You Want, Just Not Whatever You Want

The meek shall eat and be satisfied: they shall praise the Lord that seek him: Your heart shall live for ever. (Psalm 22:26)

I am astounded by the number of television advertisements that claim, *You can eat as much as you want of whatever you want and still lose weight. All you have to do is buy our "magical product."* Many of these quick-fix schemes for losing weight are traps into which too many Americans fall. When it comes to losing weight, immediate gratification (e.g., eating whatever unhealthy foods you want for pleasure today) and delayed gratification (e.g., losing weight to become fit and healthy tomorrow) cannot work together. You cannot simultaneously do both. You must choose one or the other. Even taking a "magical product" will not allow you to eat as much as you want of the unhealthy foods you love, lose weight without exercise, and then remain fit and in good health. If you take the magical product, it is likely that one of the following will occur: You will not lose weight; you will lose weight but then eventually gain back more than you lost; or you will suffer from negative side effects of the magical product.

Here is the key to losing weight: Because hunger from dieting often triggers overeating of the wrong foods, do not allow yourself to be hungry often or for long periods of time. It is possible for you to become comfortably full at each meal and still lose weight, as long as the majority—or better, yet all—of your diet does *not* consist of high empty calories. Nutritional and low-calorie foods that digest slowly in the gut are what you need to eat to lose weight. For example, you can eat an organic, green-vegetable salad complemented with a small amount of low-calorie vinaigrette dressing until you are full to the brim and still lose weight. (Although to maintain a healthy digestive system and avoid other health problems, it is best to never overstuff yourself. My parents once told me of a man with a mental condition who died from drinking too much water. Temperance is to always be congratulated.) On the other hand, if you add croutons, beef, boiled eggs, bacon bits, and a high-calorie ranch dressing to the green-vegetable salad, then there is a defined limit to how much you can eat and still lose weight.

Food cravings are usually confused with hunger; it is often difficult to identify the difference between the two. I have developed a method that helps me with this problem. I find that when I am very hungry and eat a healthy green-vegetable salad—without all of the unhealthy condiments—it usually doesn't take long before I am full. However, if I still desire to eat something else after the salad, it is usually my food cravings rearing its evil head. It is at this point that I know to put on my thinking cap and become extremely vigilant so that I will make the right choices. If I do choose to eat anything more, I try to make certain that the food is healthy and that I do not intake too many calories. It is your responsibility to become healthier. You only have one life, so make the right choices and eat right.

* * *

Work-Study: Points to Ponder

1. Have you ever tried a quick-fix diet? If so, was it successful? Did you gain the weight back or keep it off?
2. Have you ever taken a "magical product" to help you lose weight? If so, was it successful? Did you gain the weight back? Were there negative side effects?
3. Do you eat enough healthy foods to become full, or do you constantly starve yourself to lose weight?
4. Do you have a method for identifying the difference between food cravings and hunger? If so, describe your method. If not, are you willing to try my method described above in this chapter, or will you develop one of your own?

Chapter 26

Skinny Does Not Always Mean Healthy

Woe unto you, scribes and Pharisees…, which indeed appear beautiful outward, but are within full of dead men's bones. (Matthew 23:27)

I was born a healthy child and remained so until I contracted mumps when I was in the second grade; my mumps vaccination was accidentally missed by my pediatric nurse. I had all of my other vaccinations, but that one was skipped. About a year later, I was diagnosed with pancreatitis; the virus from the mumps had inflamed my pancreas. After following my doctor's instructions and completing the prescribed medicine for many months, the follow-up tests demonstrated that the symptoms of pancreatitis had ceased. Yet the doctor noticed that my pancreas was compromised and ordered me to eat a diet consisting of very little white sugar. He explained that if I did not limit the amount of white sugar in my diet, I could possibly become diabetic from the lack of insulin produced by and released from my compromised pancreas. From that point until I was a junior in high school, my parents made sure that my diet was relatively healthy.

It was difficult for me not to indulge in sweets. Since the day I was told not to eat sweets, I constantly craved them. Yet it wasn't until the fall semester of my junior year in high school that I completely fell off the wagon. I found myself eating sugar at almost every meal. In the morning, I ate sugary, fruity cereal; at lunch, I usually ate a ham and processed cheese sandwich on white bread, fries, and a big chocolate-chip cookie. In the evening, I pretended to eat my healthy supper, only to gulp down another bowl or two of sugary, fruity cereal. As my sugar cravings increased, I became addicted to sugary, fruity cereal; I wanted it all of the time. I knew that I wasn't eating healthy, but because I was losing weight, I didn't care. Constantly eating sugary, fruity cereal, although it was high in sugar, greatly reduced my calorie intake. In a short time, I was finally at my desired weight and was actually labeled as skinny by many of my peers. I used to be one of those persons who thought that people could eat as much junk food as they wanted, as long as they remained skinny. Everything seemed to be going great. But before long, I had become sick, and my ability to concentrate had greatly diminished.

My English teacher noticed a dramatic change in my personality, as my grades on class assignments dropped from all A's to also include B's and C's. This may not seem like much to some, but my teacher knew how hard I'd worked over the years to maintain a perfect grade-point average. My English teacher, who had been previously diagnosed with hypoglycemia, realized I was demonstrating many of the same symptoms that she had before she improved her diet. One day, after I turned in an incomplete essay quiz, my teacher pulled me aside, handed me a couple of apple slices and a few almonds (foods that she often snacked on to help provide energy and stabilize her blood-sugar level), and quietly explained that I was probably suffering from hypoglycemia. I then told this to one of my other favorite teachers who was also familiar with the symptoms of hypoglycemia; she recommended that I see the same physician who had diagnosed her case. After being examined by this doctor, sure enough, I was diagnosed with hypoglycemia. My compromised pancreas didn't cause me to become diabetic, as had been predicted years ago by my childhood doctor. Instead, my compromised pancreas was working overtime. Every time I ate sugar, my pancreas kicked out high levels of insulin, which immediately removed the sugar from my bloodstream.

After my parents sought the second opinion of another physician, who also diagnosed me with hypoglycemia, my diet was changed dramatically. For about two years, I ate healthy, and I felt great. When I started college, I was still eating healthy. Unfortunately, by the end of my sophomore year, my diet had regressed to being mostly white sugar and white flour. I ate unhealthy but limited my calories to keep relatively thin. I allowed a very thin friend, who ate nothing but junk food, to influence my eating habits. She ate junk in the morning, junk at lunch, junk at dinner, and junk for an evening snack. She never ate anything green or anything considered as healthy. Her diet consisted of sugar, starch, and fat. She could eat, not exercise, and never gain a pound. Many of my other friends and I were envious of her, because we had to limit our calorie intake to keep our weight down. We limited what we ate, not because we wanted to be healthy but because we wanted to be small. We wanted to eat like our friend and remain thin. We were only concerned about our present size at the time and not about our health in the future.

Approximately twenty years later and many pounds heavier, I decided to repent from my old diet and begin living a new healthy lifestyle. I lost track of my friend, but I often wonder how she is doing. I imagine she is probably still thin, but I hope she has changed her lifestyle to a healthy one and is doing well. There are many people who are thin but who are very unhealthy. Unfortunately, because they are thin, they feel they can eat whatever they want. Because they do not want to eat right, they are in denial of the fact that eating unhealthy foods is responsible for their poor health. They refuse to connect their health issues with their unhealthy diets. If you are thin and constantly eating unhealthy foods, you need to recognize that your diet is detrimental to your health—and then eat right.

* * *

Work-Study: Points to Ponder

1. If you are thin, are you healthy or unhealthy? Do you eat healthy?

2. If you are thin and eat unhealthy, what should you do to start eating right?

3. If you are presently overweight, have you ever been thin? If so, were you eating healthy at the time?

4. Do you know of anyone who is thin yet eating unhealthy? If so, what creative ways can you think of to help that person realize the importance of eating healthy?

CHAPTER 27

It Takes 21 Days to End the Food Crave

Let no man say when he is tempted, I am tempted of God: for God cannot be tempted with evil, neither tempteth He any man: But every man is tempted, when he is drawn away of his own lust, and enticed. (James 1:13–14)

Chapters 27 through 32 provide methods, skills, and tools for a healthy lifestyle that you can use to:

- Eliminate food cravings.
- Design an exercise regimen.
- Budget money and schedule time for maintaining a healthy lifestyle.
- Identify your body type.
- Calculate your ideal weight.
- Determine your daily calorie intake range.

I don't know who started the popular theory that a bad habit can be formed in twenty-one days; thus, it can also be broken in twenty-one days. I've heard this repeatedly from many people, such as church leaders, family members, friends, and coworkers, but I never attempted to test it until I was ready to stop my own cravings for unhealthy "white stuff" foods (i.e., white sugar, white flour, white pasta, white rice, and white potatoes). Many times in the past, I attempted to stop my food addictions but failed. I cannot remember the number of times I stopped and then restarted my food addictions, but I do know that this yo-yo dieting was quite frustrating.

When I repented and started my new healthy lifestyle, I was curious to see if I could quickly end my bad eating habits in twenty-one days by trying it out. Resisting the cravings was definitely a struggle at first;

I went completely cold turkey. I knew that if I wanted to break my bad eating habits and start a new lifestyle, I couldn't flirt around with the white stuff. I had to completely sever the food affair. I made certain that I did not have the white stuff in my home, office at work, and car, and when I asked my family not to buy or offer me anymore white stuff, they agreed. Before I went to the grocery store, I strategically planned my shopping route away from the bakery department. When I went to restaurants and the temptation to order the white stuff intensified, I would resist and talk back to the temptation by quoting Bible scriptures to my inner self (see chapter 13 for details), and before long, the temptation would subside. For the first three weeks, my body was upset that I had broken my daily routine of constantly eating white stuff. My brain and the rest of my body continued to crave the taste, the euphoria, and the roller-coaster ride that I experienced from the sugar rush.

Shockingly, exactly after the twenty-first day, my cravings dramatically dropped. I don't know if this was because I was mentally expecting the cravings to end after twenty-one days, or because a physical change actually occurred in my system that curbed my addiction. All I know is that it happened. For twenty-one days I was determined; I chose to listen to the voice that said eat healthy and leave the white stuff alone. For twenty-one days not only did I leave the white stuff alone, but during that time I also did not eat healthy whole grain foods, dairy products (except for plain, cultured, low-fat yogurt and aged low-fat cheese in moderation), and natural sweeteners. My diet consisted mostly of vegetables (except for no white potatoes) and fruit, and some lean meat. Before I knew it (twenty-one days later), my intense cravings for white stuff tremendously subsided.

Although the habit and intense cravings are now gone, I am not saying that I never have a desire to eat the white stuff because at times I do want it. But the main point is that I make certain that I only eat it sparingly and on rare occasions. I continue to keep my cravings for white stuff under control by adding in moderation to my diet foods that consist of whole grains, such as whole spelt flour and whole durum wheat flour, and the natural sweeteners such as stevia and xylitol. Because everyone is different, I don't know if it is possible for everyone to end their food cravings in twenty-one days. Although one's genetic makeup plays a major role in one's capacity to end food addictions, I believe one's ability to end these addictions depends more on determination than anything else. No matter if the number of days is 21 or 121 days, I believe everyone who wants to be healthy can end intense food cravings and replace them with healthy eating habits—if the desire to do so is strong enough.

* * *

Work-Study: Points to Ponder

1. Do you believe that it takes twenty-one days to form a bad habit and twenty-one days to end it? Do you know anyone who ended a bad habit in twenty-one days or a different length of time?

2. Have you ever successfully ended a bad habit? If so, how long did it take?

3. If you need to break cravings for the white stuff, are you willing to go cold turkey and consume a low simple-carbohydrate diet consisting of mostly lean meat, vegetables, fruit, and water for twenty-one days or more? After the bad habit is broken, are you willing to add healthy whole grains and other healthy foods to your diet? Describe your reasons why these steps would be something you would be willing or unwilling to do.

4. Describe any addictions or cravings for other unhealthy types of foods and beverages (e.g., foods and beverages containing saturated fat, trans fat, caffeine, and excess salt) that you need to break. Are you willing to end your cravings for these foods and beverages by totally eliminating them from your diet for twenty-one days or more?

Chapter 28

Castor Oil + Peppermint Candy = No More Peppermint Candy

Woe unto them that call evil good, and good evil; that put darkness for light, and light for darkness; that put bitter for sweet, and sweet for bitter! (Isaiah 5:20)

When I was a little girl I enjoyed eating peppermint candy, until one day I caught a terrible cold. My parents carried me to my pediatrician who prescribed cough medicine and antibiotics, which I took willingly. This is similar to what was done so many times in the past. Yet this time was different; my health did not improve. I continued to become sicker as the congestion thickened in my chest. That next evening, my mother sent my father to the nearest drugstore to buy a bottle of castor oil. I was not familiar with castor oil at the time; thus, I did not think much about it. I did not know that I was about to experience one of the worst tastes ever known to mankind. Standing patiently before my mother, I curiously watched her complete the castor-oil ritual for the very first time. She first removed the big log of Christmas peppermint candy from the cupboard, unwrapped it, and set it on a cutting board. She whacked off a good size hunk with a sharp knife, shattered the hunk into smaller pieces with the blunt end of the knife, and then rewrapped the remaining log and placed it back in storage. Next, after unscrewing the cap, she warmed up the bottle of castor oil in a pan of heated water, selected a piece of peppermint candy off the cutting board with care, and held it in tightly in her left hand. Then, she took a giant serving spoon out of the drawer and poured out the warm, thick oil into it. After testing the heat of the oil with her right index finger, she told me to *open wide*. I obediently opened my mouth, as my mother gently shoved the giant spoon into it. My mother made sure that all of the spoon's contents were emptied into my mouth by slowly removing the spoon from my pursed lips. Immediately, my face grimaced while the unexplainably horrible taste of the oily mass standing stagnant in the middle of my mouth intensified. As my mother recollected this awful taste from her childhood, her grimaced face that mirrored mine contradicted her stern reply, "Swallow, girl! You know it doesn't taste that bad."

After many unsuccessful attempts, I finally forced that nasty, oily mass down my throat. But my sufferings were long from over. Gagging with my mouth open, my mother slipped the peppermint candy from her clinched fist onto my tongue. Just a few moments earlier, I had questioned the existence of the fragmented piece of peppermint candy, but then I suddenly appreciated its purpose. Quickly swirling the candy around in my mouth, I was expecting immediate and complete relief, but it only helped for a brief moment; the nasty oily taste would not go away. I then took a napkin and began to wipe the inside of my mouth, but nothing worked; it seemed permanent. I replaced the old oily piece of peppermint candy in my mouth with a second fresh piece, but nothing ceased that nasty oily taste—except time and many trips to the bathroom.

By the next morning, it was a miracle: I felt better. The cough had subsided and the congestion was almost gone. I rose early out of bed, ready to read (I was a child that rarely played). Since that night, not only have I often shuddered at the thought of castor oil, but I have never wanted to taste, smell, or set eyes on peppermint candy again. Yet for many years after that night, as an intensely reluctant yet obedient child, I took many doses of castor oil, followed by the swirling of peppermint candy in my mouth. Each time, my disgust for peppermint candy intensified. Still, to this day, I abhor the taste of peppermint candy, and every time I see or smell it, I associate it with the horrible castor oil episodes. This association of castor oil with peppermint candy has permanently curbed my appetite for this candy. As an adult, I began using my unpleasant childhood encounters to my advantage. I realized that when I intentionally extended my distaste for castor oil and peppermint candy to other kinds of candy, I also began detesting them, just like peppermint. I tried this technique with my favorites; it worked and still works today. Whenever I crave any type of candy, I can think of the horrible castor oil episodes, and suddenly my cravings disappear.

* * *

Work-Study: Points to Ponder

1. Candy, often disguised by its sweet taste to be a good thing, is very bad for our health. Do you remember any episodes in your past that decreased your appetite for certain unhealthy foods, such as candy? Describe ways that these episodes could benefit you in eating healthier or losing excess weight.

Chapter 29

Exercise Does Not Have to Be Fun; It Just Needs to Be Done

They that wait upon the Lord shall renew their strength;…they shall run, and not be weary; and they shall walk, and not faint. (Isaiah 40:31)

Eating healthy is not the only requirement for maintaining good health. It must be paired with an exercise regimen especially designed to target the main body parts and functions that play a major role in physical fitness and health, in which there are at least seven: heart, lung, muscle, bone, fat, flexibility, and posture. Weight lifting, which commonly involves free weights and strength-building equipment, increases muscle mass and bone density, and helps with losing excess fat. Carrying light free weights or attaching wrist and ankle weights to the body are great ways to build up muscle strength during power walking or running. Pilates, yoga, and stretching routines are excellent for gaining muscle tone, flexibility, strength, and a proper posture. Aerobic exercises such as running, aerobics, biking, power walking, swimming, skiing, most other sports, and dancing are great for increasing lung capacity and muscle tone, burning off excess fat, and building a strong heart. Exercise will not only improve these seven targeted areas that require physical fitness but will also improve function of the brain, liver, kidney, digestive system, neuronal system, immune system, reproductive system, endocrine system, etc.

Everybody needs to exercise. Adults need to exercise at least thirty minutes three times a week before a significant difference in health may be observed. Physically fit adults can safely exercise as much as sixty minutes or more per day. (Note: This excludes those who are battling with the compulsive behavior of abusing their bodies with excessive exercise; if you know any individuals with this problem, advise them to seek counseling.) Healthy children need to exercise every day for at least one hour. If you are out of shape, begin exercising every day at a low intensity and for short increments of time, such as five to ten minutes, and then gradually increase the time. The most important thing is just to start moving; start slowly, and then over time, gradually increase the intensity and duration of exercise.

The old adage "no pain; no gain" is true. Yet if initially your exercise regimen is too aggressive, much pain can result in serious physical injuries and cause you to become discouraged and quit. Thus, it is important to design an exercise regimen that fits you. Your current health, weight, and age are important factors that need to be considered before designing an exercise regimen. Before beginning any type of exercise regimen, schedule an appointment for a physical examination and seek advice from your physician. This advice will help prevent physical injuries, heart complications, and other serious problems that can result from exercising. After a medical examination, ask your physician to assist you with designing an exercise regimen that focuses on improving your health and the seven targeted areas requiring physical fitness. Your physician can also help determine your current resting heart rate, the targeted heart rate you need to reach during exercise, and the optimal resting heart rate of your goal. The resting heart rate of most out-of-shape individuals is too fast and should be improved by performing aerobic exercise to obtain a slower resting heart rate from a strong and steady beating heart. Your resting heart rate should improve as endurance, exercise, and physical fitness increase. Make sure your exercise regimen not only includes the advice from your physician but also a proper routine for stretching muscles. Proper stretching will help prevent bodily injuries and keep the muscles pliable and flexible, instead of becoming hard and brittle.

Proper exercise needs to be a priority, not because it is fun or desirable (although it can be fun) but because it is required for good health. Unfortunately for many of us, exercise is not considered as a priority; thus, it is put at the end of the list of our daily activities (and many times we skip it). For this reason, it is good to start off the morning with an exercise routine such as walking or running in your neighborhood or biking to work. If you live far from work, try leaving home early enough to park away from the work site, and then walk, bike, or run the rest of the way. When at the workplace, it is important to maintain productivity, but as time permits, walk to your coworkers' offices to discuss a matter, instead of calling them on the telephone or sending them an e-mail. As often as possible, take the stairs instead of the elevator. During your lunch break, eat a small, healthy lunch, and spend the rest of the time walking, biking, or running with an exercise buddy or group of co-workers. Moreover, as you are sitting at your desk or standing at your workstation, control your posture and the amount of aggravated stress applied to your muscles by making sure that your work area is ergonomically compliant. Also during work, spare a few minutes to properly stretch and exercise your muscles, and take deep breaths to help supply your body with needed oxygen.

Parents, encourage your children to be active every day and make certain that their schools have good athletic programs. Obesity and adult onset (type II) diabetes are becoming alarmingly prevalent in our youth. Thus, it is important that you teach your children the value not only of a healthy diet but of exercise. Some children may be naturally more active than others, but it is important that you, as parents, insist that all of your children be physically active every day. Help motivate your children to join school sports. If your children are not athletically inclined but are physically capable, insist that they take a physical education class each semester. Strongly encourage your children to be physically active during recess, instead of playing sedentary games. After eating lunch at school, advise your children to play or walk around on school grounds, instead of sitting and talking. If your child's school has a low budget for physical education and athletic programs, then organize a wellness team (see chapter 23 for details) that will seek funding from private organizations and other sources to help support physical education (e.g., grants that provide salaries for P.E. teachers), maintain the different ongoing physical activities (e.g., team sports, track and field, and gymnastics), and adopt alternative forms of exercise (e.g., dance clubs, running marathons, and exercise breaks in the classroom).

It is best to exercise outside and enjoy the fresh air. However, for whatever reasons, it may be difficult for you to exercise outside.

If this is the case, there are also many ways you can exercise in your home. Instead of moving as little as possible, increase movement when completing chores. When sweeping the floor, dusting, vacuuming, or washing laundry, dishes or the car, listen to music and dance. If you have stairs in your house, put items you regularly use (e.g., coat, money, wallet, purse, and cell phone) or often enjoy (e.g., healthy snacks and CDs) on a floor other than the main floor, so that you will have to climb the stairs to reach them. If you live in an apartment, take the stairs rather than the elevator. Invest in a stationary bicycle, treadmill, or other exercise equipment—and then use them. Lift free weights. If you don't have conventional free weights, find objects in your house (e.g., jugs of milk, sacks of potatoes, and canned goods) and lift them. Put a mat down on the floor, and perform sets of floor exercises such as sit-ups, leg lifts, and push-ups. If you are extremely out of shape, sit down and move your upper body and legs as you enjoy listening to music; this will build up muscle strength and endurance. Soon you will be able to stand up and exercise your entire body (but remember to first seek advice from your physician).

After a long day at work, school, or taking care of a household, you may find yourself and your entire family "vegging out" as couch potatoes in front of the TV set by watching television or movies. It is especially difficult for unhealthy or overweight working parents and their children to develop a daily exercise regimen, but it must be done. Exercise together as a family; go for a run, walk, or run/walk combination. Together, as a family, play in the park or in an empty lot. Some villages have gyms or recreation centers with free or reasonable membership fees; join the entire family. Volunteer to be a Little League coach for your child's team. If your family lives in a village that is not safe, then play, run, and walk in your backyard. If your family does not have a yard or if the weather is bad, exercise in your home. Increase your family's exercise time by turning on music and dancing, or by teaching your family how to exercise in front of the TV set (and then turn it off afterwards so that you can help your children complete their homework and spend quality time with them). Demonstrate to your children that the family can simultaneously watch television and exercise. Show them, through your example that they do not have to be couch potatoes while watching television. Clear a space and put down mats or rugs in front of the TV to protect your floors, and let everyone march in circles or run in place. As you watch a movie, let everyone dance or do aerobics or calisthenics. Exercise while playing aerobic or Pilates DVDs, or while watching exercise shows on television. Let the entire family enjoy being in front of the TV, not as a sack of couch potatoes but as a bunch of active little rug rats!

* * *

Work-Study: Points to Ponder

1. If you already have an exercise regimen, how long and often do you exercise? Describe your exercise regimen. What improvements have you seen in your physical fitness, health, and weight?

2. Exercising with others helps to keep everyone motivated and accountable.
   Describe your experience in exercising with others. For example, do you exercise with your family, or do you have exercise buddies? Do your family members or exercise buddies need much encouragement? Or are they eager and great at motivating you to exercise? If you do not have an exercise buddy, are you willing to find one, or do you prefer to exercise alone?

3. If you are not exercising regularly, are you ready to start by designing an exercise regimen? If so, have you had your physical exam and consulted with a physician about your exercise regimen? Describe your physician's advice. If you are not ready to start exercising, explain your reasons for waiting.

4. If you are ready to design an exercise regimen, first see your physician. Ask your physician for the weight and heart rate information listed below and record it.

Current weight ____________________ lb.
Desired weight ________________________ lb.
Height _________________________in.

Current resting heart rate ____________________ (beats/min)
Targeted heart rate during exercise _________________ (beats/min)
Optimal resting heart rate (my goal) _________________ (beats/min)

5. I exercise four to six times a week, and I continually and gradually increase the duration and intensity of exercise to fit my physical needs and fitness goals. Ask your physician about the type, intensity, and duration of exercises that you need in your regimen. It is important that your exercise regimen is designed to fit your present health conditions so that you can obtain your desired weight and increase your physical fitness without the high risk of serious physical injuries and health complications. Your physician should also give you information (or direct you to someone who will give you information) on weight-lifting, aerobic, and other exercises that you require to improve the seven targeted areas requiring physical fitness. If you have a family or an exercise buddy, design together an exercise regimen that fits each of your needs, and as much as possible, choose exercises that you can perform together. Remember to add stretching to your regimen, and always stretch appropriately before and after exercising. Below is a chart that you can use to help design your and your family's exercise regimen.

Exercise Regimen

	Types of Exercise (activities)	Duration of Exercise (min.)
Monday		

Exercise Regimen

	Types of Exercise (activities)	Duration of Exercise (min.)
Tuesday		

Exercise Regimen

	Types of Exercise (activities)	Duration of Exercise (min.)
Wednesday		

Exercise Regimen

	Types of Exercise (activities)	Duration of Exercise (min.)
Thursday		

Exercise Regimen

	Types of Exercise (activities)	**Duration of Exercise (min.)**
Friday		

Exercise Regimen

	Types of Exercise (activities)	Duration of Exercise (min.)
Saturday		

Exercise Regimen

	Types of Exercise (activities)	Duration of Exercise (min.)
Sunday		

6. How often do you exercise? What differences have you seen in your health and weight since beginning your exercise regimen?

7. Does your place of employment, manager, or supervisor encourage exercise or allow time for exercise? Do you have enough time to exercise during your lunch hour? If not, do you feel comfortable with talking about this to your manager or supervisor?

8. On your job, do you feel overworked? Do you work too many hours? Do you feel you don't have enough rest-and-relaxation (R&R) time? Are you too tired or stressed out to exercise before or after work? Do you have enough time to engage in activities and exercise with your family or exercise buddies?

9. Do you own your own place of business, or are you a supervisor or a manager at your place of employment? If yes, do you provide a work atmosphere that encourages you and your employees to exercise and maintain good health? How is your and your employees' work/life balance? Are you all overworked? Do you allow yourself and your employees enough R&R time?

10. As a business owner, supervisor, or manager do you allow enough time in your schedule for you to exercise? Do you allow enough time to do activities and exercise with your family or exercise buddy? Do you plan your employees' work schedules so that they have time to engage in activities and exercise with their families or exercise buddies? If there is room for improvement in these areas, how will you make things better?

11. Is your work site, overall, ergonomically compliant? If not, what are you willing to do about it?

12. After consulting with your physician, are you ready to gradually increase your level of exercise? Are you ready to lift heavier weights and increase the sets of weight lifting? Are you willing to increase intensity and duration of aerobic exercise?

13. If you are a parent, do your children exercise every day? If not, why? If so, what type of exercise do they do and how often? Are your children healthy enough to exercise at least an hour every day? Before starting to exercise or play sports, did your children complete their annual physical exams? Do your children need to exercise more? How can you encourage them to exercise?

14. How can you become involved in your children's exercise regimen? Do your children have good physical education and athletic programs in their schools? If not, what can you do to help change this?

15. Do you or members of your family watch television every day? If so, are you all willing to start exercising in front of the TV? If the answer is yes, then begin by letting the entire family exercise together during at least one television show every day. The intensity of exercise for each family member may vary as the physical condition and age of each person are taken into consideration.

16. When you exercise with your family, are there any other individuals in your village who would benefit from exercising with you all? If so, are you willing to ask them?

17. Exercise does not have to be fun; it just needs to be done. But life is short and if you can enjoy exercising, then do it. Be creative with your family, friends, neighbors, and community, and make exercising a priority and fun. Describe ways that you could make exercising enjoyable.

18. Those of us who are parents must be responsible for the safety of our children and not let them exercise or play sports in an unsafe environment. Describe ways you could organize safe activities that would increase exercise for children, families, and adults in your village.

Chapter 30

Thrifty Today, Healthy Tomorrow

Go to the ant, thou sluggard; consider her ways, and be wise: Which having no guide, overseer, or ruler, provideth her meat in the summer, and gathereth her food in the harvest. How long wilt thou sleep, O sluggard? When wilt thou arise out of thy sleep? (Proverbs 6:6-9)

Maintaining good health costs money and time, and requires much effort and sacrifice. In today's society, immediate gratification is the essence of the average American lifestyle, thus many Americans fail to invest what it takes to maintain good health. Living in today for temporary pleasure is what many of us do best. In our minds, tomorrow is often a place where we file away all of the things we do not want to deal with or worry about today. If someone were to ask us, "Are you willing to invest in your health?" Many of us would immediately reply, "Of course! Do you think I like being unhealthy, sick, and out of shape?"

If someone were then to ask, "Are you ready to invest in your health by eating right and exercising?" Many of us would respond by giving lame excuses, such as those listed below:

- "Yes, but I can only eat soft foods that are easy to digest, like white bread, soda crackers, and cookies. My stomach is not strong enough to digest foods like raw vegetables and other roughage."
- "Yes, but I have to wait until I can afford a car. The health-food store is way across town, but my favorite fast-food joint and the corner market are only a block away."
- "Yes, but after working hard all day, I am too tired to cook and exercise. Frozen dinners are much more convenient. Besides, my favorite show is on TV tonight."

- "Yes, but I have to wait until I lose fifty pounds before I can exercise. The extra weight is too hard on my knees and back."
- "Yes, but I have to wait until I am promoted on my job, so I can afford the high prices of health food and gym membership fees."
- "Yes, but I have been wanting to buy a new _________ (fill in the blank) for months. Now, it is on sale, and I must buy it. Right now, I will just eat junk food until I can save up enough money to afford health food in the future."
- "Yes, but eating hamburgers and fries at fast-food restaurants is the only form of pleasure that I can afford. If I don't do this, then what will I do for fun?"
- "Yes, but life is too short. Both of my parents died young from heart complications. Since the same will probably happen to me, I might as well eat, drink, and be merry."
- "Yes, but first I am standing on faith and waiting to see if God will heal me. Now, I do not have the energy or strength to start. But if it is His will to heal me, then I will start to eat right and exercise." (Using words like "waiting to see," "do not have," and "if" demonstrates doubt, automatically cancels out faith, and results in no healing.)

The excuses are endless. We need to stop giving excuses that focus on immediate gratification and start making good health a priority. We need to be willing to sacrifice certain pleasures and invest in healthy lifestyles, from which we can benefit not only today but in the future.

Many of us think that we cannot afford to eat right because junk food seems to be so much cheaper than health food. Yet the reality is that eating junk will make us sick, and in the long run, the cost of prescriptions, doctor bills, and medical care will definitely outweigh the cost of health food. If we consistently eat junk food, we will find ourselves in constant debt, as we attempt to pay the ever-increasing medical bills. Consequently, we will never be able to save and invest for our retirement or in our children's future. As our health continues to deteriorate, we will find ourselves on Medicaid or disability, and eventually needing home-care assistance. The national debt will keep increasing, as the government continues to provide medical assistance to those of us who think that eating healthy is not affordable.

The reality is that we cannot afford *not* to eat healthy. We must budget our money and buy healthy foods. We must schedule our time and discipline ourselves to properly prepare our meals at home, eat our last meal of the day at least two hours before going to bed (this will help prevent excess weight gain and improve food digestion), and exercise regularly. When we do these things to improve our health, we will begin to save money, as the need for hospital care, doctor appointments, medical tests, and prescribed medicines decreases. Because we won't have as many health issues, we can shop around for health insurance with lower premiums. Before long, we can afford to save money, buy more healthy foods, and enjoy different types of exercise activities. As our health continues to improve and we gain more energy, we will increase job performance, receive job promotions, materialize creative ideas, make wise investments (e.g., buy a house), invest in our children's future, build successful businesses, and donate to charitable organizations. Better yet, we will have the energy to give our personal time to help others, and improve our villages and the villages of others to places of green pastures. As we become healthier and require less government medical assistance, our nation will have more money to provide funds for higher education and jobs in the workforce. We will then become empowered to assist in the future of our youth and insist that the government responsibly spends this money to secure provisions and resources for the next generation. Above all, we, from the youngest to the oldest, will have the strength to fulfill our God-given purpose, our reason for living!

* * *

Work-Study: Points to Ponder

1. Complete Points to Ponder 2 through 11 to help you with budgeting money for your new healthy lifestyle.

2. What are your thoughts on sacrificing temporary pleasures to gain long-term benefits? In the future, are you willing to budget your money

responsibly by spending most of your income on the essentials of life (e.g., shelter, healthy living, and bills), saving extra money (e.g., in college and retirement funds), making wise investments (e.g., buying a house), and supporting your church and other charitable organizations (e.g., paying tithes and offerings and giving money to homeless shelters and food drives)? Or are you planning to frivolously spend your income on wasteful and pleasurable items (e.g., the latest new sports car)? List the things on which you plan to spend or save your money.

3. Eating right requires being able to afford healthy groceries. Are you willing to budget your money and improve your spending habits so that you will have more money to spend on healthy groceries?

4. Buying healthy groceries and preparing dinner at home instead of eating out are ways to save money. Another way to save money is by preparing more than enough food for dinner so that you can take the leftovers to work the next day for lunch. This extra money can then be used to buy more healthy groceries. Are you willing to prepare most of your healthy meals at home and cut back on dining out? If so, what are you planning to do with the extra money?

5. Read the following description about the fictional members in the Doe family, and then observe in Table IA below the fictitious John and Jane Doe's Money Budget.

The Doe Family: John Doe, a life insurance agent and hoarder of electronic toys, is married to Jane, a hairstylist and lover of shoes. Together they have three children: Sue (age 17), a drama star and fashion addict; Leroy (age 15), a basketball player and video game junkie; and Susie (age 4), a lover of animated movies, fries, and chocolate shakes. Unfortunately, each month they spend more than their take-home income, and they consistently increase their credit card debt by eating out for lunch and dinner practically every day, going out to a movie every Friday for family night, and purchasing nonessential items (e.g., electronic toys, shoes, clothes, and video games). Yet they recently started to live a healthier lifestyle and decrease their monthly spending by preparing meals at home, renting movies on family night, and cutting back on nonessential purchases. They now have money left over each month to help pay off their credit card debt and spend on healthy groceries and fitness.

Table IA. John and Jane Doe's Money Budget

	Current Spending ($/month)	**Proposed Budget** ($/month)	**New Spending** ($/month)
Total Monthly Income (Take-Home Income)	7072.00	7072.00	7072.00
Section #1 (Constant Expenses)			
Housing (e.g., mortgage, rent, room and board, property tax, and homeowners insurance)	1220.00	1220.00	1220.00
Essential Utilities (e.g., water and sewage, gas, electric, lights, home phone, and trash collection)	375.00	375.00	375.00
Insurances (e.g., medical, vision, dental, auto, and life)	510.00	510.00	510.00
Savings, Retirement, and Investments	235.00	235.00	235.00
Transportation (e.g., car payment, gas, and bus fare)	470.00	470.00	470.00
Nonessential Utilities and Services (e.g., Internet, cable, cell phone, and satellite dish)	215.00	215.00	215.00
Children Care (e.g., daycare, babysitter, school tuition, allowances, lessons, and child support)	550.00	550.00	550.00
Others (e.g., church tithes and offerings, and monthly donations)	710.00	710.00	710.00
Subtotal #1 (Add Up Section #1)	**4285.00**	**4285.00**	**4285.00**
Section #2 (Variable Expenses)			
Medical Expenses (e.g., co-pays, prescriptions, medical tests, and dental and vision care)	110.00	110.00	100.00
Credit Card Accounts	450.00	650.00	650.00
Food Groceries (e.g., health food)	375.00	725.00	740.00
Dining Out (e.g., restaurants, fast foods, and coffee runs)	650.00	225.00	227.00
Toiletries, Household Products, Grooming, and Pet Care (e.g., toothpaste, laundry detergent, haircut, dog food, and makeup)	235.00	235.00	223.00
House Maintenance and Repairs	100.00	100.00	100.00
Fitness, Recreational Activities, and Exercise Equipment (e.g., bicycles, gym fees, skiing, golfing, and team sport fees)	55.00	90.00	90.00
Clothes	375.00	250.00	257.00
Hobbies (e.g., purchasing electronic devices, toys, video games, antiques, and paintings)	176.00	125.00	129.00
Entertainment (e.g., vacation, movies, rental movies, tickets to sport events, and concerts)	309.00	105.00	101.00
Others (e.g., charitable gifts, club membership fees, birthdays, and dry cleaning)	25.00	25.00	25.00
Subtotal #2 (Add up Section #2)	**2860.00**	**2640.00**	**2642.00**
Total Expenses (Subtotal #1 + Subtotal #2)	**7145.00**	**6925.00**	**6927.00**
Difference (Total Monthly Income – Total Expenses)	**-73.00**	**+147.00**	**+145.00**

6. As you observe the Does' Money Budget, what things do you like or dislike about it? In the upcoming months, what improvements do you suggest they make to further improve their healthy lifestyle and decrease their debt?

7. As the Does buy less junk food and nonessential items, they spend more money on health food, exercise, and paying off their credit card accounts. Like the Does, are you and your family willing to improve spending habits and become savvy shoppers so that you will have more money to spend on healthy living? Are you optimistic, believing it is possible to decrease your debt substantially by adopting a healthy lifestyle?

8. Before you can accurately determine how much money you plan to spend on healthy living, it is a good idea to first calculate your money budget. Fill in the Money Budget Worksheet in Table IB below by completing the following set of instructions. You may also use John and Jane Doe's Money Budget shown in Table IA as a tool to help complete your money budget.
   a. In the column labeled Current Spending, complete the following steps:
      i. Record your Total Monthly Income (Take-Home Income) in the provided space.
      ii. Calculate your current monthly expenses by completing Section #1 and Section #2.
      iii. Calculate the Total Expenses by adding together Subtotal #1 and Subtotal #2, and record.
      iv. Calculate the Difference (i.e., the excess or shortage of money) by subtracting the Total Expense from the Total Monthly Income, and record.
   b. As you begin budgeting money for your new healthy lifestyle, complete the column labeled Proposed Budget by following the below steps:
      i. Record your Total Monthly Income in the provided space.
      ii. In Section #1, transfer from the Current Spending column the amount of each of your Constant Expenses, which un-

der normal circumstances should basically remain the same each month.

iii. In Section #2, adjust the values of the Variable Expenses from the Current Spending column to include your new spending decisions of your new healthy lifestyle. For example, like the Does, you may decide to start spending less money on Friday nights by eating at home and renting videos, instead of going out for dinner and a movie.

iv. Calculate and record the Total Expenses, and also the Difference.

c. In the upcoming month, complete the column labeled New Spending as follows:

i. Record your Total Monthly Income in the space provided.

ii. Pay your bills and spend money according to your Proposed Budget and complete Section #1 and Section #2.

iii. Calculate and record the Total Expenses, and also the Difference.

Table IB. Money Budget Worksheet

	Current Spending ($/month)	**Proposed Budget** ($/month)	**New Spending** ($/month)
Total Monthly Income (Take-Home Income)			
<u>Section #1 (Constant Expenses)</u>			
Housing (e.g., mortgage, rent, room and board, property tax, and homeowners insurance)			
Essential Utilities (e.g., water and sewage, gas, electric, lights, home phone, and trash collection)			
Insurances (e.g., medical, vision, dental, auto, and life)			
Savings, Retirement, and Investments			
Transportation (e.g., car payment, gas, and bus fare)			
Nonessential Utilities and Services (e.g., Internet, cable, cell phone, and satellite dish)			
Children Care (e.g., daycare, babysitter, school tuition, allowances, lessons, and child support)			
Others (e.g., church tithes and offerings, and monthly donations)			
Subtotal #1 (Add Up Section #1)			
<u>Section #2 (Variable Expenses)</u>			
Medical Expenses (e.g., co-pays, prescriptions, medical tests, and dental and vision care)			
Credit Card Accounts			
Food Groceries (e.g., health food)			
Dining Out (e.g., restaurants, fast foods, and coffee runs)			
Toiletries, Household Products, Grooming, and Pet Care (e.g., toothpaste, laundry detergent, haircut, dog food, and makeup)			
House Maintenance and Repairs			
Fitness, Recreational Activities, and Exercise Equipment (e.g., bicycles, gym fees, skiing, golfing, and team sport fees)			
Clothes			
Hobbies (e.g., purchasing electronic devices, toys, video games, antiques, and paintings)			
Entertainment (e.g., vacation, movies, rental movies, tickets to sport events, and concerts)			
Others (e.g., charitable gifts, club membership fees, birthdays, and dry cleaning)			
Subtotal #2 (Add up Section #2)			
Total Expenses (Subtotal #1 + Subtotal #2)			
Difference (Total Monthly Income – Total Expenses)			

9. With regard to your money budget (see Table IB), how much do you plan to spend on groceries in your Proposed Budget versus what you actually spent in your Current Spending? In your Proposed Budget, is the Difference (Total Monthly Income - Total Expenses) more or less than that of your Current Spending? If more, great! What are you planning to do with the extra money? It is hoped that you will use it to live healthier (e.g., buy healthy groceries and running shoes) and adjust your budget accordingly. If the balance is less, then what adjustments in your budget do you plan to make in the near future?

10. If you are buying more groceries, eating healthier meals, and improving physical fitness, the amount of money spent on medical issues should eventually decrease as your monthly difference increases. When your difference and savings begin to increase, what do you plan to do with the extra money? Invest or spend it wisely, or waste it on frills?

11. In the upcoming months, follow your Proposed Budget as you modify and improve it as needed. Continue to keep track of your new spending habits until they become part of your normal routine.

12. Complete Points to Ponder 13 through 27 to help you schedule the time you plan to spend on healthy living.

13. Scheduling time to exercise and eat healthy is essential for healthy living. As you begin to live healthier and spend more money on fitness, exercise equipment, and recreational activities, are you willing to increase the time you spend exercising? Plus, as you plan to spend more money on buying healthy foods, are you also willing to dedicate the time needed to shop for groceries, prepare meals, and eat healthy?

14. Are your daily activities and habits preventing you from living a healthy lifestyle? If so, describe how. For example, do you spend so much time working on a job or attending extracurricular events

that you do not have the time and energy to exercise, shop for groceries, or prepare healthy meals? By the end of the day, are you so tired that you end up grabbing junk food from the nearest fast-food restaurant and being a couch potato in front of the TV set all evening?

15. Observe the fictitious Monday Time Schedule of John Doe in Table IIA below. Early in the morning, three times a week, John improves his physical fitness by exercising. Because the Does have decided to eat healthier and buy less fast food, John eats more home-cooked meals and sack lunches. Consequently, John now has more time during his lunch hour to exercise and spends more quality time with his family by preparing meals in the evenings. What other improvements did he make in his lifestyle habits? Like John, are you ready to increase the time you spend on healthy living?

Table IIA. John Doe's MONDAY Time Schedule

MONDAY	Week I	Week II	Week III	Week IV
6:00 AM	Wake-up; Pray and read Bible; 20 min workout on treadmill	Ditto	Ditto	Ditto
7:00 AM	Shower; Dress for work; Eat hot cereal	Ditto	Ditto	Ditto
8:00 AM	Drop daughter at daycare; Commute to work; Coffee run	Ditto	Ditto; No coffee run, drink coffee supplied at work	Ditto; No coffee, drink herbal tea supplied at work
9:00 AM	Work on job	Ditto	Ditto	Ditto
10:00 AM	↓	↓	↓	↓
11:00 AM	↓	↓	↓	↓
12:00 PM	Eat lunch at fast-food restaurant	Pick up lunch from deli	Eat sack lunch from home; Brisk walk for 20 min	Ditto; Power walk with exercise buddy for 20 min
1:00 PM	Work on job	Ditto	Ditto	Ditto
2:00 PM	↓	↓	↓	↓
3:00 PM	↓	↓	↓	↓
4:00 PM	↓	↓	↓	↓
5:00 PM	↓	↓	↓	↓

Table IIA. John Doe's MONDAY Time Schedule (cont'd)

MONDAY	Week I	Week II	Week III	Week IV
6:00 PM	Pick up fast-food cheeseburgers, fries, and shakes for family; Commute home	Commute home; Eat dinner prepared last night	Ditto	Ditto
7:00 PM	Attend son's school basketball game; Eat dinner at game	Attend son's school basketball game	Ditto	Ditto
8:00 PM	↓	↓	↓	↓
9:00 PM	Carpool son's teammates home; Put youngest daughter to bed	Ditto	Ditto	Ditto
10:00 PM	Watch TV	Prepare Tues. dinner with wife	Prepare Tues. dinner and sack lunches with family	Ditto
11:00 PM	Watch TV	Ditto	Ditto	Ditto
12:00 AM	Sleep	Sleep	Ditto	Ditto
1:00 AM	↓	↓	↓	↓
2:00 AM	↓	↓	↓	↓
3:00 AM	↓	↓	↓	↓
4:00 AM	↓	↓	↓	↓
5:00 AM	Watch TV	↓	↓	↓

16. If you are ready to spend more time on healthy living, then complete your time schedule for one month by following the below set of instructions. For your convenience, use John Doe's Monday Time Schedule in Table IIA as an example to complete your Time Schedule Worksheets (see Table IIB).
    a. Using the Time Schedule Worksheet in Table IIB as a template, assign one worksheet to each day of the week, Monday through Sunday (i.e., a complete set is a total of seven worksheets). It is up to you and your family to decide if it is best for each individual in your household to complete a separate set of worksheets or for everyone to complete one set together.
    b. For the seven worksheets assigned to each day (i.e., Monday through Sunday), fill in Week I. Then, continue to complete all seven worksheets by filling in Week II through Week IV. It is up to you to decide if it is best for you to design your schedule in advance and then follow it, or to fill in your schedule as you go or at the end of each day.
    c. Use the following list of suggested habits to help you complete your weekly schedule. As you follow the above directions in filling the worksheets for the entire month, find different ways each week to improve your lifestyle habits.

List of Suggested Habits

Work and Travel Habits

- Work at job site, place of business, or at home/attend college classes, school, or daycare
- Commute/transportation
- Work brought home from the office or job/homework/chores

Dining, Exercise, and Sleep Habits

- Shop for groceries and prepare home-cooked meals (breakfast, lunch, dinner, and snacks). Note: Try to make shopping a family event by shopping on the weekends at your favorite health-food store and then coming home to prepare a delicious meal together.
- Eat home-prepared foods (breakfast, lunch, dinner, and snacks).
- Buy and eat foods (breakfast, lunch, dinner, and snacks) from or at sit-down restaurants, school cafeterias, cafés, buffets, etc.
- Properly digest last meal of the day (should schedule at least two hours between last meal and bedtime).
- Exercise (correlate schedule with your new exercise regimen that you designed in chapter 29)
- Sleep/nap

Extracurricular Habits

- Entertainment (e.g., movies, concerts, plays, educational television, and board games)
- Activities (e.g., volunteer work, scouts, after-school activities, clubs, and church functions)
- Spiritual growth (e.g., prayer, read Bible, and church service)
- R&R (e.g., hot bath, listen to soft music, reading, and massage)
- Quality time with family (e.g., preparing dinner, exercise, and board games)
- Quality time with friends and relatives

Table II B. _________DAY Time Schedule Worksheet

______DAY	Week I	Week II	Week III	Week IV
6:00 AM				
7:00 AM				
8:00 AM				
9:00 AM				
10:00 AM				
11:00 AM				
12:00 PM				
1:00 PM				
2:00 PM				
3:00 PM				
4:00 PM				
5:00 PM				

Table II B. ________DAY Time Schedule Worksheet (cont'd)

_____DAY	Week I	Week II	Week III	Week IV
6:00 PM				
7:00 PM				
8:00 PM				
9:00 PM				
10:00 PM				
11:00 PM				
12:00 AM				
1:00 AM				
2:00 AM				
3:00 AM				
4:00 AM				
5:00 AM				

17. In the four weeks of your Time Schedule, how much time did you spend preparing meals and grocery shopping? Compared to the past, did you increase the time you spent grocery shopping and the number of meals you prepared at home? What adjustments do you need to make in the near future? If necessary, will you be able to decrease overtime work hours or extracurricular activities to give more time for healthy eating?

18. As recorded in the four weeks of your Time Schedule, how much time did you spend eating meals prepared at home versus eating meals prepared at fast-food restaurants, sit-down restaurants, cafeterias, etc.? In the following weeks, do you still need to work on increasing the time you spend eating home-prepared meals versus eating out? Do you and your family prepare meals together?

19. As you design a healthy diet that fits you, and you complete Table III in chapter 45, you will need healthy groceries. When you go grocery shopping, are the foods healthy or unhealthy? Are you willing to adjust your grocery list and meals to include more healthy foods?

20. Do you like grocery shopping, or are you reluctant to shop? If you are a reluctant shopper, try to describe ways in which you can make grocery shopping more pleasant. For example, take the entire family to the health-food store and make it a fun event, or use grocery shopping as a time of relaxation spent away from the kids or the workplace.

21. Part V of this book is a collection of my favorite healthy recipes created by my family. As you prepare healthy meals at home, it is good to have some of your own favorite healthy recipes. Are you willing to try my favorite family recipes? Do you have any healthy recipes that you use to prepare meals? Are you willing to adjust the ingredients in your favorite family recipes to healthier ones or even create healthy recipes of your own?

22. To allow enough time for proper digestion and prevent weight gain, it is best to eat at least two hours before going to bed. As you look at each day of your Time Schedule how many hours were there between eating your last meal and going to bed? If it is less than two hours, is it because you usually cook and eat dinner after arriving home late from work, school functions, sport events, etc.? If so, describe what you can do to solve this problem. For example, is there a way you can prepare dinner every night for the following day or every morning before leaving home for work? Or can you cook enough food for the entire week on your days off?

23. Continue to modify your Time Schedule in the upcoming months and constantly find ways to prepare and eat healthy meals.

24. In your Time Schedule, how much time was spent exercising? Did you use your new exercise regimen that you designed in chapter 29 to help you schedule time for exercising? Did the time spent on exercising gradually increase with each week? If so, by how much and why? If not, why?

25. In the upcoming months, continue to modify your Time Schedule (see Table IIB), and under the advice of a physician, constantly find ways to increase your exercise time.

26. Most people believe that the path to great success is to sacrifice their sleep and R&R time so that they will have more time to work, but this is not necessarily the case. Everyone needs a proper amount of sleep and R&R to maintain good health and a proper flow of creative thinking. Look at the amount of time spent on some of the other activities and habits listed in your Time Schedule, such as sleep, R&R, work, etc. Do you need to adjust your schedule so that your personal time and home life will become well balanced with your work life?

27. Continue to modify your Time Schedule in the upcoming months and constantly find ways to balance your personal life with your work life.

Chapter 31

A Pear I Am

What? Know ye not that your body is the temple of the Holy Ghost which is in you, which ye have of God, and ye are not your own? For ye are bought with a price: therefore glorify God in your body, and in your spirit, which are God's. (I Corinthians 6: 19-20)

Your shape and body type are linked to the way your body stores fat and metabolizes calories. Most people desire the perfect body type, which is the shape of a funnel for men and an hourglass for women. However, the majority of people are usually one of three most common body types, which is apple (round midsection), pear (bottom heavy), or banana (thin). Apple people are prone to accumulate more fat around the waist and upper body parts (e.g., abdomen, chest, arms, and back), whereas pear people have a tendency to accumulate more fat below the waist (e.g., thighs, legs, hips, and buttocks). Men usually carry their extra weight as apple people and women as pear people. Apple people are generally able to lose weight easier than pear people, but they are more likely to develop health problems, such as heart disease, diabetes, and cancer, than pear people. The banana people are genetically fat-burners, thus they usually have straight figures devoid of overweight fat, curves, and bulky muscle mass. They typically have fewer health issues and problems with food cravings than the apple and pear people, both of which genetically store extra fat, as they have difficulty turning down the extra calories. Many think that it is impossible for the banana people to become fat, but I know of banana people who transformed into apple, pear, or pineapple people (overweight people who are evenly fat all the way down their bodies), as their metabolism changed with the sedentary lifestyle that comes often with aging.

Remember, your ultimate goal is not to focus on sculpturing the perfect proportionate body but to gain good health. Losing weight and becoming fit do not necessarily mean you will "morph" to a different body type. Accept the body type with which God blessed you, and don't fight against it; accept it. Be content with your body type, and move forward. When overweight apple people lose weight, the chances are high that they will become smaller apple people. The main thing is to lose the extra weight, exercise, tone up, and increase upper-body muscle mass. Building strong back and abdominal muscles are essential for proper posture and overall health. When overweight pear people lose weight, chances are they will become smaller pear people. The main objective is to lose the extra weight, exercise, and tone up the lower body. Owning strong gluteus maximus muscles can be very beneficial in power walking, aerobic exercises, and sports. Banana people, not needing to lose extra weight, should exercise to increase muscle mass and transform to bulkier banana or pineapple people. (In this case, a pineapple person is overweight not because of excess body fat but because of extra muscle mass, which efficiently burns more calories.)

My heritage is mostly African American (Black) and American Indian (Native American); thus, my relatives inherited body types from both races. Some of my relatives have inherited the American Indian trait of the apple-shape body, and other of my relatives inherited the African trait of the pear-shape body, due to a large gluteus maximus. I have found peace with the fact that I am a pear person and will always be a pear person. I must watch my high intake of white stuff (not only white sugar and white flour but also white potatoes, white rice, and white pasta) and maintain a proper exercise regimen, so that I will not be an overweight pear person but a pear person who maintains a healthy weight.

A person's total body weight equals the total weight of lean body mass (e.g., muscle, bones, and organs) plus the total weight of body fat. Body weight is divided into five basic categories: underweight, normal weight, overweight, obese, and morbidly obese. The Body Mass Index (BMI) is an inexpensive and simple method used to categorize people's body weight and screen individuals who are at risk of health problems such as heart disease, diabetes, cancer, osteoporosis, and premature aging. BMI is calculated the same for men, women, adolescents, and children. Using the English system, the BMI is calculated by dividing your total body weight in pounds (lb.) by the square of your height in inches (in.) multiplied by the conversion factor 705.

The below BMI scale is used to categorize the weight of both men and women, even though women are generally smaller and fatter than men. A different BMI scale is used for adolescents and children although BMI is calculated the same for all age groups; obtain details about this from a pediatrician or nutritionist.

- **BMI < 19** is considered to be underweight; high risk for bone frailty, anemia, infertility, and osteoporosis.
- **BMI = 19–24** is considered to be at a healthy, normal weight; no or minimal risk for heart disease and diabetes.
- **BMI = 25–29** is considered to be overweight; potential risk for heart disease and diabetes.
- **BMI = 30-39** is considered to be obese; extremely high risk of heart disease, diabetes, cancer, and rapid aging.
- **BMI > 39** is considered as morbidly obese; extremely high risk of being close to death.

The body fat of a healthy adult male and female is generally about 15 percent and 25 percent of total body weight, respectively. Because the total body weight of a person and not the weight of body fat or lean body mass is used to calculate the BMI, the BMI does not directly indicate the fatness or leanness of a person. For example, a person may have a BMI of a normal-weight person but disproportionately have more fat and less lean body mass than that required to be considered healthy (e.g., a person who has a BMI of 24 but 30 percent body fat). On the flip side, a body builder with big bones may have a BMI of an overweight person but actually be very healthy because the extra weight is from the extra bone and muscle mass, and not from fat (e.g., a person with a BMI of 29 but only 10 percent body fat). Thus, a banana person can be thin (normal weight) and still be over-fat (a term used to describe excess body fat, especially that of normal weight or underweight individuals), and a pineapple person can be overweight without being over-fat. It is common for a normal-weight person with a toned body to begin losing muscle mass and become over-fat as he or she grows older and becomes more sedentary. In today's society, most jobs entail office work, which burns fewer calories than those consumed, thus resulting in decreased muscle mass. One can help reverse the aging process and maintain lean body mass by exercising regularly.

Waistline measurements are another method used to identify the risk of heart disease, cancer, diabetes, etc., in overweight or obese individuals. Having a waistline greater than 36 inches in men or 32 inches in women is more likely to cause health problems than a waistline smaller than this. It is important to accurately measure the circumference of the waist at the level of the navel. Don't let the measuring tape be loose or too tight, and don't hold in your stomach; just relax.

Years ago a television program documented the life of an anorexic patient. The patient explained that over the years, no matter how much weight she lost, she always thought she was too fat; the disease had caused her to lose touch with reality. Observing images of her tiny frame, I was amazed that it seemed like there was some truth to what she had said; she was over-fat. As she continued to lose weight, her muscle mass deteriorated and was replaced with fat. Even when the disease progressed to the point of her being almost nothing but bones, the little body weight on her bones looked like it was mostly fat. She thought that losing weight would stop her from being over-fat, but it didn't. I pray that she has conquered the disease and hope that she is alive and well and has come to the realization that eating right and exercising (not starvation) are essential to obtaining a healthy body that is not over-fat.

As one continues to exercise, a decrease in body fat versus an increase in lean body mass may result in a smaller body size. Because lean body mass is heavier than fat, exercise may not only increase lean body mass but also increase body weight. For example, if you are a person within the normal weight range, you may find as you exercise and become physically fit that you will lose fat, gain muscle, and become smaller in size, but your weight may increase. A good way to measure decrease in body size is to keep records of waist and hip measurements. As you continue to exercise and eat correctly, your hip and waistline should decrease, even if your weight does not. Furthermore, do not overexert yourself with an exercise regimen that is too intense for you. At first, it is better to exercise for longer periods with less intensity. As your physical fitness improves, increase the intensity of your exercise regimen and reward yourself (but not with food). Remember, however, that the main objective of becoming physically fit is not to provoke vanity or stroke your ego but to maintain good health.

* * *

Work-Study: Points to Ponder

1. What body type are you? Have you always been this body type?

2. Are you happy with your body type? What type of metabolism do you have?

3. How difficult is it for you to lose weight?

4. Look at the below example for calculating Body Mass Index (BMI), and then calculate your BMI (you can use your current weight and height information as recorded in chapter 29 under Points to Ponder 4).

   Formula: [Weight (lb) ÷ Height (in.)^2] x 705 = BMI
   Example: Weight = 150 lb; Height = 69 in.
   Example Calculation: (150 ÷ 69^2) x 705 = 22

   Your Calculation: [_____ lb ÷ _____ (in.)^2] x 705 = _____ BMI

5. Based on your BMI, what weight are you (i.e., underweight, normal weight, overweight, obese, or morbidly obese)?

6. Measure your waistline. Is it below or above the normal measurement of 36 inches for men and 32 inches for women? If your BMI and waistline are above the normal range and measurement, respectively, are you willing to exercise and eat right to decrease your BMI and waistline?

7. If your BMI is below the normal range, are you willing to bulk up by weight lifting and increasing your calorie intake of healthy foods?

8. If your current weight is below or above the normal range, calculate below the weight you need to target in order to reach a BMI of 22.

   Formula: [BMI x Height (in.)^2] ÷ 705 = Weight (lb)
   Example: BMI= 22; Height = 69 in.
   Example Calculation: (22 x 69^2) ÷705 = 149 lb

   Your Calculation: (22 x ____ ^{2}) ÷ 705 = Your Targeted Weight____ lb

9. Subtract below your current weight from your targeted weight, which was calculated above in Points to Ponder 8, to determine the amount of weight you will need to lose or gain in order to reach a BMI of 22. (Note: If you are underweight, subtracting your current weight from your targeted weight will give you a negative number. This number is the amount of weight you will need to gain to reach a BMI of 22.)

   Your Current Weight ______ lb – Your Targeted Weight ______ lb
   = Weight to Gain or Lose ______ lb

10. Are you willing to lose or gain the weight required to reach a BMI of 22 or somewhere within the normal BMI range (19-24)? If so, as you continue to exercise, record (approximately once a week) your BMI, waistline, and hip measurements in the following chart, and observe the changes.

Week	BMI	Waistline (in.)	Hip (in.)
1			
2			
3			
4			
5			
6			
7			
8			
9			
10			
11			
12			
13			
14			
15			
16			
17			
18			
19			
20			

Chapter 32

Silly Kid, Carrots Are for Rabbits

My knees are weak through fasting; and my flesh faileth of fatness. I became also a reproach unto them: When they looked upon me, they shaked their heads. Help me, O Lord my God; O save me according to thy mercy. (Psalm 109:24–26)

You are not a rabbit, so don't try to lose weight by eating like one. A person should eat a variety of healthy foods at a high enough quantity to gain energy, obtain the needed nutrients, and keep from being constantly hungry. It is true that weight loss requires a decrease in total calorie intake. Yet it is important to decrease the amount of calorie intake without starving yourself. Eating like a rabbit is not only unhealthy, it also never works. After losing the excess weight, it is almost impossible to maintain your desired weight by starving yourself. Years ago, I knew a young lady who was extremely overweight and became skinny by dieting. Her diet was simple, yet difficult to maintain. She was able to include her favorite types of foods in her meals, but she was only allowed to eat approximately three small bites of each one. In a matter of weeks, the fat melted away, but she was miserable. She ate like a rabbit, and she was always hungry. The hunger was more than she could bear, and in a short time the three bites increased to five, and five to ten. Soon, she had regained much of the weight, and it seemed she was in denial to the fact that she was definitely eating more than the original three bites of everything.

I also know of people who have tried to lose weight by eating only carrots, celery, and yogurt. These foods are healthy—but should be included in our diets along with many other foods. If your focus is to obtain good health, then you can lose weight by eating healthy without being hungry. When you are constantly hungry from dieting, your body thinks you are starving it, and before long you will again find yourself eating excessive amounts of foods. Manage your calorie intake by filling up your stomach with a large green-vegetable salad (complemented with a low-fat and low-sugar salad dressing, of course), instead of eating only small rations of low-calorie foods like carrots, yogurt, and celery. After a hearty salad, eat fruits, whole grain foods, lean meat, and plenty of other vegetables. When managing your diet, it is important to track the kinds of foods you eat and not just the amount of calories. A person automatically consumes fewer empty calories by eating a hearty, healthy meal than a moderate-sized meal consisting of junk food. If you are overweight, eating right will result in weight loss.

A healthy calorie intake range is the amount of daily calories required in a diet to maintain a normal weight. The daily calorie intake range required to maintain a normal weight is approximately 2500–2800 calories for the average-sized adult male and approximately 1900–2100 calories for the average-sized adult female. These daily calorie intake ranges are only guidelines to help you define your own daily calorie intake range. Everyone is different; your required calorie intake depends not only on gender but on your health, body metabolism, body size, and daily exercise regimen. When the amount of calories burned daily is less than your actual daily calorie intake, you will consistently gain weight. Yet if you want to lose weight, your daily calorie intake needs to be less than the amount of calories burned. It is advised, especially if you want to lose more than thirty pounds or have an existing health problem, that you consult your physician or nutritionist for information on the daily calorie intake required for you as an individual.

Before you improve your diet to a healthy one, record your daily calorie intake for about two weeks. Once you begin your healthy diet, record your daily intake for two more weeks. After the four weeks, do not waste your time and become an obsessive calorie-counter by tabulating your calorie intake every day. Spend that time and energy buying and preparing healthy meals. The steps required to lose weight are quite simple. If you are overweight (BMI $\geq$ 25), simply eat a hearty, healthy diet low in calories and increase daily exercise (e.g., brisk walking), and you will lose the extra pounds.

* * *

Work-Study: Points to Ponder

1. Have you ever tried losing excess weight by starving yourself? If so, did you lose the weight? Did you keep the weight off? If not, how long did it take you to regain it?

2. Did you seek the advice of a physician to determine the daily calorie intake range for someone of your gender and with your height, weight, age, metabolism, and health problems? If yes, are you willing to follow it? Are you willing to eat healthy to keep your calorie intake within this range?

3. Before you start your healthy diet, calculate and record below the approximate amount of calories you consume daily for two weeks. Packaged and canned foods and beverages should indicate the amount of calories per each serving. Surf the Internet for reliable sites that list the amount of calories in foods and beverages; the U.S. Department of Agriculture (USDA) has developed a calorie chart of foods (including fast foods) that is available online. Also, your physician or nutritionist probably has a food calorie chart to give to patients. The information provided here can be used to convert nutrients measured in grams to calories: protein: 1 calorie = 4 grams; carbohydrate: 1 calorie = 4 grams; fat: 1 calorie = 9 grams; alcohol: 1 calorie = 7 grams.

Approximate Daily Calorie Intake of Your Unhealthy Diet

Week One							
	Mon.	Tues.	Wed.	Thurs.	Fri.	Sat.	Sun.
Breakfast							
Lunch							
Dinner							
Snacks							
Total							
Week Two							
	Mon.	Tues.	Wed.	Thurs.	Fri.	Sat.	Sun.
Breakfast							
Lunch							
Dinner							
Snacks							
Total							

4. Did you keep your daily calorie intake within the range for someone of your gender, and with your height, weight, age, metabolism, and health problems?

5. Read Part III before designing your new healthy diet (see Table III in chapter 45). Then, after you start your healthy diet, calculate and record the approximate number of calories you consume daily for two weeks.

Approximate Daily Calorie Intake of Your Healthy Diet

Week One							
	Mon.	Tues.	Wed.	Thurs.	Fri.	Sat.	Sun.
Breakfast							
Lunch							
Dinner							
Snacks							
Total							
Week Two							
	Mon.	Tues.	Wed.	Thurs.	Fri.	Sat.	Sun.
Breakfast							
Lunch							
Dinner							
Snacks							
Total							

6. Compare your calorie intake of your new healthy diet to that of your past unhealthy diet. Is your calorie intake of your healthy diet more or less than that of your unhealthy diet? Is it within the range for someone of your gender and with your height, weight, age, metabolism, and health problems?

Part III: Designing a Healthy Diet That Fits You

Chapter 33

A Healthy Diet—What a Concept!

It is good and comely for one to eat and to drink, and to enjoy the good of all his labour that he taketh under the sun all the days of his life, which God giveth him: for it is his portion. (Ecclesiastes 5:18)

This chapter introduces the different types of healthy and unhealthy foods that are produced, processed, manufactured, and marketed by the food industry.

Foods

What is food, and what is its purpose? You eat food; I eat food; all of God's children eat food. We eat food to survive, and most of us eat for enjoyment. Many of us eat to gain energy so that we can earn enough money to buy food and enjoy eating all over again. However, we all should be concerned enough about the food we eat to ask questions such as: Does it really matter what we eat? Should we take responsibility for educating ourselves with regard to the food we put in our bodies? Which foods should we eat and which should we avoid? Do we actually eat healthy, or do we only think we eat healthy? Are all packaged and processed foods safe for consumption? No matter how good it tastes, if it is detrimental to our health, is it worth the pleasure?

My purpose for writing the following information is not to evoke a state of food hysteria but to help you answer the above set of questions and also increase your awareness of healthy foods, so you can begin to eat right and build villages that promote good health. After reading the following information, I anticipate that many of you will be extremely enthusiastic and take tremendous strides toward improving your diet and helping fellow villagers do the same. Some of you may be a little hesitant at first and not be ready to commit to such extreme changes, but the key to progress is to commit to doing something. A small change is progress and should be celebrated as such.

Three federal government agencies are responsible for regulating biotechnology: the United States Department of Agriculture (USDA), the Food and Drug Administration (FDA), and the Environmental Protection Agency (EPA). These agencies play a major role in the quality of life in this country; without the enforcement of their rules and regulations, our standard of living would decline dramatically. However, these agencies, like all man-made systems, are not flawless; thus, their rules and regulations are not perfect. Just because an agency has approved a particular food product to be safe enough to be put on the market does not necessarily guarantee that it is healthy and totally safe. It just means if an approved food product is consumed, we should not fall over dead in the near future from high doses of toxic poisonings, such as pathogens, pesticides, and other contaminants.

The long-term effects of certain foods on our health are sometimes but not always fully understood. Usually, it takes years of extensive research before long-term effects become evident. As time progresses, these agencies—USDA, FDA, and EPA—often become more aware of the toxic effects of certain foods on our health and revise food regulations accordingly. Yet by then, the health of a portion of the population has already been compromised. Thus, it is important that we, the consumers, are aware of the regulations used to produce, process, manufacture, and market our foods so that we can responsibly identify, buy, and consume foods that promote good health and avoid those that don't.

When ingested and metabolized, food provides our bodies with the fuel and building materials needed to stimulate growth and maintain our existence. In this book, food is divided into two main categories: health food and junk food. It is important to know the difference between the health food that we must purposely seek and the junk food that continues to saturate the food industry.

Health Food

Health food, which provides the building materials needed to maintain physically fit bodies, is a natural substance derived from the animal, plant, or fungi kingdom that consists of essential nutrients, as listed below:

- **Carbohydrates**. Organic compounds used for energy, such as starch, glucose, and other sugars. These compounds consist of carbon, oxygen, and hydrogen atoms at a ratio of one carbon (carbo) atom per one water (hydrate) molecule. Types of carbohydrates are simple, complex, and fiber (see chapters 34, 35, and 38 for more information on carbohydrates).

- **Fats**. Organic oily substances that are stored for insulation, metabolized for energy, and required for the structure of cells (see chapter 36 for more information about fats).

- **Proteins**. A large group of organic compounds composed of one or more long peptides (i.e., chains consisting of amino acids) that are folded into complex structures. Amino acids are the single units that are linked together to form the long chains of peptides. Proteins are essential for the structure and function of living organisms (see chapter 37 for more information about proteins).

- **Minerals**. Inorganic elements that are required to build human tissues (e.g., bones, muscles, and red blood cells) and regulate bodily functions (see chapter 39 for more information on minerals).

- **Vitamins**. A group of organic compounds required for metabolic reactions and normal development (see chapter 39 for more information about vitamins).

- **Phytonutrients**. Plant-derived chemicals (phytochemicals) that play important roles in fighting off sickness and disease (e.g., the common cold, cancer, and heart disease) and promoting good health (see chapters 39 and 40 for more information about phyto-nutrients).

- **Water**. A chemical compound made up of hydrogen and oxygen (H_2O). It is the most abundant substance in the body and is required for the proper function of all tissues, organs, and cells (see chapter 41 for more information about water).

Organic Foods and Whole Foods

The healthiest foods on the market are organic and whole. The USDA is responsible for defining the regulations and guaranteeing the certification and quality of organic foods. Organic foods are obtained from plants and animals that have been grown naturally, without exposure to hormones, antibiotics, pesticides, and other toxic contaminants. However, as our environment becomes more contaminated with toxic waste, it becomes more difficult to produce organic foods. An authentic organic crop is cultivated without exposure to pesticides and herbicides, and fertilized with manure that is free from hormones, antibodies, and other toxic contaminants. The healthiest organic livestock and poultry are raised on free ranges, which allow animals to eat vegetation on large pastures free of chemicals and roam without being constantly caged and confined to small areas. Because the organic animal eats vegetation and is free to exercise, its flesh consists of more protein, healthy fats, and other nutrients than the caged animal. Also, since it is free to roam on a pasture and not confined to a disease-infested cage, the organic animal is generally exposed to fewer parasites and pathogens than the caged animal. However, this does not mean the organic animal is totally free of diseases. The organic animal is not immunized with antibiotics and is susceptible to disease; thus, its flesh should be handled as such and cooked thoroughly.

A government certifier inspects the farm before the organic crop, livestock, or poultry are approved for meeting the standards set by the USDA. It is best to purchase foods that are labeled with both the USDA logo and the 100 percent organic guarantee. Foods labeled with only the organic USDA logo are guaranteed to be at least 95 percent organic. Food products labeled by the USDA to be at least 70 percent organic are made with organic ingredients that are listed on the package. However, once an organic, USDA-labeled food is placed on the market, the USDA logo does not guarantee that it is free of pathogens and safer to consume than a conventionally (inorganically) grown food. Fortunately, there are regulations set in place to help ensure the sanitary conditions for growing, shipping, and handling foods, but these regulations do not eliminate the possibility of organic, USDA-labeled foods, as well as conventionally grown foods, being contaminated with food-borne pathogens that cause food-poisoning illnesses. Because of the lack of artificial preservatives, fresh, organic foods have a short shelf life and spoil naturally. To help prevent rapid spoilage, there are a variety of organic, canned and packaged foods on the market containing the more natural preservatives such as sea salt, sugar, lemon juice, and vinegar. Yet fresh, organic foods are the healthiest nutritionally and should be eaten daily. Make sure to clean, store, and prepare fresh, organic foods properly to prevent contamination and growth of food-borne pathogens and to increase shelf life. Fresh, organic foods are sold at health-food stores, farmers markets, food co-ops, and some grocery stores and supermarkets. It is best, however, to purchase fresh, organic food as much as possible from your local farmers market because it is most likely grown and stored under organic and natural conditions, and thus, chock full of nutrients.

Whole foods are either left unprocessed and unrefined, or, at the most, minimally processed and refined; thus, the majority of the nutrients remain intact. These foods generally include whole-grain products, fresh fruits and vegetables, unprocessed meat, and non-homogenized dairy products. To identify which foods are whole or consist of whole ingredients, the FDA is responsible for determining the regulations used to define and label these foods. Based on these regulations, a whole food can be identified by observing the list of ingredients on the package; each ingredient in the list should be labeled as whole. Because of the lack of processing, most whole foods have a short shelf life and last longer if shelved in the cold when sold in stores or stored at home. Whole foods are sold at health-food stores, farmers markets, food co-ops, and some conventional grocery stores and supermarkets.

It is important to realize that just because a food is labeled as whole does not necessarily mean it is organic, and on the flip side, just because a food is organic doesn't automatically mean it is whole. For example, inorganic foods that are unprocessed and unrefined are often labeled as whole (e.g., whole wheat flour and whole brown rice), and organic foods are often found to be processed and refined (e.g., organic wheat flour and organic sugar). Furthermore, do not confuse a food that is labeled as natural with being organic or whole. This is because the USDA's standards for natural foods has many loopholes and includes only meat and poultry products, and the FDA's definition of a natural food product is extremely vague without any regulated guidelines. Thus, be aware of a food that is labeled as natural for it may consist of toxic contaminants (e.g., pesticides and hormones) and added preservatives. Therefore, the healthiest foods to purchase are those that are labeled as both organic and whole (e.g., organic whole wheat and organic whole oats).

Junk Food

The food industry designed junk food to supply the high demand of an ever-increasing population, increase the shelf life of foods, comply with modern day conveniences and technology, and satisfy the unhealthy cravings of consumers. Junk food is a substance of animal or plant origin that has been stripped of many of its nutritional components and altered from its natural form, or it contains synthetic (man-made) chemicals that originated from a natural substance (basically, everything made by man originated from something natural). These foods consist mostly of empty calories and unhealthy ingredients (e.g., white sugar, white flour, saturated fats, and trans fats), synthetic food additives (e.g., artificial sweeteners, preservatives, flavorings, and colorings), and a limited amount of nutrients (e.g., fortified or enriched minimally with vitamins, minerals, and proteins). When junk food is ingested and metabolized, our bodies receive very little nourishment and over time become unhealthy, overweight, and diseased. Thus, consumption of these foods should be regulated and monitored—or better yet, eliminated.

Inorganic Foods and Processed Foods

Junk food is defined as inorganic and processed. Inorganic foods, which are grown under unnatural conditions, are often exposed to antibiotics (which compromise our immune system and introduce antibiotic-resistant bacterial strains into the population), hormones (which lead to abnormal growth, puberty, neuronal activity, sexually reproduction, and other bodily functions), pesticides (which lead to cancer, neurological defects, etc.), and genetic engineering (which decreases the nutritional value of certain genetically modified foods). Furthermore, to increase shelf life and reduce spoilage during storage and marketing, inorganic foods are exposed to artificial preservatives (many of which are known to cause allergies, cancer, and other health issues) and irradiation (a radiation procedure which kills most of the food-borne pathogens, but does not prevent the depletion of nutrients).

Inorganic livestock and poultry are commonly treated with antibiotics and hormones, fed grain that is laced with pesticides and other toxic contaminants, and confined without exercise to disease-infested areas. The flesh of these animals, which consists of toxic contaminants, unhealthy fats, and many different types of diseases (e.g., cancer, parasites, and pathogens), is cut into meat, exposed to artificial preservatives, packaged, and possibly irradiated, and then we, the consumers, buy and eat it. Preservatives and irradiation are able to eliminate most pathogens from the exposed meat, but they do not sterilize it; thus, the meat still needs to be properly stored, handled, and cooked to prevent food poisoning illnesses.

Pesticides and other compounds are not only introduced externally to inorganic crops but are often produced internally in inorganic plants that are genetically modified. Inorganic crops are generally saturated with pesticides that were sprayed on externally or absorbed from the ground. Some inorganic plants have been genetically engineered to synthesize internal pesticides and to tolerate herbicides. Although these internally introduced pesticides and anti-herbicides have not been linked to any major health problems, the synthesis of these compounds may interfere with the natural accumulation of nutrients in produce, thus decreasing its nutritional value. A more threatening health concern is the possibility that constant exposure of the ecosystem to externally and internally introduced pesticides may result in a subset of resistant-strains of pests (i.e., super-pathogens) that can only be destroyed when crops are exposed to super-toxic pesticides. In addition to pesticides, most crops are cultivated in fertilizers composed of inorganic manure containing hormones and antibiotics, and even toxic metals such as lead, cadmium, arsenic, and mercury that leached into the environment from pollution and industrial waste. Like pesticides, plants absorb these hormones, antibiotics, and metals from the soil, which then end up in the inorganic produce. Furthermore, before put in storage and sold on the market, inorganic produce is often exposed to artificial preservatives, waxed, and sometimes irradiated to extend its fresh appearance, increase shelf life, and eliminate food-borne pathogens that cause spoilage and food poisoning. Yet artificial preservatives, waxes, and irradiation do not prevent inorganic produce from becoming old and depleted of most nutrients or guarantee that it is totally free of pathogens.

There are two main types of artificial food preservatives that are considered to be unhealthy. One type is the antimicrobial agents, such as sulfites, benzoates, nitrates, and nitrites, which help prevent spoilage caused by food-borne pathogens. The other type is the antioxidants, such as butylated hydroxyanisole (BHA) and butylated hydroxytoluene (BHT), which help to inhibit foods consisting of fat and oil from becoming rancid. In addition to their antimicrobial properties, sulfites are often added to foods (e.g., dried fruits, salads, nuts, and shrimp) as anti-browning and antioxidant agents, and nitrites and nitrates are used as color fixatives for cured meats. The majority of these antimicrobial agents and antioxidants seem to be linked to health issues such as cancer, skin disorders, asthma, headaches, severe allergies, and attention-deficit (hyperactivity) disorder (ADD or ADHD).

Irradiation is known to alter the structure of compounds in inorganic foods. The FDA claims that these compounds are not toxic and do not substantially compromise the nutritional value of foods. Consumers, however, often complain of the altered appearance and taste of irradiated foods. These undesirable effects that consumers experience may not only be the result of radiation passing through the foods and altering them from their natural form but also of irradiated foods being aged yet unspoiled and thus kept on the market long after their freshness has been lost. Fortunately, for the individuals who want to avoid irradiated foods, the FDA requires that all exposed foods be labeled with the international irradiation "radura" symbol.

Processed foods, consisting mostly of synthetic and inorganic ingredients, are altered and manufactured by a series of steps, and then, contained and sealed in packages and cans. Unfortunately, the altering and manufacturing of processed foods results in the removal of nutritional substances, such as vitamins, minerals, and phytonutrients, and the addition of artificial food additives, such as preservatives, colorings, and flavorings. All this is done to help increase shelf life, extend seasonal availability, enhance taste, and inhibit growth of microorganisms. In an attempt to restore some of its nutritional value, these foods are often enriched with a portion of the minerals and vitamins that were lost, or fortified with nutrients that were not in the original ingredients.

Foods that are inorganic and processed are commonly sold in the supermarkets and are not usually identified by a specific label. Automatically consider a food that is not labeled as organic and whole to be inorganic and processed; thus, it consists of unnatural substances or is somehow altered from its natural form. Avoid unnatural substances: pesticides, antibiotics, hormones, toxic metals, and artificial food additives such as preservatives, colorings, and flavorings. Also avoid foods that were altered by genetic engineering or irradiation. The accumulative effects of ingesting these unnatural substances in altered foods can be harmful, especially to unborn fetuses and infants. Because of these harmful effects, many expectant mothers eat organic, whole foods, and parents feed their infants organic baby foods, or better yet, buy organic foods and purée their own baby food at home.

Questions Addressed to the Nation

We know that our supermarkets and grocery stores are loaded with inorganic and processed foods that are unhealthy and lack nutritional value. This is because genetic engineering, toxic contaminants (e.g., pesticides, preservatives, antibiotics, and hormones), and irradiation are used for commercial reasons by the food industry to decrease pathogenic diseases and pest infestations, increase agricultural yields, and extend shelf life. However, we must not ignore the fact that the majority of the genetic modifications, toxic contaminants, and irradiation that are introduced to foods also help to eliminate famine and secure an adequate food supply for an ever-increasing population. Before the use of genetic engineering, toxic contaminants, and irradiation, history demonstrated episodes of widespread famine, by which organic crops and animals were often destroyed by drought and pestilence (e.g., pathogens, insects, rodents, birds, and weeds). Therefore, the food industry markets unhealthy, genetically modified, irradiated foods composed of pesticides, preservatives, antibiotics, and hormones, not only to increase profits but to secure the high demand of food.

We, as a nation, need to carefully consider the answers to the following questions: Is it possible to grow and market all foods as organic and whole, or is it essential that a certain percentage of our foods remain inorganic and processed so that there will be a large enough supply of food for everyone? Is it better to provide an ample supply of unhealthy foods, or should our nation and food industry take the risk of providing all foods as organic and whole? If it is better for the majority of our foods to remain unhealthy, then which privileged individuals in our nation will be allowed to eat the healthy foods; will they continue to be the ones that can most afford them? Because good health should always remain a priority, it is important that we face the challenge of seeking the right answers to these questions. Although many scientists and experts have been researching these questions through agricultural and applied economics for years, we still do not have all the answers. Yet I am certain God will give us the answers, when we are ready to listen and receive them. The answers definitely will come, once we understand that everyone has the right to eat healthy foods. Therefore, let us focus our attention on how to eat right and live a healthy lifestyle. Let us stay committed, continue to improve, increase in knowledge, carry this knowledge throughout our villages, and before we know it, we all will be eating healthy.

* * *

Work-Study: Points to Ponder

1. Describe how many times a day you eat health food (i.e., whole foods and organic foods) and junk food (i.e., processed foods and inorganic foods).

2. Are you ready to increase your awareness of the foods that are healthy and the ones that are not? Are you willing to buy more health food, even though it tends to be higher priced than junk food?

3. What are your thoughts on the controversial issue concerning the food industry, which markets unhealthy foods in order to keep supplying the demand of an ever-increasing population? What do you think should be done about this? What can you do about it as an individual? What should we, as a nation, do about it, and how can we go about doing this?

4. Read chapters 34 through 44, which describe the different food types, and begin building your new healthy diet. If you are very enthusiastic, you may find yourself immediately designing an extremely healthy diet; this would be outstanding. But if you decide to take things slowly, this is also good. The main thing is to start somewhere and be realistic. Do not design a diet that you are unwilling to follow. Your healthy diet should be a forever-evolving entity, as you should always look for ways to improve it.

CHAPTER 34

Sugars and Sweeteners

The full soul loatheth a honeycomb; but to the hungry soul every bitter thing is sweet. (Proverbs 27:7)

Chapters 34 through 38 will increase your awareness of the different types of foods high in carbohydrates, fats, and protein and help you identify which ones you should add to or eliminate from your diet. At the end of each of these chapters, you are given the opportunity to use this information to begin building your new healthy diet.

Saccharides

Nutritive sugars found in food derived from plants and animals are called dietary saccharides. The smallest type of dietary saccharides exists as single units of sugar called monosaccharides. Glucose, also called dextrose, is the most common monosaccharide and the main source of energy used in our bodies. Other common monosaccharides are fructose (commonly found in fruit) and galactose (commonly found in milk). Monosaccharides can be linked together to form disaccharides (i.e., two sugars linked together), oligosaccharides (i.e., short chains of several sugars), and polysaccharides (i.e., long chains of many sugars). Most of the shorter chained saccharides (i.e., disaccharides and oligosaccharides) are digested (i.e., broken down to the single-unit monosaccharides by enzymes present in the small intestines) quicker than the longer chained polysaccharides. These digestible saccharides are essential nutrients that are metabolized to provide the human body with needed fuel. Some enzymes that are required for the digestion of specific types of disaccharides, oligosaccharides, and polysaccharides are produced by certain herbivores but not by humans; thus, these saccharides are not digested in the small intestines of humans. The fate of these indigestible saccharides, such as the oligosaccharides and polysaccharides found in beans, usually follows one of two paths: either the bacteria in the lower gut metabolize these saccharides into smaller compounds that often cause gas and intestinal distress, or the saccharides pass through the bowels unchanged. Many of the indigestible polysaccharides that pass through the gut unchanged help to regulate cholesterol and sugar levels in the blood, and provide bulk for the proper movement of the bowels. All of the above mentioned types of saccharides are defined within a class called carbohydrates, a group of organic compounds that are a major energy source for living things. The carbohydrates are divided into three main types: dietary fiber, complex, and simple.

Carbohydrates

Dietary fiber is an indigestible complex carbohydrate consisting of long sugar chains (i.e., polysaccharides) that need to be consumed daily to keep healthy. This fiber makes up the structural parts of plants that are indigestible in the gut when consumed. Fiber is indigestible because the human body is not equipped to synthesize the enzymes required to break the bonds between its linked plant sugars. There are two main types of dietary fiber: water-insoluble (i.e., impossible to dissolve in water) and water-soluble (i.e., easy to dissolve in and absorb water). As it passes through the colon unchanged, insoluble fiber (e.g., cellulose, which is found in the cell walls of foods derived from plants) plays a crucial role in the movement and successful digestion of foods through the gastrointestinal system. Foods consisting of insoluble fiber are whole grains, vegetables, fruits, nuts, and seeds. As for soluble fiber, it absorbs water and swells in the gut to a gel-like substance that properly regulates digestion and the levels of sugar and cholesterol in the bloodstream. There are several different kinds of soluble fiber; two of the most common ones are pectin, which is found in apples and other produce, and gum, which is present in oats, legumes, and other plant-derived foods.

Complex carbohydrates are the long-chained digestible sugars (i.e., oligosaccharides and polysaccharides) that are broken down slowly by enzymes in the small intestines. Because of their slow digestion, complex carbohydrates are good for supplying the body with a steady stream of energy (see chapters 35 and 38 for information on different foods high in complex carbohydrates). Complex carbohydrates are slowly broken down into glucose and the other single-unit sugars, fructose and galactose; then, all of the single-unit sugars are absorbed from the small intestines into the liver. Once in the liver, glucose is either released into the bloodstream as an energy supply for individual cells or stored as an energy reserve in the liver. Also in the liver, fructose is stored as an energy reserve, and so is galactose, but more commonly, galactose is used in the structure of essential lipids and proteins. The amount of glucose that our body cells require for proper function constantly fluctuates, but our brain cells demand a steady supply of it. Produced in and secreted from the pancreas, insulin is the key player responsible for maintaining a steady state of glucose in the bloodstream, transporting glucose to individual body cells, and storing glucose in adipose tissue. Insulin is not required, however, for the uptake of glucose into the liver and brain cells.

Simple carbohydrates are the monosaccharides (e.g., glucose fructose, and galactose) and the disaccharides (e.g., sucrose, lactose, and maltose). Various combinations of the three monosaccharides are linked together to form the disaccharides. For example, glucose and fructose are linked to form sucrose, which is found in fruit and other plant-derived foods; glucose and galactose are linked to form lactose, the sugar in milk; and two glucose molecules are linked to form maltose, which is commonly found in malted barley. After consumption, the monosaccharides are quickly absorbed from the small intestines into the liver, whereas the disaccharides are first readily metabolized by digestive enzymes into single sugars and then rapidly absorbed from the small intestines into the liver. Simple carbohydrates, particularly glucose and the disaccharides, are usually labeled as "bad" carbohydrates because consuming them in high enough levels will cause surges of glucose to be absorbed into the liver and then into the bloodstream. The constant exposure of the bloodstream to these surges can become detrimental to our health. One of the major dietary issues responsible for our poor health is that the majority of the carbohydrates in our diets consist mostly of the "bad" simple carbohydrates and not the healthy dietary fiber and complex carbohydrates.

After consumption, the glucose that is not immediately transported to body cells for energy is usually stored as glycogen (long chains of glucose) in the liver. If there is still excess glucose remaining to be stored, then it is converted to and stored as fat (triglycerides) in adipose tissue. Upon fasting or lack of glucose intake, the stored glycogen in the liver and the fat in adipose tissue can be metabolized into glucose and used for fuel. On the other hand, the frequent intake of high glucose, followed by consistent surges of insulin release, can increase the storage of glycogen and fat and lead to obesity. Eventually, these consistent surges of insulin may either result in a compromised pancreas that no longer produces or releases enough insulin, or in overly exposed body cells that have become insulin-resistant (i.e., no longer affected by the presence of insulin). Consequently, the effects of either the compromised pancreas or the resistant body cells can result in adult onset (type II) diabetes, a disease in which blood glucose is not taken up properly into body cells. This improper uptake of glucose may result in a lack of glucose being supplied for energy, high-glucose and triglyceride levels in the bloodstream, and excretion of accumulated glucose in urine. Diagnosed individuals can be treated with insulin injections or oral diabetes medication. In the majority of cases, however, the symptoms of type II diabetes can be eliminated or at least controlled by eating right, losing excess weight, eliminating harmful stress, and daily exercise. Do not, however, make changes in your diet, exercise regimen, and dosage of insulin or medication without the advice of your physician.

Sugars

Sugars that sweeten foods are divided into two categories: whole and processed. Whole sugars, being unprocessed and unrefined (or at the most, minimally processed and refined), are divided into two types: intrinsic whole sugars, which remain intact in the food that naturally produced them, and extrinsic whole sugars, which are found in natural sweeteners that are added to foods. The intrinsic whole sugars (e.g., unprocessed fructose, glucose, and sucrose) contained in fresh organic fruit are low in quantity and calorie content, and therefore are called "good" simple carbohydrates. Because of the low level of sugar found in fruit, the pancreas is not overworked, the body is not overly exposed to insulin, and very little sugar is converted to and stored as fat. Also, fresh organic fruit is high in essential nutrients such as minerals, vitamins, and phytonutrients; thus, fruit is extremely healthy.

The types of extrinsic whole sugars that are found in natural sweeteners are simple (i.e., monosaccharides and disaccharides) and complex carbohydrates (i.e., oligosaccharides and polysaccharides). Raw, unfiltered honey, unprocessed fruit juice, cane-juice granules, sorghum syrup, and maple syrup are natural sweeteners high in simple carbohydrates, whereas brown rice syrup and, to a lesser degree, barley malt syrup and blackstrap molasses consist of complex carbohydrates. These natural sweeteners, which also consist of vitamins, minerals, and phytonutrients, can be relatively healthy when added in limited amounts to sweeten foods. Make sure you add natural sweeteners with caution; do not overindulge and add too much. Excessive consumption of natural sweeteners that are high in simple carbohydrates can spike sugar levels, trigger sugar cravings, increase blood levels of triglycerides, and negatively affect those diagnosed with diabetes. Unlike most natural sweeteners, brown rice syrup is high in polysaccharides, which are slowly digested in the gut; thus, it gradually increases the glucose level in the bloodstream and is acceptable for most diabetics to consume in moderation under the advice of a physician. Although brown rice syrup is a good source of extrinsic whole sugar, it still needs to be consumed in moderation. Problems arise when we extrinsically add sugar to foods; we Americans add too much. We want our food to be extremely sweet. I have found that consuming the low levels of intrinsic whole sugar found in fresh fruit does not trigger sugar cravings, nor does it cause obesity. Although consuming natural sweeteners consisting of extrinsic whole sugar has some health benefits, high consumption of them can produce health problems similar to that of processed white table sugar. Consuming much sugar—no matter what type it is—is unhealthy for your body; thus, it is best to limit the consumption of all sources of extrinsic whole sugars.

White sugar, which is also called table sugar or sucrose, is the number one processed sugar added to foods. Sucrose, derived from sugarcane and sugar beets, is processed and then bleached to form white sugar. White sugar (organic or inorganic) is an unhealthy substance, stripped of all essential nutrients and loaded with empty calories. Because the glucose in white sugar is rapidly absorbed into the bloodstream, the body experiences the negative effects of a hyper-energy high, followed immediately by a sluggish-energy low. Afterwards, the body finds itself constantly craving and eating white sugar to perpetuate this cycle. The constant consumption of white sugar leads many to a sugar addiction that results in health issues such as obesity, diabetes, hypoglycemia, depression, high triglycerides, immune deficiency, hormonal disorders, premenstrual syndrome (PMS), cancer, arthritis, yeast syndrome, allergies, sinusitis, etc.

Many people unknowingly consume too much processed sugar (i.e., "bad" simple carbohydrates) in their diets. Beware, for many packaged, frozen, and canned processed foods contain high levels of white sugar. Most people think that brown sugar is healthier than white sugar. Yet brown sugar is generally nothing more than white sugar made brown by the addition of molasses; thus, it is unhealthy. High fructose sweeteners are also unhealthy. Agave nectar, which is high in fructose, is often considered to be a healthy sweetener that is good for diabetics. This is because in the liver, fructose is usually converted and stored as glycogen, thus it doesn't spike blood-glucose levels. However, after consuming processed fructose at high concentrations, it becomes a "bad" carbohydrate that is readily converted to triglycerides (fats) and stored in adipose tissue. High triglyceride levels in the bloodstream can lead to obesity and is often associated with heart disease, high cholesterol, high blood pressure, and diabetes. Like agave nectar, concentrated fruit juice is often considered to be healthy, but in actuality, because the fructose in it is processed and highly concentrated, it should be consumed in minimal quantities. High-fructose corn syrup (sugar water made from cornstarch) is a popular and very unhealthy sweetener that is added to various processed foods and beverages such as cold cereal and fruit juice, respectively. When the fructose in agave nectar, fruit, and corn is extracted, processed, and highly concentrated, it becomes harmful to one's health, has little nutritional value, and is high in calories. Greatly reduce these sugars in your diet, as well as the packaged foods that contain them. If you want fruit juice, it is best to freshly squeeze and prepare your own from fresh, organic produce. On the package of foods and drinks, check both the list of ingredients and the Nutrition Facts label, to make certain that unhealthy sugars are added in limited quantities—or better yet, excluded.

Artificial Sweeteners

Non-sugar sweeteners (artificial or natural) are added to foods to decrease glucose intake. Artificial sweeteners are synthetic compounds with no or very few calories that should be consumed with extreme caution. Most artificial sweeteners such as saccharin and aspartame are intense (potent) in sweetness, in that it takes only a small amount to sweeten foods. Saccharin is the first artificial sweetener that I was introduced to as a child. I remember the day many years ago when I was a little girl and decided to sneak, without first asking for permission, my aunt Angie's saccharin off her table to sweeten my hot cereal (I knew if I asked, the answer would have been no). Having somewhat of an inquisitive mind, I first read the saccharin package, which was labeled with a warning that explained how using it might be dangerous to the consumer's health because it was found to cause cancer in laboratory animals. At that moment, I immediately put the package of saccharin back on the table and used the white sugar instead. I also remember when (many years later) this warning was removed, and the FDA reported that saccharin was not linked to cancer in humans. To this day, however, I still avoid saccharin.

Aspartame is another well-known synthetic sweetener that should be consumed with caution. I cannot understand why so many people consume such a large quantity of products sweetened with aspartame on a daily basis. Not only do I avoid consuming aspartame because it is artificial, but I find its aftertaste to be absolutely disturbing. I don't find anything sweet about it. Although it has no known therapeutic value, aspartame reminds me of an herbal supplement, because it tastes medicinal. Many people think the no-calorie aspartame is healthy because the FDA has approved it as safe for consumption and considered it to be non-carcinogenic in humans. Although most individuals do not complain of negative side effects from consuming aspartame, many have reported and given testimonials that aspartame causes health problems such as migraines, seizures, and other neurological disorders. Despite the complaints and controversy, the FDA eventually approved aspartame. This approval automatically suggests to the public that the data from the clinical trials and research studies performed to date does not significantly support these health complaints, nor is it compelling enough to warrant a withdrawal of aspartame from the market. I suggest that you take the time to research the approval process of aspartame; it is quite interesting. The FDA did report, however, that aspartame is toxic in individuals with phenylketonuria, a genetic disorder due to the lack of a an enzyme required to properly metabolize phenylalanine. Aspartame consists of phenylalanine, one of the nine essential amino acids that are not synthesized in the body but are required to build proteins. Phenylalanine is not harmful to the majority of the population when it is consumed in adequate quantities. But those born with phenylketonuria should restrict phenylalanine in their diets. According to FDA regulations, all foods consisting of aspartame must be labeled with the warning "beware of phenylalanine."

One of the most common artificial sweeteners on the market is sucralose, a sugar alcohol that is added to many processed foods. Sucralose is very popular, and many think it is healthy because it is a synthetic sugar alcohol that originated from natural sugar. Many fail to realize that just because it originated from sugar does *not* mean it isn't synthetic; everything that is synthetic originated from something natural. During the process of manufacturing sucralose, sugar is chemically altered to an unnatural form. Although sucralose gained approval and was labeled safe by the FDA in 1998, part of its chemical structure has caused much controversy over the years. Some scientists claim the controversial part of its structure resembles the chemical structure of table salt, whereas others believe that the controversial part is chlorinated, similar to the chemical structure found in pesticides, and that exposure to it, over time, may be toxic to the body.

As far as I'm concerned, the question remains: Is long-term exposure to sucralose, as well as to saccharin and aspartame, toxic to our health? Many years with these artificial sweeteners on the market have not yet produced enough evidence that would convince the FDA to withdraw approval or link these artificial sweeteners to cancer and other health issues. Yet we, the consumers, are unknowingly the guinea pigs that are being observed in an unorganized population study (epidemiology) that may help determine the long-term effects on our health of consuming these artificial sweeteners. If you don't mind being one of the many guinea pigs being treated with the artificial sweeteners in question, then it is okay to consume high quantities of them. If you do care, however, then be an educated and selective consumer. Because the most common sugar substitutes are artificial sweeteners, be aware of foods labeled "low in sugar" or "sugar-free." I do admit that there are times I eat foods containing sucralose, but I make sure that I eat them rarely and in extremely small quantities.

Natural Non-Sugar Sweeteners

Natural non-sugar sweeteners such as stevia, xylitol, and sorbitol have no or very few calories and are considered to be healthier than white sugar. It is very important to stress the point that these sweeteners, although natural, have no or very little nutritional value; thus, there is no dietary need to consume them. For many Americans, it is difficult to completely eliminate desserts and sweets from their diets. I am one of these individuals. The temptation of white sugar is everywhere. I have eliminated my cravings for white sugar because it is detrimental to my health. Yet I still have a desire every now and then to eat something sweet. Over the years, I have used stevia and xylitol because they satisfy my sweet tooth and help eliminate sugar cravings. With these natural sweeteners, it is possible to avoid the spiking of blood-glucose, surges of insulin released in blood, weight gain, and other associated adverse effects. But I do not abuse their use. In America, we have a habit of overdoing everything. Consuming high quantities of almost any food or food additive has the potential, over time, of causing adverse effects. Only use these natural sweeteners to help curb your appetite for sugar. Do not use them as an excuse to continue eating high quantities of sweets. If you find that you are allergic or sensitive to any one of them, stop consuming it.

Stevia, which is extracted from a plant, is very sweet and has no calories. A very small quantity of it is needed to sweeten foods. Many different brands of stevia have a slight aftertaste, due to the simultaneous extraction of a bitter substance found in its plant. This aftertaste is quite tolerable and definitely less intense than that of aspartame. Other brands processed by more advanced methods are free of the aftertaste and give a pleasant, sweet taste. Stevia has been produced commercially and marketed as a popular food additive in Japan for many decades. In Japan and many other countries, it is considered to be safe for consumption and good for preventing diabetic symptoms, obesity, and other health issues. The FDA has not approved stevia to be used as a food additive in processed food products (e.g., cookies and soda). Yet the FDA did approve stevia as a dietary supplement, which suggests that the FDA considers stevia to be safe for moderate consumption by a small percentage of the population but is not yet certain that it is safe for bulk consumption by the masses. Unfortunately, this approval issue has been a topic of much controversy for years.

Take the time to research this issue concerning stevia and that of other sweeteners; it is important to understand FDA regulations and the process used to approve food additives and dietary supplements. In the near future, I hope that the FDA will find stevia to be completely safe and approve it as a food additive. In the meantime, I regularly use stevia to sweeten drinks, like herbal tea or fresh-squeezed lemonade; hot cereals, like oatmeal; and some baked dishes. I also encourage others to test it out. When testing a new natural product, consume it in moderation and observe symptoms. If the symptoms are negative, then eliminate the natural product. If not, then continue to consume it in moderation. Even if stevia gains FDA approval as a food additive, I strongly suggest that you always consume stevia in moderation.

Xylitol is a natural sugar alcohol (which is not the same as the ethanol found in alcoholic beverages) that is extracted from corncobs, the bark of trees, and the skins of fruit. It is low in calories and has been approved by the FDA as a food additive. Most individuals claim that granulated xylitol tastes like, looks like, and is as sweet as white sugar (yet to me it tastes sweeter). After consumption, xylitol is a sugar alcohol that is slowly absorbed from the small intestines into the bloodstream. Because it is slowly absorbed into the bloodstream, it gives a low glycemic index value and requires low levels of insulin. These known effects of xylitol on the body can help reduce the risk of diabetes, hypoglycemia, and obesity. It is also known that xylitol is not properly metabolized when it is taken up by yeast and most harmful types of bacteria; thereby, the lack of energy supplied by xylitol inhibits their growth. Thus, xylitol may be excellent for the prevention of yeast syndrome, sinusitis, ear infections, tooth decay, and gum disease. Xylitol does not cause negative side effects in most individuals. But in some individuals, overindulgence may cause fermentation of it by bacteria in the large intestines and produce gas or laxative effects, similar to that experienced after consuming beans or a high-fiber diet. The best thing to do is to purchase it and test it out, and don't overindulge, but consume it in moderation.

Xylitol is marketed at health-food stores or by companies that supply and manufacture it. Because it is more expensive to manufacture xylitol than white sugar, xylitol costs considerably more than white sugar. Although it is quite expensive, xylitol is excellent for sweetening drinks, cereals, baked goods, breads, and desserts (see Part V for recipes). Yet because xylitol is not metabolized by yeast, it cannot be used to bake yeast-raised breads. There are a few food items sweetened with xylitol, such as candy, mints, chewing gum, and cookies, which can be purchased at health-food stores and in some grocery stores and supermarkets. In grocery stores and supermarkets, be careful about food items and different gums that claim to be sweetened with xylitol. This is because many food items and gums are sweetened both with xylitol and one or more of the less expensive artificial sweeteners. Read the ingredients label on these items to avoid exposure to the artificial sweeteners.

Sorbitol, mannitol, and maltitol are other natural sugar alcohols that are used to sweeten foods especially for diabetic individuals who want to decrease their sugar intake. Sorbitol is becoming quite popular and many foods in groceries stores, such as ice cream and cookies, are sweetened with it. Mannitol, because of its cooling effects, is mostly used to sweeten gum and mints. Many people, however, are afraid to consume mannitol because of its known therapeutic effects when administered intravenously by a physician. Yet when consumed, mannitol is poorly absorbed from the gastrointestinal tract into the bloodstream and does not have these therapeutic effects. Maltitol is nothing more than the alcohol form of maltose. Like xylitol, it is great for baking. The brown crystals of maltitol make a great substitute for brown sugar, and the sweet and thick maltitol syrup can be used to replace barley malt syrup. Do not abuse the use of these sweeteners or consume them in excess; consumption of them has been known to cause laxative effects in many individuals. Continue to research reliable information about these sweeteners before testing them out. Also, consult your physician, especially if you are diabetic, before using any one of these sweetener. Erythritol is another sugar alcohol that is found naturally in some fruits and fermented foods. Generally, erythritol is manufactured in bulk by a natural process used in the fermentation of sugar. It is gaining in popularity because it has fewer calories than xylitol and seems to cause minimal or no laxative effects in most individuals. So far, my experiences with erythritol have been limited, but I am looking forward to testing it more in the near future.

Although most natural sweeteners may be expensive, it is highly recommended that you purchase sweeteners such as brown rice syrup, stevia, and xylitol to replace white sugar, and then test them out to determine which ones are best for you. If your village does not have a health-food store, then order these natural sweeteners directly from the company that manufactures them. Most owners of grocery stores, food manufacturing companies, and restaurants do not provide all of the different natural sweeteners or the foods containing them. Write a letter, including signatures from loyal customers who would potentially buy these sweeteners and foods, and send it to the different owners throughout your village. Yes, purchasing these natural sweeteners can be expensive, but when your health improves, you will begin to save money as the cost of hospital bills, doctor visits, and prescribed medicines decreases. Most important, you should consider it an investment in your good health; good health is priceless.

* * *

Work-Study: Points to Ponder

1. How much white sugar do you consume in a day? In a week?

2. Describe the ways in which you might be willing to cut back on your consumption of white sugar and other processed sugars (for example, by how much?).

3. What type of foods do you eat containing intrinsic or extrinsic whole sugars? How often do you eat them? How much extrinsic whole sugar do you add to foods?

4. Do you use artificial sweeteners? If you do, how often? Are you willing to stop using them?

5. Are you willing to use the natural non-sugar sweeteners such as stevia and xylitol? If not, is it because you are uncomfortable with using them?

6. Are you willing to research the different types of sweeteners to formulate your own opinion about them?

7. I improved my health by completing the Repent 6 R's Step Process. I released certain sugar foods from my diet and replaced them, as described below:

Released	Replaced
• Consumed 3–5 desserts a day sweetened with white sugar or high fructose corn syrup (e.g., cookies, candy, ice cream, cake, doughnuts, brownies, pies, whipped cream, sherbet, and pudding).	• Eat 3 or more servings of fruit a day. Eat 1–3 desserts a week sweetened with xylitol (rarely sweetened with sucralose). Eat 1 small serving of dessert sweetened with sugar on special occasions (e.g., weddings and birthdays) and holidays. At restaurants, eat approximately 2–4 small bites of desserts sweetened with sugar on weekends.
• Purchased desserts sweetened with white sugar and high fructose corn syrup.	• Purchase desserts sweetened with xylitol, sorbitol, extrinsic whole sugars, and on occasion, sucralose.
• Baked and cooked foods sweetened with white sugar.	• Bake and cook foods sweetened with xylitol and stevia.
• Consumed drinks sweetened with white sugar, high fructose corn syrup, or artificial sweeteners daily (e.g., fruit juice, soda, ice tea, hot tea, and hot cocoa).	• Consume 8 cups (8 oz. each) of water a day. Mostly on weekends, consume drinks sweetened with xylitol or stevia. Drink fruit juice diluted with water (see Chapter 41 for details). On rare occasions, consume drinks sweetened with sucralose. Consume, at most, half a can of diet soda per week.
• Consumed hot and cold cereals coated or sweetened with white sugar.	• Consume hot and cold cereals sweetened not at all, or only with fresh fruit, xylitol, or stevia.

Determine which changes in your unhealthy diet you are committed to making with regard to white sugar, simple carbohydrates, processed sugars, and artificial sweeteners, as you focus on the Repent 6 R's Step Process. In the table below, list the foods that you are willing to release and then replace with healthier ones.

Release	**Replace**

CHAPTER 35

Wheat Flour, Cornmeal, and Cereal

Take thou also unto thee wheat, and barley, and beans, and lentils, and millet, and fitches [i.e., spelt], and put them in one vessel, and make thee bread thereof. (Ezekiel 4:9)

Complex Carbohydrates

Complex carbohydrates (starches), which are long chains of single sugars linked together, are found in whole foods such as whole grain breads, whole grain cereals, brown rice, yam-sweet potatoes (i.e., garnet yams), carrots, and beans. Digestive enzymes need to first break long complex carbohydrate chains down to glucose before absorption by the small intestines into the liver and then into the bloodstream can occur. Because of this, the absorption rate of complex carbohydrates takes longer than that of "bad" simple carbohydrates. The slow absorption rate of complex carbohydrates prevents high blood-glucose and surges of insulin into the bloodstream, supplies the body and brain cells with a consistent stream of energy, and limits the amount of excess glucose that is converted to fat (see chapter 34 for more information about complex carbohydrates).

A "good" carbohydrate (e.g., a complex carbohydrate) is identified by its slow rate of absorption into the bloodstream (i.e., the longer the absorption rate, the healthier the carbohydrate). The glycemic index is calculated to measure the absorption rate of carbohydrates in foods and used as an indicator to help determine which foods consisting of carbohydrates are healthiest to consume (i.e., the lower the glycemic index value, the healthier the food). Raw, coarse, chewy foods, consisting of much fiber and complex carbohydrates, give a low glycemic index value and should be added to your diet daily. Refined, soft, fluffy foods, consisting of "bad" carbohydrates and no fiber, give a very high glycemic index value and should be avoided. Remember that just because a particular food item has a low glycemic index value does not automatically mean that its fat content can be ignored. When adding foods to your diet, it is important to look at the Nutrition Facts label on the food product and consider both total carbohydrate and fat content (see chapter 36 for information about fat intake). About 40 to 60 percent of your daily calorie intake should consist of carbohydrates (i.e., the approximate daily carbohydrate intake should be no more than 1680 calories or 420 grams per day for the average-sized male, and no more than 1260 calories or 315 grams of carbohydrates per day for the average-sized women). Plus, make certain that the majority, if not all, of the carbohydrates you consume are the "good" ones.

Wheat and Breads

Foods made from whole grains are usually minimally refined and processed and contain a high level of nutrients. Whole grains are the seeds that are grown on the different kinds of cereal plants. One of the most common types of whole grains is wheat. Whole wheat contains complex carbohydrates, protein, fiber, oil, minerals, vitamins, and phytonutrients. The whole grain of wheat includes the outer bran covering, and the inner germ and endoderm layers. Refined grains of wheat consist of only the inner endoderm layer, without the bran and germ layers, and are devoid of much of the nutrients and fiber. Many people prefer bread made from the refined wheat flour, but bread made from the coarser whole wheat flour is the healthiest. I found that the coarser and chewier the bread, the healthier it is and lower the glycemic index. Thus, avoid soft white breads and buy coarse dark breads that contain organic, whole wheat flour, fiber, and added seeds. In life, it is best to look for long-term gratification by eating chewy, coarse, dark, whole grain breads, rather than fluffy, soft, white, refined wheat breads. You will be happier and healthier in the long run.

Spelt, which dates back to biblical times, is an ancient cousin to modern-day wheat. Unlike the genetically modified modern-day threshing wheat, ancient spelt is known for its hard hull that covers and protects its inner grain. I love to eat organic whole spelt bread, made with or without yeast. Whole spelt bread without yeast is good for improving overall health, preventing yeast syndrome, regulating the digestive system, and maintaining a constant sugar level in the bloodstream. Spelt is often a good substitute for those with a wheat allergy or intolerance. However, those who are gluten-intolerant need to avoid spelt because it contains gluten, like wheat. Whole spelt flour, because it is somewhat smoother in texture than whole wheat flour, is great for baking breads, cookies, scones, pie crusts, brownies, biscuits, rolls, muffins, and pancakes (see Part V for recipes).

It is best to greatly reduce your intake of all breads; eating too much of them can lead to weight gain and many other health issues. When you do eat them, however, make sure to eat the ones made of organic, whole grain flours, such as whole wheat and whole spelt flour, or of organic sprouted grains. Sprouted grain breads consist of whole grains (e.g., wheat, spelt, and millet) that were sprouted and then ground with all of its layers (bran and all). Because these sprouted whole grains were alive before ground, their vitamins and other nutrients are more like that of a vegetable than of a grain. As a result, their nutrients are more properly digested and absorbed by the body than those from unsprouted grains. Sprouted grain breads not only consist of an abundant amount of healthy nutrients but are usually low in preservatives; thus, they should be stored in the cold at all times. Whole grain breads can be purchased at health-food stores, food co-ops, and some grocery stores and supermarkets. Before purchasing, however, read the ingredients list to make sure that the bread is actually made of organic whole grains; in the list, the word "organic," followed by "whole" or "sprouted," must precede each grain type (e.g., organic whole wheat flour, organic sprouted spelt, and organic sprouted millet). Moreover, do not automatically assume that just because a bread is labeled as made with whole wheat flour or sprouted grain that it is entirely whole grain. For example, if the package states "made with whole wheat flour," then this generally means the bread may consist of not only whole wheat flour but also of refined wheat flour. But at least it is partially whole grain and probably healthier than the totally refined wheat flour breads. Furthermore, do not assume that multigrain and stone-ground breads are totally made with whole grains. It is not uncommon to find multigrain and stone-ground breads that are a combination of whole and refined wheat flour, or worse yet, all refined. Be aware when purchasing wheat, multigrain, and stone-ground breads; read the ingredient lists to make certain that each of the grains and flours in them is organic and whole.

An unhealthy substance that is a staple in our society is white flour. When whole wheat is ground and processed into wheat flour, the majority of its natural nutrients, oil, and fiber found in the bran and wheat germ layers are removed, and then, it is bleached into white flour. Enriched flour is not much better; it is nothing more than white flour in which a few of the removed vitamins and minerals are added back to slightly increase its nutritional value. The finely ground particles of white flour enable enzymes in the body to rapidly break down the starch to glucose, similar to the rate of many simple carbohydrates; thus, white flour is considered to be a "bad" carbohydrate. Foods consisting of both white flour and white sugar are rapidly increasing the rate of obesity and other diseases that are prevalent in America. It is essential to eliminate as many foods as possible from our diets that consist of the white sugar and white flour combination, such as white sandwich breads, white rolls, pastries, doughnuts, cookies, etc. Beware of brown-flour breads, in which most of the nutrients and fibers are removed. Many types of wheat breads consist of white flour that is made brown by adding food coloring to the white flour mixture. Even if the refined wheat flour has never been bleached, it is still an unhealthy, high-glycemic-index food that rapidly increases the glucose level in the bloodstream. Keeping whole grains as close as possible to the original state, with all nutrients and fibers intact, is what prevents fast absorption of glucose into the bloodstream.

Gluten

In certain whole grains, the main source of protein is gluten. Gluten exists in the inner (endoderm) layer of wheat (including spelt), barley, and rye. Many people, some more than others, are born intolerant to gluten. These people are born unequipped to properly break down gluten in the digestive tract and find that continual high consumption of it intensifies their distress; thus, the reason why some have adopted the gluten-free diet. Those individuals who are quite intolerant to gluten often develop health problems, such as celiac disease (an inherited disorder that results in deterioration of the inner lining of the intestines from the constant exposure to gluten), eczema, acidosis, malabsorption of minerals, heartburn, allergies, intestinal distress, osteoporosis, neurological disorders, intestinal cancer, and autoimmune diseases (e.g., rheumatoid arthritis, autoimmune hypothyroidism, autoimmune hyperthyroidism, and type I diabetes). People intolerant to gluten need to buy foods labeled as gluten-free and prepare gluten-free foods at home. I do not show symptoms of gluten-intolerance, but in my new healthy diet, I control the amount of gluten consumed. Whole wheat can be quite healthy for those who can tolerate eating it, but the typical American diet is loaded with too many wheat products. Americans are overly exposed to gluten. I think most Americans need to balance their diets by decreasing their intake of wheat- and gluten-containing products by substituting some of these products with vegetables, fruits, and gluten-free whole grains. Whole grains, such as brown rice, millet, quinoa, corn, and buckwheat, do not consist of gluten; thus, they are considered safe for gluten-intolerant people to eat. Many gluten-intolerant people find that they are not able to tolerate the consumption of oats, whereas others claim they can. Oats consist not of the same gluten that is in wheat but of a protein that closely resembles it. Many believe that their intolerance of oats is due to the similarities between the two proteins. However, others believe that their intolerance of oats is a consequence of them being contaminated with wheat and other gluten products that are usually processed at the same plant or mill. Whichever reason is correct, it seems that many gluten-intolerant individuals are able to consume oats labeled as gluten-free without any distress. But if you suspect that gluten-free labeled oats may be causing you distress, then stop eating them and discuss this issue with your physician. Flour made from corn, almonds, millet, tapioca, garbanzo beans, potatoes, rice, buckwheat, and gluten-free oats are used for baking gluten-free breads (see Part V for a recipe consisting of corn flour and oat flour). Gluten is often used as an additive to improve the stability, increase the protein nutritional value, and change the texture of processed foods. Beware: many processed foods that you would not expect to consist of gluten additives are loaded with gluten. Read the list of ingredients on processed foods to determine if gluten is included.

Corn, Cornmeal, and Tortillas

Many consider corn to be a vegetable but in actuality, corn is a grain that should be eaten in moderation. Fortunately, many who are intolerant to wheat flour find they are able to add cornmeal to their diets with no or minimal problems when the right type is consumed. Refined cornmeal is unhealthy for our bodies and should be avoided. When it is processed, the majority of the nutrients and good fibers are removed. It is best to buy and make corn bread (see Part V for corn bread recipes) with medium- or coarse-grind, organic whole-grain cornmeal, which contains the majority of its natural nutrients. Health-food stores, food co-ops, and many grocery stores carry the coarse- and medium-grind whole-grain cornmeal. Cornmeal tortillas should also be made from coarse-grind, organic whole-grain cornmeal and not the refined cornmeal. Furthermore, the darker the corn (e.g., blue corn) that is ground into meal, the healthier the meal is for diabetics. Blue cornmeal consists of more protein and less starch than yellow and white cornmeal. Whole-grain blue corn tortillas are delicious and quite healthy. White flour tortillas commonly sold in grocery stores are often made from white flour and saturated or trans fats; thus, they are very unhealthy. It is best to buy saturated or trans fat-free tortillas made from whole wheat or whole spelt flour, whole grain cornmeal, or sprouted grains. As a great alternative to sandwiches, I love to eat chicken and vegetable wraps made with thin whole spelt tortillas.

Cereals

Organic, whole grain cereals are a great source of complex carbohydrates, vitamins, minerals, protein, fiber, and phytonutrients. Yet remember that all whole grains need to be eaten in moderation. Hot, whole grain cereals, such as steel cut or coarse grain oatmeal (excellent for regulating cholesterol levels), brown rice, and barley, are a great way to start the day. Farina (prepared from refined wheat) and grits (prepared from hulled corn) are refined hot cereals that should be eaten rarely and in limited amounts and without added butter and sugar. Avoid instant or precooked cereals (e.g., instant oatmeal), which are usually high glycemic index foods. Cold, whole grain cereals can also be healthy, but it is important to look carefully at the ingredients listed on the box to make sure that all of the grains are whole, such as whole oats, whole barley, whole buckwheat, and whole rye. Most puffed and flaked cereals, such as puffed rice, puffed wheat, and corn flakes, are low in calories but are high glycemic index foods; thus, they should be consumed in very small amounts. Bran cereals that are within the low glycemic index range are great sources of fiber and other nutrients but are not whole grain cereals. This is because bran is nothing more than the outside covering of the whole grain. Granola consisting of organic whole grains (e.g., oats) and other organic whole foods (e.g., nuts and seeds) makes a good breakfast cereal or even a healthy late snack.

Determine the amount and kind of sugar that is added to cereal or granola. Check to see if the sweetener is white sugar, high fructose corn syrup, or a natural sweetener (e.g., raw, unfiltered honey, brown rice syrup, and barley malt syrup). Eliminate all of the sugar-coated cereals from your diet. Eating much of these coated cereals is just like eating a bowl of candy covered with milk. It is best to buy unsweetened cereals, and then sweeten them with added fresh fruits, raisins, stevia, or xylitol. Also, be careful, because many granolas are too sweet. Make sure that the granola is sweetened mostly with added unsweetened dried fruits and not with added sugar. It is best and easy to buy the different organic whole grains and other ingredients separately, and then combine them to make your own healthy granola. Also, check the Nutrition Facts label and ingredient list to make sure the cereal or granola does not consist of trans fats and artificial additives, such as preservatives, flavorings, and colorings.

* * *

Work-Study: Points to Ponder

1. What type of breads do you eat? How much do you eat a day? A week?

2. What are your thoughts on changing over to organic whole wheat breads? Are you willing to try organic whole spelt bread? Are you willing to decrease your consumption of products and baked goods made of white flour? If so, by how much?

3. What foods made from refined flour do you eat as snacks and desserts? Are you willing to replace the unhealthy desserts and snacks with healthy ones?

4. Are you willing to buy baked goods and other products or make bake goods at home that are made with organic whole wheat flour, organic whole spelt flour, organic sprouted wheat, or other organic whole grains?

5. Do you eat cornbread or corn tortillas? If so, are you willing to make cornbread or corn tortillas from the coarse-grind, organic whole-grain cornmeal?

6. Do you eat refined-sugar cereals? If so, are you willing to start eating organic whole grain, unsweetened cereals instead?

7. Are you gluten-sensitive or gluten-intolerant? If so, do you monitor your gluten intake? If you never were diagnosed as gluten-intolerant, but you think you have the symptoms, make an appointment to see your physician.

8. How many carbohydrate (fiber, complex, and simple) calories do you consume in a day? Are the calories within 40 to 60 percent of your total daily calorie intake? Are the calories mostly from "bad" simple carbohydrates? If so, are you willing to replace the majority of them with complex carbohydrates, "good" simple carbohydrates, and fiber? Note: Check Nutrition Facts label on foods for carbohydrate content per serving; one calorie of carbohydrates equals four grams of carbohydrates.

I improved my health by completing the Repent 6 R's Step Process. I released certain foods from my diet and replaced them as described below.

Released	Replaced
• Consumed 2–4 slices of refined white or wheat bread daily.	• Eat 2–5 slices of whole spelt bread (with or without yeast) a week.
• Consumed a doughnut or pastry for breakfast 4 times a week.	• Consume spelt sticks (or a slice of spelt bread) with low-fat cheese for breakfast 3–5 times a week.
• Consumed sweet corn bread made with refined cornmeal approximately 3–5 times a week.	• Eat corn bread made with coarse-grind whole-grain cornmeal and no added sugar 3–5 times a week (see Part V for recipes).
• Baked and cooked foods made of white flour.	• Bake and cook foods made of whole spelt flour and on occasion whole wheat flour (see Part V for recipes).
• Purchased cold refined-grain cereals sweetened with high fructose corn syrup or added white sugar.	• Purchase cold whole-grain cereals with no sugar, and sweeten with xylitol. Eat whole grain oatmeal as hot cereal sweetened with xylitol or stevia.
• Purchased white flour tortillas with trans fats or saturated fats.	• Purchase whole spelt flour tortillas and whole grain corn tortillas with no trans fats and minimal saturated fats.

<table>
<tr><td>• Purchased desserts consisting of white flour, white sugar, and trans fats.</td><td>• Purchase desserts consisting of whole spelt flour or whole wheat flour along with natural sweeteners and no trans fats.</td></tr>
<tr><td>• Ate white flour pancakes and white flour waffles 1–2 times a month.</td><td>• Eat whole wheat and whole spelt waffles or whole wheat and whole spelt pancakes about 4–6 times a year (see Part V for recipes).</td></tr>
<tr><td>• Snacked on crackers and cookies often.</td><td>• Snack on raw or roasted nuts, especially almonds, often.</td></tr>
</table>

As you focus on the Repent 6 R's Step Process, determine which changes you will commit to making in your unhealthy diet that consists of white flour and refined grains. In the following table, list the foods that you are willing to release and then replace with healthier ones.

Release	Replace

Chapter 36

Oils and Fats

For the Lord thy God bringeth thee into a good land, a land of brooks of water, of fountains and depths that spring out of the valleys and hills; a land of wheat, and barley, and vines and fig trees, and pomegranates; a land of olive oil, and honey. (Deuteronomy 8:7–8)

Fats (Triglycerides)

Fat is a lipid that is essential for good health; it is required to synthesize cell membranes, insulate organs, and supply energy. But excessive consumption of fat is very unhealthy and can lead to many major health issues such as heart disease and obesity. High consumption of fat in this country is definitely a problem. Because almost every processed food is high in fat, the majority of us consume too much of it. This is a major concern, as only 25 to 30 percent of the calories in our diets should consist of fat (i.e., the approximate daily fat intake should be no more than 840 calories or 93 grams for the average-sized male, and no more than 630 calories or 70 grams for the average-sized female). Thus, it is important that we know about the different kinds of fats and the ones that are healthiest to eat.

The structure of fat (a triglyceride) includes one molecule of glycerol (a sugar alcohol) and three molecules of fatty acids (each fatty acid is a long carbon chain). There are three major types of natural fats: saturated, monounsaturated, and polyunsaturated. Saturated fat consists of saturated fatty acids, and the two unsaturated fats are made up of unsaturated fatty acids. A saturated fatty acid is a long chain of single-bonded carbons, which are completely saturated with hydrogen, and the unsaturated fatty acids (both monounsaturated and polyunsaturated) are long chains with both single and double-bonded carbons. A monounsaturated fatty acid has only one double bond between two hydrogen-unsaturated carbons with all of the other carbons being single-bonded and saturated with hydrogen. In contrast to this, a polyunsaturated fatty acid consists of multiple (two or more) double bonds within its chain of many unsaturated carbons.

The number of carbon bonds within a fatty acid affects its fluidity. More specifically, as the number of unsaturated, double-bonded carbons increases, its fluidity increases. While in the opposite case, as the number of saturated, single-bonded carbons increases, the more it exits in the solid state. No matter if hot, cold, or at room temperature, polyunsaturated fat always remains in the liquid state (an oil); this is unlike saturated fat, which is solid at room temperature or when cold. Monounsaturated fat remains a liquid at room temperature but is solid in the cold. At high temperatures (i.e., just above body temperature or higher), all three types of fats exist in the liquid state.

After consumption, most fat remains undigested as it moves through the stomach to the small intestines as fat globules. Released from the gallbladder, bile salts enter the small intestines and separate the fat globules down to droplets to increase surface area so that lipases (water-soluble fat-digesting enzymes) can readily digest each triglyceride down to two fatty acids and a monoglyceride (a glycerol linked to one fatty acid). These fatty acids and monoglycerides are then absorbed by the intestinal wall where they are re-synthesized, once again, into triglycerides, and then, transported into the lymphatic system and eventually into the bloodstream. Once in the bloodstream, triglycerides are transported by lipoproteins (carriers of lipids) to their designated sites, where they are digested by lipases into fatty acids and glycerol. Then, these fatty acids and glycerol are either used for energy by body cells or re-synthesized and stored as triglycerides in adipose tissue.

The type and amount of carbohydrates or fats consumed affects the level of triglycerides in the bloodstream and the condition of the cardiovascular system. Excessive consumption of the "bad" carbohydrates can trigger the liver to synthesize high levels of triglycerides, which are then released into the bloodstream and transported by lipoproteins. High triglyceride levels are often associated with health issues such as high cholesterol, obesity, diabetes, high blood pressure, and heart disease. In addition to "bad" carbohydrates, high intake of saturated fats can also increase blood levels of triglycerides and lead to high cholesterol. In contrast, a balanced intake of the unsaturated fats seems to reduce high triglyceride and cholesterol levels. Unsaturated fatty acids are found in beef and other red meats. Yet because red meat is also high in saturated fatty acids and cholesterol, it is considered to be a major artery-clogging food; thus, it is *not* a good source of unsaturated fats. Plant-derived foods and cold-water fish are the healthiest sources of unsaturated fats.

Monounsaturated Fats

Monounsaturated fat (oil) consists of the healthy omega-9 fatty acids, which are monounsaturated fatty acids. Many vegetable oils derived from the fruit, seed, or nut of plants are excellent sources of omega-9 fatty acids. A major omega-9 fatty acid is oleic acid, which plays a significant role in the protection against heart disease. The most popular fruits used to produce monounsaturated oils that are suitable for cooking are the olive, typically grown in the Mediterranean, and the avocado, a native to the tropics of Central America. Oil from these fruits is not pressed from the seed but from the fleshy fruit surrounding it. Olive oil, which dates back to ancient times, is considered to be one of the healthiest oils known to man and contains high levels of oleic acid, along with phytonutrients (such as phenols) and vitamins (particularly vitamin E). It is used to help prevent a wide variety of health issues ranging from heart disease to different skin conditions. Like olive oil, avocado oil is high in healthy oleic acid, phytonutrients, and vitamin E and is great for maintaining healthy skin.

When purchasing, it is best to select an olive oil that is labeled as "organic extra virgin" or "organic virgin." Although the organic extra virgin and organic virgin oils may be quite expensive, they are well worth the money. The extra virgin and virgin oils are produced from the first press during processing; thus, they are unrefined (not exposed to high temperatures and chemicals), tastier, and healthier than the refined oils. Refined oils are chemically extracted, treated at high temperatures, and bleached to be void of nutrients, odorless, and colorless in order to increase shelf life and smoke point (the cooking temperature at which smoking occurs). Over the years, I have acquired a taste for organic olive oil (both extra virgin and virgin). I enjoy its rich and robust flavor very much. I love to dress salads and spread breads with extra virgin olive oil (which is extremely flavorful), and cook with virgin olive oil (as it is usually filtered and therefore relatively heat-stable and suitable for cooking). In my younger days, my family and I could not stand the smell or taste of olive oil. Still today, my family finds olive oil's rich and robust flavor to be less than palatable. They are in the transition stage of learning to appreciate it.

A popular oil pressed from seeds high in oleic acid is canola oil. Canola oil is derived from the seed of a canola plant, a genetic variant of the rapeseed plant. The rapeseed plant, grown for commercial use, consists of high levels of erucic acid, a toxic fatty acid when consumed in high enough quantities. Although the canola plant has been genetically modified to produce erucic acid levels that are insignificant compared to that of the rapeseed plant, some people believe canola oil is unsafe for consumption. The FDA, however, deemed the level of erucic acid in canola oil as safe and below the toxin limits set by FDA regulations. The FDA approved canola oil as healthy, low in cholesterol, and great for the prevention of heart disease.

Canola oil is suitable for cooking at relatively high temperatures, adds a mild flavor to baked goods, and has a longer shelf life than most oils. But because very little research has been completed in humans to determine the long-term cumulative effects of consuming low levels of erucic acid, it is probably best to consume canola oil in moderation. Furthermore, since the canola seed is quite hard, pressing oil out of it requires pressure produced at high temperatures. As a result of the heat, a portion of the fatty acids in canola oil is altered to an unhealthy form. I have to admit that my family and I cook and bake with canola oil quite often (see Part V for recipes). I prefer to buy the healthier expeller-pressed and cold-pressed canola oils that are filtered and thus suitable for baking and cooking at medium-high heat rather than the all-purpose canola oil that is chemically refined and typically sold in stores. During processing, the all-purpose canola oil is exposed to many different types of toxic chemicals and supposedly to more heat than the pressed oils; thus it is higher in unhealthy fatty acids and contaminants. Fortunately, I have acquired a taste for the healthy virgin olive oil. Because the taste of virgin olive oil might be too robust for baking desserts (I say "might be" because knowing me, I will probably love olive oil desserts), my family and I are looking forward to experimenting with other types of healthy oils (e.g., almond, hazelnut, and macadamia oils) to determine their properties in baking, and I encourage you to try the same.

There are many other common seed oils and also oils pressed from nuts that are high in monounsaturated fatty acids. Sesame seed oil is great for cooking at high temperatures and is an excellent source of omega-9 fatty acids and phytonutrients. High oleic sunflower and safflower oils, extracted from the seeds of genetic variants abundant in healthy oleic acid, are used to replace the more common variants consisting of mostly polyunsaturated fatty acids. Almond and macadamia oils are high in healthy omega-9 fatty acids and phytonutrients and are great for cooking as they add excellent flavor to foods. Peanut (which actually belongs to the legume family) oil is high in omega-9 fatty acids, very heat-stable, and commonly used for frying. People who are allergic to peanuts need to especially avoid foods exposed to unrefined peanut oil. Because the peanut is not very hard, expeller-pressed and cold-pressed peanut oils are extracted at temperatures that do not destroy their taste and nutrients, including their unsaturated fatty acids. This is unlike refined peanut oil in which the taste and nutrients are destroyed and altered by high heat and chemical processing. If you're not allergic, it is always better to buy unrefined and organic, expeller- or cold-pressed seed and nut oils rather than the refined ones.

Polyunsaturated Fats

Polyunsaturated fat (oil) is found mostly in foods derived from plants, fish, and animals. The polyunsaturated fatty acids are divided into two main groups: the omega-3 fatty acids and the omega-6 fatty acids. Three of the major dietary omega-3 fatty acids are:

- alpha-linolenic acid (ALA)
- eicosapentaenoic acid (EPA)
- docosahexaenoic acid (DHA)

And three of the major dietary omega-6 fatty acids are:

- linoleic acid (LA)
- gamma-linolenic acid (GLA)
- arachidonic acid (AA)

ALA (an omega-3 fatty acid) and LA (an omega-6 fatty acid), the shortest of the polyunsaturated fatty acids, are called the essential fatty acids. These fatty acids are essential because the body cannot function without them, cannot synthesize them on its own, and can only acquire them through dietary means. Because the only source of these essential fatty acids is through the diet, it is mandatory that we consume these essential nutrients daily. The body also needs the other omega-3 and omega-6 fatty acids for proper function, but these are not essential because the body can use ALA and LA essential fatty acids to synthesize the longer chained omega-3 (EPA and DHA) and omega-6 (AA and GLA) fatty acids, respectively.

Humans need to consume approximately one omega-3 fatty acid to every five omega-6 fatty acids to maintain proper health. Unfortunately, this is not the case in this country for most Americans consume approximately ten to thirty times more omega-6 fatty acids than omega-3 fatty acids. This extreme imbalance is mostly due to the American diet consisting of processed foods and inorganic meats high in omega-6 fatty acids, and of only a few foods high in omega-3 fatty acids such as cold-water fish. The high consumption of omega-6 fatty acids relative to omega-3 fatty acids is a major problem because it contributes to health issues, such as heart disease, arthritis, asthma, allergies, inflammation, thrombosis (blood clotting), diabetes, and cancer; thus, the consumption of the omega fatty acids needs to be monitored. To help balance these fatty acids, it is best to avoid processed foods and inorganic meats and consume more cold-water fish.

Consumption of dietary sources high in omega-3 fatty acids reduces the risk of health issues such as heart disease, asthma, arthritis, inflammation, high blood pressure, depression, schizophrenia, Alzheimer's disease, thrombosis, irritable bowel syndrome, diabetes, skin diseases, cancer, obesity, and high cholesterol. Highly recommended sources of the essential fatty acid ALA are flaxseeds, cold-pressed flaxseed oil, and walnuts. However, because the rate by which the essential nutrient ALA is ingested and converted to EPA and DHA is minimal in the body, it is necessary to increase consumption of foods also consisting of EPA and DHA. EPA and DHA are precursors to anti-inflammatory agents that help to prevent many health issues due to inflammation (e.g., arthritis, allergies, and backaches) and poor circulation of blood (e.g., heart disease and thrombosis). Great sources of DHA and EPA are fish oil and cold-water fish, especially salmon, herring, mackerel, sardines, tuna, and trout. It is best to purchase oil and fillets from fish that are organic and wild, as these are low in toxic contaminants and omega-6 fatty acids (see chapter 37 for more information about fish). Like fish oil, cod liver oil is high in EPA and DHA, but it is also quite high in cholesterol and thus should be avoided by those potentially at risk of acquiring heart disease. In the past, I took cod liver oil regularly, but when I found that it was high in cholesterol, I switched over to fish oil. Do not overdose on omega-3 dietary supplements (e.g., fish oil), and consult a physician for the amount that should be taken daily.

Omega-6 fatty acids, when consumed in the correct balance along with omega-3 fatty acids, promote good health. Some seed oils are great sources of omega-6 fatty acids. For those who monitor and balance their omega-6 fatty acid intake, grape seed oil (excellent on salads and for cooking) is a great healthy source of the essential fatty acid LA. High levels of LA are also found in the most common vegetable oils, such as sunflower, safflower, corn, and soybean oils. Because these common vegetable oils are usually refined and widely used in processed foods, the American diet is swamped with LA. In recent efforts to substantially decrease the high consumption of LA, more foods are being processed with olive oil and the high oleic sunflower and safflower oils instead of the ones high in LA. Unlike EPA and DHA, AA is a precursor to inflammatory agents that lead to inflammation, poor blood circulation, and many health issues (e.g., allergies, backaches, heart disease, thrombosis, diabetes, and arthritis). Not only is LA converted to AA in the body, but AA is also found in many foods common to the American diet. Because of this, individuals need to limit consumption of foods high in LA and AA, and consume ones high in EPA and DHA. AA is found in foods high in animal saturated fat such as red meat, organ meats, egg yolks, dairy products, and poultry. In contrast to AA, GLA does not lead to inflammation. It is converted to dihomo-GLA, which is a precursor to anti-inflammatory agents, and seems to help prevent health problems such as attention-deficit (hyperactivity) disorder (ADD and ADHD), eye disease, and PMS. Unlike LA and AA, GLA is generally not found in foods. Yet under normal conditions the conversion of LA to GLA should supply the body with all it requires. Many individuals, however, are deficient in GLA and may need to take dietary supplements high in it under the advice of a physician. Spirulina (blue-green algae) and uncommon seed oils, such as evening primrose oil, black currant oil, and borage oil, are sources high in GLA that are used as dietary supplements. Remember, LA, AA, and GLA are required for good health and need to be in the diet, but just not in excess.

Saturated Fats and Cholesterol

The body uses saturated fat for essential functions such as cell energy and organ insulation, and cholesterol is required to synthesize cell membranes, bile acids, and body steroids. Yet much of these lipids (saturated fat and cholesterol) do not need to be consumed because the body is able to synthesize most of what it needs in the liver. Another reason to reduce intake is because these lipids are two of the main culprits responsible for heart disease. Most consumed saturated fat and cholesterol is in excess, and the accumulation of them in arteries often leads to high cholesterol, high triglycerides, high blood pressure, and eventually, atherosclerosis. Because of this, less than 10 percent of the calories in our diets should consist of saturated fat (i.e., the approximate daily saturated fat intake should be less than 280 calories or 31 grams for the average-sized male, and less than 210 calories or 23 grams for the average-sized woman). Plus, it is important for us to consume less than 300 mg of cholesterol per day. The majority of the foods high in animal saturated fat, such as red meat, liver, poultry, butter, shrimp, dairy products, and eggs yolks, are also high in cholesterol. Cod liver oil is a dietary supplement that should be avoided by those with heart disease. Because production of cholesterol occurs in the liver, cod liver oil is high in cholesterol. Plants, on the other hand, produce no cholesterol and only trace amounts of saturated fat; thus, vegetable oils are generally free of these lipids. Coconut oil is an exception to the rule. The coconut is an unusual seed that consists of much saturated fat. Unrefined coconut oil is somewhat healthier than animal sources of saturated fat. This is because it is free of cholesterol and it is known to have anti-pathogenic properties. Coconut oil is also great for cooking at high temperatures. Yet because it is still a saturated fat, consumption of it needs to be controlled.

In the bloodstream, there are two main types of cholesterol carriers: low density lipoprotein (LDL), which transports the "bad" cholesterol; and high density lipoprotein (HDL), which transports the "good" cholesterol. Normally, LDL transports cholesterol that is produced in the liver to body cells that need it. When too much saturated fat and cholesterol is consumed, LDL deposits excess cholesterol on the walls of the arteries. If arteries are constantly exposed to high levels of cholesterol, the cholesterol may continue to build up on the arterial walls and form plaque that hardens the arteries (a disease called atherosclerosis). This plaque may clog arteries and rupture artery walls. In addition, thrombosis (blood clotting) may occur at the ruptured site and obstruct blood flow. These blood clots may block arteries feeding the heart or brain and result in a heart attack or stroke, respectively. In contrast, HDL, the carrier of "good" cholesterol, transports excess cholesterol away from the walls of the arteries and back to the liver, where it is then excreted from the body or reprocessed. A high level of HDL cholesterol decreases the risk of atherosclerosis, heart attacks, and strokes. Moreover, a LDL cholesterol level that is kept as low as possible prevents the clogging of arteries. Thus, to prevent heart disease, it is best to lower the LDL to HDL cholesterol ratio as much as possible. In most individuals, this can be achieved by decreasing the amount of saturated fats and cholesterol in the diet and replacing them with the healthy unsaturated fats. However, individuals who find it difficult to decrease their LDL to

HDL cholesterol ratio need to seek immediate attention from a physician (see Part IV for more information about high cholesterol levels).

Trans Fats

Like saturated fat, trans fat increases LDL cholesterol levels. More harmful than saturated fat, trans fat also decreases HDL cholesterol levels, thereby further increasing the risk of heart disease. Trans fats, also called hydrogenated fats, are monounsaturated or polyunsaturated fats that became toxic by a man-made process called hydrogenation. During this process, hydrogen atoms are pumped into the double carbon bonds of the unsaturated fatty acids, making them completely or partially saturated (i.e., trans-fatty acids). Commonly known unsaturated vegetable oils, such as soybean, corn, and sunflower, are often partially hydrogenated and used for preparing and cooking processed products to reduce spoilage and rancidity. These partially hydrogenated oils are commonly used commercially because they have a much longer shelf life than unsaturated fats and are great for cooking and frying at high temperatures. Although advantageous, these partially hydrogenated fats are definitely more toxic than any of the natural ones and should be reduced to trace amounts in our diets. Furthermore, margarine that is made from partially or completely hydrogenated oils is another source of toxic trans fat. When I was a child, margarine was a common part of my family's diet until my parents were informed by their homeopathic doctor that it is a toxic, synthetic substance with a chemical structure similar to plastic. After that, it wasn't long before I found butter in the refrigerator instead of margarine. It is best, however, to avoid both margarine and butter, but butter, which consists of natural saturated fat, is definitely the lesser of the two evils. If you are left to choose between butter and margarine, please eat butter. Another saturated fat that is free of trans fat is ghee. Ghee is the pure saturated fat derived from clarifying butter, a process by which fat is separated from milk solids. Because of its pure form, ghee is often considered to be healthier for the lactose-intolerant. Yet it is still pure, animal saturated fat and should be used sparingly.

Trans fat is found in many processed baked goods, microwave

popcorn, and fried foods, such as French fries. Yet less than one percent of your daily calorie intake should consist of trans fats. Before purchasing oil and processed food items, check the Nutrition Facts label on the back of the item to determine the amount of trans fat (hydrogenated fat) that is contained in them. Fortunately, within the last few years, the number of processed foods that are free of trans fat is steadily increasing. Most food items that are labeled with 0 grams of trans fat on the front of the package are shown to consist of 0 grams of trans fat in the Nutrition Facts label. But check to make sure this is the case; a food labeled as trans fat-free may actually indicate on the Nutrition Facts label that it contains low levels of trans fat, which can soon add up if you consume many servings. When a food item fails to indicate the amount of trans fat it contains per serving, you can add together the gram amounts of each listed type of fat (i.e., monounsaturated, polyunsaturated, and saturated), then subtract it from the listed total grams of fat to give you a good approximation of the total grams of trans fat. The only good news about trans fat is that the food industry is consistently increasing the number of processed food items manufactured without it.

Free Radicals and Cooking with Oil

Rancidity (oxidation) occurs when oxygen reacts at the double carbon bonds within an unsaturated fatty acid and breaks the fatty acids down to free radicals, which are extremely toxic, acidic, and carcinogenic (cancer-causing) compounds. Unsaturated fats, especially polyunsaturated fats (because of their high number of double carbon bonds) usually become rancid rather quickly when exposed to oxygen, heat, or light. As a protective measure, I usually buy unrefined, unsaturated oils (e.g., flaxseed oil, fish oil, and olive oil) that are contained in dark-colored glass bottles, and then refrigerate them at home; these steps help to decrease the rate of oxidation caused by exposure to light and heat.

Frying foods is generally unhealthy because the original state of the oil and the foods cooked in it are both altered to an unhealthy form. Excessive consumption of fried foods may increase the risk of diseases, such as cancer, obesity, arthritis, and heart disease. If you are going to fry foods, minimize the amount and absorption of excess oil by stir frying instead of deep frying, and by buying an oil spray bottle and spraying oil in the pan instead of pouring it. When frying, it is also best *not* to repeatedly reuse oil or heat it above its smoke point—the temperature at which it begins to smoke and decompose (the smoke point is often found on the label of healthy brands of oils). Although refined (chemically extracted) oils are generally unhealthy and devoid of nutrients, these oils have a higher smoke point than unrefined (mechanically extracted) oils, and thus are more suitable for deep frying and cooking at higher temperatures. There are many refined polyunsaturated oils that have high smoke points (e.g., sunflower, soybean, corn, safflower and grape seed oils). Yet polyunsaturated oils should not be used for deep frying over high heat, because once their smoke point is reached, oxidation can occur at a rapid pace due to the high number of double carbon bonds. If using unsaturated oils for deep frying, it is best to choose refined monounsaturated oils (e.g., olive, avocado, peanut, high oleic safflower, and high oleic sunflower oils) that have high smoke points and then use them only once. There are, however, many unrefined expeller-pressed and virgin monounsaturated oils that are acceptable for cooking and frying over medium to medium-high heat. Organic, expeller-pressed canola oil has a considerably high smoke point and is odorless and relatively tasteless; thus, it is suitable for cooking, baking, and frying on medium to medium-high heat. Organic, expeller-pressed avocado oil also has a moderately high smoke point and is great for frying over medium to medium-high heat. Organic, virgin olive oil, one of the healthier oils, has a medium to medium-high smoke point and can be used to cook and fry on medium heat.

As for the saturated fats, butter is great for cooking and baking because it is not rapidly oxidized. Its high animal saturated fat and cholesterol content, however, makes it unhealthy. Plus, it is not great for frying; because the milk solids in butter are easily burned, it has a low smoke point. Ghee is great for frying at high temperatures because it is pure fat, free from the milk solids that burn, but it is still high in unhealthy saturated fat and cholesterol. Coconut oil, however, is a healthier saturated fat that is free of cholesterol, not easily oxidized, and has a smoke point great for frying at high temperatures. Thus, coconut oil is the saturated oil of choice, but because it is still a saturated fat, consume it in moderation. Do not cook with hydrogenated or partially hydrogenated oils (trans fats). Although excellent for frying at high temperatures, trans fat is toxic and needs to be avoided.

* * *

Work-Study: Points to Ponder

1. Do you eat fatty foods? If so, how many times a day? A week? Do you control your triglyceride levels? If so, how?

2. What types of fats are included in your diet? Do you consume healthy unsaturated fats or the unhealthy saturated fats?

3. Do you check the Nutrition Facts label on foods for fat content before purchasing? Do you have some idea of the approximate daily amount of fat you consume? If so, is it within the 25 to 30 percent of your required daily calorie intake? Are the fats healthy or unhealthy? Note: one calorie of fat equals nine grams of fat.

4. Describe the ways in which you monitor the levels of saturated fat, cholesterol, and trans fat that are in your diet. Note: Your daily diet should consists of less than 10 percent saturated fats, 1 percent trans fats, and 300 mg of cholesterol.

5. Is your blood cholesterol level high? If so, do you manage this problem through your diet? Do you take medication to control it?

6. When I was a little girl, my family cooked with lard, shortening, and margarine; a few years later, we replaced them with butter and hydrogenated vegetable oil. Years before I started my new diet, we stopped using hydrogenated vegetable oil and began cooking with canola oil. Having acquired a taste for olive oil, I am now encouraging my family to prepare their foods with it. What is your family history of the fats you use in cooking? Are the oils that you are presently using the healthiest ones (e.g., olive oil)? If not, are you willing to change?

7. Refined olive, seed, and nut oils can be quite unhealthy, as they are devoid of healthy nutrients and consist of altered unsaturated fatty acids. I prefer the taste of organic, extra virgin or virgin olive oil, and expeller- or cold-pressed canola oil over the refined, all-purpose ones. What types of oils do you use? Do you prefer the inorganic, all-purpose oils? Do you avoid the unrefined oils because of their robust taste or expensive prices?

8. Do you use butter or margarine? If so, why? Are you willing to try coconut oil?

9. I routinely take a dose of flaxseed oil and fish oil, and I love to eat salmon. Do you eat enough foods that consist of the essential omega-3 fatty acids? If not, what foods and dietary supplements are you going to consume to increase your omega-3 fatty acid intake? (Note: Before taking dietary supplements, consult a physician.)

10. Do you eat many processed foods consisting of omega-6 fatty acids? If so, what processed foods are you going to eliminate to decrease your omega-6 fatty acid intake?

11. Which oils do you use for frying: trans fats, saturated fats, virgin oils, unrefined oils, or refined oils? How often do you fry foods? If you fry foods often, describe your thoughts on switching over to baking, steaming, grilling, broiling, or boiling foods.

12. My food weakness of the past was simple carbohydrates and not really oils or fats; thus, there were not many improvements in the area of oils or fats that I needed to include in my new diet. If oils or fats are your weakness, then determine what changes you are willing to commit to in your new diet, consisting of healthy oils or fats, and complete the Repent 6 R's Step Process. In the following table, list the oils and oily foods that you are willing to release and then replace with healthier ones.

Release	Replace

Chapter 37

Meat, Eggs, Dairy Products, and Other Protein Foods

Blessed shalt thou be in the city, and blessed shalt thou be in the field. Blessed shall be the fruit of thy body, and the fruit of thy ground, and the fruit of thy cattle, the increase of thy kine, and the flocks of thy sheep. (Deuteronomy 28:3–4)

Protein

Protein is found in meat, eggs, beans, whole grains, and dairy products and needs to be added to your diet daily. It is digested by enzymes in the gastrointestinal tract to amino acids, the building block of proteins. Once proteins are exposed to the hydrochloric acid and the enzyme pepsin in the stomach, digestion begins and then is continued in the small intestines until all proteins are broken down by enzymes to amino acids. After digestion, these amino acids are absorbed into the liver, released into the bloodstream, and then transported to body cells. In body cells, amino acids are linked together again to form peptides, which are then folded into new proteins. When there is a lack of specific enzymes in the gastrointestinal tract, certain proteins are not fully digested down to amino acids and remain either undigested or only partially-digested. As these undigested or partially-digested proteins enter the bloodstream, antibodies (i.e., immune proteins produced by previous exposures to these proteins) recognize and attack these proteins as allergens (i.e., foreign substances that trigger an allergic response), which lead to allergies or intolerance to certain foods.

Proteins are required for the structure and physiology of cells, tissues, and organs. Structural proteins, such as collagen and keratin, are the building components used to form skin, muscle, hair, etc.

Physiological proteins are active players with specialized roles that are required for proper function of the body. Examples of physiological proteins are enzymes (which catalyze, or increase the speed of, chemical reactions in the body), antibodies (which bind and aid in the removal of foreign substances in the body), receptors (which receive, translate, and signal messages in the body), and a group of hormones (which when released cause effects on specific target organs). There are approximately twenty amino acids that are needed to build proteins. Because our bodies cannot synthesize about nine of the twenty amino acids, it is essential that these nine amino acids are provided in our diets. The other amino acids are nonessential, not because the body does not need them but because the body is able to manufacture them. Approximately 0.8 grams of protein per 2.2 pounds of body weight should be consumed daily; this amount of protein is about 10 to 15 percent of the total daily calorie intake for most individuals. If you have an intense exercise or bodybuilding regimen, you may need to consume as much as 1.2 grams or more of protein per 2.2 pounds of body weight each day. Consult your physician or nutritionist about your required protein intake.

Meat and eggs are complete protein sources because they provide all of the essential amino acids, but unfortunately they also consist of high levels of saturated fat and cholesterol. Plus, high consumption of animal protein may cause acidosis (see chapter 41 for information on body pH) and malabsorption of calcium and other minerals (see Part IV for information on osteoporosis concerning mineral deficiencies). Although high consumption of plant protein can also decrease body pH and absorption of minerals, it appears to do so by a much lesser degree than that of animal protein. Because we need to limit our saturated fat and cholesterol intake, keep our body pH near neutral, and maintain proper mineral absorption, it is important that we add more plant protein to our diets. Protein foods derived from plants, however, are generally an incomplete source of the nine essential amino acids. Vegetarians and vegans need to be certain that they eat different types of plant-derived, high-protein foods in various combinations to ensure that all nine essential amino acids are included in their diets. I personally know of vegetarians who are extremely healthy and seem to be healthier than meat-eaters. This is because they took the time to educate themselves on the protein and amino acid content of plant-derived foods that they selected in their daily diets. For example, beans and whole-grain brown rice are a great combination of high-protein plant foods that provide the essential amino acids. On the other hand, I also personally know of vegetarians who became seriously ill and were instructed by their physicians to start eating meat. Before going vegetarian, consult your physician or nutritionist.

Legumes

Legumes (e.g., beans, peas, lentils, and peanuts), nuts (especially almonds) and whole grains (e.g., brown rice, oats, and whole wheat) are all great sources of protein. Beans (e.g., black, pinto, navy, and red beans) and lentils are an inexpensive yet healthy substitute for meat. Peanut butter is a delicious condiment that's high in protein and monounsaturated fats, but be aware of its high sugar content. Many stores carry peanut butter made without sugar; it is actually a quite tasty spread on bread and great for baking healthy desserts (see Part V for cookie recipe). However, those allergic to peanuts should avoid eating it. Tofu (a cheese-like high-protein food made by curdling soybean milk) is a popular source of protein among the vegetarians. The consistency and texture of tofu makes acquiring a taste for it difficult for some individuals. Yet if you take the time to educate yourself on the controversial health issues with regard to tofu (see information about soybeans in chapter 39), the different textures and kinds (such as silken or regular), and then the ways to prepare, season, and cook it, you'll find that tofu can be a quite tasty source of protein. Tofu absorbs all of the yummy juices and seasonings to which it is exposed. Mastering the art of preparing tasty tofu may be a challenging task. If prepared properly, however, it can be quite delicious, especially when it is seasoned and grilled to perfection.

Meat

The most common American meats cut from land mammals are beef, pork, and lamb; from poultry are chicken and turkey. Beef, pork, and lamb are high in saturated fat and cholesterol. Yet people who eat meat from organic, grass-fed mammals that are raised on a free range (ideally, a farm where animals are at liberty to roam around on a pasture and eat grass) are less likely to develop heart disease, inflammatory diseases, and cancer than people who eat meat from inorganic, grain-fed mammals. This is because grass-fed mammals consist of less unhealthy saturated fat, cholesterol, and omega-6 fatty acids, and more of the healthier omega-3 fatty acids than grain-fed mammals. Many grass-fed mammals are also fed flaxseeds to further increase their omega-3 fatty acid content. In contrast, inorganic, grain-fed mammals are quickly grown in cages, given a diet that increases unhealthy fat content, treated with hormones and antibiotics, and exposed to pesticides and other contaminants. Compared to organic, grass-fed mammals, these mammals are higher in unhealthy fats saturated with toxins, and lower in muscle mass consisting of protein, minerals, and vitamins. Therefore, purchase meat cut from organic, grass-fed and free-range raised mammals as much as possible. But if you decide to eat meat from grain-fed mammals, make sure that it is organic, which is at least free of toxic contaminants.

As for chicken and turkey, purchase meat from poultry that are fed organic grain and raised on a free range of vegetation. Poultry are healthiest when they consume a diet inclusive of grain, vegetation, flaxseeds, and bugs. Unfortunately, because national guidelines are loosely defined, not all free ranges are created equal. Organic animals grown on free ranges that are regulated by low standards may be caged the majority of the time in disease-infested areas, allowed to roam only occasionally in vegetation-free areas, and fed mostly grain. Before purchasing organic meat, check the labels on packages carefully and take the time to research information to determine the diet and environment of the animal.

Red Meat

Red meat, such as beef, pork, lamb, and goat, is high in protein, iron, zinc, and other nutrients. Pork is usually considered as white meat by most people. Yet because pork is red when raw, the USDA defines pork as red meat. Many cuts of red meat are high in saturated fat and cholesterol; thus, regular consumption of them can lead to heart disease. Red meat is also often linked to hypertension, high cholesterol, high triglycerides, and different types of cancer (e.g., breast, lymphoma, and prostate). Lean cuts of red meat from organic, grass-fed animals are much lower in saturated fat and cholesterol and pose less of a potential health risk than fatty meats. High quantities of purines, one of the two types of building blocks comprised in deoxyribonucleic acid (DNA), are also found in lean red meat. When digested in the body, purines are broken down into uric acid. Eating high quantities of red meat may result in an accumulation of uric acids that can lead to health problems, such as gout or the formation of kidney stones. Consumption of red meat should be limited to two or fewer servings per week, or better yet twice a month; the less of it consumed, the better your health.

Beef cut as steaks, hamburgers, prime rib, and roast is America's favorite red meat. However, eating beef has many health concerns associated with it. Most of the health issues are the consequences of cows being fed grain, soybeans, or animal by-products (e.g., the remains of animal carcasses). Cows were not created to eat grain, soybeans, and animal by-products; they have a digestive tract designed for eating grass. Generally, cases of Mad Cow Disease were not detected in cows that ate only grass but in cows that consumed animal by-products consisting of flesh and bone meal. Irradiating beef or exposing it to high temperatures does not destroy the culprits known as prions, which are proteins that eat away at the brain and cause Mad Cow Disease. The best way to prevent the risk of contracting this disease is to eat organic, grass-fed cows. Also, cows that eat corn, soybeans, and animal by-products usually have unhealthy intestinal tracts with an overgrowth of the bacteria *Escherichia coli* (*E. coli*). After butchering the cow, *E. coli* is transferred from the intestines, spread to the carcass, and then throughout the equipment in the processing plant. As the cow is being cut, the outer surface of the meat is covered with *E. coli*, and then the meat is packaged. In most packaged cuts of meat (e.g., roast beef and steak), the majority of the *E. coli* can be eliminated by washing the meat before and after thawing and then thoroughly cooking it. Yet hamburger that has been ground and processed with *E. coli*-infested equipment is one of the major sources of *E. coli* outbreaks in America. Irradiation is mainly used to prevent the spoilage of properly handled meat but does not stop the growth of *E. coli* in packaged meat that has been improperly handled and stored. Thus irradiated meat, like all meat, needs to be handled properly. To prevent *E. coli* poisoning, hamburger should be properly stored at cold temperatures, carefully thawed by sanitizing surface areas exposed to the meat and its juices, and thoroughly cooked.

Pork that is cut as ham, pork chops, spare ribs, sausages, and bacon is popular among Americans. Like beef, pork is another red meat that is associated with many health concerns. Yet the National Pork Board defines pork to be the "other white meat" (with chicken being the first) in an attempt to end the association of the negative health concerns of red beef to that of pork. However, pork has many health concerns of its own. Pork consists of much saturated fat and cholesterol. Plus, pigs are scavengers; thus, pathogens and parasites (e.g., the tapeworm *Taenia solium* and the nematode *Trichinella spiralis*) enter their bodies through their guts, and toxins accumulate in their fat. For these reasons, you should limit your consumption of pork.

Although lamb is enjoyed in many countries, such as in the Middle East, lamb (the meat from a baby sheep less than a year old) is only eaten by a small population of the people in America. Lamb is full of minerals, such as zinc and phosphorus, and protein, which make it quite healthy. Plus, lamb generally has a lesser saturated fat content—with a little less than half consisting of saturated and the rest being unsaturated—than beef and pork. Like lamb, goat meat is consumed by only a fraction of the American population and has less saturated fat and higher levels of protein and other nutrients than beef and pork. Because goat meat is a healthy source of protein, it's unfortunate that it's unpopular with most Americans. Game meats, such as buffalo, elk, and venison, are healthier red meats that are lower in saturated fat than beef. Yet hunting requires that one understand the health risk of interacting with diseased game animals and follow certain safety steps when hunting, butchering, and cooking them. Non-hunters can eliminate most of these concerns by purchasing organic, grass-fed game raised on free-range farms.

Poultry

The most common white meat in America is flightless poultry, such as chicken and turkey. Regarding the flesh of flightless poultry, there are two types of meat: dark and white. The color of dark meat is due to the high content of myoglobin, the oxygen-carriers found in the cells of active muscles that constantly demand high levels of oxygen to help generate energy for muscle contractions. The dark meat includes the legs and thighs—parts of the flightless bird that engage in long-term exercise and thus need much oxygen. The breast and wings of the flightless bird are white meat, thus low in myoglobin; this is because these body parts require only short bursts of energy. All of the meat within the flight poultry, such as duck and goose, is dark because all of the muscles are active; the breast muscles need much energy for long-term endurance during flight. Because of the high demand for energy, dark meat also has more vitamins, minerals, and other nutrients, as well as more fat than white meat; thus, white meat is best for a low-fat diet.

Many people, assuming that poultry is healthier and low in saturated fat, eat more poultry than beef. Unfortunately, because inorganic poultry are overweight, overgrown, and pumped with chemicals, their flesh is loaded with toxic contaminants, saturated fat, cholesterol, and omega-6 fatty acids. Furthermore, inorganic chickens are cramped in cages that are usually filled with waste; such poultry are often infected with bacteria such as *Salmonella* and *Campylobacter*. It is best to buy organic chickens that are free from hormones, pesticides, antibiotics, and inorganic grain. The healthiest organic chickens are fed organic grain, and raised on a free range full of vegetation and without disease-infested areas. The organic chicken meat is lean, with low levels of unhealthy fats; thus, the taste of it is quite different from conventional fatty chicken. It is not guaranteed, however, that the packaged organic chicken meat is free from bacteria. It is important to make sure that all chicken is cooked until well done and that all areas exposed to the raw chicken and its juices are sanitized.

Fish

Fish are generally the healthiest of the meats. People who are not allergic to fish should try to eat at least two to three servings of it each week. White-fleshed, non-oily fish, such as flounder, sole, tilapia, pollack, perch, cod, and orange roughy, are a great source of minerals, vitamin, and protein. Many people love to eat these lean fish because they taste less fishy than the oily ones. Yet when it comes to eating fish, people need to eat more of the cold-water, oily fish, such as sardines, herring, mackerels, salmon, tuna, and trout, which are high in healthy omega-3 fatty acids and protein. In addition, oily fish that are canned with their bones are a great source of calcium. Wild-grown fish (e.g., Alaskan salmon and mackerels) are definitely a healthier source of protein and are higher in omega-3 fatty acids than farm-raised, cornmeal-fed fish (e.g., the popular farm-raised tilapia, which is extremely high in unhealthy omega-6 fatty acids). I love to eat wild Alaskan sockeye salmon, my personal favorite; it is very healthy, flaky, and excellent for grilling.

All fish, whether store-bought or sport-caught or grown in a lake or in the sea, may be contaminated with toxins, such as pesticides, polychlorinated biphenyls (PCBs; a coolant used in electrical equipment), mercury (a trace metal released in the environment, mostly by mining), commercial oil, or other toxic chemicals. Although PCBs are no longer manufactured, these compounds are still found in our environment. Since PCBs and mercury have been shown to cause neurological defects in fetuses, infants, and young children, it is important that pregnant women, nursing women, and children use extreme caution when selecting, purchasing, and eating fish. Consumption of PCBs and mercury in fish is definitely a health hazard that should be everyone's concern, but eating fish with extremely low levels of these contaminants seems to pose less of a threat to healthy adults than to small children. Because of the nutritional value of eating fish, adults and children at the age of twelve and older are advised to eat fish at least two to three times a week, but they need to make certain the fish are raised in waters that are relatively safe and low in contaminants. Just be sure you eat a variety of fish grown in relatively safe and different water sources to decrease your chances of being overly exposed to the same types of contaminants from the same place. Research the sources of all fish in your diet, especially the oily fish like herring, mackerel, and tuna, because certain toxins such as PCBs are known to accumulate in fat. Also, it is best to eat small young fish, because over time, large adult fish are likely to have accumulated a high quantity of toxins in their bodies. It is also always important to consider the sources of fish before you go sport fishing. Surf the Internet for safety information; state advisories report the quantity of fish that can be safely consumed from different lakes or seas. If you are fishing and do not know the safety of a particular lake or sea, it is best to carefully take the fish off your hook, throw your fish back in the water, and just enjoy the sport.

Clean and Unclean Animals

Unfortunately, several of the animals that are popular in the American diet are considered to be scavengers, which eat dead and decaying things. I am a firm believer that God's Old Testament laws concerning food should still be respected today—these laws describe the types of animals that are clean and unclean to eat (see Leviticus 11 and Deuteronomy 14). Because Jesus died for the sins of the world and freed us from the bondage of the law, many believe that through faith we are free to eat all kinds of meat. I totally agree with this belief, but this freedom is only for those who have enough faith to eat all types of meat and still remain healthy. Just take the time to think: If you are unhealthy, maybe you should realize that your faith level is not great enough to eat all types of meat, especially from unclean animals; thus, you should reconsider your diet. Furthermore, if you are currently healthy, determine if your faith level is strong enough to eat unclean meat and still maintain good health until a ripe old age. If you lack the faith to be an unclean-meat eater, maybe you should limit your meat intake to clean animals and not overindulge in any type of meat. Take the time to determine your faith level and eat accordingly.

Clean mammals eat mostly grass (not other feed, such as inorganic grain), chew their cud, and have split hooves. The clean mammals that are common in America are the organic, grass-fed cow, deer, bison, lamb, and goat. Clean poultry (such as organic chicken and turkey) have a crop (i.e., the pouch in a bird's neck where food is prepared for digestion) and eat much vegetation. Fish with fins and scales are also defined as clean animals. Clean fish, which include cold-water, oily fish (high in omega-3 fatty acids) and the white-fleshed, non-oily fish (high in protein), are healthiest when grown wild and free of contaminants. Rabbits and horses are considered by many to be healthy meats, but because they do not have split hooves and their digestive systems tend to harbor toxins and pathogens, these animals are unclean. Scavengers are also unclean and should be avoided. Pigs have split hooves, but they are scavengers that constantly eat anything and everything. Different parasites, bacteria, and viruses feed in the pigs' stomachs, and toxins are stored in their fat, which can easily be passed along to us. Other scavengers that many love to eat are catfish (the pig of still waters), and shrimp, lobster, and shellfish (the three pigs of the ocean). Catfish, even those raised on a farm, eat the waste at the bottom of ponds and lakes, and have been shown to carry abundant amounts of bacteria and contaminants. However, in some fish farms or polluted waters, the clean fish (e.g., tilapia) can be just as dirty and carry as much contaminants (e.g., mercury and PCBs) as the unclean catfish. In the sea, the unclean shellfish are like little filters that can purify the water from parasites, bacteria, viruses, and toxic chemicals. Because of this, shellfish in the grocery store are often labeled as potentially dangerous for consumption. I love to eat all of these unclean scavengers, but I do so infrequently and in limited amounts. These animals were designed to help keep our environment clean, not for human consumption. If you chose to eat scavengers, it is best to do so sparingly.

Burgers, Sausages, and Bratwursts

Inorganic burgers, sausages and bratwursts are processed from scrap meats and fats, and include artificial preservatives, such as nitrites, monosodium glutamate, and BHA, and other toxic food additives. Instead of eating inorganic beef burgers, try eating organic ground turkey, buffalo, or vegetable burgers, all of which are low-fat sources of protein. Also, try eating organic sausages and bratwursts made from chicken and turkey instead of ones made from pork and beef. The shelf life of these organic meats, however, is very short, and the instructions on the label suggest that these meats should be stored properly and cooked well done to prevent food poisoning from possible pathogens. Occasionally, I have purchased from health-food stores chicken or beef bratwursts and turkey or pork sausages that tasted somewhat fresh and contained natural preservatives (e.g., sodium lactate from beets and sea salt), which are not as toxic or potent as the artificial nitrites and BHA. Nevertheless, these natural preservatives are still chemicals that are high in sodium; thus, their consumption should be limited.

Cured Meats, Hot dogs, and Cold cuts

Cured meats (e.g., cured, smoked turkey, roasted chicken, ham, bacon, corned beef, and roast beef) are processed from a higher grade of meat that is healthier than cold cuts and would be relatively healthy if it wasn't saturated with artificial preservatives (e.g., sodium nitrite and sodium nitrate), along with other additives. Because cured meats containing unhealthy preservatives may still be contaminated with pathogens (e.g., *Listeria*), it is good to heat these meats before making a sandwich or adding them to a salad. Cured meats that are free of the artificial preservatives (e.g., preserved with sodium chloride and sodium lactate) can be purchased at most health-food stores, but observe the expiration date; these meats have a short shelf life. Reduce intake of fat calories by replacing ham or bacon in a sandwich with organic roasted turkey or turkey bacon. Sliced avocados and Portobello mushrooms, which are great alternatives to sliced cured meat, make excellent, healthy vegetarian sandwiches.

Most inorganic hot dogs and cold cuts (e.g., salami, bologna, and pepperoni) are usually made from the lower grades of meat, which is generally just above dog food and loaded with artificial preservatives and other food additives; thus, they should be avoided. If you are going to eat them anyway, reduce your intake of artificial preservatives and fat calories by eating organic ones made of chicken or turkey. For example, try adding organic turkey pepperoni, instead of the regular, high-fat pepperoni, on a pizza made of whole-spelt crust. Although most hot dogs and cold cuts consist of high levels of preservatives, it is unsafe to take them directly from the package and eat them. All packaged cold cuts and hot dogs need to be cooked thoroughly to reduce the risk of being poisoned by pathogens, such as *Listeria*. Also, be careful with discarding the juices in these packages to prevent bacterial contamination.

Meat Preparation

Meat should be thawed in the refrigerator or in cold water to eliminate growth of pathogens. All surfaces exposed to the juices of raw or packaged meats should be sanitized thoroughly. The excess blood in meat is unhealthy and should be eliminated as much as possible. Thawing meat in cold water, to which vinegar, lemon juice, or organic sea salt is added, will help detoxify the meat from blood, chemicals, pathogens, and other toxins. After thawing, trim away excess fat from meat (and remove skin from chicken) to reduce fat calories. Next, wash the meat, boil it in water (a little vinegar can be added, especially if it is pork), then pour off the boiled fatty broth from the meat and wash it again. These steps help to eliminate toxins and fat. Then, the meat can be seasoned, prepared, and cooked as desired. When frying meat reduce unhealthy fat intake by spraying the pan with healthy oil, such as virgin olive oil, instead of pouring refined oil into the pan. Instead of frying or using the microwave, place meat on a rack to drain off fat drippings, and then cook it by roasting, grilling, broiling, or baking.

Eggs

Conventional, inorganic eggs consist of high amounts of vitamins, nutrients, and the nine essential amino acids. However, inorganic eggs are also high in omega-6 fatty acids, saturated fat, and cholesterol. Hens that lay eggs high in omega-3 fatty acids are fed an organic diet of grain, vegetation, and flaxseeds. Although healthier compared to inorganic eggs, organic eggs are still relatively high in unhealthy fats and cholesterol. Thus, it is best to limit the amount of eggs that are consumed, particularly if you have heart disease. Eating one to two eggs a day can be acceptable if your unhealthy fat and cholesterol levels are under control. The majority of the unhealthy fats and cholesterol is in the yolk, along with the minerals, vitamins, and flavor. Eat only the white of the egg when you want to maintain high protein levels yet reduce your unhealthy fat and cholesterol intake. If you desire the taste of egg yolks and have a big appetite, try adding only one egg yolk to several egg whites. This will give eggs a yummy flavor, maintain protein levels, decrease cholesterol intake, and fill up the stomach.

Inorganic eggs consist of pesticides, hormones, and antibiotics. Also, because inorganic hens are usually caged in disease-infested areas, *Salmonella* is a major bacteria often found in eggs. The USDA grade of an egg does not help with identifying the environment of the hen or the nutritional value of the egg; it only defines the interior (the yolk and white) and exterior (the shell) quality characteristics of the egg. When purchasing eggs, read the egg-carton label to select organic eggs laid by free-range–raised hens that are not exposed to pesticides, hormones, antibiotics, and other contaminants. When preparing eggs, make sure all eggs are cooked well done and not runny, as it is possible for both inorganic and organic hens to be infected with *Salmonella*. Thoroughly sanitize all surfaces that are exposed to the raw eggs. Keep eggs in the refrigerator, watch for expiration dates, and prepare by boiling or poaching. Vegetable omelets are great when prepared with a limited amount of fat. Avoid frying eggs; if you do fry, spray pan with one of the healthy oils.

Cow's Milk

Conventional, inorganic cow's milk and other dairy products are popular sources of calcium and protein (casein and whey proteins). Although expensive, it is better (especially for children) to purchase milk from organic, grass-fed dairy cows than from inorganic, grain-fed dairy cows. Milk from organic cows that are also fed flaxseeds is free from pesticides, antibiotics, hormones, and other contaminants and higher in omega-3 fatty acids than that from inorganic cows. Especially for the sake of your children, check the label for content information to make sure the milk is antibiotic and growth-hormone free. Store-bought cow's milk (both inorganic and organic) is usually homogenized and pasteurized. Homogenization is used to break up the fat globules and give milk its smooth appearance. Milk is pasteurized to kill pathogens transferred from milking the cows or the processing equipment. Unfortunately, homogenization and pasteurization also destroy many of the healthy nutrients in cow's milk, thus decreasing the nutritional value of it immensely. Yet because of the issues with *E. coli*, milk that is pasteurized decreases the risk of food poisoning.

Although many people are not able to properly digest cow's milk, cow's milk continues to be the number one source of calcium in the United States. Whole milk is naturally high in calcium, phosphorus, and vitamin A; it also is usually fortified with vitamin D. Low-fat and skim milk are low in natural vitamin A (being fat-soluble, this vitamin is removed with the fat), and then, are often enriched in an attempt to replace it. In a high percentage of the population, only a small portion of the calcium in cow's milk is properly absorbed by the body. This in part may be due to milk protein making the body more acidic, and then, interfering with the proper absorption of calcium (see Part IV for information on osteoporosis concerning mineral deficiencies). In order to intake the daily required amount of calcium, it may be necessary to include other sources of calcium in your daily diet.

The majority of the world's population is lactose-intolerant, especially individuals of American Indian, Middle Eastern, Mediterranean, Hispanic, Asian, and African descent—this means, after weaning, they (the lactose-intolerant) no longer synthesize the enzyme lactase, which is required to properly metabolize lactose (the sugar in cow's milk). Only most (not all) Caucasians of Northern European descent are capable of synthesizing lactase and properly metabolizing lactose. When lactose-intolerant individuals consume cow's milk, the lactose, which is metabolized mainly by intestinal bacteria, turns the intestines into a fermentation chamber. This results in digestive problems, such as excess gas, bloating, cramping, and diarrhea. Many claim that goat's milk consists of fat globules and proteins that are more easily digested than those found in cow's milk; thus, it is often substituted for cow's milk. However, like cow's milk, goat's milk is loaded with lactose and should be avoided by the lactose-intolerant. Many lactose-intolerant individuals consume cow's milk that was treated with lactase to make it lactose-free, or take lactase pills so that they can digest lactose.

Some people after consuming lactose-free cow's milk may discover that they are still suffering from distress. These individuals may be allergic to the casein or whey proteins found in cow's milk. Pasteurization has little effect on the heat-stable casein, but is known to denature (destroy the complex structure of) a large percentage of the heat-labile whey proteins. Yet, these denatured whey proteins may only reduce but not fully eliminate the distress. The allergic responses of individuals to casein and whey proteins are often due to the lack of specific enzymes that are required to fully digest them. Because of this, individuals who are allergic to these proteins need to avoid cow's milk, unfermented dairy products, and other processed foods that consist of cow's milk additives (e.g., dry milk, whey, and casein). For these individuals, calcium-fortified rice, almond, and soy milk are often used as substitutes. Of these substitutes, my preference is almond milk. Rice milk has a much higher glycemic index value than almond and soy milk; thus, it should be consumed in moderation. Those allergic to soybeans should avoid soy milk; plus, a high intake of soy milk may lead to other possible health concerns (see information about soy products in chapter 39). Instead of drinking calcium-fortified almond milk, try homemade almond milk, which is delicious, high in natural calcium, inexpensive, and easy to make (see Part V for recipe).

As an African American, I've noticed since childhood that cow's milk is not my friend. Although I constantly tried to consume it in my breakfast cereal, during school lunch as a drink, and at home as a chocolate- or strawberry-flavored dessert drink, it always made me sick. Years before I started my new healthy lifestyle, I finally gave up the cow's milk torture and completely stopped drinking it. I maintained the required calcium in my diet by consuming green leafy vegetables, broccoli, beans, canned bony fish, almonds, and almond milk, and by buying high-quality calcium supplements that are readily absorbed into the bloodstream and prescribed by my physician. Months after starting my new diet, I began testing the effects of dairy products on my system and noticed that I wasn't completely lactose-intolerant, but that I had a low tolerance for lactose. I discovered that I am able to add high-calcium dairy products, such as ripened cheese and plain, cultured, low-fat yogurt, to my diet with little or no distress.

Dairy Products

Natural, organic cheese is high in calcium, protein, other nutrients, and unhealthy saturated fat and cholesterol. After organic, whole milk from grass-fed cows is curdled (coagulated) to make natural cheese, the whey is poured off with its proteins, along with a large portion of the lactose. Then the curds, which are concentrated in casein, fats, and the remaining lactose, are left behind. Curdling with organic low-fat milk considerably reduces the fat content of curds without significantly decreasing the content of lactose and casein. Whey is used to make unripened (fresh) ricotta cheese and its protein is concentrated as a nutritive food additive. Curds are used to produce different types of ripened (aged) and unripened cheeses.

Many of the low–lactose-tolerant and mildly allergic to casein individuals may be able to eat organic, ripened cheeses with minimal distress (check with your physician to see if you are one of these individuals). Most types of ripened cheeses, such as Colby, Swiss, Cheddar, Parmesan, Feta, or Brie, are found to be low in lactose and casein. After curdling, the curds are ripened through fermentation, a process in which bacteria metabolize the majority of lactose to lactic acid (a waste product that is readily eliminated from the body) and a high percentage of casein to digestible by-products (proteins that are denatured and then broken down to peptides). Most allergic individuals are usually missing the specific enzymes needed to fully digest intact casein, but are equipped with the enzymes required to break digestible by-products down to amino acids. Thus, the digestible by-products may not trigger an allergic response in these individuals. For those who are lactose-intolerant, it is possible to purchase lactose-free unripened cheeses that are made from lactose-free curds such as cottage cheese, mozzarella, and cream cheese, or from lactose-free whey such as ricotta cheese. These lactose-free, unripened cheeses are excellent condiments that the lactose-intolerant can add to salads, fruit, or whole wheat crackers.

Lactose-intolerant individuals and those allergic to milk protein need to avoid all dairy products that contain lactose and intact protein, respectively. Be careful and check the labeled ingredients of curdled cheeses and other fermented dairy products that are expected to be relatively low in lactose, casein, and whey proteins. Many curdled or fermented dairy products consist of powdered cow's milk or milk containing additives (e.g., lactose, whey protein, and casein) that were added after the curdling or fermentation process; thus, these additives may not have been exposed to active bacteria and still remain intact. Furthermore, it is best to avoid the unhealthy, processed cheeses. Pasteurized, processed cheese is altered to an unnatural form and consists of blended cheeses, milk products (e.g., milk fat, lactose, casein, and whey) and food additives (e.g., emulsifiers, food coloring, excess salt, and flavorings). Unhealthier still is imitation cheese, which is usually made from partially hydrogenated vegetable oil, protein (e.g., casein), and a variety of cheese flavorings.

Organic, cultured yogurt is a great source of digestible proteins, calcium, and probiotics (the "good" bacteria that we need in our intestines to maintain a healthy flora). Because cultured yogurt consists of bacteria that produce lactase, many low lactose-tolerant individuals can consume cultured yogurt with minimal distress. Plus, the fermentation process also aids in breaking down casein and whey proteins to digestible by-products. Individuals who suffer from mild allergic reactions to casein and whey may discover that the digestible by-products found in yogurt do not trigger an allergic response. Yet after the fermentation process, dry milk and other milk additives are often added to thicken the consistency and increase the nutritional value of yogurt. Thus, yogurt containing cow's milk additives may be high in intact lactose, casein, and whey proteins and need to be avoided by those who are lactose-intolerant or allergic to cow's milk. Check the ingredients list of the cultured yogurt to make sure these additives are not included. Also, check the ingredient list to make certain that it consists of live probiotics and not dead ones that were destroyed by pasteurization after the fermentation process. It is especially important to consume live probiotics after the immune system has been compromised from taking antibiotics prescribed by a medical doctor. Antibiotics may kill not only the "bad" bacteria that cause the infection but also the probiotics that we need for proper digestion. The lack of "good" bacteria gives opportunity for hearty antibiotic-resistant pathogens to multiply and for the overgrowth of yeast. The fruit-flavored yogurts usually consist of high quantities of sugar that may help feed the yeast, so it is best to eat plain, cultured, low-fat yogurt. Other ways to replenish probiotics in our system are to consume unpasteurized sauerkraut; unfiltered, unpasteurized apple-cider vinegar; and probiotic capsules; these items are safe for the lactose-intolerant and sold at health-food stores.

Saturated fat consumption can be decreased by consuming low-fat cow's milk and dairy products. The high saturated fat that is removed to produce low-fat milk is used to manufacture products such as butter, sour cream, and premium ice cream; these foods should be greatly reduced in the diet, especially by those with heart disease. Try substituting butter on baked potatoes with low-fat sour cream, and replacing it on whole spelt toast with plain, cultured, low-fat yogurt (this combination was discovered by my son). These substitutions are quite tasty. If you must eat ice cream, it is best to practice self-control; try eating only one small scoop of low-fat, sugar-free ice cream sweetened with a natural sweetener (e.g., sorbitol) no more than once a week. Mixing frozen sugar-free yogurt, or better yet, plain, cultured, low-fat yogurt with fresh or frozen fruit (e.g., blueberries and peaches) is a healthier alternative to ice cream and makes a delicious dessert. Furthermore, those congested with a cold or suffering from sinusitis should exclude ice cream and other dairy products from their diets. The combination of dairy products (especially ice cream) plus sinus mucus (the breeding ground for infection) seems to trigger or agitate colds and sinusitis in many individuals. Plain, cultured, low-fat yogurt, however, is acceptable for most to eat in moderation.

* * *

Work-Study: Points to Ponder

1. Which foods in your diet are your main sources of protein?

2. If you are a meat-eater, which meats do you eat? How often do you eat them? Describe your thoughts on eating more organic meat (beef, chicken, and turkey).

3. Do you eat lean meat or meat consisting of much saturated fat? Do you or does anyone you know have cancer or heart disease? If so, how much meat is in the diet? Do you or they eat much saturated fat, cholesterol, and omega-6 fatty acids?

4. Do you eat meat from clean or unclean animals, or no meat at all? How often do you eat meat from the scavengers (pig, catfish, shrimp, shellfish, and lobster)? Are you willing to decrease your intake?

5. Do you eat burgers, sausages, and bratwursts? What about cured meats, hot dogs, and cold cuts? If so, what types and how often?

6. Do you eat eggs (organic or inorganic)? How do you eat them: fried, scrambled, poached, or boiled? Do you separate the egg white from the yolk?

7. Are you a fish eater? If so, how many times a week do you eat it? If not, are you willing to start eating the healthier types of fish? If so, what types are you willing to eat?

8. Describe your thoughts on eating less meat and increasing your protein intake by eating other foods, like beans and whole grain brown rice.

9. If you are a vegetarian, are you healthy?

10. Conventional cow's milk and cheese are popular sources of protein and calcium, but they also have a high content of saturated fat, omega 6-fatty acids, and cholesterol. Also, only a low percentage of calcium in cow's milk is properly utilized in the body. How much cow's milk and cheese do you consume in a day? In a week? Do consume organic and low-fat cow's milk and cheese? Do you consume other sources of calcium?

11. If you are lactose intolerant, do you drink lactose-free milk? Are you substituting it with other types of milk, such as almond, soy, and rice milk? Do you take calcium supplements?

12. If you are allergic to the proteins in cow's milk, casein and whey proteins, what calcium-rich foods do you consume to replace cow's milk and dairy products?

13. Do you eat plain, cultured, low-fat yogurt to maintain a healthy flora in your digestive system? What are your thoughts on trying the probiotic ("good" bacteria) capsules sold at health food stores?

14. Calculate below the approximate amount of protein that someone with your body weight should consume daily. <u>Note</u>: Approximately 0.8 gm of protein needs to be consumed per 2.2 lb of body weight. (Your body weight ________lb x 0.8) ÷ 2.2 = Daily Protein Intake _________gm

15. In the below space, add up the amount of protein that you eat in one day, and then determine if it is near your required daily protein intake. <u>Note</u>: Check Nutrition Facts label on foods for protein content: one calorie of protein equals four grams of protein.

Food type	**Amount of Protein Consumed (gm)**

Total Amount of Protein Consumed in a Day = ________ grams

16. Do you consume enough protein daily? If not, are you willing to eat more protein? Do you exercise intensely and need to consume more than the average amount of protein? If so, have you consulted a physician or nutritionist for advice?

17. Do you consume too much protein daily? Is your body too acidic from eating excessive amounts of protein? (See chapter 41 for details about checking body pH.) Are you suffering from gout or a malfunctioning kidney due to protein overload? If so, are you willing to decrease your protein intake?

18. In my past diet, my weakness was simple carbohydrates, not meats and eggs. There were not many improvements in these food types that I needed to add to my new diet. I always loved chicken, turkey, fish, and beans, whereas beef, pork, and eggs were never my favorites. Also, after my low intolerance for cow's milk and dairy products was discovered, I did not have a problem with decreasing their intake. If eating red meats, processed meats, eggs, cow's milk, and dairy products is your weakness, then determine what changes to which you are willing to commit in your new diet with regard to these items as you focus on the Repent 6 R's Step Process. Below, list the foods that you are willing to release and then replace with healthier ones.

Release	**Replace**

Chapter 38

America's Favorite Side Dishes: Pasta, Rice, and Potatoes

And every man that striveth for the mastery is temperate in all things. (I Corinthians 9:25a)

Starches

Pasta, rice, and potatoes, the starchy foods that we Americans love to include in our daily meals, are often considered to be high in "bad" carbohydrates. Yet this is not necessarily always the case. The effects of these high-carbohydrate foods on health depend on a person's metabolism, the amount of these foods consumed, the consistency of these foods, and the overall meal prepared along with these foods. Athletes, children, and adults with a banana-shaped body (who need high levels of carbohydrates for energy) can benefit from eating these foods in moderation. People who are overweight, obese, or diabetic; suffer from heart disease or hypertension; or have a pear- or apple-shaped body should limit the amount of these high-carbohydrate foods that they consume.

Pasta

Pasta can be added to the diets of most people if the right kind and amount is consumed. Generally, the darker the pasta, the more nutrients and fiber it contains, and the lighter the pasta, the more refined it is and empty calories it carries. Pasta is mostly made from durum wheat, which is a yellow grain high in protein and gluten. The most common type of pasta usually purchased at the grocery store is prepared with semolina, a coarsely ground flour made from only the inner endosperm layer of durum wheat (thus, it is not whole-grain durum wheat flour). Semolina pasta ("white" pasta) has a medium to medium-high glycemic index value and should be consumed by people with a high enough metabolism to burn it up quickly. Rice pasta is available for those who need to avoid gluten, but it has a high glycemic index value. Organic, whole grain pasta (e.g., whole grain durum wheat pasta and whole grain spelt pasta) is a complex carbohydrate that has a high content of nutrients and fiber, and a medium-range glycemic index value that is somewhat lower than that of "white" pasta. Spinach, beet, and carrot powders are often added to the different types of flours (e.g., semolina and organic whole grain) to give pasta its color and increase its nutrients. Most types of pasta have a medium glycemic index value, but the glycemic index value of pasta greatly depends on how long it is cooked. Pasta should be cooked *al dente,* which means tender and done, yet firm and slightly chewy to the bite. It should not be undercooked and hard, or overcooked and soft. The longer pasta is cooked; the softer it becomes and higher the glycemic index value. Therefore, take caution to make sure the *al dente* texture is reached. My extended family, which includes my sister's two little children, loves to eat whole-wheat and whole-spelt pasta cooked *al dente*.

The amount of pasta that one should consume also depends on the foods that are prepared with it. Pasta is a common food in Europe, where the majority of the people are thin. A typical Mediterranean meal consists of foods such as pasta, olive oil, tomatoes, vegetables, fruits, fish, and garlic. After eating a typical Mediterranean meal, the amount of unhealthy fat calories and the glycemic load (see chapter 43 for the definition) are both quite low. Plus, Europeans are known for eating small portions and sharing a meal or a dessert. At the end of a meal, Europeans are often content with consuming just a couple of bites of a pastry or a small piece of chocolate. Also, exercise is part of the Europeans' daily routine; walking and biking are common modes of transportation.

A popular American comfort food that is extremely high in calories and gives a high glycemic index value is macaroni and cheese. In America, the problem arises when pasta is consumed with cheese, creams, other fatty foods, and sugar (e.g., a meal consisting of a cheese hamburger, macaroni and cheese, and premium ice cream for dessert), followed by sitting on the couch all evening. After eating a high-calorie fatty meal like this, the digestion of high glycemic-index carbohydrates and fats results in increased sugar, triglyceride, and cholesterol levels in the bloodstream, surges of released insulin, and eventually, clogged arteries. Constantly eating like this can lead to high blood pressure, heart disease, obesity, and type II diabetes in adults and even in our youth. Because my family and I love macaroni and cheese, my sister created a healthier macaroni-and-cheese recipe that includes whole-grain spelt pasta and low-fat cheeses (see Part V for recipe). On average, my family prepares this dish twice a year, usually for our Christmas and Easter dinners. Let me repeat: we prepare this twice a year, because it is still high in fat.

Rice

Rice is a high-carbohydrate cereal that is a staple for more than half of the world's population. There are many different types of rice, but white rice is the most common in the United States. A whole grain of rice consists of many layers. White rice has been processed, polished until white, and stripped of the outer hull, bran, and germ layers, down to only the inner starchy layer, which is devoid of almost all nutrients. It should be avoided because it has a high glycemic index value and consists of almost nothing but empty calories. Brown rice, on the other hand, consists of everything but the outer hull. Very little nutritional value of brown rice is lost, and high levels of fiber are present in the bran and germ layers. In these layers are healthy oils that reduce the shelf life of brown rice. To preserve brown rice for a longer period of time, it should be stored in the refrigerator. After cooking properly, white rice is soft and sticky, whereas brown rice is stiff and chewy. Because brown rice has a medium glycemic index value, chewy brown rice digests more slowly than soft white rice. Thus, brown rice is relatively healthy and can be eaten in moderation. Also, it is best to eat rice grown in arsenic-free soil; usually, inorganic rice consists of much higher traces of arsenic than organic rice. Consumption of traces of arsenic over a long period of time can potentially cause cancer, neurological disorders, infertility, etc.

Many other different types of rice are common in the United States. Parboiled rice (converted rice) is unusual in that it has been processed and stripped of all its beneficial fibers but yet it gives a glycemic index value lower than brown rice. Parboiling rice in its hull forces the nutrients from the outer layers to the inner starchy layer. After parboiling, the inner starchy layer, which contains most of the nutrients, is found to have an extremely hard texture. The parboiled rice is then further processed to separate it from its hull and other outer layers and then polished. Because of its extremely hard texture, it takes longer to cook, and when done, it is firmer, chewier, less sticky, and healthier than white rice. Arborio, a type of Italian white rice (pearly and starchy), is used to cook creamy risotto, and sweet rice (white and gummy) is used when making sushi (both of these rice have a high glycemic index value). Jasmine long-grain rice (a high glycemic-index food) and Basmati long-grain rice (a medium glycemic-index food) have a tasty nutty flavor. Wild rice, often used to stuff poultry, is actually not rice but is the seed from a wild grass native to North America. It consists of many nutrients and gives a medium glycemic index.

It is very important when eating rice to select the proper foods to eat with it. White rice is a staple food of many different regions in Asia and Africa. Because a high percentage of the total populations in these two continents are generally thin, many people believe that their small size is due mostly to genetic factors; I beg to differ. Knowing many native Asians and Africans who now live in America, I noticed that the individuals who adopted the American lifestyle gained much more weight than the ones who continued to eat meals of their ethnicity. This suggests that although white rice is a high-carbohydrate food, if it is consumed along with healthy foods, such as vegetables and fish, one will maintain a healthy weight. As a demonstration of the typical American diet, a meal consisting of white rice along with other high-calorie foods, such as fatty beef, gravy, and biscuits, and then topped off with a slice of cheesecake and lack of exercise will result in weight gain.

Potatoes

There are many different types of white potatoes, such as the russet potato, all-purpose white potato, new potato, and red potato. White potatoes, next to white sugar and white flour, are one of the most highly consumed carbohydrates in the United States. We eat and prepare it many different ways. Baked, fried, grilled, broiled, mashed—you name it; we eat it. Unfortunately, it is common practice to make French fries by frying white potatoes in partially hydrogenated oil (trans fat) and then eat them along with a fatty cheese hamburger. French fries are slowly killing many Americans. This food is the main side dish served in fast-food chains, restaurants, schools, and the typical American household. Because the potato is a vegetable, French fries are served as vegetables to our children in schools. We also eat potato chips with our meals or as an in-between-meal snack. Like fries, chips are usually toxic because they are often cooked in partially hydrogenated oils. Check the Nutrition Facts label to determine if the chips are cooked in monounsaturated, polyunsaturated, or partially hydrogenated (trans fat) oil. Although recently many well-known brands are cooked in polyunsaturated oil, potato chips are still unhealthy and should be avoided.

The different types of white potatoes are high in complex carbohydrates (e.g., the starch amylose), but these carbohydrates rapidly increase blood glucose to levels similar to that seen with "bad" carbohydrates. Although cooked white potatoes consist of many nutrients, such as potassium, and are low in overall calories, I try to limit the amount of them I eat because of their high glycemic index value. Baked potatoes are a very high glycemic index food, and boiled, steamed, and mashed potatoes have a medium to medium-high glycemic index value. When I do eat white potatoes, I eat new potatoes, which have a lower glycemic index value than other white potatoes, and I dice, boil and slightly brown them in the oven. New potatoes are waxy and hard and do not have as much starch (amylose) as some of the other white potatoes. The skin of the new potato is smooth, thin, and a great source of fiber, which makes it good to eat along with the potato. This is unlike the skin of the russet potato, which is a great source of fiber but has a gritty texture. If you choose to eat a baked potato, it is best to eat it without many of the added toppings. Eat it with chives and a little plain, cultured, low-fat yogurt or low-fat sour cream, and nothing else. Eliminate the butter, cheese, and bacon bits. If you are longing for a French fry, try baking sliced potatoes that have been rubbed with a little bit of olive oil. If you eat mashed potatoes, prepare them with skim milk, garlic, and a little canola oil butter. Do not eat them with gravy and heavy creams.

In my meals, I like replacing the white potato with the yam-sweet potato (an orange-colored sweet potato, commonly called garnet yam). The yam-sweet potato is a complex carbohydrate food with many nutrients (such as beta-carotene), fiber, and a low glycemic index value. I like baking yam-sweet potatoes (sliced or whole) and then adding a little nutmeg and cinnamon to taste. The yam-sweet potato is already sweet, but sometimes when my sweet tooth rears itself, I add a little xylitol. Instead of eating French fries, I sometimes fry yam-sweet potato wedges in olive oil (see Part V for recipe). I also prefer to eat yam-sweet potato chips rather than white-potato chips. Many often confuse the yam-sweet potato with the sweet potato. The sweet potato is similar to the yam-sweet potato in shape and high-fiber content, but the flesh of the sweet potato is similar to the white potato in texture and is pale yellow in color. The sweet potato has a slightly higher glycemic index value and fewer phytonutrients than the orange yam-sweet potato. Purple yam-sweet potatoes are available in some stores. The skin and the flesh of these potatoes are purple and consist of phytonutrients that are similar to other purple foods, such as blueberries and purple grapes (see chapter 40 for phytonutrients found in purple foods). Generally, the darker the flesh of the tuber, the more phytonutrients it contains.

* * *

Work-Study: Points to Ponder

1. Carbohydrates white in color seem to have a higher glycemic index value than darker ones. Do you prefer your carbohydrates to be white or dark?

2. It is important to know the glycemic index values of the carbohydrates in your diet.

Here is a simple chart, including the glycemic index ranges of some of the main foods from my past and present diet. Use this chart, or alter it to fit your own dietary needs. If needed, complete below your own chart by surfing the Internet or researching reference books for the glycemic index value of foods. Because some sources are more reliable than others, it is best to find several sources and compare their information (see list of Suggested Readings for a reliable source on glycemic index values). Remember, when selecting foods in your healthy diet, the fat content should be considered along with their glycemic index value. For example, ice cream and milk chocolate are within the medium glycemic index range but are high in saturated fats; thus, these foods should be avoided.

Glycemic Index Ranges of Foods from My Past and New Healthy Diet

	Glycemic Index Range	Foods
Low glycemic index	54 or less	Fructose, most fresh fruits, most fresh vegetables, beans, raw carrots, whole grain cereals, basmati rice, parboiled (converted) rice, yam-sweet potato, grapes, whole-grain wheat bread, whole-grain spelt flour multi-grain bread, sprouted grain bread, dairy products, meat, nuts, xylitol, and stevia
Medium glycemic index	55–69	White sugar (sucrose), whole grain spelt bread, chocolate candy, corn, whole grain wheat pasta, blueberry muffins, cantaloupe, taco shells, boiled white potatoes, potato chips, blue corn tortilla chips, raisins, boiled carrots, brown rice, white pasta, ice cream, and oatmeal cookies

High glycemic index	70 or more	Glucose, cornflakes, baked white potato, watermelon, white bread, waffles, doughnuts, scones, cupcakes, white flour bagel, jelly beans, raisins, pizza, popcorn, mashed potatoes, French fries, pretzels, soda crackers, white rice, rice cakes, vanilla wafers, and graham crackers

Glycemic Index Ranges of Foods in Your Past and New Healthy Diet

	Glycemic Index Range	Foods
Low glycemic index	54 or less	

Medium glycemic Index	55–69
High glycemic index	70 or more

---

3. If you are overweight or unhealthy, are you willing to decrease your consumption of foods that give a medium or high glycemic index value?

4. Do you eat pasta? What type? Are you willing to eat whole-grain pasta?

5. Do you eat white or whole-grain brown rice? Do you eat parboiled (converted) rice?

6. Do you eat white potatoes? If so, how do you prepare them: fried, boiled, baked, or mashed? How often do you eat French fries or potato chips?

7. Are you willing to eat new potatoes—or better yet, yam-sweet potatoes? (These potatoes give a lower glycemic index value than most other types.)

8. I improved my health by completing the Repent 6 R's Step Process. I released certain foods from my diet and replaced them as described below.

Released	Replaced
• French fries 2–3 times a week	• Salad, vegetables, beans, yam-sweet potatoes, and fruit
• Mashed white potatoes 2–3 times a week	• Salad, vegetables, beans, brown rice, yam-sweet potatoes, and fruit
• Baked white potatoes 1-2 times a week	• Salad, vegetables, beans, brown rice, yam-sweet potatoes, boiled then baked new potatoes, and fruit
• White potato chips 3–4 times a week	• Salad, vegetables, beans, brown rice, yam-sweet potato, fruit, yam-sweet potato chips, and tortilla chips
• Macaroni (white pasta) and cheese 2–3 times a week	• Salad, vegetables, beans, brown rice, yam-sweet potatoes, and fruit. Twice a year, eat homemade macaroni (i.e., whole wheat or whole spelt macaroni) and low-fat cheese using family recipe (see Part V)
• Meat lasagna (white pasta) or meatballs and spaghetti (white spaghetti) approximately 4 times a month	• Vegetable lasagna (e.g., whole wheat pasta) or meatballs and spaghetti (e.g., spinach, whole wheat spaghetti, and whole spelt spaghetti) approximately 1–3 times a month (see Part V for recipes)

- White rice 4–5 times a week
- Brown rice or converted rice 2–4 times a week

Determine which changes you are willing to make in your unhealthy diet consisting of white flour and refined grains and complete the Repent 6 R's Step Process. List the foods that you are willing to release and then replace with healthier ones.

Release	Replace

CHAPTER 39

Vegetables, Including Legumes

We remember the fish, which we did eat in Egypt freely; the cucumbers, and the melons, and the leeks, and the onions, and the garlick. (Numbers 11:5)

Chapters 39 and 40 describe the different types of vegetables, fruits, nuts, and seeds and the importance of adding them to your healthy diet.

Definition of Vegetables

Vegetables are commonly identified as the edible parts of plants that include the leaves (e.g., lettuce), stems (e.g., asparagus), stalks (e.g., celery), botanical fruits (e.g., tomatoes), flowers (e.g., cauliflower), bulbs (e.g., onions), roots (e.g., beets), and tubers (e.g., potatoes). Vegetables are low in salt and fat (except for avocados and olives, which are high in monounsaturated fat) and free of cholesterol. Fresh vegetables are a very important source of complex carbohydrates, vitamins, minerals, fiber, and phytonutrients. It is almost impossible, however, to consume enough vitamins, minerals, phytonutrients, and other nutrients from today's vegetables. Today's vegetables do not consist of the high level of minerals, vitamins, and phytonutrients as those of yesterday. Crops are repeatedly grown in soil that is stripped of many minerals. The lack of minerals in the soil, the development of genetically modified foods, and exposure to pesticides, preservatives, other toxic chemicals, and irradiation has reduced the nutritional value of vegetables. Although nutritional value has decreased over the years, raw organic vegetables are still one of the major sources of minerals, vitamins, and phytonutrients in the human diet. Thus, it is important to eat at least five to seven servings of raw organic vegetables a day. Other major sources of minerals, vitamins, and phytonutrients are organic fruits, whole grains, nuts, meats, eggs, dairy products, and dietary supplements.

Minerals

It is important that we consume the amount of minerals and vitamins required for optimal health. A set of nutritional guidelines, the Directory Reference Intakes (DRIs), was recently established by the Institute of Medicine for the United States and Canada. These guidelines include and expand the reference values given in the previously established Recommended Dietary Allowances (RDAs), which were developed during World War II. The past RDAs gave guidelines for the daily intake of dietary nutrients such as minerals, vitamins, and proteins that were needed to help eliminate nutrient deficiencies and diseases. The DRIs, the improved guidelines, provide reference values to help individuals design healthy diets that prevent diseases and promote optimal health. The DRIs gives four reference values: estimated average requirements (EARs), RDAs, adequate intakes (AIs), and tolerable upper intake levels (ULs). The four reference values are specific for gender, different adult age groups, children, infants, and pregnant and lactating mothers.

Minerals (inorganic elements) are absorbed by plants from the soil. Humans consume most minerals by eating vegetables, fruits, and animals that eat plants (herbivores and omnivores). Minerals are required to build human tissues (e.g., muscles), synthesize cells (e.g., red blood cells), and regulate bodily functions (e.g., muscle contraction). Listed below are the major dietary minerals that we need to intake in relatively large quantities daily, as well as their dietary sources. The reference values of the major dietary minerals for adult age groups are defined as values > 200 mg/day. Research the DRIs (see Suggested Readings list) for specific reference values and information concerning each major mineral.

- **Calcium:** Needed for nerve transmission, heart and muscle contraction, and healthy bones, teeth, and digestive system. Dietary sources are fish with bones, almonds, homemade almond milk, broccoli, dark-green leafy vegetables, dried beans, soybeans and soy products (see information about consuming soybeans in this chapter), kelp and other sea vegetables, aged cheese, plain cultured low-fat yogurt, sesame and sunflower seeds, cow's milk (see information in chapter 37 for problems with consuming cow's milk), calcium-enriched or -fortified drinks (usually low in natural calcium) such as almond milk (made with a low quantity of almonds to make it cost-effective), rice milk (a high glycemic index value), soy milk (a large portion of the calcium naturally found in soybeans is lost; see this chapter for concerns with consuming soy products), and orange juice (high in concentrated sugar), and calcium-fortified foods such as bread and cereal. Note: The percentage of calcium that is actually absorbed into the body from enriched or fortified dietary foods is usually low, and it is often difficult to consume enough natural dietary sources to reach the daily required amount of calcium. Thus, it is necessary to consult your physician or nutritionist about including high-quality, easily absorbed calcium supplements to your daily intake.

- **Chloride (chlorine):** Essential ion needed to regulate extracellular fluid, muscle contraction, and nerve transmission, and to produce hydrochloric acid in stomach. Main dietary sources are table salt (sodium chloride) and sea salt (see chapter 42 for information about salt).
- **Magnesium:** Required for the formation of strong bones and teeth, and proper utilization of calcium. Needed for muscle contraction, nerve transmission, and brain function. Dietary sources are nuts, whole grains, green leafy vegetables, beans, and cow's milk (see information in chapter 37 for problems with consuming cow's milk).
- **Phosphorus:** Needed for formation of bones and teeth, and the synthesis of DNA nucleotides and the phospholipids found in membranes. Most foods consist of phosphorus. High dietary sources are meat, fish, legumes, nuts, eggs, yogurt, and cow's milk (see information in chapter 37 for problems with consuming cow's milk).

- **Potassium:** Needed in nerve, muscle, heart, and kidney function and for acid-base balance and stabilizing blood pressure. Dietary sources are bananas, apples, leafy greens, tomatoes, cucumbers, zucchini, potatoes, whole grains, and cow's milk (see information in chapter 37 for problems with consuming cow's milk).
- **Sodium:** Essential ion needed to regulate nerve and heart function, and extracellular fluid and mineral content throughout the body. Main dietary sources are table salt (sodium chloride), sea salt, and sodium bicarbonate. Note: Be careful not to intake in excess; most processed foods have high sodium levels (see information in chapter 42 about sodium intake levels).

The trace minerals (adults require < 200 mg/day) mostly play a role in helping enzymes (specialized proteins) catalyze (increase the rate of) chemical reactions that are required in the human body. Research the DRIs (see Suggested Readings list) for specific reference values and information concerning each trace mineral. Some of the trace minerals are listed as follows:

- **Chromium:** Plays an essential role in controlling glucose levels in the bloodstream. Dietary sources are poultry, fish, cereals, and whole grains.
- **Copper:** Required for brain function, enzyme activity, and the formation of connective tissue, red blood cells, and bone. Dietary sources are whole grains, legumes, seafood, organ meats, and dark-green leafy vegetables.
- **Fluoride (fluorine):** Incorporated into the structure of healthy bone and teeth. Dietary sources are fluoridated water (tap water), fish grown in fluoridated water, beverages made from fluoridated water, and foods grown in fluoridated soil. Note: Many physicians and dentists recommend decreasing the intake of fluoridated water and use of fluoridated toothpaste to prevent fluoride poisoning (especially in infants, small children, and elderly adults). Consult your physician or dentist about this matter.

- **Iodine:** Required for the proper function of thyroid hormones. Dietary sources are seafood (including seaweed such as kelp) and iodized table salt.
- **Iron:** Required for the formation of hemoglobin (oxygen transporter) found in red blood cells. Great dietary sources are organ meats, lean meat, poultry, and fish. Other sources are raisins, beets, prunes, green leafy vegetables, and fortified cereal.
- **Manganese:** Acts as an activator of different enzymes needed for metabolism and bone formation. Dietary sources are liver, whole grains, green leafy vegetables, and nuts.
- **Molybdenum:** A required component for certain metabolic enzymes. Dietary sources include leafy vegetables, whole grains, legumes, organ meats, and meat.
- **Selenium:** An antioxidant; regulates thyroid hormones. Dietary sources are meat, seafood, broccoli, cauliflower, Brussels sprouts, dairy products, and whole grains.
- **Zinc:** Incorporated in enzymes known for antioxidant properties, growth, and reproductive development. Dietary sources are meat, legumes, shellfish, oysters, nuts, and whole grains.

Vitamins

Vitamins are organic compounds required for essential metabolic reactions, and some vitamins (e.g., vitamins A, C, E, and K) function as antioxidants. Humans require at least fourteen essential vitamins (A, eight Bs, C, D, E, K, and choline) for proper function. The fat-soluble vitamins (A, D, E, and K) require fat for proper absorption. Vitamins C and Bs require water for proper absorption (water-soluble). The body cannot synthesize the majority of the essential vitamins (or cannot synthesize them in high enough quantities), so they must be consumed in our diets or by dietary supplements. Vitamins D, B12, and K are exceptions; vitamin D may be synthesized in the body upon exposure to direct sunlight; and vitamins B12 and K may be produced by a healthy flora of bacteria existing in the intestines. Research the DRIs (see Suggested Readings list) for specific references values and information concerning each vitamin. The vitamins are listed as follows:

- **Vitamin A (retinol):** An antioxidant; required for normal eyesight and a healthy immune system. Consumed beta-carotene (a phytonutrient carotenoid) is converted to vitamin A. Dietary sources of vitamin A are liver, fish, eggs, and cow's milk; dietary sources of beta-carotene are carrots, yam-sweet potatoes, cantaloupes, peaches, broccoli, apricots, and winter squash. Like vitamin A, carotenoids also require fat for proper absorption.
- **Vitamin C (ascorbic acid):** An antioxidant; taken to prevent or eliminate colds and allergies, and aids in the formation of bone and collagen. Dietary sources are oranges and other citrus fruits, green peppers, strawberries, tomatoes, dark-green leafy vegetables, and broccoli.
- **Vitamin D (calciferol):** Required for proper calcium and phosphorus absorption into the body, and the formation of strong bones and teeth. Vitamin D is the sunshine vitamin, which is produced in the body upon direct exposure to sunlight (ultraviolet rays). Ideally, direct exposure to sunlight without sunscreen should be the main method by which the body acquires vitamin D. Yet because of the reduction of the ozone layer, exposure to sunlight needs to be properly controlled to prevent skin damage and skin cancer. Dietary sources are fortified milk (e.g., fortified cow's, rice, and almond milk), fortified cereals, eggs, and coldwater fish (e.g., salmon, mackerel, tuna, sardines, and herring). Take high-quality vitamin D supplements as recommended by a physician to compensate for the lack of sun exposure.
- **Vitamin E:** An antioxidant; an agent in skin health and wound healing. Dietary sources are unrefined vegetable oils (e.g., olive oil, almond oil, and sunflower oil), avocados, raw nuts, seeds, and whole grains.
- **Vitamin K:** An antioxidant; needed for blood clotting and bone metabolism. Dietary sources are dark-green leafy vegetables, broccoli, liver, eggs, green tea, canola oil, olive oil, and soybean oil, and it is synthesized in humans by intestinal bacteria. <u>Note</u>: Individuals who are on anticoagulant medication need to consult their physician about reducing intake of foods consisting of vitamin K.

- **Choline:** Required for proper structure of membranes, synthesis of neurotransmitter acetylcholine, liver function, and fat metabolism. Dietary sources are legumes, liver, cow's milk, whole grains, and egg yolks.

A group of water-soluble vitamins not included in the above list are the B vitamins. This group of at least eight vitamins plays essential roles in biosynthesis, energy production, cellular metabolism, and maintaining proper function of enzymes, coenzymes, the brain, and the nervous system. In the past, the eight individual vitamins were not yet identified and were considered to be one vitamin—vitamin B; as they were identified, each was given a specific number. These eight vitamins are usually found in foods such as lean meats, organ meats, fish, whole grain cereals, cow's milk, whole wheat breads, and green leafy vegetables. Vitamin supplements that consist of the eight B vitamins define them as the B complex. These eight B vitamins are as follows:

- Vitamin B1 (thiamin)
- Vitamin B2 (riboflavin)
- Vitamin B3 (niacin)
- Vitamin B5 (pantothenic acid)
- Vitamin B6 (pyridoxine)
- Vitamin B7 (biotin)
- Vitamin B9 (folic acid, folate)
- Vitamin B12 (cobalamin)

Dietary Supplements

It is important to compensate for the deficiency of essential vitamins and minerals in our diets by taking dietary supplements, but consult your physician or nutritionist before you or your children start taking them. Do not try to single-handedly diagnosis your and your family's vitamin and mineral deficiencies; this can lead to many health problems. Your physician or nutritionist will consider your personal health issues before determining which supplements and the amount of them you need to take. Avoid vitamin and mineral overdosing or poisoning by taking your physician's advice. Do not buy cheap tablet or capsulated dietary supplements. Purchase high-quality dietary supplements that are readily absorbed and utilized by the body. Dietary supplements should be organic (free of pesticides and hormones, and not synthetic). It is important to research the different brands of dietary supplements before purchasing them. Ask your physician or nutritionist for a list of companies that supply high-quality dietary supplements. If you cannot afford to buy these dietary supplements, go to your nearest health-food store and request the best quality dietary supplements on the shelf. Take as directed by your physician, nutritionist, or as directed on the bottle; take with plenty of water.

Low-Carb Veggies

Low-starch vegetables, such as dark leafy greens, lettuce, broccoli, cauliflower, celery, bok choy, asparagus, green bean pods, and sprouts (bean and alfalfa) consist of vitamins, minerals, phytonutrients, and much fiber, and at the most, low levels of complex carbohydrates. Light-colored green leaf vegetables, such as iceberg lettuce, consist of mostly water and very little complex carbohydrates. Iceberg lettuce has minimal nutritional value, but it is a great food for filling up the stomach. One can eat fresh, organic iceberg lettuce until completely full without gaining weight. Dark leafy greens, such as spinach, collards, Swiss chards, turnip, mustards, kale, Brussels sprouts, and dark leaf lettuce (green and red) are very healthy sources of fiber, with low levels of complex carbohydrates. The darker the leaf, the more minerals, vitamins, and phytonutrients it contains. Dark-green leafy vegetables are high in calcium, iron and the phytonutrient chlorophyll, which is an antioxidant that is also good for digestion, building healthy blood, and increasing oxygenation. Spinach, kale, collard greens, romaine lettuce, and Brussels sprouts consist of the carotenoid lutein, which prevents degeneration of the macula, a part of the eye retina. Spinach also consists of an extremely high level of the phytonutrient oxalic acid, a scavenger of minerals such as calcium, magnesium, sodium, zinc, and potassium. Healthy individuals can usually eat foods consisting of oxalic acids without problems. Excess oxalic acids form oxalates (salts formed by oxalic acids combining with calcium or other minerals), which are excreted in the urine of a healthy individual. Individuals with a malfunctioning kidney (which crystallizes excess calcium salts into kidney stones) or mineral deficiencies (see Part IV for information about osteoporosis) should limit eating foods high in oxalic acids such as spinach and rhubarb. Other vegetables consisting of oxalic acids are Swiss chard, kale, celery, legumes, parsley, yam-sweet potatoes, and beets. Spinach, which is high in iron, calcium, vitamin C, and the phytonutrient flavonoids, is an excellent source of anti-cancer agents and antioxidants. Cabbage (green, red, and purple) has many minerals, vitamins, fiber, and phytonutrients and is great for building up the internal lining of the gut and improving digestion. In addition, the phytonutrient anthocyanin is found in red and purple cabbage. Unpasteurized sauerkraut (fermented cabbage) is high in probiotics; it's great for establishing a healthy balanced flora in the digestive tract.

Many types of seed-bearing fruits and spore-bearing mushrooms that are low in carbohydrates are often categorized as vegetables. Foods, like the tomato, summer squash (e.g., zucchini, and yellow and crooked neck squash), okra, pepper, eggplant, cucumber, olive, and avocado, are scientifically defined as botanical fruits but by cooking standards, these foods are prepared as vegetables. In this book, these foods are defined according to their cooking standards and are thus called vegetables. These vegetables are not only low in complex carbohydrates, but contain high levels of minerals, vitamins, and exist in a wide range of colors due to the various phytonutrients. It is important to include these vegetables in your five to seven servings per day. An organic tomato ripened naturally on a vine grown in rich soil is extremely tasteful and chock full of vitamins and phytonutrients. Tomatoes are known for their high content of two carotenoids: lycopene, an antioxidant that can help prevent cancer (e.g., prostate cancer), and lutein, an inhibitor of a macula degenerative disease. Unlike most plant-derived foods, tomatoes need to be cooked before the body can absorb and reap the full benefits of their lycopenes. Eggplant consists of the phytonutrient flavonoids, which are heart disease and cancer-preventive antioxidants. Avocados and olives, unlike most vegetables, which consist of no or very little fat, are high in healthy monounsaturated fat and a host of phytonutrients. Edible mushrooms, belonging to the biological kingdom fungi, are high in minerals, protein, and many other nutrients. Mushrooms are usually prepared and cooked as vegetables and make a great addition to salads and sautéed vegetable dishes.

Medicinal Veggies

Garlic, onions, peppers, and ginger are vegetables that have a pungent taste and an abundance of phytonutrients with medicinal qualities. Garlic, known for centuries for its therapeutic benefits, is a natural antibacterial agent that kills off infectious "bad" bacteria and viruses without eliminating the "good" bacteria in our gastrointestinal tract. Allicin is the powerful phytonutrient in garlic that is responsible for the stinky smell and the majority of its healing qualities. If my son and I consume a clove of garlic as soon as we feel the beginning symptoms of a cold, cough, congestion, or sore throat, by the next morning the problem is usually gone. In addition, garlic reduces the risk of asthma as it helps to eliminate congestion and colds, which often trigger asthmatic symptoms. Garlic also consists of phytonutrients known for lowering high blood pressure and high blood-cholesterol levels. Many people take capsules of natural organic garlic to help lower cholesterol levels (consult physician before taking garlic capsules for this).

Cooked garlic reduces the potency of allicin and gives foods (meat and vegetables) a wonderful savory flavor. Yet it is the raw natural garlic that needs to be consumed for all of the health benefits to be reaped, especially as an antibacterial and antiviral agent. Although raw garlic is very strong (pungent), it usually does not cause any digestive problems in healthy children and adults, but if any discomfort does occur, cook lightly in foods. In a healthy individual, the only side effect that may occur after the consumption of organic garlic (raw or in capsule form) is that the pungent odor will probably begin to penetrate through the pores in your skin. The smell of it may be offensive to other people who share your surroundings. If you are routinely surrounded by others at your place of employment or in a classroom, consume garlic in small quantities many hours before leaving home; this will help alleviate the stench. At home, it is best to let everyone in your household consume it. This is not just so that the entire family can reap the health benefits of garlic, but if everyone at home stinks, then no one notices or becomes offended by the pungent smell.

The onion is rarely eaten independently but is used to increase the flavor of main dishes, salads, and sandwiches. It consists of the phytonutrient quercetin, and its pungent taste is due to sulfur-containing volatile oils, which often lead to tearing of the eyes. Sharing many of the same healing qualities as its close relative, garlic, the raw onion has been claimed to help cure colds, coughs, sore throats, asthma, and sinus congestion, and prevent the symptoms of high cholesterol and high blood pressure.

Ginger, believed to be originally from Asia, has been used for centuries as a cooking spice and as a medicinal agent. A mixture of volatile oils contained in ginger is responsible for ginger's pungent taste and most of its medicinal qualities. Ginger is known for inhibiting colds, nausea, vomiting, gas, motion sickness, stomach and menstrual cramps, and morning sickness. The safety of ginger consumption for pregnant women is not fully understood, and the advice of a physician is required before taking ginger for morning sickness.

The degree of hotness in the most common peppers ranges from the no-heat bell peppers to the hot jalapeños and even hotter habañeros. The compound in peppers that is responsible for the spicy heat is the phytonutrient capsaicin. Capsaicin is known to prevent the transmission of pain (a topical cream consisting of capsaicin is often applied to inhibit pain such as in arthritic patients) and has anti-inflammatory effects. People, especially those with sinusitis or congested lungs, eat peppers to help clear and thin the mucus in sinuses and lung passages. Capsaicin is also a great agent for decreasing the intake of calories. Eating hot peppers often helps curb the appetite; thus, it can decrease excess weight gained in some individuals. Peppers are also an excellent source of vitamin C. It is best to buy organic peppers, because pesticides are found in the skins of inorganic peppers at high quantities. People who suffer from heartburn, stomach ulcers, and irritable bowel syndrome should eat hot peppers with caution; hot peppers are known to increase irritation in those who suffer from these problems. Cooking or freezing peppers does not decrease the potency of capsaicin.

High-Carb Veggies

Many vegetables are high-carbohydrate foods, which contain fiber, starch (complex carbohydrates), and sugar (simple carbohydrates) in various concentrations. These vegetables are also packed with vitamins, minerals, and phytonutrients. High carbohydrate vegetables are those of the "root" group (which is inclusive of tuber and bulb vegetables) such as white potatoes, turnip roots, jicama, onions, garlic, rutabaga, parsnips, carrots, beets, ginger, garnet yams (i.e., yam-sweet potatoes, which are orange in color), and sweet potatoes (which have light brownish skin and yellow flesh). The root vegetable highest in sugar (sucrose) is the beet, which is also high in iron, potassium, vitamin C, fiber, and phytonutrients. Beets, which are dark red due to the phytonutrients betacyanin and betaine, are known to help prevent cancer, eliminate the symptoms of fatty liver in alcoholics, and aid in the synthesis of red blood cells. When I was a little girl, I had problems with anemia. After taking supplements to rebuild my blood back to normal, my mom then fed me beets to help maintain my elevated red blood cell count. Betaine hydrochloride (the acid form of betaine, which is also derived from beets) is often taken under the advice of a physician to help individuals who are low in stomach hydrochloric acid. (Caution: Take betaine hydrochloride only if advised by a physician.) Some of the root vegetables high in starch are carrots, yam-sweet potatoes, and sweet potatoes. Other vegetables high in starch are winter squash (e.g., spaghetti, acorn, and butternut squash, and pumpkin), corn, plantains, and legumes. Carrots, yam-sweet potatoes, and winter squash are also high in the phytonutrient beta-carotene and many minerals and vitamins. Corn is actually a starchy grain that should be consumed in moderation; too much of it can increase triglyceride levels. Plantain, a relative to the yellow banana, is often cooked unripened (before the majority of its starch turns to simple carbohydrates) as a vegetable.

Legumes (e.g., split peas, kidney beans, lima beans, black-eyed peas, lentils, butter beans, sweet peas, snow peas, navy beans, black beans, and soybeans) are a family of high complex-carbohydrate vegetables that give a low glycemic index value. Many legumes, especially soybeans, also contain the phytonutrient isoflavones, which are often consumed to help provide hormone balance in women, prevent cancer, and maintain strong bones (before consuming soybeans, see information in this chapter about the soybean isoflavones controversy). Eating an adequate amount of beans along with whole grain brown rice is a great combination of fiber, complex carbohydrates, and complete protein. Bean and bean products, especially soybeans and soy products, are widely purchased by individuals and added to many processed foods to increase dietary protein levels. By eating beans, you can reduce the amount of meat (a high source of protein that is high in saturated fats and cholesterol) in your diet, and help to maintain normal blood sugar, triglyceride, and cholesterol levels. However, eating too many starchy legumes, such as lima beans, butter beans (white lima beans), and black-eyed peas, along with sugary and fatty foods, can increase the glycemic load (see chapter 43 for information about glycemic load) and calorie intake to a level that results in weight gain. I know of many sedentary overweight individuals who unsuccessfully attempted to lose weight on a legume diet, but instead, continued to gain weight by eating much sweet cornbread, pork fat, butter beans, and black-eyed peas.

Many individuals who maintain a low-carbohydrate diet and avoid eating high-carbohydrate vegetables often feel lethargic and depleted of energy. It is very important to eat starchy vegetables not only for their nutritional and fiber content but also to maintain a constant level of energy. Individuals with diabetes should carefully monitor the source and amount of starch consumed daily and help keep their blood glucose constant by adding foods such as beans and yam-sweet potatoes to their diets.

Most of the root vegetables have a moderately low to medium glycemic index value when raw. But when these vegetables are cooked until mushy, their complex carbohydrates are broken down into smaller sugars, which usually increase their glycemic index value within the high range. A baked white potato especially gives a high glycemic index value and should be consumed sparingly. Carrots give a low glycemic index value when raw but become a high glycemic index food after being boiled until soft.

Soybean Controversy

The nutritional value of soybeans and soy products is a topic of much controversy. The majority of individuals with opinions on this issue are divided into two camps. One camp argues that soybeans and soy products are very healthy to eat for the following reasons: Soybeans and soy products are excellent cholesterol-free sources of protein and calcium; thus, they are considered to be an excellent substitute for meat and dairy products. Soybeans and soy products also consist of healthy phytonutrients such as the isoflavones (which are phytoestrogens) and the phytic acids (which are present in the hulls of legumes, grains, and seeds). Generally, soy isoflavones give hormonal balance to individuals who suffer from symptoms of premenstrual syndrome (PMS) and menopause. Plus, the intake of soy isoflavones helps to prevent breast and prostate cancer, deterioration of bone density (thus may help to prevent osteoporosis), high cholesterol levels, and potential heart problems. Furthermore, phytic acids found in soy are important antioxidants that prevent free radicals from damaging the digestive system and act as anti-cancer agents in the colon. This camp also argues that basically, the only individuals who need to avoid soybeans and soybean products are those who are allergic to them.

The second camp argues that although certain fermentation methods known to modify soybeans to a more digestible form were developed in ancient Asia, these methods are not commonly used to process soybeans in our society today. Therefore, consumption of soybeans and soy products is unhealthy and should be avoided. The main culprits responsible for making soybeans and soy products unhealthy are the enzyme inhibitors (compounds that prevent digestive enzymes in the gut from properly breaking down proteins) and the phytic acids (which bind not only free radicals but also essential minerals, such as calcium, zinc, and magnesium). These enzyme inhibitors, which were broken down—along with the other soy proteins—by ancient Asian fermentation processes are high in modern-day soy products. After consumption of modern-day soy products, these enzyme inhibitors prevent digestion of soy proteins, which causes much gastrointestinal stress and triggers an allergic reaction. In addition to enzyme inhibitors and phytic acids, soybeans are high in calcium. But the binding of phytic acids to calcium and other minerals may prevent the proper absorption of minerals into the body. And if phytic acids are consumed in high enough quantities, the malabsorption of minerals may lead to malnutrition and diseases such as osteoporosis. Furthermore, this camp argues that there are possible adverse effects of soy isoflavones on hormonal balance; thereby, the intake of soy isoflavones may increase problems in breast cancer patients and the risk of breast cancer in healthy women. They believe, however, that more studies need to be performed before the carcinogenic (cancer-causing) effects of soy isoflavones can be fully understood.

Based on my own interpretation of the previous arguments and my personal experiences with soy over the years, I am between the two camps. My opinion is as follows: There is not yet enough data to significantly support the health benefits or adverse effects of soy isoflavones, enzyme inhibitors, and phytic acids concerning most health issues, so with regard to consuming soybeans and soy products, moderation is required (neither avoidance nor overindulgence). High intake of soy isoflavones may affect hormonal balance, but if one consumes soybeans and soy products in moderation, it is unlikely that this low intake will noticeably affect hormonal balance in most individuals. It is best *not* to take soy isoflavones dietary supplements for this purpose before consulting with your physician. As for the enzyme inhibitors and phytic acids, cooking and boiling will break down the majority of them in most foods. However, the quantity of enzyme inhibitors and phytic acids is so high in soy that fermentation is required to adequately reduce the levels of them. The Asians invented a fermentation process that modifies the nutrients (e.g., oligosaccharides and protein) in soybeans to a form that is easily digestible, eliminates most enzyme inhibitors and phytic acids, and allows proper absorption of minerals and other nutrients into the body. Properly fermented soybean products in the form of tempeh (fermented bean cake), miso (soybean paste used for soup), fermented tofu, and fermented soy milk are quite healthy, and the majority of the population can reap the benefits of consuming them without problems. However, most tofu is not fermented but curdled (which inadequately removes the phytic acids and enzyme inhibitors), and soy milk is usually unfermented. If consumed in moderation, unfermented tofu and soy milk still may be a relatively good source of protein and other nutrients for most individuals (those with health issues such as mineral malabsorption deficiencies may need to avoid them). Other unfermented soy products, such as soy protein, are added to many different types of processed and packaged foods. Do not overindulge in these foods. Often, when a food additive is portrayed as being nutritional (e.g., high in fortified protein, vitamins, and minerals), it is too often not properly modified to a form that is easily digestible, and then, it is added to numerous food products. As a result, we end up overeating it. If we want to be healthy, we need to practice temperance. Consume soybeans and soy products in moderation.

Cooking, Purchasing, and Growing "Veggies"

Eat plenty of raw organic vegetables daily. Raw organic vegetables are not only high in nutrients but in digestive enzymes. Digestive enzymes from raw produce (vegetables and fruit) are needed to properly breakdown consumed foods. Cooking vegetables easily destroys these digestive enzymes. Improper digestion of a cooked meal without raw produce is inevitable as only the digestive enzymes that were synthesized by the body are present in the gastrointestinal tract. As a result of improper digestion, the consumed cooked food begins to rot in the gastrointestinal tract and produce acidic and gaseous compounds. People who suffer from heartburn caused by these gaseous compounds often mistake their symptoms as the result of excess hydrochloric acid being produced in the stomach (see the section about "Heartburn and Indigestion" in Part IV).

A salad prepared with fresh organic green leafy and other vegetables is a very healthy source of digestive enzymes as long as a high-calorie salad dressing or other high-calorie condiments are not added to it. Use a little lemon juice as a dressing or one consisting of olive oil and balsamic vinegar. When steaming or boiling green leafy vegetables, such as turnip greens, mustard greens, collard greens, and Swiss chard, be certain not to overcook them. Instead of pork, try adding smoked turkey to season cooked greens (see Part V for recipe).

Cooked vegetables such as broccoli, zucchini, and green beans are acceptable when steamed, boiled, grilled, baked, or broiled, but do not overcook them. Remember, the longer vegetables are cooked, the more nutrients and digestive enzymes are destroyed. It is best *not* to fry vegetables. Frying destroys nutrients and digestive enzymes and also increases calorie intake. However, if you must fry, then stir-fry the vegetables quickly in a wok, using a small quantity of healthy oil, such as olive oil or sesame seed oil. Stir-frying requires very little oil and allows a short exposure to heat.

Again, it is best to make sure that vegetables are organically grown. Pesticides often infiltrate every cell of many types of inorganic vegetables. It is important to eat vegetables that are labeled as organic—naturally grown without being tainted with pesticides, hormones, antibiotics, or genetic modifications. Look for vegetables labeled 100 percent organic with a USDA logo. Fresh organic vegetables are more expensive and spoil quicker than inorganic vegetables, so make sure that you purchase only what you plan to eat in the near future. Plus, it is important to clean and store fresh vegetables appropriately to help prevent the growth of food-borne pathogens that are responsible for food poisoning. Health-food stores, farmers markets, food co-ops, and some conventional grocery stores and supermarkets carry organic produce; however, vegetables from farmers markets are usually the freshest.

It is acceptable for a person to eat as many low-complex carbohydrate vegetables as needed to fill up the stomach so that one is not hungry. But the amount and type of meats, carbohydrates, and fats consumed daily needs to be monitored. Dieting is often not successful because people cut their meal portions down to the point that they are constantly hungry. Then, once the diet is over, they eat a tremendous amount of all the unhealthy foods that consist of many calories, and they gain all, if not more, of the weight back. The key to losing weight is to first fill up on low-carbohydrate vegetables, specifically, the green leafy vegetables, and then, eat the high-carbohydrate vegetables and other healthy foods.

Avoid canned vegetables as much as possible; canned vegetables are usually high in preservatives, such as table salt and calcium chloride, and other additives. Plus, many nutrients are destroyed during the canning process. However, it is probably better to eat canned vegetables than no vegetables at all. Before heating, rinse the canned vegetables with water to remove unwanted salts and other additives. Most frozen vegetables, usually being free of most additives, are acceptable to consume but are not as healthy as the raw ones. Canned legumes are acceptable but dried beans are the best. Most canned beans and peas are preserved with salt. Canned baked beans are also usually high in high-fructose corn syrup and should be avoided. If you do eat canned baked beans, prepare them without adding extra sugar and syrup; if anything, add a little stevia. Canned chili beans are often high in additives such as artificial flavorings and colorings. When making chili, it is best to season regular canned beans, or better yet, start from scratch by cooking dried beans.

Dried beans and peas are high in proteins and other nutrients but consist of indigestible complex carbohydrates (e.g., oligosaccharides and polysaccharides) that produce bothersome flatulence when metabolized by bacteria in the lower gut. To reduce cooking time and hard to digest complex carbohydrates, rehydrate dried beans or peas by soaking them in water for about eight to ten hours. These gas-producing saccharides can be further reduced by adding baking soda to the beans (about ½ teaspoon per four cups of beans) while soaking, or by boiling them briefly before the soaking period. Yet because baking soda is known to cause damage to valuable vitamins such as thiamin (i.e., vitamin B1), it is probably better to not add soda but just briefly boil before soaking. Soaking the beans and peas will help soften their outer skin and allow a large portion of the indigestible saccharides to be released into the water, which then can be poured off. Yet soaking also results in the release and pouring off of the healthy minerals, vitamins, fiber, and phytonutrients along with the indigestible saccharides. Thus, if it is more important for you to retain valuable nutrients than to prevent flatulence, it is best to cook the beans and peas without soaking and pouring off the nutrients and saccharides. Cooking beans and peas over a low heat for an extended period of time without pouring off anything, however, will allow the breakdown of a large portion of the indigestible saccharides to shorter and more digestible ones and still maintain the nutrients.

If your village has no health-food stores or does not supply organic vegetables in grocery stores and supermarkets, petition for a change. Write a letter that includes a list of signatures from potential customers who will commit to purchasing organic vegetables from local stores and send them to store owners. Grow an organic vegetable garden in your own backyard (please do not use pesticides, herbicides, or inorganic fertilizers). If you don't have a yard, plant some vegetables in pots. Also, find a plot of land in your village in which you and others can grow a community garden. I know that in my village there are plots of land in which different groups (e.g., the 4-H Club, an organization that exposes the youth to agriculture) grow a garden every summer and then eat or sell the produce. Possibly as a science or home economics project, teachers and volunteers can help classes of grade school or junior high school students plant a garden in the spring, and then the students and their families can continue to cultivate it in the summer months. When growing your garden, please harvest, eat, and share your vegetables with others. Then, freeze the remaining vegetables for the winter months. The main point that needs to be understood is that everyone should eat plenty of vegetables every day to be healthy.

* * *

Work-Study: Points to Ponder

1. Do you eat five to seven servings of vegetables a day? If not, are you willing to increase your intake?

2. Do you eat fresh, organic, raw vegetables or inorganic ones? Do you eat only frozen or canned vegetables? How do you cook your vegetables?

3. How many salads do you eat a week? What ingredients and type of dressings do you add?

4. Do you eat a wide variety of vegetables to increase your consumption of minerals, vitamins, and phytonutrients? Are you willing to

add garlic, onions, peppers, and ginger to your diet?

5. Do you take vitamin and mineral supplements with or without the advice of a physician? Do you rely totally on food to supply all of your minerals and vitamins?

6. Do the grocery stores in your village provide fresh inorganic vegetables or fresh organic vegetables? Do you have health-food stores, farmers markets, or a food co-op in your village? If not, what are you willing to do about it? How do you plan to purchase your organic vegetables?

7. Do you grow your own vegetables or know someone who does? If not, are you willing to start? If so, are you willing to share with others? Are you willing to freeze some for winter months?

8. In the following chart, list the kinds of vegetables, including legumes, and the approximate number of servings of each that you presently eat per week. Then, as you begin to eat healthier and focus on the Repent 6 R's Step Process, expand the variety of vegetables in your diet, and increase your servings. Record the improvements of your new diet in the "Future" column. A serving is equivalent to approximately one cup of raw green leafy vegetables or a half-cup of other vegetables, raw or cooked.

Present		Future	
Vegetables	Servings (per week)	Vegetables	Servings (per week)

Chapter 40

Fruits, Nuts, and Seeds

As the apple tree among the trees of the wood, so is my beloved among the sons. I sat down under his shadow with great delight, and his fruit was sweet to my taste. (Song of Solomon 2:3)

Definition of Fruit

Fruit, the ripened seed-bearing part of a plant, is rightfully defined as nature's dessert. Most fruit is sweet and consists of simple carbohydrates (e.g., fructose, glucose, and sucrose). Yet because the carbohydrate and calorie contents of most types of fruit are low, fruit can be consumed in high quantities without the problem of gaining weight or increasing blood sugar to high levels. Plus, fruit is extremely healthy and consists of vitamins, minerals, phytonutrients, and fiber. We need to consume at least three to five servings of fruit every day; this may seem like a tremendous amount, but in reality it isn't. Due to genetic engineering, pesticides, herbicides, inorganic fertilizers, preservatives, and the lack of minerals in the soil, today's fruit consists of fewer nutrients than in the past. Years ago, cross-fertilization was used to alter the size, preservation, taste, color, and shape of fruit. Today, genetic engineering is used to alter the traits of fruit by inserting within its chromosomal DNA a strand of recombinant DNA that codes for the particular traits of interest. The FDA has assured that inorganic genetically modified foods that are stamped with its approval are safe and do not need to be identified or labeled as genetically modified. Yet we must bear in mind the possibility that genetic engineering may decrease nutritional value of certain foods due to the manipulation of genes and interference of pathways that produce nutrients. As a result, it is healthiest—not to mention tastiest—to eat fresh, naturally ripened, organic fruits as often as possible.

It is important to eliminate exposure to all types of pesticides by eating organic fruits instead of inorganic ones. Inorganic fruits are often genetically modified with cloned pesticide genes, and thus are saturated with internally produced pesticides. Although not known to cause any major health problems, internally produced pesticides may interfere with the natural production of nutrients and decrease the nutritional value of inorganic fruit. Many of the different types of externally introduced pesticides are bound tightly to or absorbed through the skin and inner flesh of inorganic fruits and cannot be entirely removed by washing. Some of the externally introduced pesticides are also taken up from the soil into the plant and can be found within every cell of inorganic fruits. Thus, cutting away or peeling off the skin of inorganic fruits removes some but not all externally introduced pesticides. Most inorganic fruits with soft edible skins (e.g., grapes, apples, pears, cherries, and strawberries) absorb more pesticides than those protected by tough inedible skins (e.g., bananas and pineapples). The skin of most fruits and the area directly below it consist of many fibers and the majority of the phytonutrients. It is important to always eat organic fruits so that the edible skin and the nutrients coupled with it can be safely consumed without the exposure to pesticides. The total effect of long-term exposure of our bodies to small quantities of unhealthy pesticides is not yet fully understood. Therefore, it is not wise for us to assume that consumption of low levels of pesticides is not a potential health risk.

Phytonutrients

Phytonutrients, which are chemical compounds with nutritional and therapeutic benefits, are produced by plants and found in plant-derived foods such as vegetables, fruits, grains, nuts, and seeds. Unlike protein, carbohydrates, fat, minerals, vitamins, and water, the phytonutrients are not essential for our daily existence but are extremely important in maintaining good health and preventing diseases (e.g., cancer). Many phytonutrients fight against diseases by playing the role of an antioxidant, which neutralizes free radicals and oxidants. Both free radicals and oxidants are reactive oxygen-containing chemicals that cause oxidative damage to cellular structures, similar to the way oxygen in water causes the rusting of iron. Phytonutrients are also enhancers of the immune system, killers of cancer cells, and repairers of damaged deoxyribonucleic acid (DNA). Two of the most commonly known types of phytonutrients are the carotenoids, which are responsible for the red, orange, and yellow color of vegetables and fruits; and the flavonoids, which are found in grapes, blueberries, citrus fruits, and legumes. There are many different kinds of carotenoids, but the three most well known are beta-carotene (pro-vitamin A), which is found in foods such as carrots, yam-sweet potatoes, and peaches; lycopene, which is found in foods such as tomatoes, pink grapefruit, and watermelon; and lutein, which is found in foods such as spinach and kale. Two of the most well-known flavonoids are the anthocyanins, found in grapes and berries, and the isoflavones, which are found in legumes, especially soybeans. There are many other well-known and important phytonutrients that are not mentioned here. Overall, my main intent is to increase your awareness of some of the phytonutrients and the vegetables (see chapter 39) and fruits (see information in this chapter) that consist of them. Once you change your eating habits, it would be great to further expand your knowledge by reading more about phytonutrients (see list of Suggested Readings).

Fruit Groups

Many varieties of fruits were created for our enjoyment. The different types of fruit have been scientifically categorized by botanical classifications. Yet here, I will classify fruits based on my own personal experiences with them. The most common fruits, which are supplied all year in markets, are great to eat as a snack or at any meal. This group includes bananas, apples, and grapes. A banana, a high-energy tropical food consisting of both complex and simple carbohydrates, is known for its high levels of potassium, vitamin B6, and fiber. Its outer peeling makes the banana a very convenient fruit to eat, but I find that once purchased, it doesn't last very long. It is best to buy only the amount of bananas that you plan on eating in the near future, and keep them in a cool and dark place. When I was a child, a yellow banana lasted many days before it began to spoil, but these days, I can buy a yellow banana one day and in a couple of days, it may be overly ripened.

An apple—whether green, yellow, or red—a day helps keep the doctor away is a true saying. It is very beneficial to start the day off with a fresh, naturally ripened, organic apple, as it provides the body with the flavonoid quercetin and vitamin C required to decrease inflammation and enhance the immune system, respectively. High in fiber, apples also consist of pectin (a soluble fiber that regulates cholesterol levels in the blood) and insoluble fiber (which helps to maintain a healthy digestive system). Most mornings I start off the day with an apple, and throughout the day, I eat slices of apple along with almonds to stabilize my blood glucose. I also ingest raw, unpasteurized, unfiltered, organic apple-cider vinegar, which is full of minerals, vitamins, and other nutrients. It is known for its many medicinal qualities, such as killing "bad" bacteria and yeast overgrowth, improving digestion, and metabolizing fat, and for making a great addition to salad dressings. In contrast, refined, distilled white vinegar and distilled apple-cider vinegar are devoid of nutrients. These distilled vinegars and the foods consisting of them can make a body extremely acidic and cause overgrowth of yeast; thus, these should be avoided, especially by those suffering from acidosis or yeast syndrome.

Seedless green grapes seem to taste the same all year around—sweet, yet a little sour. I have noticed that the red and purple grapes seem to be more seasonal than the green grapes. Red and purple grapes are sweet and are known to contain high levels of anthocyanins and the phytonutrient resveratrol, which give these grapes their dark, intense colors. These phytonutrients are antioxidants that may help regulate cholesterol levels in the blood, improve digestion of foods, eliminate heart disease, and prevent cancer. Red wine is an excellent source of anthocyanin and resveratrol. Yet because alcohol can lead to alcoholism and other adverse effects, it is best to avoid alcohol (see chapter 41 for more details about drinking alcohol). Resveratrol supplements can be purchased at some health-food stores, but do not take them without the advice of a physician. It is important to realize that the concentration of resveratrol that is considered to be beneficial in grapes and red wine is much lower than that supplied in dietary supplements; thus, these supplements should be taken with caution. Organic raisins (dried grapes) are a good source of phytonutrients, iron, and other minerals and make an excellent addition to cereals. Eat raisins in moderation, however, because their sugar content is highly concentrated (see Points to Ponder 6 in chapter 43 for more details).

Some common fruits may be found in the market all year around but are only sweet and delicious during the spring, summer, or early fall months. These include pears, peaches, apricots, plums, melons, berries, and the acidic fruits. Pears, high in copper, vitamin C, and fiber, give antioxidant protection and promote a healthy digestive system. The pear is a good healthy fruit for those who are allergic to other types of fruit; most people with food allergies are not allergic to pears. Peaches and apricots consist of fiber and beta-carotene. Plums and prunes (the dried version of plums) consist of fiber, vitamin C, and anthocyanins. The melons (watermelon, cantaloupe, and honeydew) are high in beta-carotenes, lycopene, and vitamin C. Watermelon has a high glycemic index value, but it consists of mostly water and a small amount of simple carbohydrates; thus, its glycemic load (see chapter 43 for definition) is low and a moderate quantity of it may be safely consumed without spiking blood glucose in most individuals.

Some of the common berry fruits are cherries, strawberries, raspberries, gooseberries, blackberries, boysenberries, bilberries, blueberries, and cranberries. Berries are packed with anthocyanins and many other types of phytonutrients, which are antioxidants that fight against cancer, prevent high cholesterol, and eliminate growth of pathogens. Extremely high levels of anthocyanins and many other phytonutrients are found in blueberries and bilberries, making them excellent sources of antioxidants. Cherries are high in anthocyanin and lycopene. Cranberries, which consist of flavonoids, are famous for eliminating urinary infections by inhibiting the attachment of *E. coli* in the urinary tract. Avoid cranberry juice that is high in sugar, which feeds "bad" bacteria and yeast and increases blood glucose levels.

The acidic fruits are oranges, tangerines, lemons, limes, grapefruits, and pineapples. Oranges are high in vitamin C and many types of phytonutrients (e.g., citrus flavonoids) that are excellent antioxidants. Fresh-squeezed organic orange juice is a great way to start the morning and an excellent source of vitamins and phytonutrients when suffering from a cold. Lemons and limes consist of citrus flavonoids that are great for digestion and are known for their antibiotic effects. Lemon and lime juice are often added to foods as a method to eliminate the growth of pathogens. Grapefruits give excellent antioxidant protection, aid in weight loss by speeding up body metabolism, and contain high levels of vitamin C and lycopene. Pineapple is well known for its enzyme, bromelain, an anti-inflammatory compound that heals bruises and burns and promotes digestion by breaking down proteins. Eat fresh pineapples; bromelain is destroyed during the canning process.

Exotic tropical fruits are not as common in the States but are very delicious and contain many vitamins, minerals, fibers, and phytonutrients. This group includes fruits such as the papaya (high in digestive enzymes), kiwi, pomegranate, acai (high in anthocyanins), guava (extremely high in vitamin C), black sapote, kumquat, persimmon, lychee, passion fruit, figs, and mango (high in carotenoids). Although much research has been completed, more research needs to be done to further identify and understand the role of the different phytonutrients found in these and all fruits.

Nuts and Seeds

Organic raw nuts are an excellent source of protein, healthy unsaturated fats, fiber, and phytonutrients. Most nuts have no or low levels of carbohydrates and a glycemic index value near zero. Almonds are amongst the healthiest of the nuts and are an excellent source of omega-9 fatty acids (e.g., oleic acid), protein, and vitamin E. Almond butter, also high in these nutrients, is a great substitute for peanut butter and an excellent spread on bread and celery sticks. Snacking on almonds along with apples between meals and before bedtime is a great way to inhibit abnormal fluctuations in blood glucose and insulin release. People suffering from diabetes and hypoglycemia should snack on almonds and apples regularly. I often eat a handful of raw almonds and slices of apple before bedtime, or when there is a long period of time between meals, to help maintain a steady blood-glucose level. Along with a host of healthy phytonutrients, almonds consist of the phytonutrient phytic acids. The potential risk of phytic acids inhibiting the absorption of minerals in individuals with mineral deficiencies (see Part IV for information about osteoporosis) can be reduced by roasting or removing the outer hull layer of almonds. Many other nuts, such as pecans, Brazil nuts, pistachios, macadamias, and hazel nuts, are also high in healthy proteins, phytonutrients, and omega-9 fatty acids, thus making them a healthy snack. The walnut is an unusual nut in that it has a very high content of healthy omega-3 fatty acids. Cashews and peanuts contain healthy phytonutrients, omega-9 fatty acids, and low levels of carbohydrates but are often covered with mold, which is a problem for those suffering from yeast syndrome. Furthermore, peanuts are not really nuts but belong in the legume family and consist of isoflavones (which are also commonly found in soybeans). Individuals with asthma or food allergies should avoid eating peanuts. Coconuts also are not nuts but are actually large seeds consisting of cholesterol-free saturated fat and phytonutrients that help to protect the body from pathogenic infections. Other organic seeds, such as flax, sesame, sunflower, and pumpkin seeds, consist of unsaturated fatty acids (flax seeds are high in omega-3s, sesame seeds in omega-9s, and sunflower and pumpkin seeds in omega-6s), minerals, vitamins, protein, and phytonutrients.

Purchasing and Preparing Fruits, Nuts, and Seeds

Fruits, nuts, and seeds that are fresh and organic are high in vitamins, minerals, phytonutrients, and digestive enzymes. Eat fresh, naturally ripened, organic, whole, unpeeled fruit as much as possible. It is the skin and the area directly underneath the skin that carries the majority of the fibers and phytonutrients. Cutting and smashing fruit exposes it to oxygen and light, which destroys much of its phytonutrients. To help reduce the loss of nutrients, do not select fruits that are under ripened, ripened by unnatural means, or overly ripened and bruised. Make certain to wash and store fresh fruits appropriately to prevent growth of food-borne pathogens that cause food poisoning. Avoid spoilage of fruits by refrigerating them or storing them in a dark cool place, and purchase no more than will be consumed in the near future. In order to increase the shelf life of fresh, inorganic fruit and make it look more appealing as it ages and loses its nutritive content, it is often covered with a waxy paint-like substance before it is put on the market. A few times in the past, I found that something like shellac was chipping off the outer peeling of inorganic oranges and the internal slices had a chemical taste. This problem was easily eliminated by buying organic oranges.

Canned or frozen fruit is usually limited in its nutritional value as it is no longer fresh and often preserved and sweetened with sugar. Canned fruit can be found packed in either heavy syrup (i.e., corn syrup and sugar), light syrup (i.e., sugar and water), fruit juice (e.g., juice concentrate diluted in water), or water sweetened with an artificial sweetener (e.g., sucralose). The color of canned fruit is often preserved with natural additives that are considered to be relatively safe to consume, such as citric acid (the acid found in lemons and other citrus fruits) and ascorbic acid (vitamin C). Like canned fruit, it is not uncommon to find packaged frozen fruit sweetened with sugar and its color preserved with ascorbic acid and citric acid. In short, canned and frozen fruit are not as healthy as fresh fruit, but are definitely better than no fruit at all. Make sure to purchase canned and frozen fruits that are organic, and before eating them, rinse them off with water to remove excess sugar and other additives.

Dried fruits such as raisins, prunes, figs, pineapples, apricots, bananas, and cranberries are concentrated in phytonutrients, minerals, vitamins, and fiber because most of the liquid is removed. But the intrinsic whole sugar in dried fruits is also concentrated; plus, they are usually preserved and further sweetened with added white sugar. Moreover, during the drying process, unhealthy sulfites are often added as a preservative. Read the ingredients and Nutrition Facts label to determine the amount of sulfites that are added to dried fruits; unfortunately, many products do not give this information. Avoid sulfite intake by drying organic fruits at home and using ascorbic acid and citric acid as color preservatives—do this only if you are willing to learn to properly dry fruits without the use of artificial preservatives so that they are free of harmful food-borne pathogens.

Cooking organic fruits or roasting peanuts, nuts, and seeds is not as nutritional as eating them fresh or raw. But if the freshness of these foods is slightly questionable and you cannot bring yourself to toss them out, it is best to kill possible food-borne pathogens by cooking or roasting these foods rather than eating them raw. Also, if you are mildly allergic to any of these foods, you may find that exposing them to heat may prevent an allergic reaction. However, even if you are only mildly allergic to these foods, especially peanuts and nuts, be extremely cautious because cooking and roasting them may not destroy the allergens adequately enough to be considered safe. If you are allergic to a particular food, it is safest to avoid it.

Support your local farmers market, food co-op, and health-food store. If your village does not have grocery stores, supermarkets, or health-food stores that market organic fruits and nuts, then petition for a change. Write letters and obtain signatures of potential customers who are willing to commit to purchasing organic fruits. Then, send the letters to the grocery store owners in your village. Learn how to freeze and can organic fruits for the winter months. Eat a peach, and plant the pit in your backyard. Grow strawberries, watermelons, and sunflowers in your garden or in pots. Instead of having shade trees in the yard, try planting fruit and nut trees.

* * *

Work-Study: Points to Ponder

1. Do you consume three to five servings of fruit a day? If not, are you willing to do so?

2. Are you willing to pay the higher prices of organic fruits and nuts in order to avoid eating inorganic ones? If not, is it because you think you cannot afford them? (See chapter 30 for discussion on the financial benefits of buying healthy foods.)

3. What types of fruits do you enjoy? Do you eat them as snacks, desserts, or with your meals?

4. Are you willing to replace a sugary desert with a piece of fruit?

5. Do you eat a wide variety of fruits to increase your intake of phytonutrients, minerals, and vitamins?

6. Do the grocery stores and supermarkets in your village sell an adequate amount of fresh fruits? If not, what are you willing to do about it?

7. Do the grocery stores and supermarkets in your village sell organic fresh fruits? Does your village have health-food stores? Is there a farmers market or food co-op nearby? If not, are you willing to do something about it? What changes are you going to make so that you will begin purchasing organic fruit?

8. In the following table, list the different kinds of fruits, nuts, and seeds and the approximate amount of each that you presently eat per week. Then, as you plan to eat healthier and focus on the Repent 6 R's Step Process, expand your list of fruits, nuts, and seeds, and increase serving size in the Future column. One serving is equivalent to approximately one whole apple, banana, or orange; a half-cup of fruit (chopped raw, canned, or cooked); or a quarter-cup of nuts, seeds, or raisins.

Present		Future	
Fruits, Nuts, and Seeds	Servings (per week)	Fruits, Nuts, and Seeds	Servings (per week)

CHAPTER 41

Water and Other Beverages

He turneth the wilderness into a standing water, and dry ground into water springs; and there He maketh the hungry to dwell, that they may prepare a city for habitation. (Psalm 107:35-36)

Chapters 41 and 42 explain the importance of consuming healthy types of water and salt in appropriate quantities to maintain good health. These chapters also define the different types of beverages, spices, and condiments that should be added to or eliminated from a healthy diet.

Water: Essential to Life

When I was in middle school, my science teacher called all the students in the class "big drips." He continued to explain that our bodies are made up of approximately 70 percent water; thus, it is essential that we consistently drink plenty of it. A person's daily water intake (in ounces) should be equal to about 50 percent of his or her total body weight (in pounds). Based on the above, an adult weighing between 120 and 160 pounds needs to drink around 60–80 ounces (approximately eight to ten 8-oz. cups) of water daily, and a person weighing 260 pounds should drink about 130 ounces (approximately sixteen cups) of water daily. Because drinking that many cups (e.g., sixteen cups) of water would probably be a difficult task for most, it is recommended that adults drink at least eight 8-oz. cups a day. Unfortunately, most people do not drink even the minimum requirement of water; they live the majority of their lives partially dehydrated. Many unknowingly suffer from symptoms of dehydration, such as constant thirst, headaches, extremely dark urine (urine should be a light pale yellow; not clear or dark), constipation, acidosis (see information in this chapter on body pH), water retention, and toxins trapped in the body. Because many people are not familiar with the symptoms of dehydration, they often confuse their thirst with hunger. When you haven't had anything to drink in a while and you feel hungry, drink water first, and then eat later. This will not only help keep the body hydrated but control overeating. If your stomach is full of water, there is not as much room for food.

We need to constantly replenish our bodies with water, not only to keep hydrated but to wash away toxins and pathogens to which our bodies are constantly exposed. Leave it to humans to have polluted two of the most essential substances we need to exist: water and air. This makes it challenging to provide everyone with clean drinking water. Fortunately, the safety standards of drinking water—tap and bottled water—are regulated by the government—the EPA and the FDA, respectively. Many believe that bottled water is purer than tap water. This may be true in some instances, but the purity of bottled water, just like tap water, depends on the location of the water well and the purification process. In some places, certain bottled water companies pump their water from wells positioned in inner cities. I have difficulty understanding how this water could possibly consist of fewer pollutants than water from the tap. Basically, this bottled water (labeled as purified drinking water) is nothing more than city water that has been disinfected and purified by a bottled-water treatment plant.

Bottled Water

I personally have problems with the plastic bottles manufactured to contain water. During many years at the bench in research laboratories, it has been etched in my brain not to perform experiments with solutions contained in plastic bottles. This is because it is well understood that the chemicals within the plastic of bottles will leach into the contained solutions and affect experimental data. Every time I drink bottled water, I automatically assume that I am also consuming toxic plastic. The plastic of recyclable water bottles leaches into the contained water, especially when exposed to increased temperatures and stored over time. Although not economically feasible, it would be much healthier to purchase water bottled in sterile glass or food-grade stainless steel containers (glass or stainless steel doesn't leach into water) rather than in plastic ones. When purchasing water bottled in plastic containers, do not store it for long periods of time (only buy what you plan to drink in the immediate future), and do not store bottled water at high temperatures (especially avoid exposing it to direct sunlight or sunlight through a car window). The longer bottled water is stored and exposed to heat, the more plastic will leach into the water. Plus, take the time to research the different types of plastic used in water bottles; not all plastic is created equal. Take the time to learn about the recycling codes labeled on the bottom of bottles; certain bottles tend to be made from higher grades of plastic that leaches into water at a slower rate than other grades.

Artesian water, purified drinking water, well water, mineral water, and spring water are the most common types of bottled water. The purest type of bottled water to purchase is sometimes hard to identify. It is important that you do your homework to determine which type of bottled water is best. My personal preference is artesian water because the method by which it is pumped out of the ground is known to remove more contaminants from water than most other methods. However, just because bottled water is artesian does not automatically guarantee that it is free from all contaminants; different brands and sources are purer than others. Again, do your homework. It's not only important to purchase the best type of bottled water but to also select the best source, treatment process, and brand of bottled water. Furthermore, although disinfected during the treatment process, bottled water is non-sterile, thus possibly exposed to bacteria during processing and bottling. It is best to refrigerate bottled water to prevent bacterial growth.

Like purity, the mineral concentration of bottled water also depends on the type, treatment process, brand, and source of the water. The mineral content of natural water should consist only of its original minerals, with no additional minerals added during processing. Yet certain types of bottled water contain minerals such as calcium, magnesium, and sodium that were added during the treatment process. A person's mineral deficiencies may help determine the amount of these added minerals that should be consumed, but these water additives are usually not as nutritive as those found naturally in food or in high-quality dietary supplements. In addition, because most diets contain excessive amounts of sodium, the majority of people should avoid water with added sodium. Ideally, most types of bottled water should be free of the minerals chlorine (which is used to disinfect tap water) and fluoride (which is added to tap water to help prevent tooth decay and maintain strong teeth). This is not always necessarily the case, as some bottled water has not been completely purified of these minerals. There is a growing concern that constant exposure to chlorinated and fluoridated tap water can be a potential health risk to many individuals, especially to children and the elderly. I know of many individuals who were advised by their physicians and dentists to drink bottled water instead of tap water in an attempt to decrease exposure to chlorine and fluoride.

Many physicians recommend drinking distilled water and cooking with it because it is free of all minerals and most contaminants. Others advise their patients not to drink distilled water or cook foods in it because it may cause malabsorption of essential minerals (see information on osteoporosis in Part IV) and acidosis. Because distilled water is pure, they claim that drinking it draws and depletes electrolytes and minerals out of the body and into the urine, and boiling food in it draws minerals out of the food into the water (i.e., it causes diffusion). If you choose to drink and cook with distilled water, consult your physician about possibly taking supplements to replenish the body of depleted minerals.

Carbonated water (e.g., seltzer and sparkling water) is pumped with carbon dioxide, which dissolves into carbonic acid (the bubbly fizz) in the presence of water by a process called carbonation. Although carbonated water is nothing more than a no-calorie fizzy beverage (usually consisting of very low levels of sodium; approximately 10 mg per 8 oz.), it is best to drink in moderation. Drinking much carbonated water and other carbonated beverages (such as soda and sparkling cider) may make the body extremely acidic, which prevents proper absorption of minerals. Plus, many individuals avoid drinking carbonated beverages because they claim that swallowing the acidic gas in it builds up stomach gas and causes indigestion and heartburn.

On the other hand, many others drink carbonated beverages as a way to help relieve indigestion and heartburn after eating a big meal. They claim that the bubbly acidic gas interacting with stomach gas produces enough pressure to push the mixed gas out through the esophagus. I used to agree with those who believe that carbonated beverages help to relieve stomach gas. Throughout my past, I often mistakenly used carbonated beverages to help with indigestion and heartburn. However, after I started my healthy diet and realized that it was one of the causes of my indigestion, I decreased the amount of carbonated water I drink (no more than 16 ounces in a week) to protect my body from becoming too acidic. In one day, it is best not to drink an entire glass of carbonated water; only drink a small amount at a time. Try adding a small amount to a beverage (e.g., add approximately 1–2 oz. of carbonated water to 6 oz. of a beverage, such as homemade organic fruit juice).

A temporary yet effective remedy for decreasing stomach gas after a big meal and preventing acidity in the body is to add baking soda to water (approximately 1/2 tsp. per 4–8 oz. of water under the advice of a physician), or take organic digestive enzymes and other organic dietary supplements, as directed by your physician. Be careful not to overdo the baking soda because too much of bicarbonate may cause the body to become too alkaline and prevent proper stomach digestion. Plus, do not exceed the maximal daily intake of 2.3 grams of sodium (see information in chapter 42 about total daily sodium intake) from consuming baking soda (1/2 tsp. of baking soda consists of approximately 600 mg of sodium). Too much sodium can lead to health issues such as high blood pressure. If you are at risk of developing high blood pressure or require specific sodium restrictions, first consult your physician before consuming baking soda. A more effective and permanent solution to decrease gaseous symptoms and prevent acidity is to eat organic fermented food products containing probiotics and fresh organic produce consisting of fiber and digestive enzymes. At first, you may find it is difficult to digest these healthy foods and will need to take dietary supplements to alleviate the gaseous symptoms. But as you continue to consume these foods, and develop a healthy digestive system and bacterial flora in the intestines, health issues such as heartburn, indigestion, and acidosis will begin to disappear.

Tap Water

If you decide to drink water from the tap, research the information concerning the purity of water in your local area to make certain that the water purity falls within the EPA regulations. Contact your local water officials and have them test a sample of your tap water for impurities. When possible, have a certified state lab listed by the EPA test a sample of tap water directly from your faucet. If you can afford it, a wise investment would be an EPA-approved water purifier and filter system for your home faucet, such as one consisting of reverse-osmosis filtration (i.e., a method by which pressure forces water through a membrane that retains the contaminants). This is an excellent way to ensure that you are supplied with safe drinking water that is free of chlorine, lead, mercury, pesticides, pathogens, and most other impurities!

Water pH

The pH (potential of hydrogen concentration) level of the water we drink is also important. The pH scale, ranging from 0.0 to 14.0, is used to measure the acidity or alkalinity of a solution. A solution with a pH less than 7.0 is acidic (high in cations—positive charged ions), while a solution with a pH higher than 7.0 is alkaline (high in anions—negative charged ions). A solution with a pH of 7.0 is neutral (neither acidic nor alkaline). Pure water that is healthy to drink should have a pH near 7.0. As our bodies are mostly water, the overall pH of our saliva and urine should be near neutral. If water goes in the body at a pH of about 7.0, it should come out of the body at a pH near 7.0. The pH values for urine and saliva are slightly acidic for most individuals; urine and saliva with a pH between 6.4 and 7.2 and blood with a pH at 7.4 are considered to be relatively healthy.

The pH of tap and bottled water is not tightly regulated by the EPA and FDA, respectively. Tap water from many locations and different brands of bottled water are often found to be too acidic or alkaline. It is important to test the pH of your drinking water. Contact local water officials and have them test the pH of your tap water, along with the level of contaminants. Buy pH paper and use it to check the pH of your drinking water. If your tap water is purified by a certified purifier filter system and is still too acidic or alkaline, then you might want to consider changing your method of purification or start buying bottled water. If the pH of the bottled water you are drinking is far from neutral (e.g., water with a pH not between 6.8–7.2), then change brands and types of bottled water until you find one with a pH that is near neutral.

Body pH

The acidic versus alkaline balance in the body is extremely important. The water we drink and the foods we consume help to determine the pH of our saliva, blood, and urine. Many people suffer from the pH of their urine, saliva and blood being either too acidic or alkaline. Everyone can determine the pH of their bodies by checking the pH of their saliva and urine. Buy a kit from the health-food store consisting of pH paper, a pH chart, and a list of acidic and alkaline foods. Test the pH of the first pass of your urine early in the morning and of your saliva after keeping your mouth free from any substances for at least two hours. If you discover that your urine and saliva are consistently too acidic or alkaline (out of the pH range of 6.4–7.2), then it is best to seek the advice of your physician (especially one who practices with a holistic approach) or a nutritionist.

Many Americans, suffering from the body being too acidic, need to drink more water and alter their diets (e.g., by consuming less animal protein, which is very acidic) in order to bring their body pH closer to neutral. Some of the symptoms of being too acidic are acidosis (i.e., a pathologic condition caused by the accumulation of acid or increased concentration of hydrogen ions in the body), heartburn, acid reflux, tension, inflammation, obesity, osteoporosis, arthritis, gout, menstrual cramps, infected gums, tooth decay, muscle spasms, constipation, irritable bowel syndrome, allergies, bacterial infections, yeast syndrome, sinusitis, migraine headaches, acne, atherosclerosis, nervousness, irregular heartbeats, mineral malabsorption, and a lack of oxygen being supplied to the body. Moreover, if you have a pathogenic (e.g., bacterial or yeast) infection, it is difficult for your body to reach neutral, unless the infection is eliminated. The opposite is also true; it is difficult for pathogens to die off and remain gone unless the body becomes less acidic and reaches a pH near neutral. The best way for your body to reach and maintain a pH near neutral is to adopt an alkaline-forming diet that is low in the acidic-forming foods and beverages. Examples of common acidic foods and beverages are white flour, refined grains, sugar, meat (especially red meat and other meat that is high in protein), wheat, caffeine, cow's milk, most dairy products, coffee, and carbonated beverages. Generally, alkaline foods such as raw vegetables, greens, fruits, almonds, wheatgrass, green tea, and stevia will help bring an acidic body to a pH near neutral. Some of the foods that are great for bringing an acidic body closer to neutral may be somewhat surprising. For example, after digestion, acidic fruits—such as oranges, limes, lemons, grapefruits, and pineapples, and organic fermented food products like unpasteurized, unfiltered apple-cider vinegar; unpasteurized sauerkraut; and plain, cultured, low-fat yogurt—will help bring an acidic body near neutral. However, a person with heartburn issues should minimize irritation of the stomach by eating small amounts of acidic fruits and fermented food products at first, and then gradually eating more as digestion improves and the stomach becomes less sensitive.

For many years, I had suffered from symptoms of being acidic (which were caused by my past diet of white sugar and white flour and continually taking prescribed antibiotics). In my new healthy diet, I work at keeping my body pH within the healthy range by balancing my diet with the right amount of both healthy acidic-forming foods (e.g., poultry, whole grains, and beans) and alkaline-forming foods (e.g., green-leafy vegetables, fruits, and plain, cultured, low-fat yogurt). At times when my body pH is still too acidic, I often add to my daily intake of water certain organic or natural alkaline-forming substances such as liquid chlorophyll (free of alcohol); unpasteurized, unfiltered, apple-cider vinegar; slices of fresh lemon sweetened with stevia; or baking soda (about 1/2 tsp. to 64 oz. of water). When consuming baking soda, be careful not to exceed the maximum daily intake of 2.3 g of sodium (read information in chapter 42 about sodium intake).

Water–Drinking Tips

The following are a few water-drinking tips that have been handed down to me from past generations. My family uses these tips to help improve (not cure) digestive problems that produce stomach gas and acidic toxins in our bodies. Water is neutral, so we drink it to dilute and help neutralize these acidic toxins. Plus, we drink most of our water at room temperature rather than drinking ice water. Enzymes in the stomach have the highest activity at body temperature. Cold water can slow down enzyme activity and decrease digestion. Occasionally, a couple of hours after a big meal, we add baking soda to our water as a temporary relief of gaseous symptoms (see previous information on baking soda in this chapter; add to water only if advised by your physician). Gas and flatulence is often caused by constipation, and mild cases of constipation can often be relieved by drinking one to three glasses of warm water. During a meal, we do not drink excessive amounts of water because too much water can dilute the hydrochloric acid in the stomach and decrease rate of digestion (normal pH of gastric juices is between 1.0—2.0). We drink the majority of our daily water in between meals.

Other Beverages

Most purchased beverages should be avoided. Soda, processed fruit juices, and other bottled drinks consisting of extremely high quantities of sugar or high fructose corn syrup are unhealthy. Diet beverages are unhealthy because of the artificial sweeteners. Since processed fruit juices are concentrated with sugar, it is best to squeeze your own orange juice or lemonade from organic oranges and lemons. Use blenders and processors to make homemade organic fruit and vegetable juices. If want to sweeten juice, use natural sweeteners, such as xylitol and stevia. Blend plain, cultured, low-fat yogurt with fruit and fruit juices to make smoothies (see Part V for recipe). If you decide to purchase juices, buy organic vegetable juices, green juices (e.g., wheatgrass and chlorophyll), and frozen and bottled fruit juices with no added sugar. When diluting frozen concentrated fruit juices, add twice as much volume of water to the juice than that instructed on the package (this will lower the sugar content). Also, dilute bottled fruit juices with water by adding approximately 6 oz. of water to 2 oz. of juice, and make sure that you drink *no more* than half a glass (4 oz.) of bottled fruit juice per day. Diluting bottled fruit juice with excess water will not decrease your sugar intake if you end up consuming the entire frozen container or bottle in one day. When it comes to bottled fruit juice, I drink no more than two cups, 16 oz. or less, per week—8 oz. of fruit juice diluted with 24 oz. of water, and the other 8 oz. of fruit juice added to a smoothie (see Part V recipe); one smoothie takes me two or more days to complete. If you want to give your bottled fruit juice a little fizz, add a small amount of carbonated water to it (e.g., dilute 2 oz. of juice with 2 oz. of carbonated water and 4 oz. of regular water). Remember, carbonated water is acidic and should be consumed with caution. Also, when purchasing organic fruit juice (especially orange juice), it is often safest to buy bottled fruit juice that is pasteurized (even though this destroys many healthy nutrients) to prevent exposure to food-borne pathogens.

Avoid beverages containing additives, such as caffeine and other stimulators. Caffeinated beverages (e.g., coffee, soda, and tea) can lead to a caffeine addiction, dehydration, acidic effects in the body, and other health issues. Unsweetened decaffeinated herbal teas, such as green tea or ginger tea, may be good to drink for their medicinal benefits. Green tea consists of powerful antioxidants and is known to increase fat metabolism (for the medicinal properties of ginger, see chapter 39). If you decide to sweeten these herbal teas, use natural sweeteners, such as xylitol and stevia. Instead of hot coffee and teas, try drinking a hot cup of water with a twist of lemon (see Part V for recipe).

Avoid drinking alcohol (all types). Many people believe moderate consumption of red wine, which is high in the phytonutrients anthocyanin and resveratrol, is great for preventing heart disease, reducing stomach indigestion, and relieving other common ailments. Although I do not drink alcohol, I do believe that these benefits exist. However, the many health problems (e.g., alcoholism, weight gain, liver deterioration, diabetes, high triglycerides, acidosis, yeast syndrome, cancer, heart problems, neurological disorders, and high blood pressure) that stem from excessive alcohol drinking outweigh the benefits. There exists a thin line between moderate (one or two 5 oz. glasses a day for the average-sized adult male) to excessive drinking (three or more 5 oz. glasses a day for the average-sized adult male) of wine. The best way to eliminate the temptation of overindulgence and prevent alcoholism and the health problems associated with it is not to drink.

* * *

Work-Study: Points to Ponder

1. How much water do you drink a day? Do you ever suffer from dehydration? Do you drink at least eight cups (8 oz. each) of water a day?

2. Do you think you frequently confuse being dehydrated with hunger? If so, are you willing to drink water when feel hungry?

3. Do you drink bottled or tap water? If you drink bottled water, do you drink it within a couple of weeks of buying it? Or is it stored for long periods of time?

4. What type and brand of bottled water do you drink? Have you researched the different types, sources, and brands of bottled water to determine which ones are the best? Have you researched the different type of plastics used to make the bottles? If so, describe what you found out.

5. Do you drink tap water? If so, have you researched the purity of the water in your area? Have you had a sample of your tap water tested?

6. A water purifier and filter system consisting of reverse-osmosis filtration usually removes more pathogens and impurities than a basic water filter or purifier. Do you have a purifier and filter system? If not, are you willing to purchase a system consisting of or equivalent to reverse-osmosis filtration in the future?

7. Do you check the pH of your body regularly? If not, are you willing to start? If your urine pH is consistently out of the healthy range (6.4–7.2), are you willing to change your diet and consult a physician about your problem? Explain.

8. Do you drink soda and other carbonated beverages? If so, how often? Are you willing to stop drinking soda? Are you willing to decrease your intake of carbonated water?

9. Do you drink fruit juice or vegetable juice often? If you drink much fruit juice, are you willing to prepare and squeeze your own, instead of purchasing it from the store? Are you willing to dilute purchased fruit juice with extra volumes of water and limit the amount consumed?

10. How often do you drink coffee or caffeinated soda? If you are addicted, are you willing to break the habit?

11. Do you drink tea often? If so, is it caffeinated, decaffeinated, herbal, or other?

12. Do you drink alcohol often? If so, are you addicted? Are you willing to stop? Do you drink alone, or are you a social drinker? Explain.

13. Calories from beverages (including spirits) high in sugar, fat, or alcohol can quickly add up if you drink too much of them. If most of the beverages in your diet are high in calories, then add up the amount of sugar, fat, or alcohol calories that you consume daily from them. Note: Check Nutrition Facts label on beverages: one calorie of carbohydrate (sugar) equals four grams of sugar; one calorie of fat equals nine grams of fat; and one calorie of alcohol equals seven grams of alcohol.

Beverage type	Amount of Calories Consumed (kcal)

Total Amount of Calories from Consuming Beverages in a Day = ______ kcal

14. How many calories a day do you drink? Do these beverages take you out of your daily calorie intake range? If so, are you willing to replace these beverages with water?

15. I improved my health by completing the Repent 6 R's Step Process. I increased my water intake, released certain beverages from my diet, and replaced them, as described on the next page.

Released	Replaced
• Water (tap and bottled) 2–5 cups (8 oz. each) a day	• Water (tap and bottled) 8 cups (8 oz. each) a day. Add chlorophyll, a slice of lemon, baking soda, unpasteurized, unfiltered apple-cider vinegar, or stevia to water when needed to help keep my pH near neutral.
• Soda approximately 5-7 cans (12 oz. each) a week	• Diet soda approximately 6 oz. (less than half a can) once a week; carbonated water no more than 16 oz. total in one week (including amount added to fruit juices).
• Much sweetened cranberry juice every day	• Bottled fruit juice about 16 oz. total per week. Dilute a total of 8 oz. with tap water and carbonated water per week, and add about 8 oz. to a smoothie (see Part V for recipe) about once a week.
• Sweetened iced tea 5 times a week	• A cup of decaffeinated unsweetened iced tea (preferably herbal tea) 3–5 times a week; sweetened often with xylitol or stevia.

• Hot caffeinated or herbal tea sweetened with white sugar every day	• Hot decaffeinated herbal tea (sweetened with xylitol or stevia) few times a month; drink hot lemon water often (see Part V for recipe).

Determine to which changes you are willing to commit in your daily intake of water and other beverages as you focus on the Repent 6 R's Step Process. In the following table, list your improvements and the beverages that you are willing to release and then replace with healthier ones.

Release	Replace

CHAPTER 42

Salt, Spices, Herbs, and Condiments

Salt is good: but if the salt have lost his saltness, wherewith will you season it? Have salt in yourselves, and have peace one with another. (Mark 9:50)

Salt, Sodium, and Daily Intake

Salt, a compound composed of the minerals chloride and sodium, is essential for all living things. The difference between the types of salt depends on how it is handled and processed. Food-grade salts, which are used to preserve and season foods, consist mainly of two types: table and sea salt. Table salt is processed from raw rock salt and refined into unnaturally shaped crystals that are bleached white, and depleted of its moisture, trace minerals, and everything it originated with except the sodium chloride. Just to make its appearance appealing to the consumer, table salt is processed into an unnatural substance that is difficult for the body to properly utilize. Unlike table salt, organic sea salt consists of crystals that are naturally shaped, dull colored, and composed of many trace minerals and moisture. Because it is organic, it is healthier, tastier, and better utilized by the body than table salt. Be aware that not all salt labeled as "sea salt" is organic and unrefined. It is important to look at the properties of sea salt (i.e., its color, texture, and shape) to determine if it is organic or refined.

Check the label on the package to see if the salt is supplemented with iodine (an essential mineral required for the proper function of the thyroid) by a process called iodization. Plain table salt does not consist of iodine, and organic sea salt generally contains very little. Most manufacturers supply both plain and iodized salt. A minimal amount of daily iodine is needed to maintain proper function of the thyroid and prevent iodine-deficiency diseases, but the dietary intake of iodine is usually in excess, as iodized salt is consumed in high quantities. However, those who are avoiding salt because of the health issues associated with it may need to include other sources of iodine to their diets. Seafood (including seaweed) contains high levels of iodine naturally, but if enough of it is not consumed, iodine supplements may need to be taken under the advice of a physician. It is important to seek medical advice before taking these supplements because a deficiency as well as an overdose of iodine may lead to a malfunctioning thyroid.

It is essential for our bodies that we consume salt. Our bodies need sodium and chloride electrolytes for proper function of the digestive system, neuronal (nervous) system, muscles, heart, brain, etc. The problem is, however, that we usually consume more salt than the body requires. Healthy foods can become unhealthy with the addition of too much salt. Sodium is the culprit in salt that needs to be monitored to prevent health issues such as high blood pressure. Your total sodium intake in one day should be no more than 2.3 grams, which is equivalent to the amount found in about one teaspoon (approximately a total of 6 grams) of table salt. The sodium found in baking soda (sodium bicarbonate; one teaspoon contains approximately 1200 mg of sodium), baking powder (sodium aluminum sulfate; one teaspoon contains approximately 480 mg sodium), and preservatives (e.g., sodium nitrite, sodium sulfite, sodium phosphate, and monosodium glutamate) should also be included when calculating the total daily intake of sodium. As table salt and other additives consisting of sodium are used as seasonings and preservatives, the large quantities of sodium that are found in processed, canned, and packaged foods are amazing. If many processed, canned, and packaged foods are included in your diet, it becomes extremely difficult to keep your total sodium intake below the maximum limit of 2.3 grams a day.

Many steps can be taken to help eliminate the intake of excess sodium. Read the Nutrition Facts label on foods to determine the amount of sodium that is in each serving. Select foods such as canned vegetables and soup that are labeled as reduced salt, no salt, or low sodium. Some of the excess sodium can be removed from certain processed, canned, and packaged foods by rinsing them several times with water.

Processed meats can be soaked in water to remove excess sodium. Dilute the sodium content of soups by adding extra volumes of water. Most processed sauces and gravies have a high quantity of sodium and should be avoided or at least diluted. Soy sauce that is fermented properly would be a healthy food additive if it wasn't for its high salt content; because of this, it should be used sparingly when seasoning foods. Unpasteurized sauerkraut is an excellent source of probiotics, but the intake of its high salt content needs to be monitored. Those who need to reduce their salt intake should select other low-sodium sources of probiotics, such as plain, cultured, low-fat yogurt; unfiltered, unpasteurized, apple-cider vinegar; and probiotic capsules. At restaurants, request that foods be prepared without salt and monosodium glutamate (MSG), a preservative that is high in sodium and in glutamate, which can cause major problems in brain and neuronal function; and ask that sauces and gravies be served on the side. Eat foods free of sodium, such as fresh, organic vegetables and meat. If not fresh, buy frozen vegetables and meat, which have less sodium than canned vegetables and processed meat. Add salt only to foods free of sodium, and use organic sea salt—this is the healthiest of the salts. Even though organic sea salt is healthier than table salt, don't add it in excess; add just enough of it to barely enhance the taste.

Spices and Herbs

Instead of just adding organic sea salt, it is important to make healthy foods taste good with added spices. If your taste buds are satisfied, you will more likely stick with your healthy diet and not crave junk food. Season foods with spices such as organically grown cinnamon, cloves, chili pepper, nutmeg, ginger, paprika, sesame seed, celery seed, mustard seed, curry, garlic, onion, basil, black pepper, oregano, sage, cilantro, dill weed, parsley, rosemary, and thyme. If you use seasoning blends, make sure that these blends do not contain salt. Most spices are herbs that have medicinal effects when taken at a high enough dosage. When added in small quantities to enhance the taste of foods, herbs usually do not significantly affect bodily functions. Organic non-irradiated herbs can be a great alternative to synthetic medicine when correctly understood and researched. In order to reap full benefits and avoid possible adverse effects, medicinal herbs must be taken at the correct dosage prescribed by a physician (usually one practicing with a holistic approach). Some of the most common types of medicinal herds are aloe vera, ginseng, nettle, chamomile, licorice, green tea, raspberry leaf, slippery elm bark, saw palmetto, Echinacea, dandelion, peppermint, turmeric, ginkgo biloba, grape seed extract, and spirulina. Do not diagnose your own medical case or take herbs for their medicinal benefits before you consult your physician. When I was a little girl, my family's homeopathic doctor advised us to take a high-quality aloe vera juice as a preventive remedy for overall gastrointestinal and digestive health. Today, my family is still reaping the benefits as we continue to take it for this reason.

Condiments

Healthy foods that are low in calories can quickly become very fattening with the addition of unhealthy condiments. For example, a healthy, green-vegetable salad with tomatoes, onions, cucumbers, carrots, a lean skinless chicken breast, and vinegar-oil dressing can soon gain many calories if you also add ingredients such as croutons, crackers, bacon bits, beef, grated processed cheese, and a high-calorie dressing. Add a low-calorie dressing to salads, such as organic lemon juice, a low-fat ranch dressing combined with plain low-fat yogurt, or a vinaigrette dressing made up of vinegar (e.g., unpasteurized, unfiltered, apple-cider vinegar or balsamic vinegar) and oil (e.g., extra virgin olive oil or flaxseed oil). Prepare sandwiches with hummus, horseradish, mustard, low-fat mayonnaise, extra virgin or virgin olive oil mayonnaise, mayonnaise plus plain, low-fat yogurt combination, reduced-sugar ketchup, and ketchup plus tomato paste combination, instead of using condiments loaded with unhealthy fats and sugar. When cooking, add low-fat and low-sugar condiments to foods. Use lemon and lime slices, chili peppers, salsa, and unpasteurized, unfiltered, apple-cider vinegar to add zest to foods. It is best to avoid creams, creamed sauces, and gravies, but if eaten occasionally, you can prepare creams and sauces with mostly low-fat milk instead of using all light cream, and make gravies with defatted meat drippings and whole wheat flour instead of with white flour browned in saturated fat. At a fast-food or sit-down restaurant, request that the condiments be put on the side, and then do not add all of them. Add just enough to enhance the flavor.

* * *

Work-Study: Points to Ponder

1. Do you eat a lot of processed, packaged, or canned foods? Do you take the time to calculate the approximate amount of salt you consume daily? If so, is it less or more than the required one teaspoon a day?

2. Have you been diagnosed with high blood pressure? If so, how much sodium do you consume in a day? Is it more or less than the 2.3 grams per day limit?

3. Most processed, canned, and packaged foods consist of a high quantity of sodium. When preparing processed, canned, or packaged foods, do you add more salt? Do you rinse or soak these foods with water before eating them to help remove excess sodium? Do you buy foods that consist of no or low sodium?

4. The best way to decrease your intake of sodium is to buy fresh, organic foods that are free of sodium. Describe ways in which you are willing to increase your consumption of these foods.

5. Which type of salt do you use to prepare your food: table salt or organic sea salt? If you commonly use table salt to season foods, are you now willing to use organic sea salt? Describe ways in which you would be willing to use other types of spices.

6. How do you maintain the required daily intake of iodine? Do you use iodized salt? Do you consume seafood or take dietary supplements?

7. When eating at home or in a restaurant, do you add more salt to your plate of food? If so, why?

8. At a restaurant, do you request that your meals be prepared without salt? Do you request that creams, dressings, gravies, and other condiments be added on the side?

9. If you are using high-calorie condiments, what changes are you willing to make in your condiment selections to decrease calorie intake? Are you willing to prepare and eat condiments with fewer calories and less sodium?

10. List below the foods that you consumed for one day and the amount of sodium in them. Then add up the total amount of sodium consumed in one day. If your daily sodium intake is more than 2.3 grams, continue to adjust your diet accordingly.

Food type	**Amount of sodium per serving (gm)**	**Number of servings consumed**	**Total sodium consumed (gm)**

Total Amount of Sodium Consumed in a Day = ______ grams

Chapter 43

Snacks, Desserts, and Sweets

They found an Egyptian in the field, and brought him to David, and gave him bread, and he did eat; and they made him drink water; and they gave him a piece of a cake of figs, and two clusters of raisins; and when he had eaten, his spirit came again to him: for he had eaten no bread, nor drunk any water, three days and three nights. (I Samuel 30:11-12)

This chapter lists different types of snacks, desserts, and sweets that are relatively healthy to eat and can be added to your diet if you are willing to practice self-control.

Snacks

Unhealthy (junk-food) snacks are one of the major ways that many of us consume empty calories consisting of white sugar, white flour, trans fat, saturated fat, caffeine, and other additives. We eat unhealthy snacks during a work break, as a reward for any job well done, or just for personal enjoyment. After eating the unhealthy snacks, we immediately reach an intense high, followed by a sluggish lull. Soon, we find ourselves eating more unhealthy snacks to repeat the process all over again. At night, we love to sit in front of the TV set or curl up with a book, and eat countless calories of enjoyable unhealthy snacks.

Unhealthy snacks should be avoided and replaced with healthy ones. Healthy snacks can be used to help maintain a constant sugar level in the bloodstream. If you have problems with your blood-sugar level dropping throughout the night, eat a healthy snack before going to bed. I discovered that eating a handful of almonds and a few slices of apple before going to sleep increases my undisturbed sleep time by approximately two to three hours. Healthy snacks between meals can also be beneficial in maintaining blood-sugar levels, thus providing the energy required to keep active throughout the day. The healthy snacks (e.g., almonds, fruit, and carrots) may not always be as appealing as snacks high in unhealthy fats (e.g., a bag of potato chips or a bowl of buttery popcorn) or simple carbohydrates (e.g., saltine crackers and chocolate chip cookies), but much of the healthy ones should be eaten anyway.

Some processed snacks are healthier than others, but even these healthier processed snacks should be eaten in moderation (see Points to Ponder #2 at the end of this chapter for a list of some of the acceptable processed snacks). These healthier processed snacks may give a glycemic index value that is within the low or medium range. But if these healthier snacks are consumed in high enough quantities, the total carbohydrate intake may spike blood-glucose, release surges of insulin, and increase triglyceride levels. The overall effect on blood-glucose levels from a specific snack or any other food can be determined by measuring the glycemic load, which is dependent on both the glycemic index value of a specific food and the total amount of carbohydrates packed in one serving size of it. Calculating the glycemic load of certain enjoyable foods that give a low or medium glycemic index value but are packed with carbohydrates can help you determine the amount of these foods you can safely eat in a day. As a result, this can help you control your overeating habits and prevent the spiking of your blood-glucose levels. It is also important not to overindulge in healthier snacks that are rich in fats. Remember that only 25 to 30 percent of your total calorie intake should consist of fat. Eating too much of a good thing (e.g., a snack high in "good" carbohydrates or healthy fats) will still cause you to gain weight. When eating healthier snacks, temperance must be applied.

Desserts and Sweets

For the average American, desserts and sweets are eaten at almost every meal and then between meals as snacks—this should not be done. Do not buy, bake, or eat unhealthy desserts. Avoid white sugar, white flour, and unhealthy fats and additives by observing the list of ingredients on the label of unhealthy desserts and sweets. Buy, bake, and eat only "healthier" desserts and sweets, which are desserts and sweets consisting of healthy ingredients such as whole grains, whole wheat flour, whole spelt flour, whole almond flour, unsweetened cocoa, and natural sweeteners (e.g., xylitol, stevia, and brown rice syrup), and don't eat them every day. Bake and bring a healthier dessert to special functions and holiday dinners. Make your own fruit yogurt smoothies (see Part V for recipe) and granola, and share them with your family. Buy unsweetened dark chocolate-covered almonds, but eat in moderation. Unsweetened dark chocolate made with cocoa is high in saturated fat, especially when it is made with food-grade cocoa butter, but it is also high in healthy flavonoids. Also, unsweetened cocoa makes excellent homemade desserts (see Part V for brownie recipe).

Hide these healthier desserts and sweets to help control overindulgence. *Out of sight, out of mind* is an old adage that can help reduce overeating. Put healthier store-bought or homemade cookies in a special cookie jar, place the jar in back of the pantry behind other food items, and only take one cookie at a time. Seal healthier pastries and breads in containers, and place them in cupboards behind pots and pans or in the back of the refrigerator. Bake a large batch of healthier baked goods, eat a small amount, and then divide the rest into sealable bags and freeze it for a later date. These steps will keep the healthier goodies out of sight as well as making them more difficult to retrieve, thus helping to limit the amount consumed.

If you do decide to eat unhealthy desserts, only eat them on special or rare occasions, such as your birthday. Don't celebrate everyone's birthday and every holiday by eating unhealthy desserts and sweets, or you will be eating them almost every day. Make sure you only eat a few bites, and chew each bite very slowly. I have developed the art of taking twenty minutes to consume three bites of my favorite unhealthy dessert. Afterwards, I am satisfied and do not want any more of it. Remember, we do not eat desserts (healthy or unhealthy) for the nutritional value but for the enjoyment, so eat them slowly and sparingly.

* * *

Work-Study: Points to Ponder

1. Describe your snacking habits. How often do you eat snacks? Do you eat healthy or unhealthy snacks? Are your snacks mostly junk food? Are you willing to stop eating unhealthy snacks?

2. Here is a list of snacks that I used to eat but now avoid and have replaced with healthy or healthier snacks.

Released	Replaced
• Potato chips, corn chips, caramel flavored rice cakes, and cheese puffs	• Sweet potato chips and yellow and blue corn tortilla chips
• Ranch dip and French onion dip	• Homemade guacamole dip, salsa, sour cream, hummus, and plain, cultured, low-fat yogurt
• Soda crackers and cheese	• Spelt sticks, whole wheat crackers, whole grain crackers, and low-fat aged cheeses
• Caramel corn and buttered popcorn	• Plain popcorn lightly salted and barely buttered with canola butter
• Pizza rolls and battered cheese sticks	• Whole spelt tortilla rolls and homemade salsa (see Part V for recipe)
• Granola bars	• Homemade granola
• Caramel apples	• Apples, carrots, other fruits, and fruit salads (see Part V for recipe)
• Candy bars, candy corns, Boston baked beans, and jelly beans	• Almonds, walnuts, unsweetened chocolate-covered almonds, sunflower seeds, raisins, xylitol mints, and xylitol or sorbitol sweetened gum

Below is a table for you to make a list of snacks that you usually eat but should avoid. Next, as you focus on the Repent 6 R's Step Process, list the healthy or healthier snacks that you plan to eat as you replace the old unhealthy snacks with healthier ones. Remember, the healthy snacks are fruits, vegetables, seeds, and most nuts. Healthier processed snacks should be eaten in moderation.

Release	Replace

3. Describe your dessert habits. How often do you eat desserts and sweets? Do you eat healthier or unhealthy desserts and sweets? Do you eat them daily or on special occasions? How might you bake healthier desserts and sweets? (See Part V for recipes.)

4. Here is a list of desserts and sweets that I used to eat but now avoid and have replaced with new, healthier ones.

Released	Replaced
• Ice cream, pudding, sherbet, and Popsicles	• Yogurt with blueberries; fruit smoothies (see family recipe in Part V); a scoop of low-fat, no-sugar ice cream sweetened with sorbitol (only on special or rare occasions).
• Gelatin desserts	• Fruit salad with sour cream (see family recipe in Part V).
• Chocolate-chip cookies, frosted shortbread cookies, and many other types of cookies.	• Homemade cookies (see family recipes in Part V) such as oatmeal raisin, chocolate-chip, ginger, and fruit cookies.
• Cakes, pastries, doughnuts, and brownies	• Homemade bread and pastries, such as banana bread, zucchini bread, scones, turnovers, and brownies (see Part V for family recipes). Homemade whole spelt doughnuts 1–2 times a year (see Part V for family recipe). Very small piece of unhealthy cake on special or rare occasions, such as birthday, weddings, and Christmas. Total of 1–3 small bites of unhealthy desserts ordered at restaurants.

Below is a table for you to make a list of desserts and sweets that you usually eat but should avoid. Next list the healthier desserts and sweets that you plan to eat as you focus on the Repent 6 R's Step Process and replace the old unhealthy ones. Remember, all desserts and sweets should be eaten rarely and sparingly.

Release	Replace

5. Read below to learn how to calculate the glycemic load of foods. The glycemic load of a food can be calculated for a particular serving size by using the following formula:

   Glycemic Load = (Glycemic Index Value ÷ 100)
   x Carbohydrate content per serving size (grams)

   The glycemic loads of foods are divided into three range groups:

   - low glycemic load (0–10)
   - medium glycemic load (11–19)
   - high glycemic load (20 and above).

   A glycemic load within the low range is the healthiest.

6. Below are the calculated glycemic loads for a standard serving size of blue corn tortilla chips and raisins (two healthier snack foods that I love to eat; each one with a medium glycemic index estimated to be around 65).

   Blue corn tortilla chips: A serving size of about 28 g (10 chips) contains about 18 g of carbohydrates.

   Formula: (Glycemic Index Value ÷ 100) x Carbohydrate content per serving size (g) = Glycemic Load

   Calculation: (65 ÷100) x 18 = 0.65 x 18 = 12

   The glycemic load for blue corn tortilla chips at this serving size is approximately 12, which is within the medium glycemic load range.

   Raisins: A serving size of about 40 g (¼ cup) contains 31 g of carbohydrates.

Formula: (Glycemic Index ÷ 100) x Carbohydrate content per serving size (g) = Glycemic Load

Calculation: (65 ÷100) x 31 g = 0.65 x 31 g = 20

The glycemic load for raisins at this serving size is approximately 20, which is within the high glycemic load range.

These calculations demonstrate that although both of these foods give a similar glycemic index value, I can only eat slightly over an 1/8 cup of raisins to reach a glycemic load similar to that after eating approximately 10 blue corn tortilla chips.

7. Calculate the glycemic load of the healthier snacks and desserts that you often enjoy so that you will know what size serving of them you can safely eat. The amount of carbohydrates in a standard serving size of a packaged food can be located in the Nutrition Facts label, and the glycemic index value of foods can be obtained from many different sources found on the Internet and in reference books (see list of Suggested Readings for a reliable source on glycemic index values).

   Your Favorite Snack Food ______________: A serving size of about ______ g contains _______ g of carbohydrates.

   Formula: (Glycemic Index Value ÷ 100) x Carbohydrate content per serving size (g) = Glycemic Load

   Calculation: (______ ÷ 100) x _______ = ______

8. To make sure your fat intake is not more than 30 percent of your total daily calorie intake (see chapter 36 for more details about fat intake), add up the amount of fat calories that are in your healthier snacks and desserts. Note: Check Nutrition Facts label on foods and oils for fat content; one gram of fat equals 9 calories of fat.

Type of Snack or Dessert	Amount of Fat Calories Consumed (kcal)

Total Amount of Fat Calories from
Consuming Snacks and Desserts in a Day = ______ kcal

Chapter 44

Restaurant Tips (Fast-Food, Sit-Down, and Buffet)

Whether therefore ye eat, or drink, or whatsoever ye do, do all to the glory of God. (I Corinthians 10:31)

Chapter 44 gives suggestions on how to eat relatively healthy meals when dining out at some of your favorite restaurants.

Preparing meals at home with organic, whole foods is the safest way to help control what we put in our bodies. Because most of us are caught up in fast-paced lifestyles, we often go out to grab quick-fixed, unhealthy meals. Yet if we take the time and effort to watch what and how much we eat, eating out can be relatively healthy. Here are a few tips to help us eat healthier while enjoying an occasional meal at our favorite fast-food, sit-down, or buffet restaurants.

Fast-Food Restaurant Tips

- Eat sandwiches in which the meat is broiled or grilled and not breaded or fried.
- Request condiments to be added on the side.
- Bring healthy whole grain bread from home to replace hamburger buns and bread on sandwiches.
- Eat only one slice of whole grain bread per sandwich, instead of two slices.
- Ask for extra lettuce or other vegetables on sandwich.
- Eat a green-vegetable salad instead of fries, and do not add processed cheese and croutons to the salad. If you desire dressing, ask for ranch, and only add half or less of the packet to the salad. If

you do not want salad, it is better to eat a baked potato (remember, however, this is a high glycemic index food), chili, or soup than an order of fries. Do not add processed cheese, butter, or bacon bits to a baked potato. Add only a small amount of sour cream (about half of one packet).

- Bring mini-carrots and sliced apples from home. Avoid ordering sliced fruits from fast-food menus, because a high quantity of preservatives and additives are added to sliced fruits to keep them looking fresh.
- Bring from home whole grain wheat tortillas or whole grain corn tortillas made with unsaturated fat to replace white flour tortillas. Order just the burrito filling (naked burrito) and eat it as is, or wrap it up in a whole grain tortilla.
- Avoid soda and juice all together. Drink water. If you order unsweetened drinks, sweeten with packets of xylitol and stevia brought from home.
- If you are allergic to preservatives such as sulfites and monosodium glutamate, it is important to avoid the food items that consist of them. Ask the restaurant cook or the manager how the food is prepared and which preservatives are added.

Sit-Down Restaurant Tips

- Bring healthy whole grain bread from home instead of eating white bread served with the meal. Some restaurants serve coarse, chewy whole grain breads that are good to consume.
- Request that all condiments, gravies, salad dressings, and sauces be added to the side; then, do not add all of them to your food. Use only enough to enhance flavor.
- Choose lean-cut meats and fresh fish as entrées. Make sure meat is cooked well done.
- Request that foods be prepared free of salt and preservatives such as sulfites and monosodium glutamate (MSG).
- Add minimal salt to foods cooked with no salt. Squeeze lemon juice on fish and chicken for seasoning. If you decide to order beef (although it's better to eat fish or chicken), ask for minced garlic or

horseradish as a condiment.

- Split an entrée with someone in your party, and then each order a separate salad.
- Order soups containing many vegetables and very little cream or cheese.
- Eat grilled, broiled, baked, and sautéed foods, instead of fried and breaded.
- Ask for extra lettuce on sandwiches, and replace white bread with one slice of whole grain bread from home.
- Order vegetables (raw, grilled, or steamed).
- Eat brown rice or a baked yam-sweet potato instead of mashed potatoes and gravy or fries. A small baked potato with a little sour cream is usually healthier than whipped mashed potatoes with added cream gravy. Yet remember that the glycemic index value of a baked potato is very high. Diced garlic potatoes should give a lower glycemic index value (within the medium range) than a baked potato.
- Avoid sodas, juices, and spirits. Drink water; add a slice of lemon for flavor. If you want to sweeten unsweetened drinks, bring packets of xylitol and stevia from home.
- Enjoy the atmosphere and the company. Eat slowly and engage in conversation. If dining alone, read a book, magazine, or newspaper.
- Do not overeat. As soon as you reach the point of feeling comfortably full, stop. Box the remainder of the food and take it home for the next meal.
- Say no to desserts. Encourage others at your table to avoid dessert. But if you must have a dessert, buy only one dessert, share it with everyone at the table, and eat it slowly. Do not buy a dessert and eat it all by yourself.
- Instead of drinking caffeinated coffee after a meal, enjoy a small bowl of hot chicken and rice soup or a cup of hot water with a slice of lemon.

Restaurant Buffet Tips

- If you are going to eat bread, bring healthy bread from home.
- Drink water. If you want to sweeten an unsweetened drink, bring your own packets of xylitol or stevia from home.
- Let the first serving consist of salads, fresh vegetables, and fresh fruits. Eat a green-vegetable salad and use dressings like lemon juice, balsamic vinegar, and a little olive oil. It is acceptable to go back and eat seconds of these foods.
- If you're sensitive to sulfites and other preservatives, ask if the food is prepared with them so that you can avoid eating it. Sulfites and monosodium glutamate are often added to foods, such as salads, fruits, potatoes, and shrimp, to keep them looking fresh.
- Eat soups containing many vegetables and very little cream or cheese.
- The entrée plate can include lean meats (grilled, broiled, or baked) and cooked vegetables (steamed, sautéed, or grilled). Try not to go back for seconds.
- When comfortably full, stop eating. Don't stuff yourself.
- Avoid fried foods.
- Avoid white potatoes and foods high in simple carbohydrates.
- Avoid desserts. If you eat dessert, enjoy only a few small bites.
- Instead of drinking caffeinated coffee after a meal, enjoy a cup of vegetable soup or hot water with a slice of lemon.

* * *

Work-Study: Points to Ponder

1. Describe your eating-out habits. How often do you go out to eat in a week? Is it before, during, or after work hours? Is it on the weekends?

2. When going out to eat, you don't need to be obsessive and pull out a calculator to count calories. It is a good idea, however, to remain in control and keep your daily food intake within your calorie range

(see chapter 32). Describe your method of ordering meals when you eat out. Do you obsessively count calories, responsibly estimate and monitor your fat and sugar intake, or carelessly order and eat whatever you want?

3. When dining alone, do you take something to read and then enjoy reading it as you eat slowly? Or do you quickly gorge down anything and everything that is set before you?

4. At fast-food restaurants, are you willing to eat a salad rather than fries? Are you willing to drink water instead of soda? Describe your thoughts on bringing food items from home to make your meal healthier, such as bringing your own whole-grain bread, carrot sticks, or natural sweeteners.

5. Think about your dining-out experiences. When you go to a sit-down restaurant, do you take your time to order a meal that is relatively healthy (e.g., condiments added to the side and no added salt)? Do you ask the right questions and request for your food to be prepared healthy? Or do you eat foods that are high in calories, simple carbohydrates (sugar), fat, and salt?

6. At a sit-down restaurant, do you split an entrée with someone else, or do you eat it all by yourself? If you order a dessert, do you eat only a few small bites, or do you eat it all? Once full, do you continue to eat, or do you take the rest home for the next meal?

7. At a buffet restaurant, are you aware of the types and amount of food you eat? Do you pace yourself and enjoy the company of family or friends?

8. Describe your thoughts on following the majority of the tips listed for eating at fast-food restaurants, sit-down restaurants, and buffets. What other tips do you think should be added to the list?

Chapter 45

Practice Makes Perfect (Design Your New Healthy Diet)

But let patience have her perfect work, that ye may be perfect and entire, wanting nothing. (James 1:4)

Now it is time for you to design your own personal healthy diet as you begin your healthy lifestyle. Use the information in the previous chapters and complete the following tables to plan and design your new healthy diet. If you or your family members take medication or have health problems, read Part IV and see your physician before designing your new healthy diet.

* * *

Work-Study: Points to Ponder

1. In the Replace column in the following table (Table III), list the foods that you plan to buy and eat in your new healthy diet, as you focus on the Repent 6 R's Step Process. Combine the information from the Release-Replace charts that you already completed in Part III to help fill out Table III for each food type. As time progresses, your diet should evolve. Continue to gain more knowledge and improve your diet; let it be a forever-changing entity. If you have health issues or take any prescribed medicine, consult your physician about your new healthy diet. In Part IV, there is a list of common health problems that are often affected by diet. If you have any of these listed health issues, you may use the information in Part IV under the advice of your physician to help design your new healthy diet.

Table III: My New Healthy Diet

	Replace
Sugars and Sweeteners (see Chapter 34)	
Wheat Flour, Cornmeal, and Cereal (see Chapter 35)	
Oils and Fats (see Chapter 36)	

Table III: My New Healthy Diet (cont'd)

	Replace
Meat, Eggs, Dairy Products, and Other Protein Foods (see Chapter 37)	
America's Favorite Side Dishes: Pasta, Rice, and Potatoes (see Chapter 38)	
Vegetables and Legumes (see Chapter 39)	

Table III: My New Healthy Diet (cont'd)

	Replace
Fruits, Nuts, and Seeds (see Chapter 40)	
Water and Beverages (see Chapter 41)	
Salt, Sodium, Spices, Herbs, and Condiments (see Chapter 42)	
Snacks and Desserts (see Chapter 43)	

2. Next, in Table IV, plan your weekly meals for you and your family. Continue to do this for as many weeks as needed, until eating healthy becomes a way of life. If you have health problems or concerns, consult your physician and nutritionist about your new healthy diet. Part V lists some of my favorite healthy recipes created by my family. Use these recipes and your own favorite healthy recipes to help plan meals.

Table IV: Planned Meals for a Week

	Breakfast	Lunch	Dinner	Snacks
Monday				
Tuesday				
Wednesday				
Thursday				

Table IV: Planned Meals for a Week (cont'd)

	Breakfast	Lunch	Dinner	Snacks
Friday				
Saturday				
Sunday				

3. Below is a list of the dishes and baked goods that I released from my past and replaced with new healthier recipes created by my family (see Part V for family recipes).

Released	Replaced
• All kinds of cakes and muffins	• Spelt banana bread, zucchini bread, and blueberry muffins
• Glazed croissants	• Spelt scones
• Caramel apples covered with walnuts	• Apple walnut salad
• Flakey buttermilk biscuits	• Spelt biscuits and Coats (gluten-free biscuits)
• Sweet potato pie	• Sweet potato pie (This is my mom's secret recipe, so it's not included in Part V. She hopes these pies will be supplied for your enjoyment in the near future!)
• Candied sweet potatoes	• Xylitoled sweet potatoes
• Fluffy cornbread muffins and Southern hot water cornbread	• Coarse cornbread muffins and coarse hot water cornbread
• Battered fried chicken	• Fried chicken and sautéed chicken
• Pizza rolls and battered cheese sticks	• Spelt tortilla rolls with homemade salsa
• Pancakes and waffles	• Spelt pancakes and waffles
• Glazed fruit turnovers	• Xylitoled fruit turnovers
• Fruit gelatin desserts with whipped cream	• Fruit salad
• Shakes and floats	• Smoothies
• Chocolate Frosted Cream Cheese Brownies	• Cocoa Cream Cheese Brownies

• All kinds of cookies	• Ginger cookies, peanut butter cookies, oatmeal raisin cookies, dark chocolate-chip cookies, and fruit cookies made with whole grain flour and xylitol
• Macaroni and cheese	• Whole spelt macaroni and low-fat cheese
• Meat lasagna	• Vegetable lasagna
• Greens with ham hocks	• Greens with smoked turkey
• Fried catfish	• Zesty fish fillets
• Meatballs and spaghetti	• Meatballs and spelt spaghetti
• Hot cocoa and hot sweetened tea	• Hot lemon warmer-upper
• Cow's milk	• Homemade organic almond milk shake
• French fries	• Fried sweet potatoes

You may find it extremely difficult to completely annihilate all memories of the foods that you love from your past diet. In the Release column of the following table (Table V), list the unhealthy dishes, desserts, and other baked goods that you love to eat but plan to replace with new healthier recipes. Use my family recipes listed in Part V and recipes from other sources, or create your own new recipes to replace the old ones. Make sure that your new recipes remind you of dishes that you loved in your past unhealthy diet. Your collection of new recipes will play an important role in preventing cravings and helping you maintain your new diet of healthy living. As you focus on the Repent 6 R's Step Process and begin to collect and create healthy recipes, list them in the Replace column. Take your time, and be creative.

Table V. List of Your Old Unhealthy Recipes vs. New Favorite Healthy Recipes

Release	Replace

4. Congratulations! You made it! You have successfully reached your next designation! You are now on the path of healthy living. As you begin your new journey, be vigilant and take each step with enthusiasm. Don't be afraid to make mistakes, because it is certain that you will. When you make a mistake, just slap your hand lightly, forgive yourself totally, and move forward courageously. Learn from your mistakes. Remember that courage triggers determination, determination initiates practice, and practice makes perfect. But fear will paralyze the mind, inhibit action, and stagnate growth. Keep practicing as you continue your journey of healthy living, and enjoy eating in green pastures!

Part IV: Medicine, Common Health Issues, and Diet

Chapter 46

The Truth about Medicine

Is any sick among you? Let him call for the elders of the church; and let them pray over him, anointing him with oil in the name of the Lord: And the prayer of faith shall save the sick, and the Lord shall raise him up; and if he have committed sins, they shall be forgiven him. (James 5:14-15)

Chapter 46 defines the advantages and limitations of medicine. We are a nation of unhealthy people that is attempting to solve the obesity epidemic and other health issues with medical techniques and pharmaceuticals. I have come to understand that medicine is important for sustaining life in this country, but it is not the solution to our nation's health dilemma. Accepting our gift of good health and then maintaining a healthy lifestyle is the answer to solving our health problems.

Medicine

Thank God for medicine! Medicine has truly benefited many people throughout history, and its advancements will continue to improve the quality of lives in the ages to come. Medicine is a great tool when used as a lifesaver or bridge in the crossover from sickness and disease to good health. It also helps to relieve or prevent the symptoms of different abnormalities, handicaps, and injuries. There are two types of medicine: conventional and alternative. Conventional medicine is the common practice of treating each health issue independently through the use of synthetic drugs, surgery, radiation, and other modern-day therapies. Health-insurance providers help to cover the cost of treatments with synthetic drugs because these drugs are manufactured in bulk, marketed by pharmaceutical companies, and approved by the Federal Drug Administration (FDA). In contrast, alternative medicine is based on the holistic approach to healing. The holistic approach focuses on healing the whole person (a person's spirit, soul, mind, and body) through alternative methods such as with a healthy lifestyle and medicinal herbs rather than treating each injured body part and diseased physiological system separately with synthetic drugs and surgery. Treating patients with medicinal herbs, which consist of therapeutic compounds derived from plants, trees, and herbs, can be traced back to biblical times (see Ezekiel 47:12). Today, the use of medicinal herbs is typically not covered by the majority of health-insurance providers, nor is it approved by the FDA. However, as more individuals seek medicinal herbs, more health insurance companies provide coverage for alternative medicine.

There are many different types of alternative medicine, such as homeopathy, chiropractic medicine, traditional Chinese medicine, ayurvedic medicine, osteopathy, and naturopathy. Four of the most common alternative ones practiced in the States are osteopathic medicine, chiropractic medicine, homeopathy, and naturopathy. Osteopathy is based on the premise that the health of the entire body is directly linked to the condition of the musculoskeletal system. In the United States, osteopathy has evolved to osteopathic medicine, which has adopted a more conventional approach. Having licensure in all fifty states, doctors of osteopathic medicine (DOs) are known to practice in all medical specialties (e.g., internal medicine, family practice, emergency medicine, and surgery). With a few similarities to osteopathy, chiropractic medicine primarily revolves around maintaining proper alignment of the musculoskeletal system to prevent health issues arising from an altered nervous system. Chiropractors commonly treat the body by manipulations to the spine and joints, and often include natural medicine, diet, and exercise as part of their treatment. Another type of alternative medicine is homeopathy, which is defined by the theory that like can cure like. In more specific terms, homeopathic medicine is based on the theory that a natural substance (i.e., a substance found in plants, herbs, humans, animals, soil, seawater, etc.), which causes a particular health disorder when it is exposed to the body at high quantities, can heal the same disorder when taken at extremely small dosages. Although this practice by which homeopathic physicians treat patients with low doses of natural substances is believed by many to be credible, it is generally not accepted today by conventional physicians. Finally, naturopathy (i.e., natural medicine) is focused on healing the body and maintaining wellness through the use of medicinal herbs, diet, exercise, and other natural treatments. As natural medicine and the holistic approach has become more popular, the number of states in which naturopathic doctors (NDs) are licensed to practice has consistently increased. The holistic approach to healing is the main premise not only for many different types of alternative medicine, but it also has expanded to the practices of medical doctors (MDs). Across the nation, there are many MDs that recognize the significance of the holistic approach and have successfully adapted it to their daily practice of conventional medicine.

We are experiencing a dilemma in today's society in that when we say "medicine," we automatically think of synthetic drugs, with medicinal herbs being totally excluded from our minds. Both synthetic and medicinal herbs, however, have advantages and limitations. Medicinal herbs, if taken properly, often produce the desired results with fewer side effects than those seen with synthetic drugs. Some synthetic drugs, such as antibiotics and vaccinations, are lifesavers that our society cannot afford to do without. The majority of synthetic drugs, however, are only Band-Aids that usually produce the desired effects by masking (not curing) the problem for a while. If taken long-term, these drugs often cause negative (adverse) side effects. Adverse effects can be short-lived (acute), or they can be long-term (chronic). As chronic adverse effects become evident, it is often too late to fully recover from them. Before taking any type of prescribed medicines (synthetic or herbal), it is important to fully discuss their effects with your physician. I am not a physician; my purpose here is not to convince you to choose between synthetic drugs or medicinal herbs. Thus, my reference to "medicine" is a general term that is inclusive of both synthetic drugs and medicinal herbs.

We must be aware that medicine has its proper place and limitations. Before taking a prescribed medicine, it is essential that you ask your physician to explain the therapeutic use, the mechanism of action, and the adverse effects (both tolerable and intolerable) that are associated with it. It is also important to ask about alternative treatments or therapies other than taking medicine. Most importantly, make it a priority to listen to and follow the voice that says: *Change your lifestyle to a healthy one. But make sure you find a physician who is willing to help you work toward your goal of reaching and maintaining good health.*

Many people, without ever considering the need of investing time and effort in living a healthy lifestyle, think that medicine is a magical aid or cure for all health issues and that taking it is the only way they can ever feel better. They do not realize—or they purposely ignore the fact—that medicine often has adverse effects. It is important to understand that medicine has two main sites of action: the target site(s) and the secondary site(s). When administered, the medicine binds or interacts at the target site(s), which produces the desired therapeutic effect(s). For example, if one takes an aspirin for a headache, the pain should subside as the medicine acts at the target site(s). The problem is that medicine also triggers responses at secondary site(s) of action, which often give adverse effects. For example, aspirin commonly taken for a headache can also cause thinning of the blood (prevention of blood clotting). In some individuals with heart disease, this is a positive side effect, because it inhibits blood clots that can cause strokes or heart attacks. However, in others, thinning of the blood is an adverse effect that may lead to internal bleeding and death. Depending on the type and dosage of medicine and the physical condition of the patient, it may take some time before the adverse effects from taking medicine actually show up. Many FDA-approved medications that are on the market may unknowingly cause adverse effects in some patients, and unfortunately, it may take years before these adverse effects become associated with the medications in question.

In today's society, too many of us develop a dependency on prescribed drugs without ever adopting a plan to become healthy and whole. Too many of us depend on medicine to eliminate pain or to give us a sense of euphoria, without making good health a priority. Blindly using medicine as a Band-Aid, many of us just continue to remove the old Band-Aid from our health problems and slap on a new one. As the wound becomes deeper and more infected, it is replaced with a bigger and more durable Band-Aid. Before long, the wound, oozing infectious pus, demands more assistance than that provided by a mere Band-Aid. We consistently use medicine as a Band-aid without asking the proper questions or seeking second opinions about alternative methods. As our health issues continue to worsen, we just blindly take the medicine. Our drug dependency deepens as we take increased doses of medicine or resort to more potent types of prescribed drugs. If anyone asks us why we are on medication, we simply reply, "Because my doctor gave it to me. Without question, I trust that my doctor knows what to do, and besides, I want to take the medicine."

In addition to drug dependency, tolerance is another serious problem that often develops from repetitively taking medicine. As the body becomes adapted to a particular drug dosage, the desired therapeutic effects are weakened. An increased dosage is required before optimal desired therapeutic effects can be reached again. For example, taking one aspirin for a headache may ease the pain. Yet after months of taking only one aspirin each time for a headache, the dosage of aspirin may need to be increased to two or even more before the pain will stop. As a result, tolerance to the desired effects of aspirin has been developed. Now that the dosage is increased, the target and secondary sites are exposed to more aspirin, and both tolerance and adverse effects will continue to increase. If aspirin is consistently taken, eventually the pain may not cease unless the dosage has been increased to an excessive amount.

Clearance, the process by which the body breaks down and eliminates medicine from the body, can often cause much stress and health complications. This is particularly a problem with long-term administration of medicine. Normally, processes occur in the liver, kidney, and other organs that break down and eliminate medicine from the body. However, as these processes become exhausted from constant exposure to medicine, the organs begin to fail. Physicians try to control this problem by administering the correct dosage of medicine, but after long-term exposure, major health issues and organ failure often occur.

Faith and Medicine

Using medicine as a bridge to acquire better health, my family and I understand that medicine has its advantages and limitations, and that it should not be taken blindly without much consideration. For example, many years ago my dad was diagnosed with hypothyroidism (which means the thyroid produced thyroxin at low levels) and had developed a goiter (an enlarged thyroid) that was surgically removed. Because his body no longer produces thyroxin naturally, it is essential that he takes medication daily.

A few years later, Dad was also diagnosed with diabetes. His physician told him that he needed to start taking daily insulin injections. Dad, not liking the sound of this, asked the doctor if there was an alternative to insulin injections. The doctor replied that there was, but it required changing his lifestyle to a healthier one. After much prayer and listening to the correct voice, he decided to live a healthier lifestyle and not take the insulin. He is still living that lifestyle today. He monitors his blood-glucose level daily with a home device, eats correctly, and exercises. He and his physicians continue to check his blood-glucose level and find it within the normal range over 95 percent of the time. On occasion, when it exceeds the upper limit of the desired range, he goes back to the drawing board and tweaks his diet and exercise habits until his blood-glucose level is within the normal range again. Over the years, as he was examined by different physicians, they would ask him if he wanted to start taking insulin, but his response would always be that he didn't think so because he was doing quite well without it. His physicians agreed to respect his decision as long as he kept up the good work. For over a decade, my dad has controlled his blood-glucose level by eating a proper diet and exercising, instead of taking insulin. He takes medication for his absent thyroid, uses home equipment to daily test his blood-glucose level, and visits his physicians on a regular basis. Instead of ignoring his responsibility for improving his health, he has decided through faith to perform the work required to maintain better health as he continues to complete his God-given purpose. A few years back, God gave Dad a vision to construct a new building for the church that he and my mom established many years ago. Now that the new building is finished, he is still fulfilling his pastoral duties and is planning to continue to do so for many years to come.

As a young child, my mom developed serious heart problems, which ceased when she accepted her healing and began eating a healthy diet. However, as Mom became an adult, she returned to unhealthy eating habits, and eventually, certain heart issues resurfaced that remained difficult for her physicians to diagnose as they tested different types of medication on her. Tired of the heart complications, she started listening to the right voice and changed her diet to a healthy one again. These heart complications have subsided tremendously over the years, and now she takes heart medication on a daily basis. As a result of prayer and eating a healthy diet, she has been able to take this same medication at an extremely low dosage for years without ever developing tolerance or experiencing adverse effects.

Soon after the birth of my youngest sister, Mom was diagnosed with rheumatoid arthritis. Throughout the years, she has never given in to the pain and its crippling effects. She constantly keeps busy, exercises, and learns of and avoids foods that trigger rheumatoid arthritis. Many physicians throughout the years had advised Mom to take corticosteroid injections routinely to control the symptoms of rheumatoid arthritis. After praying and listening to the correct voice, she realized that these routine injections were not going to cure it, but would probably eventually lead to stronger dosages as a result of tolerance, and ultimately, cause many adverse effects. She decided to fight the pain through prayer, various activities, regular exercise, and a healthy diet. After many years, her determination has allowed her to outlive the disease. By faith, she conquered it, instead of letting it conquer her. Now in her winter years, she is determined not to stop until her God-given purpose is completed. She is a busy grandmother, a devoted wife and mother, a sincere server of others, and an active minister in the church. Just recently, she answered God's call to preach and joined Dad in the pulpit as she delivered her first sermon, the first of many more to come.

Soon after her marriage, my sister was diagnosed with hypothyroidism and had her thyroid surgically removed. She accepts the fact that she will probably be taking synthetic thyroxin for the rest of her life. Due to her first pregnancy ten years later, my sister was diagnosed with high blood pressure and high triglycerides. During a physical examination, her physician pulled out a prescription pad and was ready to prescribe medicine for her condition. My sister immediately asked her physician if there was an alternative to taking the medication. Her physician said, "Yes, you can control your blood pressure and triglyceride levels through a healthy diet, but most people are not willing to take this step."

My sister listened to the right voice and decided to simultaneously take the prescribed medicine and change her diet. Seeking advice and reading several books, she expanded her knowledge about healthy diets, the glycemic index value of foods, and the kinds of high carbohydrate foods that increase triglyceride (fat) levels. As she improved her diet and continued with physical checkups, her physician found that her blood pressure and her triglyceride levels were consistently back to normal. Under the doctor's supervision, she gradually decreased the dosage of medicine as she continued to eat healthy. About five months later during a physical checkup, her physician explained that her blood pressure and triglyceride levels were still normal and she no longer needed to take the medicine. Today, her regular physical exams still show that her blood pressure and triglyceride levels are normal. She pays close attention to her body signals. If she eats a particular food that is not good for her condition, she usually detects adverse effects right away and eliminates that food from her diet. By faith, she soon gets back on track as she walks with God and continues her journey to healthy living. She is now a loving mother of two, a devoted wife, and a server of Jesus Christ.

My son was born with asthma. At the time of his infancy, I was studying to become a pharmacologist and had learned about the dangers of asthmatic symptoms, the different therapies used to treat asthma, and the importance of controlling it with prescribed medications. Whenever my son started to show asthmatic symptoms, my family (which includes my parents) and I would always give him albuterol as prescribed, and then immediately take him to see his pediatrician. By the time my son grew into a young child, his pediatrician also discussed the possibility of treating him with corticosteroids, as a preventive method, along with the albuterol. I was concerned that prescribed corticosteroids might lead to adverse effects that would eventually affect normal growth and development in my son. After praying in faith and listening to the right voice, my family and I agreed that my son would not take corticosteroids but would only continue with the albuterol. Through the years, we constantly monitored his breathing patterns by measuring his lung capacity with a home device and making sure he was examined regularly by his physician. We eliminated foods from his diet, and his exposure to chemicals and airborne allergens that triggered asthmatic symptoms. Then, we learned of foods that are good for eliminating asthma and building healthy lungs, airway passages, and immune systems. Today, my son, by faith, has not had an asthma attack for many years. He has grown into a strong, wise, healthy young man who believes that God heals and that everyone needs to accept his or her responsibilities for maintaining good health.

Since early childhood, yeast overgrowth had been a reoccurring problem for me. I frequently had colds and sinus infections, and after completing antibiotics prescribed by my physician, I would soon acquire problems with yeast. The worst overgrowth of yeast to ever occur was when I, as an adult, had a tonsillectomy. Several days after the surgery, I had a thin white coating covering my mouth and throat (i.e., thrush) that became more pronounced after taking antibiotics, chewing gum, drinking juice and soda, and eating soft noodles, white bread, vanilla ice cream, and pineapple sherbet. The antibiotics, along with the white-stuff diet, triggered the overgrowth of yeast in my mouth and throat that kept me miserable for over a week. After listening several years later to the voice of the Good Shepherd and changing my diet to a healthy one, my yeast problems have disappeared and reoccurrences of sinus infections have tremendously decreased. The majority of the times when I do have a sinus infection, I eat raw garlic and take an over-the-counter decongestant without the need of antibiotics. By faith, I am looking forward to the day when I only need to consume raw garlic for sinus infections, and then to the day when I no longer have sinus infections at all.

I also discovered that with the change in my diet, my allergies decreased substantially. Beginning as a young child, I was intensely allergic to pollen, grass, plants, trees, dust, dander, and to many types of fruits. However, after eliminating the white stuff (e.g., white sugar and flour) from my diet for less than three months, my allergic responses to fruits ceased and most of the other allergens stopped triggering my allergies as intensely. Although most fruits consist of sucrose, a natural sugar that is a simple carbohydrate composed of fructose plus glucose,

I was able to add fruit back to my diet. Surprisingly, the glucose in fruits did not lead to a reoccurrence of yeast overgrowth in my system. This is a blessing because fruit contains many different phytonutrients that play a significant role in good health. Choosing to clean my system from white sugar and white flour allows me to eat fruits, remain free of yeast issues, and eliminate certain allergies. By faith, I believe one day all my allergies will be gone and I will serve God in complete wellness.

My purpose for giving a brief description of my family's medical history is to demonstrate some of the steps involved in our steady progress toward better health. There are many other examples of miraculous healings and also times when we resorted to medicine. Throughout our lives, we have been treated by medical physicians and also by doctors of osteopathic medicine, naturopathic physicians, homeopathic physicians, chiropractors who practiced kinesiology (the study of the mechanics of body motion in relation to health), etc. Yet through it all, God has truly blessed us. Many might be confused by my family and me, asking, "What is your stand? Do you and your family believe in medicine or not? If you all have faith and believe that God heals, then why use medicine in the first place?"

These questions involve delicate issues that deserve a clear and well-defined answer. First of all, the Bible says that God loves and cares for man so very much. We must believe this by faith. In the book of Psalms, David asks, "What is man that God is so mindful of him?" (Psalm 8:4). Like David, I sometimes wonder the same thing, but I am very grateful that He is so mindful of us. As a result of His love, God wants us to live in wellness. Yet it is up to us to choose Him as our Good Shepherd and listen to His voice that teaches us what we must do to be healed and maintain good health. God also knows everything about us. He knows the state of our health; He even knows the number of hairs on each of our heads (see Matthew 10:30). Therefore, God knows our exact level of faith. He knows if we have the faith or not to accept our God-given gift of good health, and then, to follow His instructions on how to maintain it. Some of us may want to obey God, but our faith has not yet matured to the level required to consistently make the right choices. Thankfully, God is extremely patient with us and gives us much mercy and grace. When our faith is not great enough, God does not ignore us but continues to nurture us until our faith reaches maturity. He starts off by feeding us words of milk and then of soft foods, and He continues until we are able to eat solid words of meat. He serves us soft foods as He speaks, "My child I am not through with you yet. You have much room to grow. Go ahead and take the medicine; go ahead and have the surgery, *but* you must eat healthy and exercise and continue to grow in faith (by praying, fasting, hearing My voice, and obeying the Word) as you become strong enough to accept my gift of complete healing."

There is a guaranteed way to always know when it is God's voice and not that of the Evil One advising us to go ahead and take the medicine or have surgery. When God gives His permission to take the medicine or have surgery, He always follows it with a "but" and a set of conditions that we must perform and complete to grow in faith and improve our health. For example, He may give instructions such as *Take the medicine; have the surgery, but you must accept your gift of good health and change your lifestyle to a healthy one.* The Bible says that *faith without works is dead* (James 2:26b). The only way our faith can be perfected to maturity is if we combine our faith with works by completing His instructions. We must obey God's words through our actions of accepting and maintaining good health.

There are two main tactics by which the Evil One tempts us to depend solely on medicine to fix all of our health problems. One tactic is that he convinces us that we are not held accountable for our health or our future. He persuades us to believe that taking the medication or undergoing surgery is all we need to do and can do. Unlike the Good Shepherd, the Evil One doesn't give us a "but" followed by a list of conditions. He gives us an "and" that precedes words of dead faith. The Evil One deceives us and brings thoughts in our minds like, *Go ahead and take the medicine; have the surgery, and whatever will be will be. If you die, you die. If you live, you live.* As a result, he triggers fear and doubt with no hope of a progressive future, no faith in gaining good health, and no acceptance of our responsibilities. Another deceitful tactic that the Evil One uses is that he convinces us that we can have the faith needed to receive good health without doing anything. The Evil One will plant thoughts like: *Take the medicine; have the surgery, and don't change a thing. You already have great faith so just sit back and wait for God to heal you.* In my life, I have seen many people die while listening to this voice and waiting on dead faith without taking action. They died because after taking the medicine and undergoing surgery, they showed no works, actions, or lifestyle changes to demonstrate their faith in God for healing.

Medicine standing alone without faith and works will often result in no healing or even death, but combining medicine with faith and works will heal. In short, medicine is a tool used in the healing process, whereas faith, combined with works, is the key to the healing process. Through our faith and works, we can be either healed with the aid of medicine or miraculously healed without it. It is important to understand, however, that God's best is for us to accept our God-given gift of good health and remain in wellness by living a healthy lifestyle without ever being sick in the first place. Thanking God for medicine and realizing that our faith is stronger in certain areas than others, we must keep the faith and grow to maturity as we work with determination toward fulfilling our God-given purpose and reach wellness.

* * *

Work-Study: Points to Ponder

1. Do you have health problems for which you take prescribed medication? If so, how long have you taken the medication? Does it still give the desired therapeutic effects? Have you developed dependency or tolerance? Has your dosage increased? Have you felt any adverse effects or positive side effects from the medicine?

2. Every time your doctor prescribes medicine, advises surgery, or suggests medical treatment, do you follow his or her instructions without question? If so, why? Do you ask your doctor for facts on how the medicine will help you and its potential adverse effects? Have you ever asked your doctor about the health risk of the surgery or treatment? Are you willing to seek a second opinion or an alternative method of treatment?

3. It is extremely important that our faith is supported by our actions. This means we listen to God's instructions, and then we completely follow them. God always gives us responsibilities. If we want good health, He will instruct us on how to receive and maintain it through faith.
   a. Do you listen to God's voice and allow Him to help you make medical decisions? Or do you listen to the voice of the Evil One when making medical decisions?
   b. Do you depend completely on the medicine and the skills of your doctor? Or do you obey God's words and follow His instructions? Do you believe God will heal you without there being any responsibilities on your part?

CHAPTER 47

Common Health Issues and Diet

And ye shall serve the Lord your God, and He shall bless they bread, and they water; and I will take sickness away from the midst of thee. (Exodus 23:25)

Once we have accepted our gift of healing and begin living a healthy lifestyle, many diseases may be prevented, controlled, or even eliminated by eating right. Below, in alphabetical order, is information about some of the most common health problems that are affected by the foods we eat. This information is not shared to help you diagnosis your own case; allow your physician to do that for you. Furthermore, the list of foods to eat and avoid, as suggested under each type of health problem, is not presented to replace the advice of your physician. Consult your physician (preferably one who has adopted a holistic approach to his or her practice) about your diet and the types of medicines (synthetic and herbal), alternative treatments and therapies, exercise regimen, weight maintenance, and dietary supplements that you need. Be aware that certain foods and dietary supplements counteract the effects of certain medicines; therefore, it is important to consult your physician about your diet intake. Use the following information as a tool to help you design a new diet that improves your health problems. Designing a healthy diet may require many attempts. You may find that the effects of eating particular foods may differ between individuals. Foods that may be safe for one individual with a particular health problem may trigger symptoms in another individual with the same health problem. For example, most people with gout can eat beans in moderation with minimal problems, but some people must avoid beans to prevent gout attacks. Be patient, and take the time to determine the effects of certain foods on your body. If you have more than one health problem, designing a healthy diet may be quite challenging. As you work closely with your physician, you will find that a healthy diet will ultimately result in a healthier you.

* * *

Work Study: Points to Ponder

1. List the health problems that your physician has diagnosed, as well as the prescribed medications.

2. Read through the information that follows about the different health problems, and then list the health problems for which you think you show symptoms but which your physician has not diagnosed. Visit your physician, explain your symptoms, ask questions, and seek answers.

3. Based on the diagnosis of your physician, use the information listed below, combined with that of your physician, to design a healthy diet (see chapter 45) and exercise regimen (see chapter 29). <u>Caution</u>: If you are taking any type of medication, make certain to consult your physician about your diet and dietary supplement intake. This is to inhibit the adverse or toxic effects that can be caused by the interactions of medications with certain foods and dietary supplements.

<u>List of Common Health Issues and Diet</u>

Acne

Acne is infectious pimples coupled with cysts that erupt, usually on the face, due to bacterial or yeast growth in clogged pores. This is most commonly found in individuals near puberty or adolescents, who are experiencing hormonal changes and consume high quantities of junk food. As the American diet consists of much junk food, many adults also have problems with acne. Most acne can be controlled or diminished by eating a healthy diet such as that listed here.

List of Healthful Suggestions:

- Eat plenty of organic fresh fruits and vegetables, especially dark-green leafy vegetables.
- Eat organic lean chicken, turkey, and wild fish. Consume organic lean beef in moderation.
- Avoid all junk food.
- Avoid sugar and all foods consisting of simple carbohydrates such as white sugar and white flour.
- Avoid all sweetened drinks.
- Avoid soda (both regular and diet).
- Avoid coffee and caffeinated drinks.
- Avoid saturated fats and trans fats.
- Monitor intake of dietary sources high in omega-6 fatty acids, such as corn oil, soybean oil, safflower oil, sunflower oil, and foods derived from grain-fed animals.
- Yeast overgrowth can lead to acne. Eat yeast-free foods (described in this section under "Yeast Syndrome Candidiasis") to eliminate and control these symptoms.
- Maintain a healthy flora by consuming plain, cultured, low-fat yogurt (no sugar), unpasteurized sauerkraut, and unpasteurized, unfiltered, apple-cider vinegar. Under the advice of a physician, also take probiotic (friendly bacteria) capsules, which can be purchased in health-food stores.
- Consume dietary sources high in oleic acids and vitamin E, such as olive oil and avocados.
- Intake dietary sources high in omega-3 fatty acids, such as cold-water fish, flaxseeds, walnuts, flaxseed oil, and fish oil.
- Eat organic beans, nuts, and seeds.
- Eat plenty of garlic.
- Eat whole grains and other foods high in fiber to avoid constipation.
- Avoid acidosis by adjusting urine pH within the normal range of 6.4–7.2 (see chapter 41 for the types of foods and drinks that can help eliminate acidosis).
- Avoid fried foods, like chips and French fries.
- Avoid the hormones, antibiotics, pesticides, and artificial sweeten-

ers, preservatives and other food additives found in inorganic, processed, and packaged foods.

- Avoid foods that cause allergic reactions; these foods may vary for each individual. (See "Allergies" in this section for more information.)
- Drink plenty of water (about eight 8-oz. cups daily) that is free of contaminants and at the correct pH (see chapter 41 for details).
- Exercise and sweat regularly.
- Wash and lightly scrub face daily.
- Take high-grade multivitamins and other dietary supplements as recommended by your physician.
- There are many medications available for acne, but it is best to work together with your physician to control acne through your diet.
- Read below the list of foods and liquids to avoid and consume, and use it as a tool to help you design your healthy diet with your physician. Before you start, make certain to inform your physician about any medications you are taking.

Avoid	**Consume**
• Junk foods, processed and packaged foods, and artificial sweeteners, preservatives and other additives	• Organic raw vegetables (especially green leafy vegetables and garlic) and organic fresh fruit
• Omega-6 fatty acid dietary sources such as corn oil, safflower oil, sunflower oil, soybean oil, and foods derived from grain-fed animals	• Cold-water fish, flaxseed oil, flaxseeds, walnuts, fish oil, olive oil, and avocados
• Saturated fats and trans fats	• Organic lean meat (e.g., chicken, turkey, and wild fish); organic lean beef in moderation
• Coffee and caffeine	• Organic beans, nuts, and seeds

• Fried foods, such as chips and French fries	• Unpasteurized sauerkraut, plain, cultured, low-fat yogurt, and unpasteurized, unfiltered, apple-cider vinegar
• White flour and wheat flour	• Xylitol and stevia
• Sugar (white sugar, brown sugar, high fructose corn syrup, glucose, and sucrose) and foods high in simple carbohydrates	• Whole grains such as whole wheat (if not allergic or sensitive to it) and brown rice
• Soda and sweetened beverages	• Plenty of water (eight cups, 8 oz. each daily) free of contaminants and at the correct pH

Allergies

An allergy is a state of hypersensitivity that is triggered by repeated exposure of the immune system to an allergen (a substance that triggers an allergic or immune response). Allergies give symptoms such as itchy and watery eyes, scratchy throat, rashes, sneezing, runny nose, bronchial spasms (especially if allergic to nuts, peanuts, or seafood), stomach pains, and headaches.

List of Healthful Suggestions:

- Avoid food allergens. Allergens vary between individuals and are usually the foods that are craved the most. Many are intolerant, sensitive, or allergic to foods, such as sugar, peanuts, soybeans, soy products, nuts, black pepper, red meat, wheat, gluten, corn, yeast, fish, seafood, shrimp, cow's milk, dairy products, citrus fruit, chocolate, eggs, white potatoes, and tomatoes.
- Avoid artificial preservatives, food colorings, and other artificial additives added to processed foods.
- Avoid monosodium glutamate (MSG), sulfites, and other preservatives added to foods served in restaurants.
- If wheat is an allergen, test to see if you are able to eat spelt. Many who are sensitive to wheat are able to eat spelt with no problems.

- Gluten-intolerant individuals should avoid wheat (including spelt), rye, barley, and gluten contaminated foods.
- Avoid cow's milk and dairy products if lactose-intolerant or allergic to casein or whey proteins. Consume other sources of calcium, such as fish with bones, almond milk, almonds, broccoli, kelp and sea vegetables, dark-green leafy vegetables, and sesame seeds, if not allergic to these sources. Individuals with a low-tolerance to dairy can eat organic, low-fat cheese and plain, cultured, low-fat yogurt in moderation.
- Eat organic vegetables and fruits that are high in phytonutrients. Avoid the ones that cause allergic response. Most individuals are not allergic to pears.
- Eat foods high in vitamin C, such as oranges, peppers, pears, tomatoes, strawberries, and broccoli.
- Eat organic lean meat (e.g., chicken, turkey, and wild fish) and beans. Eat organic lean beef in moderation.
- Avoid processed, packaged, and fried foods.
- Avoid acidosis by adjusting pH of urine pH within the normal range of 6.4–7.2 (see chapter 41 for different types of foods and drinks that can help eliminate acidosis).
- Build a healthy flora by consuming plain, cultured, low-fat yogurt (no sugar), unpasteurized sauerkraut, and unpasteurized, unfiltered, apple-cider vinegar. Under the advice of a physician, also take probiotic (friendly bacteria) capsules, which can be purchased in health-food stores.
- Avoid saturated fats and trans fats.
- Eat organic and whole foods.
- Consume dietary sources high in monounsaturated fats such as olive oil and avocados.
- Monitor intake of dietary sources high in omega-6 fatty acids, such as corn oil, soybean oil, safflower oil, sunflower oil, and foods derived from grain-fed animals.
- Intake dietary sources high in omega-3 fatty acids, such as cold-water fish, flaxseeds, flaxseed oil, walnuts, and fish oil.
- Consume natural sweeteners such as raw honey (especially that produced by local bees, which may help to reduce allergies), stevia, xylitol, and sorbitol in moderation if not allergic to them.

- Avoid white sugar and white flour products.
- Avoid carbonated and sweetened beverages.
- Avoid alcohol, caffeine, coffee, and teas (herbal teas are acceptable).
- Keep hydrated—drink plenty of water (about eight cups, 8 oz. each daily) that is free of contaminants and at the correct pH (see chapter 41 for details).
- Avoid airborne allergens, such as dust, dust mites, molds, pollen, paint fumes, fur, dander, cigarette smoke, perfume, cleaning products, and chemicals.
- Avoid skin contact to allergens.
- Clean sinuses with nasal saline daily. Using a neti pot, a pot resembling a genie's lamp, filled with saline solution is a popular method these days. The neti pot can be purchased at most health-food stores and some drug stores.
- Sleep seven to nine hours a day.
- Design and continue an exercise regimen.
- Take high-grade multivitamins and other dietary supplements as recommended by your physician.
- Consult a physician and try to control allergies without taking medication by eliminating exposure to allergens.
- Many who eat healthy, exercise regularly, take dietary supplements to build up the immune system, and avoid food allergens find that, over time, specific food allergens no longer trigger an immune response, and they are able to add these foods back into their diets. (Note: Make sure to add back only the healthy foods.)
- Read the following list of foods and liquids to avoid and consume, and use it as a tool to help you design your healthy diet with your physician. Before you start, make certain to inform your physician about any medications you are taking.

Avoid	Consume
• Sugar (white sugar, brown sugar, high fructose corn syrup, glucose, and sucrose) and foods high in simple carbohydrates	• Organic fresh vegetables and fruits that are not allergens
• White flour and wheat flour	• Organic lean meats (e.g., chicken, turkey, and wild fish) and beans; organic lean beef in moderation
• Fruit juice, and sugar-sweetened and carbonated beverages (soda)	• Natural sweeteners such as xylitol, stevia, sorbitol, and raw honey (if not allergic to them)
• Food allergens such as peanuts, wheat, cow's milk, gluten, etc. This may vary between individuals. Identify specific allergens and then eliminate them.	• Calcium food sources, such as fish with bones, almond milk, almonds, broccoli, low-fat yogurt, organic low-fat cheese, dark-green leafy vegetables, kelp and other sea vegetables, and sesame seeds (if any of these foods are allergens, avoid them)
• Junk food, processed and packaged foods, and artificial sweeteners, preservatives, and other food additives	• Plain, cultured, low-fat yogurt, unpasteurized sauerkraut, and unpasteurized, unfiltered apple-cider vinegar
• Coffee, caffeine, and teas (decaffeinated herbal teas acceptable)	• Whole grains (e.g., whole oats, and brown rice) and nuts (e.g., almonds and walnuts) that are not allergens. If allergic to whole wheat, try whole spelt.

- Omega-6 fatty acid dietary sources such as corn oil, safflower oil, sunflower oil, soybean oil, and foods derived from grain-fed animals
- Saturated fats and trans fats

- Omega-3 fatty acid dietary sources such as cold-water fish, flaxseeds, flaxseed oil, walnuts, and fish oil
- Olive oil and avocados
- Plenty of water (eight cups, 8 oz. each daily) at the right pH and free of contaminants and added minerals

---

Arthritis

Arthritis (rheumatism) is inflammation of the joints that results in swelling and pain. There are many types of arthritis, but most types fall within two classes: osteoarthritis and rheumatoid arthritis. Osteoarthritis is when the cartilage in joints begins to deteriorate and wear away. Rheumatoid arthritis is an autoimmune disease (i.e., an abnormal condition in which the body attacks itself) that causes inflammation of the joints and bone deformities.

<u>List of Healthful Suggestions:</u>

- Discover the foods that trigger arthritic symptoms in your case and eliminate them from your diet. Start off by eliminating the foods that are the common suspects for triggering arthritic symptoms. Then test these foods by adding them back to your diet one at a time. If an added food is found to trigger symptoms, then remove it from your diet permanently. Common foods known to trigger arthritic symptoms are white flour, white sugar, wheat, red meat, white potatoes, corn, tomatoes, peppers, cow's milk, dairy products, etc. Test white potatoes. White potatoes, belonging to the nightshade plant family, consist of alkaloids that are known to trigger arthritic symptoms. Also, take the time to determine if tomatoes, peppers, eggplant, and other members of the nightshade family (consisting of alkaloids) trigger arthritic symptoms. If these foods do trigger symptoms, then eliminate them from your diet.
- Eat organic raw vegetables and fresh fruits.

- Eat many foods high in fiber, such as beans, oatmeal, and brown rice, and clean out your system by frequent fasting (consult your physician about how long you can fast; this is dependent on your overall health).
- Build a healthy flora by consuming plain, cultured, low-fat yogurt (no sugar), unpasteurized sauerkraut (remember, this is high in sodium, thus its intake needs to be monitored), and unpasteurized, unfiltered, apple-cider vinegar. Under the advice of a physician, also take probiotic capsules, which can be purchased in health-food stores.
- Avoid acidosis by adjusting pH of urine within the normal range of 6.4–7.2 (see chapter 41 for different types of foods and drinks that can help eliminate acidosis).
- Eat foods high in calcium, such as fish with bones, almond milk, almonds, broccoli, dark-green leafy vegetables, plain, cultured, low-fat yogurt, and sesame seeds, to help build up strong bones.
- Eat foods high in magnesium (e.g., nuts, whole grains, green leafy vegetables, and beans) and vitamin D (e.g., cold-water fish, such as salmon, mackerel, tuna, herring, and sardines, fortified almond milk, fortified rice milk, and fortified cereals) to help the body utilize calcium properly.
- Exposure to sunshine (ultraviolet light) is the best method for stimulating production of vitamin D in body, but intense or constant exposure is potentially dangerous due to the hole in the ozone layer. Thus, all exposure to sunlight needs to be properly controlled to reduce the risk of skin cancer.
- Purchase high-quality calcium, magnesium, vitamin D supplements, high-grade multivitamins, and other dietary supplements that are readily absorbed and recommended by your physician. It is important not to overdose on dietary supplements.
- Eat foods and dietary supplements high in omega-3 fatty acids, such as cold-water fish, flaxseeds, walnuts, flaxseed oil, and fish oil. Consume oleic acid such as that found in olive oil and avocados. These fats, especially the ones in fish oil, cold-water fish (DHA and EPA), and olive oil (oleic acid) help to eliminate arthritic symptoms as they prevent inflammation. Avoid cod liver oil, as it consists of high levels of cholesterol.

- Monitor intake of dietary sources high in omega-6 fatty acids, such as corn oil, soybean oil, safflower oil, sunflower oil, and foods derived from grain-fed animals. More specifically, limit foods high in arachidonic acid (AA), such as red meat, organ meats, dairy products, and egg yolks; AA can trigger inflammation in joints.
- Eliminate wheat, gluten, and corn from diet and other foods if trigger arthritic symptoms or an allergic response.
- Eliminate foods such as white sugar, white flour, and high simple carbohydrates.
- Avoid junk food, processed and packaged foods, and preservatives and other food additives.
- Avoid fried foods and foods consisting of saturated fats and cholesterol such as red meat.
- Eat organic, lean chicken and turkey (in moderation), and wild fish.
- Avoid margarine and other trans fats.
- Avoid excess salt and sodium. Consume no more than 1 teaspoon of salt daily; sea salt is preferable to table salt.
- Avoid artificial sweeteners.
- Drink plenty of water (about eight 8-oz. cups daily) that is free of contaminants and added minerals (e.g., fluoride and chlorine) and at the correct pH (see chapter 41 for details). Consult your physician about the type of water that is best to drink and which contaminants and minerals you need to avoid.
- Lose overweight fat to prevent joints from bearing excess weight.
- Exercise and keep active daily. Avoid bodily injury and excess pain, but keep active. Do not let symptoms keep you inactive. Design an exercise regimen that will not cause joint and other bodily injury. When ready to design an exercise regimen, consult your physician.
- Keep warm, and avoid damp weather.
- Consult a physician about your treatment options. If possible, avoid treatment with corticosteroids. Corticosteroids are very powerful drugs with many potentially adverse effects. Under the care of a physician, avoid medication as much as possible and try to treat through diet and physical activities.
- Read the following list of foods and liquids to avoid and consume,

and use it as a tool to help you design your healthy diet with your physician. Before you start, make certain to inform your physician about any medications you are taking.

Avoid	Consume
• White flour, wheat flour, white rice, white pasta, and white potatoes and possibly other nightshade foods	• Whole grains such as oatmeal and brown rice—<u>Exception</u>: whole wheat (whole spelt) may trigger rheumatoid arthritis in some individuals
• Sugar (white sugar, brown sugar, high fructose corn syrup, glucose, and sucrose) and foods high in simple carbohydrates	• Organic beans, fresh fruits, and raw vegetables—<u>Exception</u>: do not eat those that trigger rheumatoid arthritis (e.g., white potatoes, other nightshade foods, and corn)
• Omega-6 fatty acid dietary sources such as corn oil, safflower oil, sunflower oil, soybean oil, and foods derived from grain-fed animals, and especially, AA in red meat, organ meats, cow's milk, egg yolks, and dairy products	• Olive oil, avocados, and omega-3 fatty acid dietary sources such as flaxseeds, walnuts, flaxseed oil, and especially, EPA and DHA in fish oil and cold-water fish such as salmon, mackerel, tuna, sardines, and herring
• Saturated fats, cholesterol, trans fats, and margarine	• Organic lean chicken and turkey in moderation and wild organic fish
• Junk food, processed and packaged foods, and preservatives and other food additives	• Foods high in calcium, such as fish with bones, almond milk, almonds, broccoli, plain, cultured, low-fat yogurt, dark-green leafy vegetables, and sesame seeds

• Corn, wheat, gluten, and other foods that trigger arthritic symptoms or allergies	• Foods high in magnesium (e.g., nuts, whole grains, green leafy vegetables, and beans) and vitamin D (e.g., coldwater fish, fortified almond milk, fortified rice milk, and fortified cereals)
• Salt and sodium (consume no more than 1 teaspoon of salt daily; sea salt is preferable to table salt)	• Plain, cultured, low-fat yogurt, unpasteurized, unfiltered, apple-cider vinegar, and unpasteurized sauerkraut
• Artificial sweeteners	• Natural sweeteners xylitol, stevia, and sorbitol
• Alcohol, caffeine, soda, carbonated beverages, and coffee	• Plenty of water (about eight cups, 8 oz. each daily) free of contaminants and added minerals (e.g., fluoride and chlorine), and at the correct pH

Asthma

Asthma is a chronic condition in which breathing is frequently obstructed by muscle spasms in the bronchial tubes that leads to mucus secretion in the lungs. A person with these symptoms often suffers from an asthma attack when exposed to certain triggers, such as food, airborne or environmental allergens, exercise, stress, cold air, and pathogens.

<u>List of Healthful Suggestions:</u>

- Avoid food allergens, which vary for each individual. (See suggestions in this section under "Allergies" for a list of of possible allergens.)
- Avoid foods that lead to heartburn and indigestion, which can produce pressure on the lungs and trigger asthmatic systems. (See suggestions in this section under "Heartburn (Indigestion)" for possible foods.)
- Maintain a healthy flora by consuming plain, cultured, low-fat yogurt (no sugar), unpasteurized sauerkraut, and unpasteurized, un-

filtered, apple-cider vinegar. Under the advice of a physician, also take probiotic (friendly bacteria) capsules, which can be purchased at health-food stores.

- Avoid artificial food additives, such as preservatives (especially sulfites), food colorings, and flavorings. Sulfites are known to trigger asthmatic symptoms. Be aware that sulfites are often added to processed foods such as dried fruit, guacamole, and potato salad and other salads. Also, in restaurants, be cautious of sulfites that may be added to foods such as sliced fruits, salads, shrimp, and prepared potatoes.
- Eat garlic, onions, and foods spiced with hot pepper (first ensure you are not allergic to these foods).
- Eat plenty of organic vegetables, fruits, beans, whole grains, and other high-fiber foods daily. Make sure to eat only those foods that are not allergens.
- Eat foods high in vitamin C, such as oranges, peppers, grapefruits, green leafy vegetables, tomatoes, strawberries, and broccoli.
- Avoid cow's milk. Eat other foods high in calcium, such as fish with bones, almond milk, almonds, broccoli, plain, cultured, low-fat yogurt, organic, low-fat cheese, dark-green leafy vegetables, kelp and other sea vegetables, and sesame seeds, if not allergic or intolerant to these foods.
- Eat foods and take dietary supplements high in omega-3 fatty acids such as cold-water fish, flaxseeds, walnuts, fish oil, or flax seed oil to build up lungs.
- Consume monounsaturated fats such as that found in olive oil and avocados.
- Avoid saturated fats and trans fats.
- Monitor intake of dietary sources high in omega-6 fatty acids, such as corn oil, soybean oil, safflower oil, sunflower oil, and foods derived from grain-fed animals.
- Eat organic lean chicken, turkey, and wild fish. To prevent gas pressure that can trigger asthmatic symptoms, consume red meats and properly prepared beans in moderation (see chapter 39 for details on how to cook dried beans).
- Avoid junk food, and processed and packaged foods.

- Avoid acidosis by adjusting pH within the normal range of 6.4–7.2 (see chapter 41 for different types of foods and drinks that can help eliminate acidosis).
- Keep hydrated and drink much water (eight cups, 8 oz. each daily) free of contaminants and added minerals, and at the correct pH (see chapter 41 for details).
- Avoid airborne allergens. (See suggestions in this section under "Allergies" for a list of possible airborne allergens.)
- Avoid skin contact to allergens.
- Avoid swimming if asthma is induced by chlorinated water.
- Do not smoke, and avoid second-hand smoke.
- Avoid breathing in cold air and eating cold foods. Cold triggers asthma in certain individuals. Dress warmly and cover mouth with a scarf.
- Monitor exercise. Exercise triggers asthma in many individuals.
- Build up lungs and body with aerobic exercise. Consult a physician about designing an exercise regimen that will not trigger asthma attacks.
- Avoid contracting colds and the flu.
- Use a humidifier and keep it clean.
- Sleep seven to nine hours at night.
- Clean nasal passages with nasal saline spray or nasal irrigation daily (a neti pot is an excellent system to use).
- Monitor breathing daily. Keep devices and equipment used to monitor and treat asthma clean.
- Take high-grade multivitamins and other dietary supplements as recommended by your physician.
- See a physician and take medication as prescribed. Consult physician for alternatives to conventional medicine (especially corticosteroids, which have many potential adverse effects).
- Read the following list of foods and liquids to avoid and consume, and use it as a tool to help you design your healthy diet with your physician. Before you start, make certain to inform your physician about any medications you are taking.

Avoid	Consume
• Food allergens such as wheat, peanuts, eggs, and gluten, etc. This varies between individuals.	• Organic raw vegetables, fresh fruit, whole grains, and nuts that are not allergens
• Sugar (white sugar, brown sugar, high fructose corn syrup, glucose, sucrose) and foods high in simple carbohydrates	• Garlic, onions, and hot pepper (do not eat if they trigger allergies)
• White flour and refined wheat flour	• Organic lean meats (e.g., chicken, turkey, and wild fish); organic lean beef and properly prepared beans in moderation
• Junk food, processed and packaged foods, and artificial sweeteners, preservative and other food additives	• Olive oil, avocados, cold-water fish, flaxseeds, walnuts, flaxseed oil, and fish oil
• Omega-6 fatty acid dietary sources such as corn oil, safflower oil, sunflower oil, soybean oil, and foods derived from grain-fed animals	• Foods high in vitamin C, such as oranges, peppers, green leafy vegetables, grapefruits, tomatoes, strawberries, and broccoli
• Cow's milk and dairy products (Exceptions: aged cheese, cottage cheese, plain, cultured, low-fat yogurt is acceptable, if not allergens)	• Calcium food sources, such as fish with bones, almond milk, almonds, broccoli, organic, low-fat cheese, organic, low-fat cottage cheese, plain, low-fat yogurt, dark-green leafy vegetables, kelp and other sea vegetables, and sesame seeds (avoid if any of these foods are allergens)

• Saturated fats and trans fats	• Plain, cultured, low-fat yogurt, unpasteurized sauerkraut, and unpasteurized, unfiltered, apple-cider vinegar
• Alcohol, sweetened and carbonated beverages, and concentrated fruit juice	• Plenty of water (about eight cups, 8 oz. each daily) free of contaminants and added minerals, and at the correct pH

Atherosclerosis

Atherosclerosis is the hardening of the arteries due to the formation of plaque caused by cholesterol deposited on the arterial walls. The rupturing of hardened artery walls causes the formation of blood clots (thrombosis) that may block arteries feeding the heart or brain and result in a heart attack or stroke, respectively. In many cases, atherosclerosis can be prevented by eating a healthy diet and exercising.

List of Healthful Suggestions:

- High cholesterol and high triglycerides can cause atherosclerosis. Follow the suggestions listed in "High Cholesterol" to control or eliminate these symptoms.
- High blood pressure can lead to atherosclerosis. Follow the suggestions listed in "High Blood Pressure" to control or eliminate these symptoms.
- High blood-glucose levels can lead to atherosclerosis. Follow the suggestions listed in "Diabetes Mellitus (Type II)" to control or eliminate the symptoms of high blood-glucose levels.
- Eat fruits such as grapes and berries that are high in the phytonutrient resveratrol, which is known to prevent cholesterol buildup on arterial walls.
- Avoid alcohol. Drinking alcohol in moderation, especially red wine, may be good for the heart and help inhibit atherosclerosis, but the adverse effects of alcohol may cause more problems than benefits (see chapter 41 for more details).

- Avoid foods high in saturated and trans fats.
- Eat organic lean chicken, turkey, wild fish, and beans. Reduce intake of organic lean beef.
- Monitor intake of dietary sources high in omega-6 fatty acids, such as corn oil, soybean oil, safflower oil, sunflower oil, and foods derived from grain-fed animals. More specifically, limit foods high in AA, such as red meat, organ meats, dairy products, and egg yolks; AA can trigger thrombosis.
- Intake dietary sources high in omega-3 fatty acids, such as cold-water fish, flaxseeds, flaxseed oil, and fish oil. Do not consume cod liver oil because it consists of high levels of cholesterol.
- Consume dietary sources high in oleic acids such as olive oil.
- Avoid cow's milk and most cheeses. Replace cow's milk with foods high in calcium, such as fish with bones, almond milk, almonds, dark-green leafy vegetables, plain, cultured, low-fat yogurt, and sesame seeds.
- Eat whole grains, such as whole wheat and whole spelt (in moderation), oats, and brown rice. Also, eat other complex carbohydrates such as yam-sweet potatoes.
- Avoid acidosis by adjusting pH within the normal range of 6.4–7.2 (see chapter 41 for different types of foods and drinks that can help eliminate acidosis).
- Build a healthy flora by consuming plain, cultured, low-fat yogurt (no sugar) and unpasteurized, unfiltered, apple-cider vinegar. Under the advice of a physician, also take probiotic (friendly bacteria) capsules, which can be purchased at health-food stores.
- Drink plenty of water (about eight 8-oz. cups daily) that is free of contaminants and added minerals (e.g., fluoride and chlorine), and at the correct pH (see chapter 41 for details).
- Take high-grade multivitamins and other dietary supplements as recommended by your physician.
- Eliminate cigarette smoking.
- Lose excess body weight, especially excess upper-body fat.
- Consult a physician and design an exercise regimen that includes aerobic and weight-bearing exercise. Exercise regularly.
- Consult a physician and take medication as prescribed. Work with

a physician to determine when it is possible to eliminate or control symptoms through diet and exercise, and without medication.

- Read below the list of foods and liquids to avoid and consume, and use it as a tool to help you design your healthy diet with your physician. Before you start, make certain to inform your physician about any medications you are taking.

Avoid	Consume
• Red meat (beef and pork), organ meats, shrimp, and cod liver oil for their cholesterol and saturated fats	• Organic, fresh vegetables and fruits (especially grapes and berries high in resveratrol)
• White potatoes, white rice, and white pasta with or without gravies and cream sauces	• Organic, lean meats (e.g., chicken, turkey, wild fish) and beans
• Omega-6 fatty acid dietary sources such as corn oil, safflower oil, sunflower oil, soybean oil, and foods derived from grain-fed animals, and especially, AA in red meat, egg yolks, organ meats, and dairy products	• Omega-3 fatty acids in cold-water fish, fish oil, flaxseeds, and flaxseed oil
• Salt and sodium (consult a physician; organic sea salt is preferable to table salt but still needs to be reduced)	• Whole grains (oatmeal, brown rice, and whole wheat)
• Saturated fats, trans fats, and cholesterol	• Oleic acids such as that found in olive oil
• Cow's milk and cheeses	• Yam-sweet potatoes

- Sugar (white sugar, brown sugar, high fructose corn syrup, alcohol, glucose, and sucrose) and foods high in simple carbohydrates
- White flour and wheat flour
- Artificial sweeteners
- Alcohol, carbonated beverages, soda, and caffeine

- Foods high in calcium, such as fish with bones, almond milk, plain, cultured, low-fat yogurt, dark-green leafy vegetables, and sesame seeds
- Foods high in potassium, such as bananas, legumes, and whole grains
- Garlic and onions
- Plain, cultured, low-fat yogurt and unpasteurized, unfiltered, apple-cider vinegar
- Nuts (almonds and walnuts)
- Plenty of water (about eight 8-oz. cups daily) free of contaminants and added minerals (e.g., fluoride and chlorine), and at the right pH

Attention Deficit (Hyperactivity) Disorder (ADD/ ADHD)

Attention deficit (hyperactivity) disorder is characterized by the inability of an individual to sustain concentration, coupled with disruptive patterns of behavior, and often with excessive physical activity. This disorder is most prevalent in children and teens (it is especially identified in boys), and is often continued and characterized with modified behaviors throughout adulthood. In many cases, parents have found that this disorder is due to the toxic effects of certain foods on the brain chemistry of their children and have been able to successfully control it through diet without prescribed medications.

<u>List of Healthful Suggestions:</u>

- Avoid inorganic, processed, and packaged foods.

- Eat organic and whole foods.
- Avoid artificial food preservatives, such as nitrates, nitrites, sulfites, monosodium glutamate (MSG), and butylated hydroxyanisole, food colorings, food flavorings, and other artificial food additives found in processed foods.
- Avoid artificial sweeteners.
- Avoid junk food.
- Avoid monosodium glutamate, sulfites, and other additives added to foods served in restaurants.
- Eliminate white sugar, white flour, and all foods high in simple carbohydrates.
- Avoid food allergens. Allergens vary between individuals. See suggestions in this section under “Allergies” for list of possible food allergens.
- If wheat is an allergen, test to see if you are able to eat whole spelt. Many who are sensitive to wheat are able to eat spelt with no problems.
- Gluten-intolerant individuals should avoid wheat (including spelt), rye, barley, and gluten contaminated foods.
- Avoid cow’s milk and most dairy products if lactose-intolerant, or allergic to casein or whey proteins. Consume sources of calcium, such as fish with bones, almond milk, almonds, plain, low-fat yogurt, broccoli, kelp and sea vegetables, dark-green leafy vegetables, and sesame seeds, if not allergic to these sources.
- Test to see if able to substitute cow’s milk with goat’s milk. Many parents find that children who are allergic to the proteins in cow’s milk are not allergic to the ones in goat’s milk. However, the lactose intolerant need to avoid goat’s milk; it is loaded with lactose.
- Eat organic vegetables and fruits that are high in phytonutrients. Avoid the ones that cause allergic response. Most individuals are not allergic to pears.
- Eat foods high in vitamin C, such as oranges, peppers, pears, tomatoes, strawberries, and broccoli.
- Eat foods high in B vitamins, such as lean meats, organ meats, fish, whole grain cereals, whole wheat breads, and green leafy vegetables.
- Eat foods high in magnesium, such as nuts, whole grains, green leafy vegetables, and beans.

- Eat organic, lean meat (e.g., wild fish, if not allergen, chicken, and turkey) and beans. Reduce intake of organic, lean beef.
- Avoid acidosis by adjusting pH of urine within the normal range of 6.4–7.2 (see chapter 41 for different types of foods and drinks that can help eliminate acidosis).
- Build a healthy flora by consuming plain, cultured, low-fat yogurt (if not allergen), unpasteurized sauerkraut, and unpasteurized, unfiltered, apple-cider vinegar. Under the advice of a physician, also take probiotic (friendly bacteria) capsules, which can be purchased in health-food stores.
- Through diet and advice of your physician, treat diseases that cause improper digestion, malabsorption of nutrients into the body, and food toxicity, such as irritable bowel syndrome, yeast syndrome, Crohn's disease, and celiac disease.
- Avoid saturated fats, trans fats, and fried foods.
- Monitor intake of dietary sources high in omega-6 fatty acids, such as corn oil, soybean oil, safflower oil, sunflower oil, and foods derived from grain-fed animals.
- Consume dietary sources high in monounsaturated fats such as olive oil and avocados.
- Intake dietary sources high in omega-3 fatty acids, such as cold-water fish, flaxseeds, walnuts, flaxseed oil, and fish oil (if not allergens).
- Under the advice of a physician, take evening primrose oil, black currant oil, or spirulina dietary supplements that are high in GLA. Do not take without doctor's recommendation.
- Consume natural sweeteners such as stevia, xylitol, and sorbitol in moderation if not allergic to them.
- Avoid all carbonated and sweetened beverages.
- Avoid alcohol, caffeine, coffee, and teas (herbal teas are acceptable).
- Keep hydrated—drink plenty of water (eight cups, 8 oz. each daily) free of contaminants and added minerals (e.g., fluoride and chlorine), and at the correct pH (see chapter 41 for details).
- If possible, avoid constant exposure to medications, which may have toxic effects on brain chemistry.

- Pregnant mothers and parents: avoid cigarette smoking.
- Consume dietary sources high in monounsaturated fats such as olive oil and avocados.
- Avoid airborne allergens. Allergens vary between individuals. See suggestions in this section under "Allergies" for list of possible airborne allergens.
- Avoid exposure to toxic metals such as lead and mercury.
- Avoid skin contact to allergens.
- Avoid stressful situations and maintain healthy family relationships.
- Design and continue an exercise regimen.
- Take high-grade vitamins and minerals (e.g., vitamin B complex, vitamin C, and magnesium), and other dietary supplements (e.g., ones containing omega-3 fatty acids and GLA) as recommended by your physician to help build up a strong nervous system.
- Discuss with your physician possible alternative methods other than taking prescription medications such as methylphenidate, which is commonly prescribed for ADD/ADHD. This medication may cause serious adverse effects, especially in children. Fortunately, after identifying and eliminating exposure to food and environmental toxins that cause the disorder, many parents find that their children no longer need to take medication.
- Read below the list of foods and liquids to avoid and consume, and use it as a tool to help you design your healthy diet with your physician. Before you start, make certain to inform your physician about any medications you are taking.

Avoid	**Consume**
• Sugar (white sugar, brown sugar, high fructose corn syrup, glucose, and sucrose) and foods high in simple carbohydrates	• Organic fresh vegetables and fruits that are not allergens

• White flour and refined wheat flour; if gluten intolerant, avoid all wheat	• Organic lean meats (e.g., chicken, turkey, and wild fish) and beans; organic, lean beef in moderation
• Caffeine, coffee, tea, soda, carbonated beverages, and fruit juice	• Natural sweeteners such as xylitol, stevia, and sorbitol (if not allergic to them)
• Food allergens such as peanuts, wheat, cow's milk, gluten, etc. This may vary between individuals. Identify specific allergens and then eliminate.	• Calcium food sources, such as fish with bones, almond milk, almonds, broccoli, plain, cultured, low-fat yogurt, organic, low-fat cheese, dark-green leafy vegetables, kelp, and other sea vegetables, and sesame seeds (if any of these foods are allergens, avoid them); also try goat's milk
• Artificial preservatives, food coloring, sweeteners, and other additives	• Plain, cultured, low-fat yogurt, unpasteurized sauerkraut, and unpasteurized, unfiltered apple-cider vinegar
• Coffee, caffeine, and teas (decaffeinated herbal teas acceptable)	• Whole grains (e.g., whole wheat, oats, and brown rice) and nuts (e.g., almonds and walnuts) that are not allergens. If allergic to whole wheat, try whole spelt.
• Omega-6 fatty acid dietary sources such as corn oil, safflower oil, sunflower oil, soybean oil, and foods derived from grain-fed animals (Note: reduce intake of all dietary sources of omega-6s except for GLA)	• Omega-3 fatty acid foods such as cold-water fish, flaxseeds, walnuts, flaxseed oil, and fish oil
• Saturated fats and trans fats	• Oleic acid in olive oil and avocados

- GLA in spirulina, primrose oil, and black currant oil under the advice of a physician
- Foods high in vitamin C, such as oranges, peppers, pears, tomatoes, strawberries, and broccoli
- Foods high in B vitamins, such as lean meats, organ meats, fish, whole grain cereals, whole wheat breads, and green leafy vegetables
- Foods high in magnesium, such as nuts, whole grains, green leafy vegetables, and beans
- Plenty of water (eight cups, 8 oz. each daily) free of contaminants and added minerals (e.g., fluoride and chlorine), and at the correct pH

Diabetes Mellitus (Type II)

Diabetes mellitus (type II) is indicated by the consistent high level of blood glucose that is the result of either the body becoming resistant to its own insulin or not producing enough insulin. As a result, glucose is not utilized or stored properly in the body. Type II diabetes is common among overweight adult individuals. However, as individuals are becoming overweight at an earlier age, type II diabetes is often seen in children.

List of Healthful Suggestions:

- Avoid sugar and high simple-carbohydrate foods with a high glycemic index value, especially ones consisting of white sugar and white flour (see chart for glycemic index ranges of foods in chapter

38 under Points to Ponder #2). Eat carbohydrates with a moderate glycemic index value in moderation.

- Eat plenty of salads consisting of dark-green leafy vegetables and a splash of olive oil and balsamic vinegar.
- Eat organic, raw vegetables and fresh fruits (with a low glycemic index value). Eat fruits such as watermelon and cantaloupe in moderation.
- Individuals with diabetes often have high triglycerides. Control triglyceride levels in bloodstream by reducing intake of unhealthy fats and simple carbohydrates. Reduce intake of simple carbohydrates by avoiding foods with a high glycemic index value, such as white sugar, white potatoes, white flour, white pasta, and white rice. Eat foods with a moderate glycemic index value in moderation (see chart for glycemic index ranges of foods in chapter 38 under Points to Ponder # 2).
- Eat foods high in dietary fiber such as raw vegetables, beans, and whole grains.
- Eat organic lean chicken, turkey, and wild fish. Reduce intake of red meat.
- Reduce intake of cow's milk. Replace with other foods high in calcium, such as fish with bones, almond milk, almonds, plain, cultured, low-fat yogurt, organic, low-fat cheese, broccoli, kelp and sea vegetables, dark-green leafy vegetables, and sesame and sunflower seeds, if not allergic to these foods.
- Avoid rice milk, which has a high glycemic index value.
- Avoid saturated fats, cholesterol, and trans fats.
- Avoid junk food, and processed and packaged foods.
- Reduce salt and sodium intake. Consult physician about daily sodium intake.
- Avoid alcohol and caffeine.
- Avoid artificial sweeteners. Use natural sweeteners xylitol, stevia, brown rice syrup, and sorbitol in moderation.
- Monitor intake of dietary sources high in omega-6 fatty acids, such as corn oil, soybean oil, safflower oil, sunflower oil, and foods derived from grain-fed animals.
- Avoid acidosis by adjusting pH within the normal range of 6.4–7.2

(see chapter 41 for different types of foods and drinks that can help eliminate acidosis).

- Build a healthy flora by consuming plain, cultured, low-fat yogurt (no sugar) and unpasteurized, unfiltered, apple-cider vinegar. Under the advice of a physician, also take probiotic (friendly bacteria) capsules, which can be purchased in health-food stores.
- Eat complex carbohydrates in moderation, such as whole grains (e.g., whole wheat, whole spelt, oats, and brown rice) and yam-sweet potatoes.
- Intake dietary sources high in omega-3 fatty acids, such as flaxseeds, fish oil, walnuts, and flaxseed oil in moderation.
- Consume olive oil and other monounsaturated fats in moderation.
- Drink plenty of water (about eight 8-oz. cups) that is free of contaminants and added minerals, and at the correct pH throughout the day (see chapter 41 for details).
- Do not skip a meal. Make sure each meal is healthy and balanced.
- Snack between meals and before sleeping at night to stabilize blood-sugar levels. Make sure snacks are healthy (e.g., almonds, apples, carrots, and plain, cultured, low-fat yogurt).
- Take high-grade multivitamins and other dietary supplements as recommended by your physician.
- Exercise daily (e.g., brisk walking, running, biking, and swimming). After eating, it is amazing how a brisk walk will help return a high blood-glucose level back to normal.
- Design an exercise regimen with your physician that includes both aerobic and weight-lifting exercises.
- Lose excess weight, especially around waist, and maintain normal weight.
- Take care of eyes. Have vision checked regularly.
- Avoid stress.
- Stop smoking.
- Take special care of feet and toes. Do not bruise or blister.
- Trim toenails properly and avoid ingrown toenails.
- Do not obscure blood circulation in limbs, hands, and feet.
- Monitor blood-sugar level daily at home, as advised by physician.
- See your physician regularly. Those who succeed in the above steps

under the supervision of a physician often find that they do not need insulin injections and can live a life free of diabetic symptoms. If diabetic symptoms are prevalent, however, take your medication, and eat and exercise as directed by your physician.

- At times, many diabetics suffer from hypoglycemic episodes after insulin injections. Consult a physician for the foods and beverages to consume (e.g., orange juice) during a hypoglycemic episode and the steps required to avoid insulin shock.
- Read below the list of foods and liquids to avoid and consume, and use it as a tool to help you design your healthy diet with your physician. Before you start, make certain to inform your physician about any medications you are taking.

Avoid	Consume
• Sugar (white sugar, brown sugar, high fructose corn syrup, glucose, and sucrose) and foods high in simple carbohydrates	• Organic raw vegetables, dried beans, and other foods high in fiber
• White flour and refined wheat flour	• Organic fresh fruits (Exceptions: watermelon and cantaloupe should be eaten in moderation)
• White semolina pasta	• Organic, lean chicken, turkey, and wild fish
• White rice	• Whole grain brown rice and whole grain oatmeal
• White potatoes	• Yam-sweet potatoes
• Salt and sodium (consult physician)	• Whole grain breads (whole wheat and whole spelt), whole grain pasta, and whole grain cereals in moderation
• Artificial sweeteners	• Nuts (almonds and walnuts) and sunflower seeds

• Beef (eat sparingly) and pork	• Natural sweeteners such as xylitol, stevia, sorbitol, and brown rice syrup
• Saturated fats, trans fats, and cholesterol	• Fish oil, flaxseeds and flaxseed oil, cold-water fish, walnuts, and olive oil
• Omega-6 fatty acid dietary sources such as corn oil, safflower oil, sunflower oil, soybean oil, and foods derived from grain-fed animals	• Calcium food sources, such as fish with bones, almond milk, almonds, broccoli, organic, low-fat cottage cheese, plain, cultured, low-fat yogurt, dark-green leafy vegetables, and sesame and sunflower seeds
• Cow's milk and rice milk	• Plain, cultured, low-fat yogurt and unpasteurized, unfiltered, apple-cider vinegar
• Alcohol, caffeine, coffee, tea, fruit juices, and carbonated beverages	• Plenty of water (about eight 8-oz. cups daily) free of contaminants and added minerals, and at the correct pH

Gout

Gout is a form of arthritis caused by crystals that are produced from excess purines breaking down to uric acid and accumulating in joints. Many individuals who suffer from gout also suffer from uric acid crystallizing into kidney stones.

<u>List of Healthful Suggestions:</u>

- Eat healthy and develop a list with your physician of the rich purine foods that you need to avoid. Rich purine foods are high in animal-derived protein.
- Avoid meats rich in purines, such as red meats, organ meats, poultry, fish (e.g., catfish, sardines, mackerels, anchovies, and herring), caviar, and seafood. Completely eliminate beef from diet. Most can

eat chicken in moderation without a problem. Some can eat small portions of pork, turkey, and some types of fish (e.g., wild tuna, salmon, and trout) without triggering symptoms. Yeast is also high in purines; avoid baked goods high in baker's yeast, and beer and other products high in brewer's yeast.

- As excellent sources of protein, add to your diet plain, cultured, low-fat yogurt and other low-fat dairy products. Although these foods are high in protein, most individuals with severe gout find that these foods are safe to eat.
- With your physician, develop a list of moderately high purine foods and the amount of them that you can eat in a day. Some of these foods are dried beans, peas, soybean products (tofu), whole grains, dark-green leafy vegetables (especially spinach), asparagus, cauliflower, and mushrooms. The amount of these foods that is safe to eat depends on the severity of your gout. For example, a person with a mild case of gout may be able to eat certain moderately high purine foods in small portions; whereas, a person with a more severe case may need to completely eliminate them. Once you discover that a small ration of a specific food is triggering symptoms, eliminate it from your diet.
- Eat foods and take dietary supplements high in omega-3 fatty acids, such as flaxseeds, walnuts, fish oil, and flaxseed oil.
- Consume olive oil and other foods high in oleic acids.
- Reduce intake of omega-6 fatty acid dietary sources such as corn oil, safflower oil, sunflower oil, soybean oil, and foods derived from grain-fed animals.
- Develop a list with your physician of low purine foods that are safe to eat. Eat plenty of raw vegetables that are on your low purine list. Eat fresh fruits, especially berry fruits (e.g., cherries and strawberries are good for gout).
- Do not eat much of low purine foods consisting of sugar, unhealthy fats, and simple carbohydrates; this is because it is important to maintain a healthy weight to control gout symptoms and prevent other health issues.
- Avoid acidosis by adjusting pH within the normal range of 6.4–7.2 (see chapter 41 for different types of foods and drinks that can help eliminate acidosis).

- Build a healthy flora by consuming plain, cultured, low-fat yogurt (no sugar) and unpasteurized, unfiltered, apple-cider vinegar. Under the advice of a physician, also take probiotic capsules, which can be purchased in health-food stores.
- Avoid excess salt and sodium. Consult physician about sodium intake.
- Drink plenty of water (about eight 8-oz. cups) that is free of contaminants and added minerals (e.g., fluoride and chlorine), and at the correct pH throughout the day (see chapter 41 for details).
- Avoid saturated fats and trans fats.
- Avoid alcohol, including beer.
- Avoid caffeine, soda, carbonated beverages, and coffee.
- Exercise regularly but avoid intense exercise that may cause bodily injury or excess stress to joints.
- Lose excess weight, especially around the waist. Do not lose weight abruptly; avoid fasting.
- Keep feet comfortable. Wear sandals when warm.
- Keep warm. Avoid cold and damp weather.
- Consult physician and control symptoms as much as possible with a low-purine diet. Do not take medicine just to continue eating a rich purine diet. Eat right. Take calcium and dietary supplements as directed by physician. Work with a physician, and if possible, try to eliminate symptoms without taking gout medication; this medication can result in many adverse effects.
- Read the following list of foods and liquids to avoid and consume, and use it as a tool to help you design your healthy diet with your physician. Before you start, make certain to inform your physician about any medications you are taking.

Avoid	Consume
• Beef, organ meats, mutton, gravies, pork, and turkey (some can eat small portions of turkey and pork such as ham)	• Organic chicken in moderation
• Caviar, seafood, and fish such as catfish, mackerels, sardines, herring, and anchovies (some can eat small portions of fish such as wild tuna, trout, and salmon)	• Organic fruits, especially cherries and other berries
• Sugar (white sugar, brown sugar, high fructose corn syrup, glucose, and sucrose) and other foods high in simple carbohydrates	• Plain, cultured, low-fat yogurt (excellent source of protein), low-fat dairy products, almond milk, and almonds
• Dried beans, peas, soybeans, soy products, and tofu (some can eat these foods in moderation; whereas, others cannot eat these foods at all).	• Organic vegetables, such as green beans, tomatoes, yam-sweet potatoes, and zucchini (<u>Exceptions</u>: some people need to avoid spinach and other dark-green leafy vegetables, cauliflower, mushrooms, and asparagus)
• Foods high in yeast (e.g., baker's yeast and brewer's yeast)	• Olive oil, flaxseeds, flaxseed oil, walnuts, and fish oil
• Alcohol (including beer), caffeine, soda, carbonated beverages, coffee, and tea	• Whole grains, such as whole wheat and oatmeal (some people need to avoid these foods, most can eat in moderation)

- Salt and sodium (consult physician)
- Omega-6 fatty acid dietary sources such as corn oil, safflower oil, sunflower oil, soybean oil, and foods derived from grain-fed animals
- Saturated fats and trans fats
- Nuts and seeds
- Plenty of water (a minimum of about eight 8-oz. cups daily) free of contaminants and added minerals (e.g., fluoride and chlorine), and at the correct pH

Gum Disease and Tooth Decay

Gum disease or tooth decay is the deterioration of gums or teeth due to growth of unfriendly bacteria. Bacteria growth is usually the result of consuming a diet high in sugar and other simple carbohydrates.

List of Healthful Suggestions:

- Avoid sugars, white flour, junk food, candy, sweets, desserts, and other foods high in simple carbohydrates.
- Eat foods low in simple carbohydrates, such as vegetables, fruits, nuts, seeds, whole grains, meats, and beans.
- Eat organic, raw vegetables and fresh fruits.
- Eat healthy snacks, such as almonds, carrots, apples, and seeds. Chewing raw, crunchy snacks cleans teeth and gums.
- Eat foods high in calcium, such as fish with bones, almond milk, almonds, dark-green leafy vegetables, plain, cultured, low-fat yogurt, aged, low-fat cheese, kelp and other sea vegetables, and sesame and sunflower seeds.
- Avoid bacterial growth in mouth by adjusting pH of saliva and urine within the normal range of 6.4–7.2 (see chapter 41 for different types of foods and drinks that can help eliminate acidosis).
- Maintain a healthy flora by consuming plain, cultured, low-fat yogurt (no sugar), unpasteurized sauerkraut, and unpasteurized, unfiltered, apple-cider vinegar. Under the advice of a physician, also take probiotic (friendly bacteria) capsules, which can be purchased in health-food stores.

- Consume natural sweeteners, such as xylitol, stevia and sorbitol.
- Avoid coffee, tea, soda, sugary gum, and fruit juice.
- Milk can cause tooth decay, especially in toddlers; milk drinkers should brush teeth frequently.
- Drink plenty of water (about eight 8-oz. cups) that is free of contaminants and at the correct pH throughout the day (see chapter 41 for details).
- Chew gum, consume mints, or brush teeth with toothpaste consisting of xylitol. Xylitol is excellent for eliminating gum disease and tooth decay.
- Brush teeth at least twice a day and floss regularly. It's best to brush teeth after every meal and after eating snacks. Do not go to bed without brushing teeth.
- Brush teeth with baking soda or fluoridated toothpaste. Fluoride is essential for healthy teeth. However, consult a physician or dentist to avoid fluoride poisoning caused by overexposure to fluoridated toothpaste and water; children and the elderly are especially susceptible to fluoride poisoning.
- Gargle daily with warm salt water or antiseptic mouthwash.
- Take high-grade multivitamins and other dietary supplements as recommended by your physician.
- See dentist regularly. Clean teeth frequently.
- Read below the list of foods and liquids to avoid and consume, and use it as a tool to help you design your healthy diet with your dentist. Before you start, make certain to inform your dentist about any medications you are taking.

Avoid	**Consume**
• Sugar, white flour, candy, sweets, desserts and other foods high in simple carbohydrates	• Organic raw vegetables and fresh fruits
• White flour, white potatoes, white pasta, and white rice	• Whole grains and beans

- Coffee, tea, caffeinated drinks, fruit juices, soda, and other sweetened beverages

- Healthy raw snacks, such as apples, carrots, almonds, and sunflower seeds
- Foods high in calcium, such as fish with bones, almonds, almond milk, plain, cultured, low-fat yogurt, low-fat aged cheeses, dark-green leafy vegetables, kelp and other sea vegetables, and sesame and sunflower seeds
- Organic, lean meat
- Natural sweeteners, such as xylitol, stevia, and sorbitol
- Plenty of water (about eight 8-oz. cups daily) free of contaminants and at the correct pH

Heartburn (Indigestion)

Heartburn is a burning sensation or pain that occurs right below the rib-cage in the center of the chest. This is often (but not always) the result of gastroesophageal (or acid) reflux disease, which is due to weakened muscles in the lower end of the esophagus permitting excess acid to be pushed up from the stomach into the esophagus. This excess acid is usually the result of improper digestion after a big or unhealthy meal. After eating, some sufferers release too much hydrochloric acid in the stomach. This often leads to indigestion (burning in the stomach), gastroesophageal reflux (acid reflux), and then heartburn. Most others do not release enough hydrochloric acid or digestive enzymes, and as a result, the improper digestion of food in the gastrointestinal tract produces an excessive amount of acidic gas (consisting mostly of lactic acid), which causes indigestion and then pushes up into the esophagus and causes heartburn.

<u>List of Healthful Suggestions:</u>

- Inhibit foods and beverages that trigger heartburn and produce gas. Some foods and liquids (as listed on the following pages) are commonly known to produce gas, whereas others are individual-dependent.
- Avoid spicy foods, gravies, and sauces to decrease irritation of the stomach.
- Avoid alcohol and caffeine.
- Avoid drinks such as coffee, teas, soda, and fruit juices (especially citrus).
- Avoid saturated fats, trans fats, and fried foods.
- Avoid red meat, such as beef and pork.
- Monitor intake of dietary sources high in omega-6 fatty acids, such as corn oil, soybean oil, safflower oil, sunflower oil, and foods derived from grain-fed animals.
- Eliminate foods that trigger allergic reactions (see list of suggestions in this section under "Allergies").
- Lactose-intolerant individuals need to avoid cow's milk and dairy products. Most lactose-intolerant individuals are able to eat plain, cultured, low-fat yogurt and low-fat aged cheese in moderation.
- Gluten-intolerant individuals should avoid wheat (including spelt), rye, barley and other gluten-containing foods.
- Some natural sweeteners such as xylitol and sorbitol may produce gas in some individuals. Avoid, if this is the case.
- Build a healthy flora by consuming plain, cultured, low-fat yogurt (no sugar), unpasteurized sauerkraut, and unpasteurized, unfiltered, apple-cider vinegar. Under the advice of a physician, also take probiotic (friendly bacteria) capsules, which can be purchased in health-food stores. A healthy flora is extremely important because this will help improve digestion of the healthy foods (e.g., raw vegetables, fresh, citrus fruits, and whole grains) that irritate a weak gastrointestinal tract but provide essential digestive enzymes and fiber.
- Eat foods high in fiber, such as organic vegetables, fruits, and whole grains. Make sure to chew foods adequately. Prevent constipation and improve digestion by eating high-fiber foods.
- Eat foods high in digestive enzymes such as organic, raw vegeta-

bles and fresh fruits, especially pineapples and papayas. Grapefruits and lemons are also great for proper digestion of foods.

- Try eating cabbage—it consists of nutrients that help build the internal lining of the gut—but if it produces too much gas and causes irritation, reduce intake until improve intestinal flora.
- Eat an organic apple the first thing in the morning. This helps improve proper digestion of foods and elimination of toxins.
- Legumes are good to eat but they must be prepared properly to prevent gas (see chapter 39 for preparation of legumes).
- Eat organic lean chicken, turkey, and fish.
- Eat foods and take dietary supplements high in omega-3 fatty acids such as cold-water fish, flaxseeds, walnuts, fish oil, or flaxseed oil.
- Consume olive oil and other dietary sources of monounsaturated fats.
- Check pH level of urine and saliva. If it's acidic, see a physician and eat foods, such as vegetables and fruits that will help make the body less acidic (see chapter 41 for more details).
- Eat foods high in calcium, such as fish with bones, almond milk, almonds, dairy products, dark-green leafy vegetables, plain, low-fat yogurt, aged, low-fat cheese, kelp and other sea vegetables, and sesame and sunflower seeds.
- Add ginger to foods or drink ginger tea.
- Drink plenty of water (about eight 8-oz. cups daily) that is free of contaminants and added minerals, and at the correct pH (see chapter 41 for details).
- Adopt proper eating and drinking habits. Eat healthy, and decrease meal sizes. Do not overeat.
- Eat sitting upright; do not slouch. After eating, sit up. Do not lie down, because this pushes the acid into the esophagus.
- Eat and chew food slowly. Do not gulp food down.
- Chew gum sweetened with natural sweeteners frequently to increase release of saliva with enzymes that help to digest starch.
- Do not constrict stomach with tight clothes, especially when eating.
- Do not eat late at night. If you do, make sure to stay up for at least two hours or until your food is digested before going to bed.
- Drink water instead of carbonated drinks; this will help dilute the burning sensation caused by gas and acidic conditions.

- Do not drink iced water. Drink room temperature or warm water to keep enzymes active and avoid constipation.
- When eating, do not drink much water or other beverages. Drink before or after eating a meal so that that hydrochloric acid will not be diluted in the stomach.
- Exercise regularly. Design an exercise regimen that consists of weight-lifting, aerobic, and abdominal exercises. Make sure to wait about 90 minutes before exercising after a meal.
- Do not smoke cigarettes.
- Prevent taking medications such as ibuprofen and aspirin. These medicines trigger heartburn and indigestion.
- It is important to see a physician to diagnose your symptoms of heartburn (i.e., too much hydrochloric acid or not enough). Depending on your diagnosis, take dietary supplements, such as bromelain and other digestive enzymes, betaine hydrochloride, low doses of baking soda, and unpasteurized, unfiltered apple-cider vinegar under the advice of a physician. Make sure to take dietary supplements (especially betaine hydrochloride and baking soda) under the advice of and at the dosage prescribed by your physician.
- Many people may abuse their intake of prescribed or over-the-counter antacids. Make sure not to overdose on them. Better yet, avoid taking them, if at all possible.
- Work as a team with your physician to eliminate the problem without taking medication. If symptoms persist or you feel symptoms other than a burning sensation, see your physician immediately to make certain there are no heart issues or other serious problems.
- Read below the list of foods and liquids to avoid and consume, and use it as a tool to help you design your healthy diet with your physician. Before you start, make certain to inform your physician about any medications you are taking.

Avoid	**Consume**
• Red meat (beef and pork)	• Organic lean chicken, turkey, and wild fish

• White flour, wheat (spelt), barley, and rye for gluten-sensitive individuals	• Organic, raw vegetables (e.g., cabbage) and fresh fruits (e.g., pineapples and papayas)
• Sugar (white sugar, brown sugar, high fructose corn syrup, glucose, and sucrose) and foods high in simple carbohydrates	• Properly prepared legumes (prepared to prevent gas; if they trigger symptoms, avoid)
• Gravy, spicy seasonings, and hot peppers	• Whole grains (e.g., oatmeal and brown rice), nuts, and seeds
• Coffee, teas, soda, carbonated beverages, and fruit juices, especially citrus juices	• Foods high in calcium, such as fish with bones, almonds, almond milk, green leafy vegetables, plain, cultured, low-fat yogurt, aged, low-fat cheese, kelp and other sea vegetables, and sesame and sunflower seeds (if not allergic to these foods)
• Alcohol and caffeine	• Ginger and ginger tea
• Cow's milk and dairy products for lactose-intolerant individuals	• Fiber rich foods (fresh vegetables and fruits, and whole grains)
• Saturated fats, trans fats, and fried foods	• Olive oil, cold-water fish, flaxseeds, flaxseed oil, walnuts, and fish oil
• Omega-6 fatty acid dietary sources such as corn oil, safflower oil, sunflower oil, soybean oil, and foods derived from grain-fed animals	• Plain, cultured, low-fat yogurt, unpasteurized sauerkraut, and unpasteurized, unfiltered, apple-cider vinegar
	• Plenty of water (about eight 8-oz. cups daily) free of contaminants and added minerals, and at the correct pH

High Blood Pressure (Hypertension)

Hypertension (high blood pressure) is a high measurement of pressure (equal to or higher than 140/90 mm Hg) that the blood exerts against the wall of arteries when the heart beats (systolic pressure; 140 or higher) versus when the heart is at rest (diastolic pressure; 90 or higher). A normal blood pressure is 120/80 or lower. Prehypertension is a measurement of pressure between 120/80 and 140/90. If high blood pressure is left untreated, it may lead to other problems, such as atherosclerosis, heart attack, stroke, and blindness.

List of Healthful Suggestions:

- High cholesterol often leads to high blood pressure. Eliminate saturated fats, cholesterol, and trans fats from your diet. Avoid eating gravy, red meat, organ meats, shrimp, and egg yolks.
- Individuals with high blood pressure often have high triglyceride (fat) levels. Control triglyceride levels in bloodstream by reducing intake of unhealthy fats and simple carbohydrates. Reduce intake of simple carbohydrates by avoiding foods with a high glycemic index value, such as white sugar, white potatoes, white flour, white pasta, and white rice. Eat foods with a moderate glycemic index value in moderation (see chart for glycemic index ranges of foods in chapter 38 under Point to Ponder #2).
- Eat plenty of organic raw vegetables, fresh fruits, beans, and other foods high in fiber.
- Eat organic fresh grapes and berries, high in the phytonutrient resveratrol.
- Avoid alcohol. Some believe that drinking alcohol, especially red wine, is good for the heart and vascular health, but the adverse effects of alcohol may cause more problems than the benefits (see chapter 41 for details).
- Control intake of salt and sodium. Consult a physician about dietary salt and sodium intake.
- Consume dietary sources high in oleic acids such as olive oil.
- Intake dietary sources high in omega-3 fatty acids, such as coldwater fish, flaxseeds, flaxseed oil, and fish oil. Do not consume cod liver oil because it consists of high levels of cholesterol.

- Monitor intake of dietary sources high in omega-6 fatty acids, such as corn oil, soybean oil, safflower oil, sunflower oil, and foods derived from grain-fed animals. More specifically, limit foods high in AA, such as red meat, organ meats, dairy products, and egg yolks.
- Eat whole grains such as whole wheat and whole spelt (in moderation), and whole grain oats and whole grain brown rice. Also, eat other foods high in complex carbohydrates such as yam-sweet potatoes.
- Add garlic and onions to foods.
- Eat organic lean chicken, turkey, wild fish, and beans.
- Check pH level of urine and saliva. If it's acidic, see a physician and eat foods such as vegetables and fruits that will help make the body less acidic (see chapter 41 for more details).
- Maintain a healthy flora by consuming plain, cultured, low-fat yogurt (no sugar) and unpasteurized, unfiltered, apple-cider vinegar. Under the advice of a physician, also take probiotic capsules, which can be purchased in health-food stores.
- Avoid cow's milk and most cheeses. Replace cow's milk with foods high in calcium, such as fish with bones, almond milk, almonds, dark-green leafy vegetables, plain, cultured, low-fat yogurt, and sesame seeds.
- Eat foods high in potassium such as bananas, apples, green-leafy vegetables, tomatoes, cucumbers, zucchini, and whole grains.
- Drink plenty of water (about eight 8-oz.cups daily) free of contaminants and added minerals (e.g., fluoride and chlorine), and at the correct pH (see chapter 41 for details).
- Exercise regularly, and design an exercise regimen with your physician. Gradually increase aerobic exercise. It's important to monitor your heart rate before and during exercise.
- Lose excess weight and maintain weight in the healthy normal range. Excess weight increases blood pressure.
- Keep hypertension treated to avoid heart disease and other serious problems.
- Monitor your blood pressure daily if it's above 140/90. Consult your physician and learn how to take your blood pressure with a home device.

- Reduce stress. Control anxiety, anger, and other stressful emotions.
- Take high-grade multivitamins and other dietary supplements as recommended by your physician.
- Consult a physician to find out if need to take calcium and potassium supplements.
- Avoid taking medicines that increase blood pressure and heart rate. Consult your physician on which medicines are safe.
- Consult your physician and take medication as prescribed. Under the advice of your physician, try to control or eliminate high blood pressure through diet and exercise.
- Read below the list of foods and liquids to avoid and consume, and use it as a tool to help you design your healthy diet with your physician. Before you start, make certain to inform your physician about any medications you are taking.

Avoid	Consume
• Red meat (beef and pork), organ meats, shrimp, cod liver oil, and egg yolks	• Organic raw vegetables and fresh fruits (especially grapes and berries)
• White flour, white potatoes, white rice, and white pasta, complemented with or without gravies and cream sauces	• Organic lean chicken and turkey, wild fish, and beans
• Omega-6 fatty acid dietary sources such as corn, safflower, sunflower, and soybean oil, and foods derived from grain-fed animals, and especially, AA in red meat, organ meats, cow's milk, egg yolks, and dairy products	• Omega-3 fatty acid dietary sources such as flaxseeds and flaxseed oil, and especially EPA and DHA in fish oil and cold-water fish, such as salmon, mackerel, tuna, sardines, and herring

- Salt and sodium (consult physician about dietary salt and sodium intake)
- Alcohol, fruit juices, carbonated beverages, caffeine, and coffee
- Cow's milk and cheeses
- Sugar (white sugar, brown sugar, high fructose corn syrup, glucose, and sucrose) and other foods high in simple carbohydrates
- Saturated fats, trans fats, and cholesterol

- Whole grains (oatmeal, brown rice, whole wheat), yam-sweet potatoes, nuts (almonds and walnuts), and seeds
- Olive oil and other dietary sources of oleic acids
- Garlic and onions
- Foods high in calcium such as fish with bones, plain, cultured, low-fat yogurt, almonds, almond milk, dark-green leafy vegetables, and sesame seeds
- Foods high in potassium such as bananas, legumes, green-leafy vegetables, and whole grains
- Plenty of water (about eight 8-oz. cups daily) free of contaminants and added minerals (e.g., fluoride and chlorine), and at the correct pH

High Cholesterol

High cholesterol is due to elevated levels of LDL ("bad") cholesterol—and in many cases also due to low levels of HDL ("good") cholesterol—in the bloodstream (see chapter 36 for more details). Some people with high cholesterol inherited the problem of a high LDL to HDL cholesterol ratio that is intensified by dietary fats such as trans fat, saturated fats, and cholesterol, but most people with high cholesterol can blame it on their unhealthy lifestyles. High cholesterol levels may lead to other problems, such as atherosclerosis, high blood pressure, heart attacks, and strokes.

List of Healthful Suggestions:

- Avoid junk food such as fried, processed, and packaged foods.
- Eliminate saturated fats, cholesterol, and trans fats from your diet. Some foods that may contain these fats are crackers, chips, French fries, egg yolks, cookies, margarine, butter, pastries, and cakes.
- Avoid eating gravy, red meats, organ meats, and shrimp. Eat organic lean chicken and turkey, wild fish, and beans. Remove skins from meat, and cut away all visible fat.
- Do not consume excess salt and sodium. Consult a physician about dietary salt and sodium intake.
- Individuals with high cholesterol levels usually have high triglyceride (fat) levels. Control triglyceride levels in bloodstream by reducing intake of unhealthy fats and simple carbohydrates. Reduce intake of simple carbohydrates by avoiding foods with a high glycemic index value, such as white sugar, white potatoes, white flour, white pasta, and white rice. Eat foods with a moderate glycemic index value in moderation (see chart in chapter 38 under Point to Ponder #2 for glycemic index ranges of different foods).
- Eat plenty of organic raw vegetables and fresh fruits, especially grapes and berries, high in the phytonutrient resveratrol.
- Avoid alcohol. Drinking alcohol in moderation, especially red wine, may be good for the heart and help to inhibit the buildup of cholesterol on arterial walls, but the adverse effects of alcohol may cause more problems than benefits (see chapter 41 for more details).
- Avoid caffeine, coffee, tea, soda, fruit juice, and carbonated beverages.
- Do not fry foods; bake, grill, broil, or steam them.
- Consume dietary sources high in oleic acids such as olive oil.
- Eat foods high in omega-3 fatty acids such as cold-water fish, and flaxseeds, and intake other dietary sources such as flaxseed oil and fish oil under the advice of a physician. Do not take cod liver oil because it is high in cholesterol.
- Monitor intake of dietary sources high in omega-6 fatty acids, such as corn oil, soybean oil, safflower oil, sunflower oil, and foods derived from grain-fed animals. More specifically, limit foods high in AA, such as red meat, organ meats, dairy products, and egg yolks.

- Eat whole grains, such as whole wheat and whole spelt (in moderation), oats, and brown rice. Also, eat other complex carbohydrates such as yam-sweet potatoes.
- Eat organic lean chicken, turkey, wild fish, and beans.
- Avoid cow's milk and cheese. Replace cow's milk with foods high in calcium, such as fish with bones, almond milk, almonds, dark-green leafy vegetables, plain, cultured, low-fat yogurt, and sesame seeds.
- Check pH level of urine and saliva. If it's acidic, see a physician and eat foods, such as vegetables and fruits that will help make the body less acidic (see chapter 41 for more details).
- Build a healthy flora by consuming plain, cultured, low-fat yogurt (no sugar) and unpasteurized, unfiltered, apple-cider vinegar. Under the advice of a physician, also take probiotic (friendly bacteria) capsules, which can be purchased in health-food stores.
- Add garlic and onions to foods.
- Drink plenty of water (about eight 8-oz.cups daily) free of contaminants and added minerals (e.g., fluoride and chlorine), and at the correct pH (see chapter 41 for details).
- Exercise regularly, and design an exercise regimen with your physician. Gradually increase aerobic exercise. It's important to monitor your heart rate before and during exercise.
- Lose excess weight (especially upper-body fat) and maintain weight within the healthy range.
- Take high-grade multivitamins and other dietary supplements as recommended by your physician.
- Have your blood cholesterol levels tested routinely. If the results of these tests are within the high range, take your prescribed medicine, and design a diet and exercise regimen with your physician based on your physical conditions. Also, work with your physician to determine if it is possible to get off the medication by eating right and exercising.
- Read the following list of foods and liquids to avoid and consume, and use it as a tool to help you design your healthy diet with your physician. Before you start, make certain to inform your physician about any medications you are taking.

Avoid	Consume
• Red meats (beef and pork), shrimp, organ meat, cod liver oil, and egg yolks	• Organic lean chicken, turkey, wild fish, and beans
• White flour; white potatoes, white rice, and white pasta, complemented with gravies and cream sauces	• Organic raw vegetables and fresh fruits (especially red grapes and berries high in resveratrol)
• Omega-6 fatty acid dietary sources such as corn, safflower, sunflower and soybean oil, and foods derived from grain-fed animals, and especially, AA in red meat, organ meats, cow's milk, egg yolks, and dairy products	• Dietary sources of omega-3 fatty acids such as flaxseeds and flaxseed oil, and especially, EPA and DHA in fish oil and cold-water fish such as salmon, mackerel, tuna, sardines, and herring
• Salt and sodium (consult physician about dietary intake levels)	• Olive oil and other dietary sources of oleic acids
• Cow's milk and cheeses	• Garlic and onions
• Alcohol, carbonated beverages, fruit juices, and caffeine	• Whole grains (oatmeal, brown rice, and whole wheat), yam-sweet potatoes, and almonds
• Sugar (white sugar, brown sugar, high fructose corn syrup, glucose, sucrose) and other foods high in simple carbohydrates	• Foods high in calcium, such as fish with bones, almonds, almond milk, dark-green leafy vegetables, plain, cultured, low-fat yogurt, and sesame seeds
• Saturated fats, trans fats, and cholesterol	• Plain, cultured, low-fat yogurt (no sugar) and unpasteurized, unfiltered, apple-cider vinegar

- Plenty of water (about eight 8-oz. cups daily) free of contaminants and added minerals (e.g., fluoride and chlorine), and at the correct pH

Hypoglycemia

Hypoglycemia occurs when the blood-glucose level drops below the normal range, which is the range required to properly fuel the body. Symptoms of hypoglycemia are dizziness, blurred vision, confusion, loss of concentration, hypothermia, tremors, irritability, headaches, cold sweat, hallucinations, and coma. The standard definition of hypoglycemia, in which blood glucose falls below the normal range, is not a typical health problem. However, many Americans suffer from symptoms similar to hypoglycemia due to a high white sugar and white flour diet, which causes sudden elevations and drops of blood-glucose levels within the normal range. These hypoglycemic-like symptoms can usually be avoided by maintaining a constant blood-glucose level through diet and exercise. If you demonstrate hypoglycemic symptoms, however, consult a medical physician and have blood-glucose levels tested. Unfortunately, the symptoms are sometimes difficult to diagnose. Most who suffer from these symptoms are diagnosed as having blood-glucose levels within the normal range, and thus are not considered to be hypoglycemic. But if you are suffering from these symptoms and suspect that you have been misdiagnosed, try getting a second opinion from other physicians who have adapted the holistic approach into their practice.

<u>List of Healthful Suggestions:</u>

- Eat plenty of organic, raw vegetables, fresh fruits, and beans.
- Eat complex carbohydrates, such as whole grains (e.g., oats and brown rice), whole wheat bread, whole spelt bread, whole wheat pasta, and yam-sweet potatoes.
- Avoid white sugar, white flour, refined cereals, and other foods high in simple carbohydrates (see chart for glycemic index ranges of foods in chapter 38 under Point to Ponder #2).

- Avoid white potatoes. If you do eat potatoes, eat new potatoes.
- Avoid foods that trigger allergies (see the list of healthful suggestions in this section under “Allergies”).
- If lactose-intolerant, avoid cow’s milk and dairy products.
- Avoid rice milk; it is a high glycemic food.
- Gluten-intolerant individuals should avoid wheat (including spelt), rye, barley and other gluten-containing foods.
- Avoid fruit juices, sodas, and other sugar-sweetened drinks.
- Eat natural sweeteners such as stevia, xylitol, and sorbitol.
- Avoid drinking alcohol.
- Avoid junk food, processed and packaged foods, and artificial sweeteners, preservatives, and other additives.
- Avoid saturated fat and trans fat foods.
- Consume sources consisting of monounsaturated fats such as olive oil and avocados.
- Intake dietary sources high in omega-3 fatty acids, such as cold-water fish, flaxseeds, walnuts, fish oil, or flaxseed oil. If you take medicine for hypoglycemia, consult a physician before ingesting dietary sources of omega-3 fatty acids.
- Monitor intake of dietary sources high in omega-6 fatty acids, such as corn oil, soybean oil, safflower oil, sunflower oil, and foods derived from grain-fed animals.
- Eat foods high in calcium, such as fish with bones, almond milk, almonds, dark-green leafy vegetables, plain, cultured, low-fat yogurt, aged, low-fat cheese, kelp and other sea vegetables, and sesame and sunflower seeds.
- Check pH level of urine and saliva. If it’s acidic, see a physician and eat foods, such as vegetables and fruits that will help make the body less acidic (see chapter 41 for more details).
- Build a healthy flora by consuming plain, cultured, low-fat yogurt (no sugar), unpasteurized sauerkraut, and unpasteurized, unfiltered, apple-cider vinegar. Under the advice of a physician, also take probiotic (friendly bacteria) capsules, which can be purchased in health-food stores.
- Eat small frequent meals (approximately four to six small meals) throughout the day, or eat snacks between breakfast, lunch, and

dinner. Make sure snacks are healthy, such as almonds, carrots, and apples. Also, before going to bed at night, eat healthy snacks, and if you wake up in the middle of the night, eat a few almonds.

- Drink plenty of water (about eight 8-oz. cups) that is free of contaminants and added minerals, and at the correct pH throughout the day (see chapter 41 for details).
- Exercise regularly. Regulate stress levels. Keep at a healthy weight.
- Take high-grade multivitamins and other dietary supplements as recommended by your physician.
- Read below the list of foods and liquids to avoid and consume, and use it as a tool to help you design your healthy diet with your physician. Before you start, make certain to inform your physician about any medications you are taking.

Avoid	Consume
• White flour and refined wheat flour	• Organic raw vegetables
• Sugar (white sugar, brown sugar, high fructose corn syrup, alcohol, glucose, sucrose) and other foods high in simple carbohydrates	• Organic fresh fruits (especially apples)—Exceptions: watermelon and cantaloupe should be eaten in moderation
• White semolina pasta	• Organic, lean meats and other protein foods
• Rice milk	• Almond milk, plain low-fat yogurt, and low-fat aged cheese
• White rice	• Yam-sweet potatoes
• White potatoes	• Whole grain foods (whole oats, brown rice, whole wheat, whole spelt, whole grain pasta, and whole grain cereals)

- Table salt (consume 1 teaspoon or less of salt per day; sea salt is preferable)
- Coffee, tea, fruit juices, and sodas and other carbonated beverages
- Artificial sweeteners
- Alcohol
- Omega-6 fatty acid dietary sources such as corn oil, safflower oil, sunflower oil, soybean oil, and foods derived from grain-fed animals

- Nuts (almonds and walnuts) and sunflower seeds
- Natural sweeteners such as xylitol, stevia and sorbitol
- Monounsaturated oil such as olive oil
- Cold-water fish, walnuts, flaxseeds, flaxseed oil, and fish oil (If you take medication for hypoglycemia, consult a physician before consuming these oils)
- Foods high in calcium, such as fish with bones, almonds, almond milk, dark-green leafy vegetables, plain, low-fat yogurt, aged, low-fat cheese, kelp and other sea vegetables, and sesame and sunflower seeds
- Plain, cultured, low-fat yogurt (no sugar), unpasteurized sauerkraut, and unpasteurized, unfiltered, apple-cider vinegar
- Plenty of water (about eight 8-oz. cups daily) free of contaminants and added minerals, and at the correct pH

Irritable Bowel Syndrome

Irritable bowel syndrome (IBS) is due to an irritated digestive system that results in cramps, gas, diarrhea, or constipation. In the majority of people, sensitivity to certain foods triggers IBS.

<u>List of Healthful Suggestions:</u>

- Identify which foods and beverages trigger IBS, and eliminate them from your diet. These foods and beverages are usually cow's milk, dairy products, wheat, sugar, eggs, red meats, saturated fatty foods, fried foods, processed foods consisting of trans fats, alcohol, soda, carbonated beverages, and white potatoes.
- Avoid cow's milk and cheese if lactose intolerant. Replace cow's milk with foods high in calcium, such as fish with bones, almonds, almond milk, dark-green leafy vegetables, plain, cultured, low-fat yogurt, kelp and other sea vegetables, and sesame and sunflower seeds. Some individuals may be able to eat low-fat, aged cheese in moderation. People allergic to casein or whey proteins should avoid cow's milk.
- Gluten-intolerant individuals should avoid wheat (including spelt), rye, barley and other gluten-containing foods.
- Avoid all foods that trigger allergies (see the list of healthful suggestions in this section under "Allergies").
- Some natural sweeteners such as xylitol and sorbitol may produce gas in some individuals. Avoid them if this is the case.
- Build a healthy flora by consuming plain, cultured, low-fat yogurt (no sugar), unpasteurized sauerkraut, and unpasteurized, unfiltered, apple-cider vinegar. Under the advice of a physician, also take probiotic capsules, which can be purchased at health-food stores. A healthy flora is extremely important because this will help improve digestion of the healthy foods (e.g., raw vegetables, fresh, citrus fruits, and whole foods) that irritate a weak gastrointestinal tract but provide essential digestive enzymes and fiber.
- Prevent constipation and improve digestion by eating high-fiber foods, such as organic vegetables, fruits, yam-sweet potatoes, and whole grains (e.g., whole oats and brown rice).
- Properly soak and prepare beans before eating them (see chapter 39 for details). This will help prevent gas production, which can irritate the digestive system.
- Eat foods high in digestive enzymes such as organic raw vegetables and fresh fruits, especially pineapples and papayas.
- Try eating cabbage—it consists of nutrients that help build the in-

ternal lining of the gut—but if it produces gas and causes irritation, reduce intake.

- Check pH level of urine and saliva. If it's acidic, see a physician and eat foods, such as vegetables and fruits that will help make the body less acidic (see chapter 41 for more details).
- Consume dietary sources high in monounsaturated fats such as olive oil.
- Intake dietary sources high in omega-3 fatty acids, such as cold-water fish, flaxseeds, walnuts, fish oil, or flaxseed oil.
- Monitor intake of dietary sources high in omega-6 fatty acids, such as corn oil, soybean oil, safflower oil, sunflower oil, and foods derived from grain-fed animals.
- Drink plenty of water (about eight 8-oz. cups daily) free of contaminants and added minerals, and at the correct pH (see chapter 41 for details).
- Chew food thoroughly, and eat slowly. Do not gulp down food. Take a long time to eat a meal.
- Do not overeat or stuff yourself. When your stomach is full and content, stop eating.
- While eating, do not drink much water or other beverages. Drink after eating.
- Do not drink iced water. Drink room temperature or warm water. If you have problems with constipation, drink warm water.
- Monitor your stress level. Too much stress can trigger IBS.
- Exercise (both aerobic and weight training) regularly. Exercise relieves stress, keeps the digestive system strong and functioning properly, and maintains muscle strength.
- Consult a physician. Take dietary digestive enzymes, dietary fiber, multivitamins, and other dietary supplements under the advice of a physician. As a team, try to prevent IBS symptoms through diet, without medication.
- Read the following list of foods and liquids to avoid and consume, and use it as a tool to help you design your healthy diet with your physician. Before you start, make certain to inform your physician about any medications you are taking.

Avoid	Consume
• Red meat (beef and pork)	• Organic lean chicken and turkey, and wild fish
• Saturated fats, trans fats, and fried foods	• Complex carbohydrates such as yam-sweet potatoes
• Wheat, barley, and rye for gluten-intolerant individuals	• Properly prepared legumes (prepared to prevent gas)
• White flour, sugar (white sugar, brown sugar, high fructose corn syrup, glucose, and sucrose), and foods high in simple carbohydrates	• Whole grains such as oats and brown rice—Exceptions: if gluten-intolerant, avoid whole wheat and other gluten containing foods.
• Cow's milk and dairy products for lactose-intolerant individuals	• Foods high in fiber, such as organic, raw vegetables and fresh fruits
• Coffee, teas, carbonated beverages, and fruit juices	• Cold-water fish, flaxseeds, flaxseed oil, walnuts, fish oil, and olive oil
• Omega-6 fatty acid dietary sources such as corn oil, safflower oil, sunflower oil, soybean oil, and foods derived from grain-fed animals	• Foods high in calcium, such as fish with bones, almonds, almond milk, dark-green leafy vegetables, plain, cultured, low-fat yogurt, kelp and other sea vegetables, and sesame and sunflower seeds (if not allergic to these foods)
• Gravy, spicy seasonings, and hot peppers	• Plain, cultured, low-fat yogurt, unpasteurized, unfiltered apple-cider vinegar, and unpasteurized sauerkraut

- Alcohol and caffeine
- Plenty of water (about eight 8-oz. cups daily) free of contaminants and added minerals, and at the correct pH

Obesity

Obesity is the condition of accumulating excess body fat and having a BMI greater than 29 (see chapter 31 for details). Obesity often leads to other health issues, such as premature aging, heart disease, atherosclerosis, cancer, diabetes mellitus, high blood pressure, high triglycerides, and high cholesterol.

List of Healthful Suggestions:

- Eat organic raw vegetables and most organic fresh fruits. Consume watermelon and cantaloupe in moderation.
- Eat plenty of salads made with dark-green leafy vegetables and a splash of olive oil and balsamic vinegar.
- Consume fresh acidic and citrus fruits such as pineapples, lemons, and grapefruits, and unpasteurized, unfiltered apple-cider vinegar to help increase metabolism and the breakdown of fat.
- Avoid sugar, white flour, and foods high in simple carbohydrate foods. Diabetes mellitus and obesity often occur, simultaneously. See the diet described in this section under "Diabetes Mellitus (Type II)."
- Avoid cholesterol and foods that increase triglyceride levels. High cholesterol, high triglycerides, and obesity often occur simultaneously. See the diet described in this section under "High Cholesterol."
- Avoid unhealthy fatty foods, especially those consisting of saturated fats and trans fat. Do not eat fried foods. Eating a diet that causes obesity often leads to atherosclerosis. See the diet described in this section under "Atherosclerosis."
- Avoid excess salt and foods that cause high blood pressure. Obesity often leads to high blood pressure. See the diet described in this section under "High Blood Pressure."
- Monitor intake of dietary sources high in omega-6 fatty acids, such

as corn oil, soybean oil, safflower oil, sunflower oil, and foods derived from grain-fed animals.

- Avoid cow's milk, especially if you are lactose intolerant. If you consume cow's milk, purchase skim milk. Replace cow's milk with foods high in calcium, such as fish with bones, almonds, almond milk, dark-green leafy vegetables, plain, cultured, low-fat yogurt, and sesame seeds.
- Avoid consumption of rice milk; it has a high glycemic index value.
- Eat organic lean chicken and turkey, and wild fish. Avoid beef, pork, and shrimp.
- Eat complex carbohydrates, such as whole grains (e.g., whole wheat, whole spelt, oats, and brown rice) and yam-sweet potatoes in moderation.
- Eat foods high in fiber such as raw vegetables and beans.
- Avoid junk food such as fried, packaged, and processed foods.
- Avoid snacking. If you snack, eat healthy snacks, such as raw carrots, almonds, and apples.
- Do not drink alcohol, soda, caffeinated coffee and tea, fruit juice, carbonated beverages, and sugar-sweetened drinks.
- Avoid acidosis by adjusting pH within the normal range of 6.4–7.2 (see chapter 41 for a list of foods and drinks that can help eliminate acidosis). It is extremely difficult to lose weight if body pH is below the normal range.
- Build a healthy flora by consuming plain, cultured, low-fat yogurt (no sugar), unpasteurized sauerkraut, and unpasteurized, unfiltered, apple-cider vinegar. Under the advice of a physician, also take probiotic (friendly bacteria) capsules, which can be purchased at health-food stores. This will help improve digestion and decrease weight gain.
- Consume dietary sources of monounsaturated fats such as olive oil in moderation.
- Intake dietary sources of omega-3 fatty acids, such as fish oil, flaxseeds, and flaxseed oil in moderation, and also cold-water fish.
- Drink plenty of water (about eight 8-oz. cups daily) free of contaminants and added minerals, and at the correct pH (see chapter 41 for details).

- At mealtime, do not take second helpings unless it is raw vegetables or certain fresh fruits (such as apples and other fruits with a low glycemic index value).
- Avoid eating late at night. Finish eating your last meal at least two hours before bedtime.
- Take high-grade multivitamins and other dietary supplements as recommended by your physician.
- Do not attempt to lose weight by starvation, fad diets, or medications. Lose excess weight through a healthy diet and regular exercise, and see your physician routinely.
- With your physician, design an exercise regimen that will allow you to lose weight but not cause any heart problems, bodily injury, or harm.
- Be careful to avoid bodily injury. Bodies with excess fat are easy to bruise and seriously injure.
- Read below the list of foods and liquids to avoid and consume, and use it as a tool to help you and your physician design a diet that fits your physical condition. Before you start, make certain to inform your physician about any medications you are taking.

Avoid	**Consume**
• White flour and wheat flour	• Organic raw vegetables and fresh fruits
• White potatoes, white rice, and white pasta, with or without gravies and cream sauces	• Organic lean chicken and turkey, wild fish, and beans
• Saturated fats, trans fats, and cholesterol	• Fish oil, flaxseeds, and flaxseed oil in moderation, and cold-water fish
• Table salt and sodium (consult a physician for sodium intake)	• Olive oil in moderation

• Omega-6 fatty acid dietary sources such as corn oil, safflower oil, sunflower oil, soybean oil, and foods derived from grain-fed animals	• Whole grains (oatmeal, brown rice, whole wheat, and whole spelt) and almonds in moderation
• Cow's milk, cheeses, and most other dairy products	• Yam-sweet potatoes
• Sugar (white sugar, brown sugar, high fructose corn syrup, glucose, and sucrose) and foods high in simple carbohydrates	• Foods high in calcium, such as fish with bones, almonds, almond milk, low-fat cheeses, plain, cultured, low-fat yogurt, green leafy vegetables, and sesame seeds
• Red meats (beef and pork), organ meats, cod liver oil, egg yolks, and shrimp	• Plain, cultured, low-fat yogurt and unpasteurized, unfiltered, apple-cider vinegar
• Artificial sweeteners	• Natural sweeteners such as xylitol, stevia, and sorbitol
• Alcohol, fruit juice, soda and other carbonated beverages, caffeinated coffee and tea, and sweetened drinks	• Plenty of water (about eight 8-oz. cups daily) free of contaminants and added minerals, and at the correct pH

Osteoporosis

Osteoporosis is the loss of bone mass (density), which causes bones to be porous and fragile. Many factors may be responsible for osteoporosis, such as the malabsorption of calcium and other minerals, poor diet, aging, lack of activity, malnutrition, and an imbalance of hormone secretion. In this country, osteoporosis is most prevalent in postmenopausal, underweight women (BMI < 19) with a poor absorption of calcium. Although protein is required for proper bone formation, most Americans consume too much animal protein, especially that found in red meat and cow's milk. A diet rich in animal protein can decrease the absorption of calcium, a major mineral required for bone formation. In contrast, the consumption of plant protein seems to inhibit calcium absorption to a lesser degree than that of animal protein, and thus, is considered to be a good source of protein. Plant-derived foods, however, also often consist of the phytonutrients phytic acids and oxalic acids, which are known to cause malabsorption of calcium. For instance, certain plant-derived foods such as whole grains, legumes (especially soybeans), nuts, and seeds are excellent sources of calcium, protein, and other nutrients required for bone formation but are also high in phytic acids. Phytic acids that occur naturally in the hull of plant-derived foods can cause malabsorption of calcium (and other minerals) by combining with these minerals to form salts that are excreted in the urine. In most foods, phytic acids can be destroyed by cooking, but fermentation is required to substantially reduce that found in soybeans. Besides protein and calcium, fiber is also important in bone formation: it helps to maintain healthy digestion and increase absorption of nutrients. But some high-fiber foods such as spinach and rhubarb consist of oxalic acids, which are naturally occurring chemicals in plants that combine with calcium and other minerals to form salts. Like those formed with phytic acids, these mineral salts are excreted in the urine and inhibit absorption of minerals within the body. Therefore, to increase and maintain bone density, it is important to start eating a healthy diet—the younger you are, the better—that will will provide the body with enough protein and fiber and still allow proper absorption of the required levels of calcium and other minerals.

List of Healthful Suggestions:

- Eat a healthy diet consisting of much foods high in nutrients, such as vegetables (exceptions: reduce intake of spinach, rhubarb, and soybeans), fruits, and nuts.
- Eat foods rich in calcium (e.g., fish with bones, dark-green leafy vegetables, homemade almond milk, fortified almond milk, fortified rice milk, broccoli, kelp and other sea vegetables, and sesame and sunflower seeds), magnesium (e.g., nuts, whole grains, green leafy vegetables, and beans), and vitamin D (e.g., fortified rice milk, fortified almond milk, fortified cereals, and cold-water fish such as salmon, mackerel, tuna, herring, and sardines) to help build up bone density.

- Exposure to sunshine (ultraviolet light) is the best method for stimulating production of vitamin D in body, but intense or constant exposure is not highly recommended due to the hole in the ozone layer. Thus, all exposure to sunlight needs to be properly controlled to reduce the risk of skin cancer.
- Consume sufficient levels of protein required for healthy bones, but do not overindulge in foods that are rich in animal protein, such as red meat and cow's milk. Eat organic chicken, turkey, and wild fish in moderation. Aged cheese and cultured yogurt are excellent sources of digestible proteins that may be eaten in moderation. Consult a physician about the amount of animal protein that someone at your age and size and with your health conditions can safely consume.
- Plant protein is a good source of protein. Eat beans and other foods high in plant protein in moderation, but because of the phytic acids, it may be best to reduce your intake of soybeans and soy products. Tempeh, miso, and tofu that are fermented are acceptable to eat. But most tofu is curdled, not fermented; thus, it consists of phytic acids that should be avoided. Seek advice from your physician about which foods you should eat to avoid high levels of phytic acids and obtain the amount of protein and calcium required for someone at your age and size and with your health conditions.
- Consuming soybeans is somewhat controversial for several reasons (see chapter 39 for details). Soybeans are not only high in protein, protein enzyme inhibitors, calcium, and phytic acids, but they also consist of the phytonutrient isoflavones, which may help to prevent bone loss in menopausal women at high concentrations. Consult your physician about consuming soybeans and soy products.
- Have your physician design for you a balanced diet consisting of foods high in calcium, and fiber but low in oxalic acids. Many high-fiber foods, such as spinach and rhubarb, are high in oxalic acids. Other foods high in oxalic acid are chocolate, cocoa, wheat, black pepper, nuts, beets, legumes, and Swiss chard.
- If gluten-intolerant, avoid whole wheat, whole spelt, rye and barley. This often leads to celiac disease and the malabsorption of calcium and other nutrients.

- Avoid acidosis by adjusting pH within the normal range of 6.4–7.2 (see chapter 41 for a list of foods and drinks that can help eliminate acidosis). Acidic conditions decrease the absorption of calcium and other minerals into the body.
- Build a healthy flora by consuming plain, cultured, low-fat yogurt (no sugar), unpasteurized sauerkraut, and unpasteurized, unfiltered, apple-cider vinegar. Under the advice of a physician, also take probiotic (friendly bacteria) capsules, which can be purchased in health-food stores.
- Avoid saturated fats and trans fats.
- Consume healthy fats found in dietary sources such as olive oil, avocados, fish oil, flaxseeds, cold-water fish (in moderation), walnuts, and flaxseed oil.
- Monitor intake of dietary sources high in omega-6 fatty acids, such as corn oil, soybean oil, safflower oil, sunflower oil, and foods derived from grain-fed animals.
- Avoid processed and packaged foods, and food additives.
- Avoid such bad habits as excess salt and sodium in the diet; cigarette smoking. These habits can cause bone loss.
- Drink plenty of water (about eight 8-oz. cups daily) free of contaminants, low in added minerals (e.g., fluoride and chlorine), and at the right pH (see chapter 41 for details). Consult your physician about what type of water that someone with osteoporosis should avoid (e.g., distilled water and chlorine and fluoride poisoning may lead to malabsorption of minerals).
- Do not drink alcohol, soda and other carbonated beverages, and caffeinated coffee and tea; these beverages can lead to bone loss.
- Purchase high-quality calcium, magnesium, and vitamin D supplements, multivitamins, and other dietary supplements that are readily absorbed and recommended by your physician. It is important not to overdose on dietary supplements.
- Exercise regularly (weight-bearing, weight-lifting, and aerobic exercises) to increase muscle mass and bone strength. Consult your physician in designing an exercise regimen that will not cause bodily injure and fracture or damage bones.
- Use a back brace, if necessary, to reduce injury during exercising.
- Through diet, exercise, and the advice of a physician, prevent or

treat the diseases that inhibit absorption of calcium and other nutrients into the gut, such as irritable bowel syndrome (IBS), Crohn's disease, yeast syndrome, and ulcerations in the digestive tract due to inflammation.

- Consult a physician to determine if you need to increase estrogen levels. Natural remedies and dietary supplements such as soy isoflavones may help with low estrogen levels. (See chapter 39 for information on soybeans. Take soy isoflavones only under the advice of a physician).
- If you take corticosteroids, research the adverse effects. Long-term exposure to corticosteroids taken for health problems, such as asthma and arthritis, can cause osteoporosis. Check with your physician about corticosteroids and other medications that are known to cause osteoporosis.
- Consult a physician to see if you can control osteoporosis with diet and exercise, without taking medicine. If not, there are medications that can help decrease the progression of the disease.
- Read the following list of foods and liquids to avoid and consume, and use it as a tool to help you and your physician design a diet that fits your physical condition. Before you start, make certain to inform your physician about any medications you are taking.

Avoid	Consume
• Reduce intake of red meat, cow's milk, and dairy products (Exception: cultured yogurt and aged cheese)	• Organic fresh vegetables, especially ones rich in calcium such as dark-greens and broccoli (Exceptions: reduce intake of spinach and rhubarb)
• Soda and other carbonated beverages	• Plenty of organic fresh fruits and nuts

• Omega-6 fatty acid dietary sources such as corn oil, safflower oil, sunflower oil, soybean oil, and foods derived from grain-fed animals	• Calcium foods such as fish with bones (eat in moderation), dark-green leafy vegetables, broccoli, and almond and rice milk, kelp and other sea vegetables, plain, cultured yogurt, aged cheese, and sesame and sunflower seeds
• Salt and sodium (contact physician for levels of intake)	• Olive oil, avocados, fish oil, flaxseeds, walnuts, and flaxseed oil. Eat cold-water fish (e.g., sardines, mackerels, salmon, herring and tuna) in moderation.
• White flour, sugar (white sugar, brown sugar, high fructose corn syrup, glucose, and sucrose), and foods high in simple carbohydrates	• Protein foods—organic lean meat, such as chicken, turkey, and wild fish in moderation (<u>Exception</u>: avoid red meat), and beans (<u>Exception</u>: avoid soybeans)
• Alcohol	• Whole grains such as brown rice, oats, and barley; whole wheat and whole spelt and gluten containing foods in moderation (if gluten intolerant avoid wheat, barley, and rye)
• Saturated fats and trans fats	• Plain, cultured yogurt (no sugar), unpasteurized sauerkraut, and unpasteurized, unfiltered, apple-cider vinegar

• Reduce intake of spinach, rhubarb, soybeans, and soybean products	• Foods high in magnesium such as nuts, whole grains, green leafy vegetables, and beans; and foods high in vitamin D such as fortified rice milk, fortified almond milk, fortified unsweetened cereals, and cold-water fish
• Caffeine, coffee, tea, and distilled water	• Plenty of water (about eight 8-oz. cups daily) free of contaminants and other added minerals (e.g., fluoride and chlorine), and at the correct pH

Sinusitis, Chronic (Chronic Sinus Infection)

Chronic sinusitis is the frequent reoccurrence of an infection (bacterial, viral, or yeast) in the sinuses, the cavities located above (frontal sinuses) and below (maxillary sinuses) each eye and also between the eyes (ethmoid sinuses).

<u>List of Healthful Suggestions:</u>

- Eat plenty of organic raw vegetables and eat most organic fresh fruit in moderation.
- Avoid fruits that are allergens. If have a yeast infection, eliminate fruits from diet. When the infection is gone, add fruits back to diet gradually.
- Avoid white flour, white sugar, and foods high in simple carbohydrates.
- Allergies and allergens can trigger sinusitis. Follow suggestions and diet described in this section under "Allergies" to eliminate or control allergies.
- Yeast syndrome can trigger sinusitis. Follow the suggestions and yeast-free diet described in this section under "Yeast Syndrome (Candidiasis)" to eliminate and control these symptoms.

- Eat garlic (especially raw), onions, hot peppers, and horseradish regularly, but if allergic to these foods, avoid them.
- Check pH level of urine and saliva. If it's too acidic, see a physician and eat foods, such as vegetables and fruits that will help make the body less acidic (see chapter 41 for more details).
- Avoid cow's milk and dairy products, especially ice cream. Dairy coupled with excess mucus appears to irritate the sinuses. Mucus is a breeding ground for bacteria, viruses, and yeast. However, plain, cultured, low-fat yogurt (a good source of probiotics) is acceptable.
- Substitute cow's milk with foods high in calcium, such as fish with bones, almond milk, green leafy vegetables, plain, cultured, low-fat yogurt, kelp and other sea vegetables, and sesame seeds.
- Eat vegetables high in fiber and complex carbohydrates such as yam-sweet potatoes and beans, but avoid white potatoes. Make sure dried beans are properly prepared (see chapter 39 for details on how to cook beans).
- Eat whole grains (e.g., oats, brown rice, whole wheat, and whole spelt) high in fiber and complex carbohydrates. When suffering from sinusitis, avoid whole grains until symptoms are eliminated; then consume in moderation. Rotate whole grains throughout the week, and do not eat the same ones everyday. If wheat is an allergen, always avoid it.
- Consume healthy monounsaturated fats such as olive oil.
- Intake dietary sources high in omega-3 fatty acids, such as cold-water fish, flaxseeds, walnuts, fish oil, and flaxseed oil.
- Monitor intake of dietary sources high in omega-6 fatty acids, such as corn oil, soybean oil, safflower oil, sunflower oil, and foods derived from grain-fed animals.
- Eat hot chicken and brown rice soup often.
- Avoid pork and fatty beef. Eat organic lean chicken, turkey, and wild fish. Reduce intake of organic, lean beef.
- Eat foods high in vitamin C, such as oranges, peppers, grapefruit, green leafy vegetables, tomatoes, strawberries, and broccoli.
- Maintain a healthy flora. After completing prescription of antibiotics, it is important to replenish flora by consuming plain, cultured, low-fat yogurt (no sugar), unpasteurized sauerkraut, and unpasteurized, unfiltered, apple-cider vinegar. Under the advice of a physi-

cian, also take probiotic (friendly bacteria) capsules, which can be purchased at health-food stores.

- Prevent constipation and control irritable bowel syndrome. Follow suggestions and diet described under "Irritable Bowel Syndrome."
- Avoid caffeine and carbonated beverages.
- Reduce salt and sodium intake to prevent dehydration.
- Eliminate alcohol drinking and cigarette smoking.
- Keep your body hydrated with water. Drink plenty of water (at least eight 8-oz. cups daily) free of contaminants and added minerals, and at the correct pH (see chapter 41 for details).
- Keep sinuses hydrated and washed with saline spray. Xylitol spray is great because yeast and bacteria cannot metabolize xylitol for fuel; thus, it kills them off.
- Keep sinuses hydrated by using a humidifier or washed by irrigation. Using a neti pot (a pot resembling a genie's lamp) filled with saline solution is a popular method. The neti pot can be purchased at most health-food stores and some drug stores. Also, try adding a small pinch of baking soda or xylitol to the saline solution.
- Wash hands consistently.
- Avoid cold and dry air. This triggers sinus problems in many individuals.
- Avoid catching colds or the flu.
- Take high-grade multivitamins and other dietary supplements as recommended by your physician.
- Limit the use of over-the-counter decongestants and other medication. Medication will often weaken the immune system and lining of the sinuses, thus perpetuating sinus problems.
- Under the advice of a physician—medical, osteopathic, naturopathic, etc.—take conventional antibiotics and decongestants to conquer stubborn sinus infections. But if you decide to consistently take these conventional medicines for an infection, it is inevitable that a weak immune system will cause a sinus infection to reoccur.
- Read the following list of foods and liquids to avoid and consume, and use it as a tool to help you and your physician design a diet that fits your physical condition. Before you start, make certain to inform your physician about any medications you are taking.

Avoid	Consume
• Sugar (white sugar, brown sugar, high fructose corn syrup, glucose, and sucrose,) and foods high in simple carbohydrates	• Organic raw vegetables, especially green and leafy vegetables (if they are not allergens)
• White flour, wheat flour, white potatoes, white rice, and white pasta	• Organic fresh fruits (Exceptions: melons and grapes) in moderation (avoid fruits if fruits are allergens)
• Fruit juice and sweetened or carbonated beverages	• Organic lean chicken, turkey, and wild fish; organic, lean beef in moderation
• Canned, packaged, processed, and junk foods, and artificial sweeteners, preservatives, and other food additives	• Natural sweeteners such as xylitol, stevia, and sorbitol
• Food allergens, such as peanuts, milk proteins, wheat, etc. This will vary with each individual. Gluten intolerant, avoid wheat (spelt), barley, rye, and other gluten-containing foods.	• Foods rich in omega-3 fatty acids such as cold-water fish, flaxseeds, walnuts, flaxseed oil, and fish oil, and in monounsaturated fatty acids, such as olive oil
• Grapes, watermelon, cantaloupe (may add these fruits back into diet after eliminating sinusitis and yeast overgrowth) and dried fruits (always avoid)	• Plain, cultured, low-fat yogurt, unpasteurized, unfiltered apple cider vinegar, and unpasteurized sauerkraut
• Reduce salt and sodium intake (less than 2.3 grams of sodium daily)	• Nuts (if not allergens); Exceptions: avoid peanuts and cashews)

- Omega-6 fatty acid dietary sources such as corn oil, safflower oil, sunflower oil, soybean oil, and foods derived from grain-fed animals
- Foods consisting of molds, such as aged cheese, grapes, peanuts, cashews, and mushrooms
- Saturated fats, trans fats, and cholesterol
- Fermented and curdled foods, such as beer, tofu, cheese, cottage cheese, buttermilk, and distilled apple cider and white vinegar
- Yeast foods, such as certain breads and beer
- Cow's milk and dairy products
- Pork and fatty beef

- Whole grains, such as whole grain brown rice, whole wheat pasta, and whole spelt bread in moderation (if not allergens and sinuses are under control). Rotate whole grains throughout a week, and do not eat the same ones every day. The ones that are allergens, always avoid. If suffering from sinusitis avoid whole grains, especially wheat and spelt, until under control.
- Garlic and hot peppers (if they are not allergens)
- Chicken and brown rice soup
- Foods high in calcium, such as fish with bones, almond milk, dark-green leafy vegetables, plain, cultured, low-fat yogurt, and sesame seeds
- Properly prepared legumes (prepared to prevent gas)
- Foods high in vitamin C, such as oranges, peppers, pears, tomatoes, strawberries, and broccoli
- Vegetables high in complex carbohydrates and fiber such as yam sweet potatoes and beans (Exception: avoid white potatoes)

- Alcohol, caffeine, coffee, tea (some herbal teas are acceptable)
- Plenty of water (eight 8-oz. cups daily) free of contaminants and added minerals, and at the right pH

Yeast Syndrome (Candidiasis)

Yeast syndrome (candidiasis), often called yeast toxicity syndrome, is the chronic overgrowth of yeast (i.e., *Candida albicans*, which is fungi) in the body. Yeast is a common inhabitant in our bodies, especially in the intestines, mouth, and reproductive system (both male and female). Appropriate growth of probiotics, good bacteria, is required in our bodies to maintain a healthy flora and inhibit the overgrowth of yeast. Problems arise when probiotics die off, and yeast begins to overgrow and invade the entire body. One of the major problems of yeast overgrowth is leaky gut syndrome, which is the result of yeast metamorphosing into its plant form. The plant form bores holes in the intestinal wall, which causes its contents (including yeast and other toxins) to leak out into the bloodstream. Yeast overgrowth and yeast toxins can lead to digestive and menstrual problems (such as cramps, bloating, headaches, and nausea) and symptoms in the joints, sinuses, mouth, throat, lungs, skin, muscles, reproductive system, etc. Because of the unhealthy American diet (which feeds the yeast) and the constant use of antibiotics (which kills the good bacteria), I believe many Americans (both male and female) unknowingly suffer from yeast overgrowth and yeast toxins. Do not diagnose this problem yourself. If you suspect that you have yeast syndrome, consult your physician. Yeast syndrome, however, is often missed or misdiagnosed. In most cases, it requires that you remain persistent and see many different types of physicians (preferably ones that practice with a holistic approach) before the problem is identified and properly treated.

List of Healthful Suggestions:

- Eat plenty of vegetables, especially organic, green-leaf vegetables.

- Avoid simple carbohydrates (high glycemic index foods), especially foods consisting of white sugar and white flour. It can be quite difficult to eliminate these foods from your diet because most who suffer from yeast syndrome have an intense craving for them, especially white sugar and white flour. The best thing to do is eat a diet that will simultaneously eliminate the craving for white stuff (see chapter 27 for diet) and inhibit yeast overgrowth.
- Check pH level of urine and saliva. If it's acidic, see a physician and eat foods, such as vegetables and fruits that will help make the body less acidic and decrease growth of yeast (see chapter 41 for more details)
- Prevent constipation and control irritable bowel syndrome. Follow the recommendations and diet described under "Irritable Bowel Syndrome."
- Avoid foods that contain yeast, such as yeast-raised breads and beer.
- Eat organic and whole foods. Avoid processed, canned, and packaged foods, and artificial sweeteners, preservatives, food colorings, and other food additives.
- Avoid most fruits, especially grapes, watermelon, and dried fruits. Once yeast overgrowth is under control, you can add fruits back into your diet. Exception: it is best to always reduce intake of dried fruits.
- Eat garlic as it is a natural killer of unfriendly bacteria and unwanted yeast.
- Allergies triggered by food and other allergens can lead to yeast overgrowth. Follow suggestions and diet described in this section under "Allergies" to eliminate allergens.
- Avoid cow's milk and dairy products (exception: plain, cultured, low-fat yogurt is acceptable). Dairy coupled with excess mucus seems to irritate the sinuses and provide an environment where yeast loves to grow.
- Substitute cow's milk with almond milk, but avoid rice milk (it consists of high levels of simple carbohydrates). Also eat foods high in calcium, such as fish with bones, almonds, dark-green leafy vegetables, plain, cultured, low-fat yogurt, and sesame seeds.

- Eat vegetables high in fiber and complex carbohydrates such as yam-sweet potatoes and beans, but avoid white potatoes. Make sure beans are properly prepared (see chapter 39 for information about cooking beans).
- Avoid refined, distilled white and apple-cider vinegar and foods that contain them, such as dill pickles, vinaigrette salad dressing, and mustard.
- Avoid eating foods that have mold growing on them. Watch for mold on foods, such as aged cheese, peanuts, mushrooms, and grapes.
- Avoid most fermented or curdled foods, such as hard and soft cheeses, and tofu. Once yeast overgrowth is eliminated, you can eat these foods in moderation.
- Take the steps required to maintain a healthy and balanced flora in your digestive tract by eating plain, cultured, low-fat yogurt (no sugar), and by taking under the advice of a physician dietary supplements of probiotics (friendly bacteria), which can be purchased at health-food stores. It is also good to consume unpasteurized sauerkraut and unpasteurized, unfiltered, apple-cider vinegar. These particular fermented foods help to build a healthy flora and prevent yeast overgrowth.
- When suffering from yeast overgrowth, avoid whole grains, especially whole wheat and whole spelt, until symptoms are eliminated; then consume in moderation. Rotate whole grains (e.g., oats, brown rice, wheat, and spelt) throughout the week, and do not eat the same ones every day. Reduce intake of breads made with yeast. If wheat is an allergen, always avoid it.
- Avoid foods consisting of gluten such as wheat, spelt, barley, and rye. Once yeast overgrowth is under control, you may find that you are able to eat gluten-containing foods in moderation. Yet, if you are gluten intolerant, always eliminate these foods from your diet.
- Eat organic lean chicken, turkey, and wild fish. Also, eat organic lean beef in moderation. Eliminate pork and fatty beef.
- Avoid foods consisting of saturated fats, cholesterol, and trans fats.
- Consume dietary sources of monounsaturated fats, such as olive oil and avocados.

- Intake flaxseeds, walnuts, flaxseed oil, fish oil, and cold-water fish to increase omega-3 fatty acid intake.
- Monitor intake of dietary sources high in omega-6 fatty acids, such as corn oil, soybean oil, safflower oil, sunflower oil, and foods derived from grain-fed animals.
- Avoid caffeine, soda, carbonated beverages, coffee, and tea (some herbal teas or acceptable).
- Avoid all alcohol, including beer.
- Drink plenty of water (eight 8-oz. cups daily) free of contaminants and added minerals, and at the correct pH (see chapter 41 for details).
- Avoid moldy, damp places.
- Eliminate cigarette smoking.
- Control emotional stress.
- Monitor effects of birth control pills. Female hormonal imbalances can trigger yeast overgrowth. Females may even see an increase in yeast growth prior to or during their menstrual cycles.
- Avoid antibiotics. Yet, if take antibiotics, it is important to inhibit yeast overgrowth by replenishing healthy flora with plain, cultured, low-fat yogurt (no sugar), unpasteurized sauerkraut, and unpasteurized, unfiltered, apple-cider vinegar. Under the advice of a physician, also take probiotic capsules.
- Avoid corticosteroids and other drugs that depress the immune system.
- Exercise regularly to maintain a healthy weight and build up your immune system.
- Take high-grade multivitamins and other dietary supplements, as suggested by a physician to help build up immune system and inhibit overgrowth of yeast.
- If you believe you have symptoms of yeast syndrome, consult your physician (medical, osteopathic, naturopathic, homeopathic, etc.), and work together as a team to combat yeast overgrowth. Be patient; the treatment can be long and tedious. It will require much persistence and effort, but the reaped rewards will be well worth it.
- Read the following list of foods and liquids to avoid and consume, and use it as a tool to help you and your physician design a diet that

fits your physical condition. Before you start, make certain to inform your physician about any medications you are taking.

Avoid	Consume
• Cow's milk and dairy products	• Organic raw vegetables, especially green and leafy vegetables
• Pork and fatty beef	• Organic lean chicken, turkey, and wild fish; organic, lean beef in moderation
• Sugar (white sugar, brown sugar, high fructose corn syrup, glucose, and sucrose) and other foods high in simple carbohydrates	• Organic fresh fruits eat in moderation. If have yeast overgrowth, avoid all fruits (especially melons and grapes) until it is eliminated. Always avoid fruits that are allergens.
• Grapes, watermelon, cantaloupe (you may add these fruits back into your diet after eliminating yeast overgrowth) and dried fruits (always consume sparingly)	• Vegetables high in complex carbohydrates and fiber such as yam sweet potatoes and beans (<u>Exception</u>: avoid white potatoes)
• Food allergens, such as peanuts, milk proteins, wheat, etc. This will vary with the individual. Gluten intolerant, avoid wheat, barley, rye, and other gluten-containing foods.	• Whole grains, such as whole grain brown rice, whole grain oats, whole wheat pasta, and yeast-free whole and sprouted grain breads in moderation, if not allergic to them. Rotate whole grains throughout a week, and do not eat the same ones every day. Always avoid the ones that are allergens. If suffering from yeast overgrowth, avoid whole grains, especially wheat and spelt, until under control.

• Artificial sweeteners	• Natural sweeteners such as xylitol, stevia, and sorbitol
• Saturated fats, trans fats, and cholesterol	• Olive oil and avocados
• Foods consisting of molds, such as aged cheese, grapes, peanuts, cashews, and mushrooms	• Foods rich in omega-3 fatty acids, such as cold-water fish, flaxseeds, walnuts, flaxseed oil, and fish oil
• Omega-6 fatty acid dietary sources such as corn oil, safflower oil, sunflower oil, soybean oil, and foods derived from grain-fed animals	• Foods high in calcium, such as fish with bones, almond milk, dark-green leafy vegetables, plain, cultured, low-fat yogurt, and sesame seeds
• Yeast-containing foods, such as yeast-raised breads and beer	• Garlic (if not allergen)
• Fermented or curdled foods, such as cheese, beer, wine, tofu, cottage cheese, buttermilk, and distilled apple-cider and white vinegar	• Properly prepared legumes (prepared to prevent gas) and nuts (if not, allergens)—<u>Exceptions:</u> No peanuts and cashews
• Canned, packaged, and processed foods and preservatives, food coloring, and other food additives	• Plain, cultured, low-fat yogurt; unpasteurized, unfiltered apple cider vinegar; and unpasteurized sauerkraut
• Alcohol, caffeine, coffee, and tea (some herbal teas are acceptable), soda, carbonated beverages, and sweetened drinks	• Plenty of water (eight 8-oz. cups daily) free from contaminants and added minerals, and at the correct pH

Part V: My Favorite Recipes Created by My Family

List of Healthy Family Recipes

Below is an alphabetical list of my favorite recipes created by my family, mostly by my mom and sister. My dad and son created one food recipe each, and my brother-in-law created the recipe for a hot lemon drink, which is great for a cold morning. I love these recipes, and I really enjoy eating them. My family is convinced that I think their recipe creations are delicious for two reasons: one, their creations are healthy (or at least healthier than the foods of my past); and two, I was not the one who put the time and effort in creating them. I do not enjoy cooking, so because I didn't have to cook or work to create these recipes, I loved it. Regardless, my family recipes are priceless to me—they are what helped me stay away from the "white stuff." Each one of these recipes replaced a food that I released from my past. I believe that these recipes are delicious and I hope that you will enjoy them as much as I do.

The recipes are not complicated, but it does take some effort to become familiar with using healthy ingredients. For example, to most, the sweetness of xylitol is equal to that of white sugar. However, to me, the sweetness of xylitol is more potent than that of white sugar, so in these recipes only about half as much xylitol was added to sweeten a food than if sugar was used (e.g., in these recipes, approximately a half-cup of xylitol is equivalent to approximately one cup of white sugar). Furthermore, the texture of whole wheat flour is coarser than that of white flour, so baking with whole wheat flour requires practice. If you prefer a whole grain flour that gives a lighter consistency to breads and desserts than whole wheat flour, use whole spelt flour. In these recipes, most emphasis is put on using whole grain ingredients, it also is essential to use fresh, organic, and unrefined ingredients as much as possible. Plus, many of these recipes include canola oil, which is usually better than most hydrogenated oils but is definitely not the healthiest of oils (see chapter 36 for details). If you prefer, test and replace canola oil with one of the healthier oils, such as olive oil or coconut oil. Keep practicing, and don't give up. Appreciating the healthier foods made with the healthy ingredients is sometimes an acquired taste. If you don't succeed at first, just keep working at it, and eventually you will appreciate the taste and texture of healthy ingredients. *Bon appétit*!

Appetizers

Homemade Salsa (created by my sister)

4 medium tomatoes, coarsely chopped
½ medium onion, coarsely chopped
½ bell pepper or Anaheim mild pepper (if you want it spicy, use jalapeño pepper), finely chopped
2 garlic cloves, finely chopped
5 cilantro stalks, finely chopped
½ large lime, squeezed (save juice)
Sea salt and black pepper to taste

Mix the chopped tomatoes, onion, pepper, garlic, cilantro, the juice from half of a lime together in a medium bowl with a medium spoon. Add salt and pepper to taste, and stir again. Chill until ready to serve.

Tip: Makes an excellent condiment to serve with the spelt tortilla rolls (see recipe below).

Spelt Tortilla Rolls (created by my sister)

4 oz. low-fat cream cheese
¾ cup 1% or 2% low-fat Colby and/or cheddar cheese, shredded
3 green onions, diced
1 can (2¼ oz.) chopped black olives, drained
4 whole spelt tortillas, 8 inches in diameter
1 cup tomato salsa

Mix cheese, cream cheese, and olives in a small bowl. Spread one-quarter of the mixture (about ½ cup) on each tortilla. Roll up each tortilla. Wrap each roll separately with plastic wrap and refrigerate for about 1 hour. Unwrap plastic from each roll and slice each roll into about 16 slices (each ½-inch thick). Serve with salsa (see recipe for homemade salsa above).

Biscuits and Breads

Banana Bread (created by my sister)

½ cup xylitol
6 Tbsp. butter, softened
2 eggs
3 to 4 ripe bananas, mashed
⅓ cup water
⅔ cup whole spelt flour
1 cup whole wheat flour
1 tsp. baking soda
½ tsp. salt
¼ tsp. baking powder
½ cup chopped nuts

Heat oven to 350°F. Grease bottom only of a 9x5x3-inch loaf pan with cooking spray. Mix xylitol and butter in medium bowl. Stir in eggs until blended. Add bananas and water; beat 30 seconds. Stir in remaining ingredients, except for nuts, just until moistened; then stir in nuts. Pour into pan. Bake about 55 to 60 minutes or until wooden toothpick inserted in center comes out clean. Cool and loosen sides of loaf from pan; remove from pan. Cool completely before slicing.

Tip: Make extra loaves and freeze. Wrap each loaf individually in aluminum foil and then put wrapped loaf in a freezer bag and seal.

Biscuits—Spelt Flour (created by my mom)
Makes about 15 biscuits

2 cups whole spelt flour, plus 2 Tbsp. whole spelt flour
3 tsp. baking powder
½ tsp. salt
6 Tbsp. canola oil, plus 1 tsp. canola oil
1 tsp. xylitol
½ tsp. butter
½ cup whole milk

Mix dry ingredients in a medium bowl and then add milk, water, and 6 Tbsp. oil. Stir well. Rub 1 Tbsp. of spelt flour on pastry board. Turn dough onto it and knead. Keep sprinkling more flour (approximately 1–2 Tbsp. total) onto dough and knead about 8 times. Pat out dough with floured hands and roll out dough to ¼ inch thickness with floured rolling pin. Preheat oven to 400°F. Grease cookie sheet with ½ tsp. of butter, place in oven until heated, and then remove from oven. Use a 3-inch diameter glass to cut out biscuits. Lift trimmings away from biscuits. Transfer biscuits to greased cookie sheet, about ½ inch apart. Lightly press dough trimmings together. Pat out and cut out as before. Arrange biscuits on cookie sheet. Brush canola oil lightly on top of biscuits (approximately 1 tsp. total of canola oil). Bake in oven at 400°F for 10–12 minutes.

Blueberry Muffins (created by my sister)
Makes about 1 dozen muffins

¾ cup 1% low-fat milk
½ cup canola oil
1 egg
1 cup whole wheat flour
1 cup whole spelt flour
¼ cup xylitol
3 tsp. baking powder
1 tsp. salt
1 cup fresh or drained canned blueberries, or ¾ cup frozen blueberries, thawed and well drained
½ cup chopped walnuts, optional

Heat oven to 400°F. Grease bottom of 12-medium well muffin pan (each well 2½ x1¼) with cooking spray, or line with paper baking cups. Beat milk, oil, and egg in medium bowl. Add in flours, xylitol, baking powder, and salt all at once, and stir just until flour is moistened (batter will be lumpy). Fold in blueberries and nuts. Divide batter among muffin wells. Bake until golden brown, 18 to 20 minutes. Immediately remove from pan.

Coats (Corn-Flour and Oat-Flour Biscuits)—Gluten-Free (created by my dad)
Makes about 10 cakes (each about 2½ inches in diameter)

1 cup whole corn flour (gluten-free)
1 cup whole oat flour (gluten-free)
1½ tsp. baking powder
½ tsp. xylitol
½ tsp. salt
3 Tbsp. canola oil
1 egg
½ cup low-fat milk

Heat oven to 350°F. Grease cookie sheet with canola oil and place in oven until cookie sheet is hot. Mix all dry ingredients in a medium bowl. Then, add oil, egg, and milk, and mix well by stirring. Make one large ball of dough. With hands, separate small balls of dough from large ball, and then shape into small, flat, round cakes about 2 inches in diameter. Place cakes on greased cookie sheet, about ½ inch apart. Cook for 20–25 minutes or until golden brown.

Note: Make sure that oat flour is made from gluten-free oats. Many manufacturing mills contaminate oats with gluten. If suspect that oats trigger symptoms of gluten-intolerance, then try replacing oat flour with gluten-free flour made from almonds, rice, buckwheat, millet, tapioca, garbanzo beans, or potatoes (these other flours have not yet been tested as substitutes).

Coarse Cornbread Muffins (created by my mom)
Makes approximately 12 muffins

2 cups of medium- or coarse-ground yellow cornmeal
1 cup of regular stone-ground yellow cornmeal
½ cup whole spelt flour
2¼ Tbsp. baking powder
1 tsp. salt
1 Tbsp. xylitol sweetener
⅓ cup canola oil
2 cups whole milk

Mix all dry ingredients (cornmeal, flour, baking powder, salt, and xylitol) together in a large bowl; do not sift ingredients. Add canola oil and milk and mix very well. Grease 12–well muffin pan (each well 3 inch in diameter) and preheat at 350°F. Fill each well of muffin pan two-thirds full. Bake at 350°F for 10 minutes. Then increase oven temperature to 400°F, and bake until golden brown.

Hot-Water Cornbread (created by my mom)
Makes approximately 10 hot-water cornbread patties

2 cups medium-ground yellow cornmeal
1 cup coarse-ground yellow cornmeal
½ cup whole spelt flour
¼ cup whole corn flour
2 tsp. baking powder
½ tsp. salt
2½ Tbsp. canola oil
½ cup canola oil for frying
2¼ cups boiling water

Add both cornmeals, spelt flour, corn flour, baking powder, and salt to a large bowl, and mix well with a large spoon. Do not sift cornmeal; make sure to leave in husk and fiber. Then add canola oil (2½ Tbsp.) and boiling water to dry ingredients (measure boiling water directly from stove). Mix all ingredients together very well with a spoon. Once cooled down enough to be able to touch, mix well by hand. Using hands, form balls of meal and then flatten out into small oval-shaped patties. Each patty should be about 3½ inch long, 2½ inch wide, and 1 inch thick. Add ½ cup of canola oil to a large, nonstick skillet and heat on medium heat. Add patties to preheated skillet. (Before adding patties, make sure oil is hot enough. Test by dropping a small piece of dough into oil. If dough begins to fry immediately, then oil is ready). Fry patties on medium heat until golden brown and crisp on each side and dough inside of patty is soft yet completely done. Remove patties from oil and place in a pan. If patties are golden brown before completely cooked all the way through, bake patties in oven at approximately 250°F until well done. Do not overcook; patties should be hard and crisp only on the outside and not in the middle. Make sure the dough inside is soft yet not raw. If not sure patties are done, observe the inside of one by breaking it in half.

Pancakes (created by my sister)
Makes about 7–9 medium-sized pancakes

1 egg
½ cup whole spelt flour
½ cup whole wheat flour
¾ cup 1% or 2% low-fat milk
½ Tbsp. xylitol
2 Tbsp. canola oil
3 tsp. baking powder
½ tsp. salt

Beat egg until fluffy; beat in remaining ingredients just until smooth. If desire thinner pancakes, stir in additional ¼ cup low-fat milk. Grease griddle or skillet with cooking spray and heat on medium heat.

For each pancake, pour about 3 Tbsp. batter from large spoon onto hot griddle or skillet. Cook pancakes until dry around edges. Turn and cook other side until golden brown.

Scones (created by my sister)
Makes about 15 scones

⅓ cup butter
1 cup whole spelt flour
¾ cup whole wheat flour
1½ tbsp. xylitol
2½ tsp. baking powder
½ tsp. salt
1 egg beaten
½ cup dried unsweetened fruit (e.g., cranberries and raisins)
6 to 8 Tbsp. 1% or 2% milk
1 egg, beaten

Heat oven to 400°F. Mix flours, xylitol, baking powder, and salt together in a large bowl. Cut butter into flour mixture with pastry blender, until mixture forms fine crumbs. Stir in 1 egg, the fruit and just enough milk so dough leaves sides of bowl.

Turn dough onto lightly floured surface. Knead lightly 10 times. Roll with pin, or pat with hand until dough is ½ inch thick. Cut with floured 2-inch round cutter, or cut into triangle shapes with sharp knife. Place on ungreased cookie sheet. Bake until golden brown, 10 to 12 minutes. Immediately remove from cookie sheet; cool.

Waffles (created by my sister)
Makes about 6-8 (5-6 in.) waffles

2 eggs
1 cup whole wheat flour
1 cup whole spelt flour
½ cup canola oil
2 cups 1% or 2% milk
½ Tbsp. xylitol
4 tsp. baking powder
½ tsp. salt

Heat waffle iron. Beat eggs until fluffy; beat in remaining ingredients just until smooth. Pour batter onto center of hot waffle iron. Cook until steaming stops, or for about 5 minutes. Remove waffle carefully.

Zucchini and Carrot Bread (created by my sister)
Makes one loaf

1 cup whole spelt flour
½ cup whole wheat flour
⅜ cup xylitol
2 tsp. baking powder
½ tsp. baking soda
¼ tsp. salt
2 eggs, beaten slightly (or 4 egg whites)
½ cups canola oil
½ cup grated carrots
1¾ cups grated zucchini
½ cup golden raisins (optional)
½ cup walnuts (optional)

Preheat oven to 365°F. Grease and flour a 9x5x3-inch loaf pan; set aside. In a medium bowl, combine the eggs and oil; mix well. Mix the dry ingredients into a large bowl. Gently stir the egg mixture into the dry ingredients. Stir in the zucchini, carrots, raisins, and walnuts into the mixture. Pour the mixture into the pan and bake for about 55 minutes, or until a toothpick comes out clean. Remove from the oven and let cool for 5 minutes. Remove from pan when completely cooled.

Tip: Make extra loaves and freeze. Wrap each loaf individually in aluminum foil, and then put wrapped loaves in freezer bags and seal.

Desserts and Sweets

Apple or Cherry Turnovers (created by mom)
Makes about 8 turnovers

Prepare apple or cherry filling (see recipes below) and set aside. Then prepare pastry crust (see recipe below).

Apple Filling
3 large organic Red Delicious apples
¼ cup water
½ cup xylitol sweetener
1 tsp. brown cinnamon
¼ cup (4 Tbsp. or ½ stick) butter, melted or soft

Peel, remove core, and dice apples into medium-sized cubes. Add apple cubes and water to a small pan, and cook on low heat until tender and all juice is gone. If there is still juice when apples are tender, pour it off. Mash apples with a potato masher. Add cinnamon, butter, and xylitol to apples and mix well. Set aside.

Cherry Filling
3 cups frozen tart cherries (Montmorency)
1¼ cup xylitol
¼ cup water
¼ stick butter
1 tsp. lemon juice

1 Tbsp. spelt flour
1 pinch salt

Pit cherries, place in pan, add water, and cook over low heat until tender. Pour out extra juice from cooked cherries. Add butter, xylitol, lemon juice, and salt to cherries. Place flour in a separate small cup and stir in enough water to make a paste. Then add paste to cherry mixture to thicken. Mix well and set aside.

Pastry Crust
2 cups whole spelt flour
1 tsp. xylitol
¼ tsp. baking powder
¼ cup canola oil
½ tsp. salt
½ cup plus 1 Tbsp. ice water
½ cup canola oil or ½ cup butter for frying (optional)
1 tsp. butter
Xylitol for sprinkling (optional)

Mix dry ingredients (flour, xylitol, baking powder, and salt) together in large bowl. Add ¼ cup of oil and ½ cup of ice water to dry ingredients, and mix well with hands. Knead dough in bowl with hands. If it's too stiff to knead properly, add 1 tsp. to 1 Tbsp. of ice water (add only enough water to make all the flour stick together). Continue to knead dough until it forms one large ball. Then divide into approximately two balls of equal size.

Sprinkle flour on clean surface and roll out dough with floured rolling pin until thin (approximately ⅛ inch thick). Cut dough into approximately four equal parts (or squares) with a knife. Spoon out approximately 2 Tbsp. of apple or cherry filling and place on the center of each square. Use the 1 tsp. of butter to put a dot of butter on top of the fruit, then fold the dough over until edges meet. Press dough with fork all around edges.

Baked Turnovers: Place turnovers on greased cookie sheet, and bake in preheated oven at 400°F for 20 minutes or until golden brown. Sprinkle each turnover with a small pinch of xylitol while still hot.

Fried Turnovers: Preheat ½ cup of butter or ½ cup of canola oil in large nonstick skillet. Fry pies over medium heat until golden brown on each side. Remove turnovers from skillet, and sprinkle each with a small pinch of xylitol while hot.

Cocoa Cream-Cheese Brownies (created by my sister)
Makes approximately 16 squares

¾ cup xylitol
¾ cup butter, softened
2 Tbsp. canola oil
8 oz. cream cheese (1/3 less fat), softened
1 tsp. vanilla
2 eggs
⅔ cup whole spelt flour
½ cup cocoa
½ cup chopped walnuts
½ tsp. baking powder
½ tsp. salt

Preheat oven to 350°F. Mix xylitol, butter, canola oil, cream cheese, vanilla, and eggs until smooth and creamy. Stir in remaining ingredients. Spread batter evenly into a greased square pan (8x8x2). Bake 25 to 30 minutes. Let cool, and cut into 2-inch squares.

Dark Chocolate-Chip Cookies (created by my sister)
Makes about 2 dozen

1 cup unsalted butter, softened
1 cup xylitol
1 egg
2 cups whole spelt flour
1 tsp. baking soda
½ tsp. salt
½ cup coarsely chopped walnuts
1 package (12 oz.) bittersweet chocolate chips

Preheat oven to 375°F. Mix butter, xylitol, and egg in medium bowl. Stir in flour, baking soda, and salt (dough will be stiff). Stir in nuts and bittersweet chips. Drop dough by rounded teaspoonfuls onto ungreased cookie sheet, about 2 inches apart. Bake 8 to 10 minutes, until light brown (centers will be soft.) Cool slightly; remove from cookie sheet.

Doughnuts (created by my sister)
Makes about 1 dozen

1½ cups whole spelt flour
1 cup whole wheat flour
½ cup xylitol
¾ cup low-fat milk
2 Tbsp. butter
3 tsp. baking powder
½ tsp. salt
½ tsp. ground cinnamon
¼ tsp. ground nutmeg
2 eggs
Canola oil for frying
Xylitol for sprinkling (optional)

Add oil 2 to 3 inches deep to a deep fryer, and heat to about 375°F. Beat flours and the remaining ingredients in medium bowl with an electric mixer at low speed, scraping bowl constantly for 20 seconds. Then, beat at medium speed, scraping bowl occasionally, for 2 minutes.

Turn the dough onto floured board or floured clean flat surface; roll dough around lightly to coat with flour. Gently roll out with rolling pin 3/8 inch thick. Use a floured 2-inch diameter doughnut cutter to cut out doughnuts. Lift trimmings away from doughnuts, reshape trimmings together, roll out, and cut out doughnuts. Carefully place doughnuts into hot oil. Turn doughnuts as they rise to surface. Fry until golden brown, about 1 to 1½ minutes on each side. Remove carefully from oil (do not prick surfaces); drain. Serve plain or sprinkle on a little xylitol on each one.

Note: Use a cooking thermometer to make sure oil has reached the correct temperature. If oil is too hot, foods will brown before they are cooked thoroughly; if too cool, foods will become soaked with grease.

Fruit Cookies (created by my sister)
Makes approximately 2 dozen

¼ cup xylitol
1 cup butter, softened
3 large eggs, separated
¼ cup water
1½ tsp. vanilla extract
¼ tsp. salt
2 cups whole spelt flour
2 cups chopped pecans
1 cup 100% fruit spread (no added sugar)
No-stick cooking oil spray

Preheat oven to 350°F. Spray cookie sheets with no-stick cooking oil spray. Beat the xylitol and butter with an electric mixer at medium speed for 2 minutes or until fluffy. Scrape down sides of bowl. Add egg yolks, water, vanilla, and salt; beat by hand until well combined. Next, add flour to mixture while on low speed until dough is well blended. Then, beat egg whites separately in a small shallow bowl until foamy. Place pecans in a separated shallow bowl. Divide dough by rounded spoonfuls into about 24 equal parts. Form each spoonful into a ball by rolling in palms of hands. Dip each dough ball into the beaten egg whites, then roll into the pecans and place on the prepared cookie sheet. Using the back of a teaspoon, make a rounded indentation on top of each cookie. Bake cookie for 10 minutes; remove from oven. If indentation is no longer visible, it may be necessary to press the indentation once again. Fill each indentation on top of the cookies with ½ teaspoon of fruit spread. Return cookie to oven, bake another 5–7 minutes, or until lightly browned on the bottom. Remove from oven. Let cookies cool on baking sheet.

Ginger Cookies (created by my sister)
Makes about 2 dozen

½ cup xylitol
¾ cup butter, softened
¼ cup molasses
1 egg

1 cup whole wheat flour
1¼ cups whole spelt flour
2 tsp. baking soda
1 tsp. ground cinnamon
1 tsp. ground ginger
½ tsp. ground cloves
¼ tsp. salt
Small bowl of xylitol

Mix xylitol, butter, molasses, and egg in medium bowl. Stir in flours, baking soda, cinnamon, ginger, cloves, and salt. Cover and refrigerate at least 1 hour.

Preheat oven to 375°F. Shape dough by rounded teaspoonfuls into balls. Dip tops of balls in bowl of xylitol. Place balls, xylitol sides up, about 3 inches apart, on lightly greased cookie sheet. Bake cookies just until set, or about 10 to 12 minutes. Immediately remove from cookie sheet.

Oatmeal Raisin Cookies (created by my sister)
Makes about 2 dozen

1 cup (½ pound, 2 sticks) butter, softened
¾ cup xylitol
2 eggs
1 tsp. vanilla
¾ cup whole wheat flour
½ cup whole spelt flour
1 tsp. baking soda
1 tsp. cinnamon
½ tsp. salt (optional)
2½ cups whole grain oatmeal, uncooked
1 cup raisins
½ cup walnuts, chopped

Preheat oven to 350°F. Beat together butter and xylitol until creamy. Add eggs and vanilla; beat well. Add flours, baking soda, cinnamon, and salt to mixture; mix well. Stir in oats, raisins and nuts; mix well. Drop by rounded tablespoonfuls onto ungreased cookie sheet. Bake 10 to 12 minutes or until golden brown. Cool 1 minute on cookie sheet before removing.

Peanut Butter Cookies (created by my sister)
Makes about 3 dozen cookies

½ cup xylitol
½ cup natural, creamy peanut butter (unsweetened, no added sugar)
½ cup butter, unsalted and softened
1 egg
1¼ whole spelt flour
¾ tsp. baking soda
½ tsp. baking powder
¼ tsp. salt

Mix xylitol, peanut butter, butter, and egg in medium bowl. Stir in remaining ingredients. Cover and refrigerate at least 3 hours.

Preheat oven to 375°F. Shape dough into 1¼ in. balls. Place about 3 inches apart on ungreased cookie sheet. Flatten, using fork dipped in flour to make crisscross pattern. Bake 9–10 minutes until light brown. Cool 2 minutes; remove from cookie sheet.

Drinks

Homemade Organic Almond Milk Shake (created by me)
Makes one serving

¼ cup raw almonds
1 cup water
Xylitol or stevia (add to taste)
Sea salt (dash)

Add about ¼ cup of organic almonds and one cup of water into a blender. Blend well; then, add xylitol or stevia to taste and a dash of sea salt. Chill (optional).

Note: If want to make almond milk, pour shake through a tea strainer.

Hot Lemon Warmer-Upper (created by my brother-in-law)

Water
Fresh lemon, sliced
Stevia or xylitol (optional)

Boil water. Pour in coffee cup or mug. Squeeze juice from 1 or more slices of lemon into water. If desire, sweeten with xylitol or stevia to taste.

Smoothies (created by my sister)

1½ cup crushed ice
1 cup plain, cultured, low-fat yogurt
1 cup fresh strawberries, diced
1 cup blueberries (fresh or frozen)
⅓ cup 100% orange juice (approximately 2.5 oz.)
⅓ cup 100% fruit juice (grape, cranberry, or apple)
⅓ cup water
Stevia or xylitol (optional)

Add all ingredients to blender. Blend until well blended. If you desire more sweetness, add stevia xylitol to taste.

<u>Tip:</u> Any fresh or frozen fruit may be substituted, according to individual desired taste. Bananas, peaches, nectarines, grapes, oranges, apricots, apples, pears, cherries, plums, and carrots are also great (make sure remove pits and seeds from fruit).

<u>Meat Dishes</u>

Fried Chicken (created by my mom)
Makes 6 servings

2 to 2½ pounds of chicken pieces (breasts, thighs, wings, and drumsticks)
¼ cup whole spelt flour, optional (I like it with or without whole spelt flour)
2 Tbsp. of soy sauce
½ tsp. paprika
½ tsp. garlic powder
½ tsp. chili powder
½ tsp. onion powder
¼ tsp. pepper
½ cup of canola oil or olive oil (depends on personal taste; I prefer virgin olive oil)

Clean and wash chicken thoroughly; pat dry. In a plastic bag combine spelt flour (optional), spices, and pepper. Add chicken pieces to bag and shake to coat. In a large skillet, heat oil on medium to medium-high heat (do not reach smoke point). Add chicken to the hot oil in skillet, placing meaty pieces toward the center. Pour on or baste pieces with soy sauce while frying. Fry over medium heat for 10–15 minutes, turning to brown evenly. Preheat oven to 375°F. Drain chicken pieces of excess oil, then transfer to pan. Bake chicken uncovered for about 20–25 minutes or until well done (meat will no longer be pink).

Note: If fry with expeller-pressed canola oil or virgin olive oil, make sure smoke point is high enough (approximately 375°F or higher).

Sautéed Chicken (created by my mom)
Makes 6 servings

2 to 2½ pounds of chicken pieces (breasts, thighs, wings, and drumsticks)
2 Tbsp. of soy sauce
½ tsp. paprika
½ tsp. garlic powder
½ tsp. chili powder
½ tsp. onion powder
¼ tsp. pepper
2 Tbsp. of olive oil or canola oil
Water

Clean and wash chicken thoroughly. Add chicken parts to a pot and cover with water. Boil chicken on medium heat until no longer pink. Drain water off of chicken. Add seasonings to chicken (make sure to cover all parts). Pour oil to the bottom of pot; add water, 1 in. deep, to pot and cover partially with lid. Simmer at medium to low heat until chicken parts are well done and tender (meat falling off bone). Then sauté lightly in juices until slightly brown and most of juices disappear.

Zesty Fish Fillets (my own creation)

1 pound fresh or frozen white-fleshed fish fillets (wild orange roughy, cod,

Pollack, etc.) ¼ to ½ in. thick
¼ tsp. pepper
2 Tbsp. soy sauce
½ tsp. chili pepper or paprika
¼ cup olive oil
Approximately 1 tsp. of cocktail sauce per fillet

Thaw fish, if frozen. Wash fish thoroughly and pat dry. Season fillets with spice, pepper, and soy sauce. In a large skillet, add oil. On medium heat, fry fish in a single layer for approximately 1 minute on each side (add more oil if necessary). Turn carefully with large spatula. Drain fillets, then place in a pan. Preheat oven to 350°F. Spread cocktail sauce over the top surface of each fillet. Bake until fillets are golden brown around edges.

Pasta Dishes

Macaroni and Cheese (created by my sister)

1 lb. whole wheat or whole spelt macaroni (uncooked)
2 ½ cups 1% milk
4 oz. low-fat cream cheese
2 cups 2% sharp cheddar cheese, shredded
3 cups 2% Monterey Jack and Colby cheese combined, shredded
¼ cup canola spread
Additional 1 cup of shredded 2% cheese and 1 ¾ cup of 1% milk (save to put on top)

Mix the 5 cups of shredded cheeses together in a bowl and set aside. Cook macaroni according to instructions on package until *al dente*. Drain, cool, and set aside. In a large saucepan, heat canola spread until melted on medium-low heat. Add ½ cup milk and 1 cup of the mixed shredded cheese to the canola spread; stir constantly until cheese is melted into milk and canola spread. Keep adding milk (½ cup at a time) and shredded cheese (1 cup at a time) stirring constantly, until all of the cheese (5 cups) and milk (2 ½ cups) is added, and the cheese is completely melted and dissolved into the milk and canola spread. Add cream cheese and stir constantly until the cream cheese is melted into the cheese mixture. Once the cheese mixture is smooth, without any lumps, pour cooked macaroni into the large saucepan of cheese mixture and stir gently. Pour macaroni/cheese mixture into 13x9x2 glass baking dish. Sprinkle 1 cup of additional cheese and pour ¾ cup of additional milk on top; cover and bake at 350°F for about 1 hour or until baked all the way through. Remove cover, stir, and bake an additional 10 minutes. (If too dry when remove from oven, immediately pour an additional ½ to 1 cup of milk over the top).

Vegetable Lasagna (created by my sister)
Make 10–12 servings

Pasta
1 pkg. whole wheat or whole spelt lasagna, uncooked (approximately 18 large pieces of pasta; enough for 3 layers)

Vegetable Sauce
2 small zucchini, diced
1 medium onion, chopped
2 cups chopped spinach (frozen or fresh)
2 cups broccoli, chopped
2 cups carrots, thinly sliced
1 small red bell pepper, diced
3 cups spaghetti sauce
1 tsp. oregano
⅓ cup fresh parsley, chopped
2 cans (14 oz. each) diced garlic tomatoes
3 garlic cloves, chopped
Sea salt and black pepper to taste
1½ cup water

Cheese Mixture
1¾ cups (15 oz.) ricotta cheese
2 eggs
1½ cup low-fat Italian cheese, shredded
¼ cup low-fat Parmesan cheese, grated
¼ cup parsley, chopped
½ tsp. sea salt
¼ tsp. black pepper
Topping
Low-fat Parmesan cheese, grated
Low-fat Italian cheese, shredded

Cook pasta according to directions on package until *al dente*. Drain well, separate, and lay individual pieces of pasta on aluminum foil or on clean dish towel to keep from sticking. Set aside.

In a large sauce pan, add all "vegetable sauce" ingredients and cook on medium-low heat, stirring constantly. Cook until vegetables are semi-tender (be careful not to overcook vegetables). In medium bowl, stir together all "cheese mixture" ingredients for cheese filling. Preheat oven to 350°F. Spread one-quarter of vegetable sauce on bottom of 13x9x2 baking dish. Arrange pasta pieces lengthwise over sauce layer. Spread one-quarter of vegetable sauce, then half of cheese mixture over pasta. Arrange pasta pieces over cheese mixture layer. Repeat layering with one-quarter of vegetable sauce and then the second half of cheese mixture. Add another layer of pasta. Top with remaining vegetable sauce; sprinkle top with shredded Italian cheese and grated Parmesan cheese. Cover with foil and place in oven. Bake for about 15 minutes, until zucchini and carrots are tender. Let stand at least 10 minutes before serving.

Meatballs and Spaghetti (created by my mom)
Make approximately 6 servings

1 pound ground beef
¼ pound pork sausage
⅓ cup onions, chopped
2 cloves garlic, minced
2–3 medium tomatoes, diced
½ tsp. pepper
1 tsp. onion powder
½ tsp. garlic powder
¼ cup 2% milk
1 beaten egg
2 Tbsp. Worcestershire sauce
1 Tbsp. xylitol
¾ cup whole wheat crackers
½ cup whole spelt flour
8 to 12 ounces dried whole wheat spaghetti with spinach powder or whole spelt spaghetti
½ cup canola oil
1 jar (33.5 oz.) traditional spaghetti sauce

Prepare sauce in a large pot. Pour in spaghetti sauce. Stir in 1 Tbsp. of Worcestershire sauce, xylitol, and diced tomatoes. Add water to sauce until thickness of sauce is as desired (if you prefer really thick sauce, do not add water). Bring to a boil; reduce heat, and let simmer for approximately 15 min. In a separate bowl, add whole wheat cracker crumbs, chopped onion, onion powder, garlic powder, 1 Tbsp. of Worcestershire sauce, egg, pepper, milk, minced garlic, sausage, and beef in bowl, and mix well. Shape into 1½-inch round meatballs. Roll each meatball in whole spelt flour.

Pour oil in nonstick skillet and preheat over medium heat until oil is hot. Place meatballs in oil over medium heat. Turn meatballs until brown, and cook until well done (about 15–20 minutes). Cook spaghetti as instructed on package or until *al dente.* Drain spaghetti. Drain oil off of meatballs, add meatballs to sauce and stir gently. If you desire, add meatballs and sauce to the pot of spaghetti, or keep it separate and add meatballs and sauce on top of spaghetti as serve each plate.

Salads and Vegetables

Apple Walnut Salad (created by my son)
Makes about 3 main-dish servings

1 large head red leaf lettuce
1½ cup (about 12 oz.) cooked chicken breast, finely chopped (optional)
½ cup walnuts, chopped
2–3 medium organic red apples, diced and unpeeled
½ cup green onions, thinly sliced
½ cup whole wheat croutons, crushed
Balsamic or raspberry vinaigrette dressing

Break up clean lettuce in a large bowl. Add all other ingredients except salad dressing and toss well. Carefully, pour just enough dressing to lightly cover, not drench, salad and then toss again. Chill until ready to serve.

Fried Sweet Potato Wedges (created by my mom)
Make 4–6 servings

4 medium yam-sweet potatoes (peeled)
Canola oil or olive oil (I prefer virgin olive oil)

Cut peeled potatoes into ½-inch or ¼-inch slices. In a heavy large pan add oil about ½ inch deep, heat oil on medium to medium-high heat (do not reach smoke point). Carefully add slices to hot oil with a spoon. Fry and turn with a spatula until partially brown or for about 5–6 minutes. Remove potatoes from oil and drain on paper towels. If potato slices are not completely done (still not tender), bake in oven at 350°F until done.

Note: Use oil with a high enough smoke point (around 375°F or higher) so that potatoes can be browned quickly without soaking up too much grease.

Fruit Salad (created by my mom)
Make approximately 12 side-dish servings

1 8-oz. can mandarin orange sections, drained
1 15-oz can fruit cocktail (no added sugar or artificial sweeteners), drained
1 medium fresh apple, diced
1 15-oz. can pineapple chunks, or 1 cup fresh pineapple, diced and drained
½ cup shredded coconut
⅓ cup walnuts, finely chopped
½ cup (4 oz.) sour cream (may use less, if desired)
½ cup (4 oz.) plain, cultured, low-fat yogurt (may use less, if desired)

Mix all ingredients together in a large bowl with a spoon. Chill until ready to serve.

Greens with Smoked Turkey (created by my sister)

10–12 cups greens (collard, Swiss chard, mustard, and/or turnip) washed and torn
1–2 smoked turkey necks or ¼ package of turkey bacon
½ Anaheim mild pepper, chopped (if you want it spicy, use jalapeño)
½ tsp. sea salt

¼ tsp. black pepper
Canola oil for frying turkey bacon

Break smoked turkey necks in half, place in a large pot, and add about 1½ inch of water to bottom of pot. Cover the pot and let the necks simmer over medium-low heat until water level has decreased to about ¼ inch.

Note: Smoked turkey necks are sometimes hard to find in the grocery store; you can also use turkey bacon. Barely cover the bottom of a large pot with canola oil, and fry turkey bacon in bottom of pot until done and lightly browned. Then add ½ inch of water to pot and let simmer for about 5 minutes.

Add greens, pepper, black pepper, and salt to turkey necks or turkey bacon. Then add more water to pot until the water level is just over half full. Cook over medium heat until greens are tender. Do not overcook; greens should not be soft and mushy.

Tip: Greens with hot water cornbread (see above recipe) make an excellent meal.

Xylitoled Sweet Potatoes (created by my mom)
Make about 6 servings

4 medium yam-sweet potatoes, approximately 3½ lbs.
½ cup xylitol
½ stick (8 Tbsp.) butter, softened
2 Tbsp. imitation vanilla or 1 Tbsp. of vanilla extract
1½ tsp. nutmeg

Peel and cut potatoes into ½-inch slices. Place potatoes in a pot, and cover with water. Boil in water for 25–30 minutes or until tender (able to stick fork through slices). Place slices in a single layer in a 13x9 casserole dish. Spread butter on slices with knife. Mix xylitol and nutmeg in a small cup. Sprinkle xylitol-nutmeg mixture over potatoes. Pour vanilla into spoon and drizzle over all of the slices. Bake uncovered at 375°F until edges of potatoes become brown, approximately 40–45 minutes. (Unlike sugar, the xylitol on the potatoes will not caramelize or become candied, but it will melt).

NOTES

1. All of the Bible scriptures referenced in this book are from the King James Version except for one. This one scripture, Daniel 1:11-16 presented at the beginning of Chapter 20, is from the New Century Version.

References

Barker, K., D. Burdick, J. Stek, W. Wessel, R. Youngblood, ed. Study Bible, King James Version. Grand Rapids: Zondervan, 2002.

World Bible Translation Center. The Youth Bible, New Century Version. Texas: Word Publishing, 1991.

Suggested Readings

Adams, A. *Health, Nutrition and Fitness*. Dallas, TX: International Institute of Holistic Healing, 2006.

Balch, J.F., M. Stengler. *Prescription for Natural Cures*. Hoboken, NJ: John Wiley and Sons, Inc., 2004.

Balch, P.A. *Prescription for Nutritional Healing,* 4th ed. New York: Penguin Group, 2006.

Bowden, J. *The 150 Healthiest Foods on Earth.* Gloucester, MA: Fair Winds Press, 2007.

Brand-Miller J., T.M.S. Wolever, K. Foster-Powell, S. Colagiuri. *The New Glucose Revolution.* New York: Marlowe and Company, 2003.

Cousin, P.J., K. Hartvig. *The Complete Guide to Nutritional Health.* New York: Sterling Publisher Co., Inc., 2004.

Duyff, R.L. *American Dietetic Association Complete Food and Nutrition Guide*, 3rd ed. Hoboken, N J: John Wiley & Sons, Inc., 2006.

Farina, H.G., M. Pomies, D.F. Alonso, D.E. Gomez. "Antitumor and antiangiogenic activity of soy isoflavone genistein in mouse models of melanoma and breast cancer." *Oncology Reports.* 2006. 16: 885–891.

Gaby, A.R., J.V. Wright, F. Batz, R. Chester, G. Constantine, L.D. Thompson, ed. *The Natural Pharmacy,* 3rd ed. New York: Three Rivers Press, 2006.

Golbitz, P. "Traditional soyfoods: processing and products." *Journal of Nutrition.* 1995. 125: 570S–572S.

Graf, E., J.W. Eaton "Antioxidant functions of phytic acid." *Free Radical Biology and Medicine.* 1990. 8:61–69.

Graf, E., J.W. Eaton. "Suppression of colonic cancer by dietary phytic acid." *Nutrition and Cancer.* 1993. 19:11–19.

Heald, C.L., M.R. Ritchie, C. Bolton-Smith, M.S. Morton, F.E. Alexander. "Phyto-oestrogens and risk of prostate cancer in Scottish men." *British Journal of Nutrition.* 2007. 98: 388–396.

Hull, J.S., *Sweet Poison: How the World's Most Popular Artificial Sweetener Is Killing Us.* New Jersey: New Horizon Press, 1999.

Ivker, R.S., *Sinus Survival: The Holistic Medical Treatment for, Allergies , Colds, and Sinusitis* , 4th ed. New York: Tarcher/Putnam, 2000.

Messina, M., W. McCaskill-Stevens, J.W. Lampe. "Addressing the soy and breast cancer relationship: review, commentary, and workshop proceedings." *Journal of the National Cancer Institute.* 2006. 98:1275–1284.

Messina, M., V. Messina. "Soyfoods, soybean isoflavones, and bone health: a brief overview." *Journal Renal Nutrition.* 2000. 10:63-68.

Messina, M.J., C.L. Loprinzi. "Soy for breast cancer survivors: a critical review of the literature." *Journal of Nutrtion.* 2001. 131: 3095S–3108S.

Messina, M.J., C.E. Wood. "Review: Soy isoflavones, estrogen therapy, and breast cancer risk: analysis and commentary." *Nutrition Journal.* 2008. 7:17-29.

Murray, M., J. Pizzorno, L. Pizzorno. *The Encyclopedia of Healing Foods.* New York: Atria Books, 2005.

Otten, J.J., J.P. Hellwig, L.D. Meyers, ed. *Dietary Reference Intakes: The Essential Guide to Nutrient Requirements.* Washington DC: The National Academic Press, 2006.

Sacks, F.M., A. Lichtenstein, L. Van Horn, W. Harris, P. Kris-Etherton, M. Winston. "Soy protein, isoflavones, and cardiovascular health." *Circulation*. 2006. 113:1034–1044.

Setchell, K.D.R., E. Lydeking-Olsen. "Dietary phytoestrogens and their effect on bone: evidence from in vitro and in vivo, human observational, and dietary intervention studies." *American Journal of Clinical Nutrition*. 2003. 78:593S–609S.

Song, W.O., O.K. Chun, I. Hwang, H.S. Shin, B.G. Kim, K.S. Kim, S.Y. Lee, D. Shin, S.G. Lee. "Soy isoflavones as safe functional ingredients." *Journal of Medicinal Food*. 2007. 10:571–580.

Verghese, M., D.R. Rao, C.B. Chawan, L.T. Walker, L. Shackelford. "Anticarcinogenic effect of phytic acid (IP_6): apoptosis as a possible mechanism of action." *Swiss Society of Food Science and Technology*. 2006. 39:1093–1098.

Vucenik, I., A.M. Shamsuddin. "Cancer inhibition by inositol hexaphosphate (IP_6) and inositol: from laboratory to clinic." *Journal of Nutrition*. 2003. 133:3778S–3784S.

Wood, C.E., T.C. Register, A.A. Franke, M.S. Anthony, J.M. Cline. "Dietary soy isoflavones inhibit estrogen effects in the postmenopausal breast." *Cancer Research*. 2006. 66:1241-1249.

Zhou, J.R., E.T. Gugger, T. Tanaka, Y. Guo, G.L. Blackburn, S.K. Clinton. "Soybean phytochemicals inhibit the growth of transplantable human prostate carcinoma and tumor angiogenesis in mice." *Journal of Nutrition*. 1999. 129: 1628–1635.

CPSIA information can be obtained at www.ICGtesting.com
Printed in the USA
BVOW072005110412

287465BV00002B/20/P

9 781936 107490